The **GOP-Hater's** *Handbook*

The GOP-Hater's Handbook

---

378 REASONS NEVER TO VOTE

FOR THE PARTY OF

REAGAN, NIXON, AND BUSH AGAIN

JACK HUBERMAN

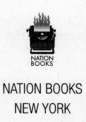

NATION BOOKS

NEW YORK

Published by Nation Books, A Member of the Perseus Books Group
116 East 16th Street, 8th Floor
New York, NY 10003

Nation Books is a co-publishing venture of the Nation Institute and the
Perseus Books Group.

Designed by Simon M. Sullivan and Maria Fernandez

Library of Congress Cataloging-in-Publication Data

Huberman, Jack.
    The GOP-haters handbook : 378 reasons never to vote for the party of
Reagan, Nixon, and Bush again / Jack Huberman.
        p. cm.
    Includes bibliographical references and index.
    ISBN-13: 978-1-56858-376-1
    ISBN-10: 1-56858-376-1
    1. Republican Party (U.S. : 1854-) 2. Conservatism—United States. 3.
United States—Politics and government—1989- I. Title.
JK2356.H83 2007
324.273402'07—dc22
                                        2007033960

10 9 8 7 6 5 4 3 2 1

Contents

*To my mother, bless her liberal, tolerant,
compassionate heart*

INTRODUCTION

H aving failed in two previous attempts* to put every single reason to hate the GEORGE W. BUSH administration into one modest-size book, I decided to try again, only this time to widen my focus to the Republican Party as a whole. What you are holding in your left hand** is the result: another magnificent failure.

If I fell short of my goal, it was, once again, the Republicans' fault: not only because of the fantastic *volume* of Grand Old Party mischief and malfeasance, but also because of its wonderful holographic quality, which makes any small piece of the picture seem to contain the whole. A single Bush White House misdeed—for example, leaking a CIA agent's identity—can highlight this administration's mendacity, contempt for law, reckless disregard for national security, blundering foreign policy, ferocious partisanship, and savagery toward critics, all at once. By the same token, I found I could start digging almost anywhere in the GOP field and strike a rich lode of corruption, sleaze, and stupidity. I made unexpected discoveries of delightfully awful personalities and episodes. Digressions became dissertations. Before I knew it I'd used up all my available space and time and still hadn't touched on areas of GOP villainy I'd intended to cover.

*The Bush-Hater's Handbook and Bushit!
**Only a Republican would regard what you're doing with your right hand as anyone's business but your own.

I don't think any important topic is *entirely* missing. There is no separate Reagan section, for example; but see IGNORANCE AND IDIOCY; COMPASSION; IRAN-CONTRA; and GOPONOMICS. No Nixon section, but see SOUTHERN STRATEGY. No civil rights section, but see HELMS and THURMOND. No Iraq section as such, but see O.I.L. No *environment* section, for God's sake—but see GRILES, WARMING, WATT, WHITMAN, and LITTLE FURRY ANIMALS. No Christian Right section, but see SEX PERVERTS.

THESE small caps, by the way, are the way sections are cross-referenced throughout the text. I must point out, however, that some of these cross-references are to sections I had to cut or never got around to writing, but which, in my traumatized mind, still exist, like phantom limbs, and whose headings still seemed to serve a purpose—rhetorical, ironical, whimsical . . . (I trust you're not, like the Republicans, anti-whimsy. Or as they term it, "pro-serious.") These virtual sections are indicated THUS (no boldface). Highlighted the same way, purely for visibility, are topics and names you might otherwise search the book for in growing ANGER AND DESPERATION because it wouldn't occur to you to look in the index. (I mean, how do I know? You may be a Republican.)

With the end of the Bush administration drawing nearer and the Democrats back in control of Congress, I wondered as I began this new offensive whether I brought the same passion and sense of urgency to the task as I had the first time. I am pleased to tell you I can still get my dudgeon up. Or rather, the Republicans can. And do. Pretty much daily. Sometimes twice. It's called *having a healthy vex life*. You ought to try it.

We are, after all, still quagged in the mire of Iraq—who knows for how many more years, lives, and dollars—and

that was a quite effective daily reminder of GOP loathsome-
ness. Another reminder was Bush's June 2007 veto—his first
since taking office—of a bill to remove restrictions on federal funding for potentially life-saving stem cell research: an
anti-life act to appease the GOP's core voting bloc of "pro-
life" religious nuts.*

Still others were the administration's firing of eight U.S.
attorneys who clung to the old-fashioned notion that their
job was to pursue justice rather than to serve the White
House's hyperpartisan political agenda; and the GOP presidential candidates' debate in May 2007, in which nine of the
ten candidates said *Roe v. Wade* should be overturned (RUDY
GIULIANI just said that would be "okay"), and three—Kansas
senator SAM BROWNBACK, former Arkansas governer **MIKE
HUCKABEE**, and Colorado representative TOM TANCREDO—
raised their hands like eager five-year-olds when the moder-
ator asked who did not believe in evolution. (They made me
wonder yet again whether *I* do.)

For me, many old, familiar Bush-GOP outrages are forever young: the rush from day one to hand over to corporate
buddies every piece of public land, every vital government
function that wasn't bolted down; the entrusting of environmental regulation to the polluters, of energy policy to oil and
gas drillers, and so on down the line; the post-9/11 assault on
civil liberties; the hugely expanded federal debt Bush will
leave behind, imperiling federal finances and social
spending for years if not decades to come—*as intended*; the
widening wealth gap between the top and the bottom—

*Americans support federal funding of embryonic stem cell research by a 2
to 1 margin, according to a June 2007 ABC News/Beliefnet poll. House
Republicans voted nearly 4 to 1 against it.

indeed, top and middle—which Republicans are not merely indifferent to but, I believe, quite pleased about, and certainly largely responsible for; the tripling of oil prices, which didn't just *happen* to occur under an administration led by two oilmen.

Then there's my demented refusal to simply forget that, here in the birthplace of democracy (*Was* that Greece? Sorry), the last two presidential elections were stolen, by means of systematic suppression of the Democratic vote, differential discarding of ballots, and perhaps even more sinister, uh, *machinations*.

Gore Vidal once called the U.S. the United States of Amnesia. Our short national attention span is the Republicans' best friend. Fortunately, when they tauntingly told Democrats to "get over it" after the 2000 election theft, a lot of us didn't listen; "Thanks, but fuck you, too," we said. With every subsequent GOP leadership failure, from the Bushies' failure to prevent 9/11 (as they could, should, and would have, had their priority been the nation's safety rather than their own political-ideological agenda) to the fraudulent Iraq war and all its related skulduggery, to HURRICANE KATRINA— the Repugs continue to resist every effort to investigate, and dispense the same idiotic counsel: "Move on." One imagines a criminal defendant importuning the court not to dwell on the past. Hello? *Accountability?* Finding out who screwed up and how, both for the sake of justice *and* so that maybe it can be prevented next time? No—that's the last thing that the party that preaches personal responsibility wants. It was the same during Nixon's and Reagan's scandals; but the Bush White House has waged a particularly fanatical war against OVERSIGHT AND ACCOUNTABILITY.

You just don't get it, do you. Fighting this national scourge, amnesia, is one thing that keeps my nose to the grindstone. Another is that I can't afford rhinoplasty. A third is that, even with the Repugs back in the minority in Congress and Bush's approval ratings below 30 percent, I still don't think most of the public *gets it.*

Take the Iraq debaq: Americans have been slow to realize it isn't about incompetence as such. The Bushies have been all too competent. Obviously, the intelligence "failures" were nothing of the kind; the administration "found" the intelligence it needed to sell the war. Whether the war as a whole is a failure depends on what the aims were. If they were to establish democracy, bring peace to the region, free the Iraqi people from fear and violence, defuse anger at the United States for supporting regional despots, or make America safer and stronger, then of course the war is a colossal failure. But were those the principal aims? See **O.I.L. (OPERATION IRAQI LIBERATION).** When Bush and Cheney say that if they knew then what they know now they'd still have gone to war, you can believe it. (When they say they'd do some things differently, *don't* believe it.)

Moderate Republicans (like **CHRISTINE WHITMAN**) may deny it all they like, but the Bush administration is no aberrational, monster strain of Republicanism; it is, rather, its perfection, its apotheosis, its foul-smelling flower. The Republicans' prolific **CRIME, CORRUPTION, AND CRONYISM** is not a collection of unrelated screw-ups and ethical lapses that might as easily have occurred in either party, but rather, an outgrowth of what the GOP *is.* The Republicans have not been *betraying* their principles, but acting on them.

Serving powerful and deep-pocketed interest groups first and foremost, collecting great piles of money from them, and using it to secure a permanent stranglehold on power in order to sell *more* favors and attract *more* money and gain *more* power . . . this is only the most salient of GOP principles. The increasing concentration of wealth and power in fewer hands, the nation's political polarization, the Bushies' failure to protect and defend the Constitution and to respect the system of checks and balances on which our democracy is built—these are not failures. These are GOP *goals*.

Repugs themselves may only be half-conscious of what they're up to. (Who *does* know what drives him?) A George W. Bush would of course insist that he truly believes upper-income tax cuts are ultimately in everyone's best interest. But first he'd have to admit his tax cuts *have* gone mainly to the richest Americans. He denies that. There is no more convincing liar than one who believes his own lies. In what sense, then, *are* they lies? As a *New York Times* editorial had it, Bush believed in Saddam's WMDs out of a terrifying "capacity for politically motivated self-deception." You could say there are three kinds of Republican politician— those who know but don't care that what they espouse is bullshit; those simply too dumb to know, and who really *believe*; and in between, those who "believe" whatever is politically expedient to "believe." If you ask me, *knowing* you're doing wrong is less corrupt than convincing yourself it's in a noble cause.

Co-President **DICK CHENEY** seems less deluded than the messianic Bush. Cheney knows he wants to restore the "imperial presidency." This is what the Bushies' fanatical secrecy is about. For Cheney and Bush both, there is no such thing as too much presidential power. They've arrogated to themselves more executive power than any British monarch has enjoyed since Charles I. Perhaps they're confident no Democrat will ever again occupy the Oval Office. (See DIEBOLD.)

Conservatism and democracy have always been opposing principles. Smaller government, lower taxes, less regulation, and a return to "traditional values" are things most GOP supporters believe in and think their leaders believe in. But the soul of conservatism remains what it always was: opposition to all movement in the direction of social and economic equality, personal and cultural freedom, intellectual and scientific enlightenment. The modern conservative movement was built on a backlash against the gains in racial, gender, and class equality and in political and sexual freedom made in the 1960s and '70s. Indeed, what's left of the New Deal is marked for destruction, while religious conservatives would like to cancel the Age of Enlightenment. Probably also the Renaissance. Surrealism and Situationism, obviously. Between religious and economic conservatives, there is a continuum: collectively, they hark back to a time when whites, men, the upper class, and Christians ruled and everyone else knew her or his place (the kitchen, the closet, the other side of the tracks, the other side of the border . . .).

Conservatives have tried to block or reverse every bit of social and political progress for at least two centuries. If they'd had their way at each step, we'd still have slavery, aristocracy, and monarchy everywhere; little freedom of speech, the press, or religion; no universal suffrage; no social safety net. This vision, this nostalgia lives on in the hearts of conservatives. They watch for every opportunity to turn the clock back a bit more. Like their Islamist counterparts (see DINESH D'SOUZA for frank, explicit linkage), *our* conservatives' vision is a long-range one. They are patient.

Under Reagan, Bush, and Bush, they've had a field day. I'm confident they will lose in the end. But trust me, the threat is far from gone. That's why you must stop standing there, disengage that right hand, and take this book up to the cashier this instant.

And I hope it's as good for you as it was for me.

By the way—regarding my advertised "378 Reasons" never to vote Republican again: You're probably too shrewd not to notice that this book contains fewer than 378 *sections*. But there are among them exactly 378 *reasons*. They have been counted and recounted. It's time for the counting to stop and for the country to move on.

ABORTION AND BIRTH CONTROL: OPERATION BAREFOOT AND PREGNANT

*My pro-life position is I believe there's life . . . therefore the
notion of life, liberty and pursuit of happiness.*
　　　　　—George W. Bush (But is there *intelligent* life?)

It may be hard to convince you that the GOP's antiabortion-
rights policies are wrong if you believe abortion is murder.
(In which case you probably also believe in the DEATH
PENALTY . . . ergo, rev up the pro-life gas chambers, electric
chairs, and syringes! Around 850,000 legal abortions are performed every year in the United States, and there's a woman
and a doctor involved in almost every one.)

Now, crucify me, but there's no way *I* see a blastocyst—
the ball of 16, 32, or 64 cells that is the "baby" in its earliest
stages—as a human being. So, at what point does it become
one? There are pro-choice clergy who interpret Genesis
2:7—"the Lord God formed the man from the dust of the
ground and breathed into his nostrils the breath of life, and
the man became a living being"—to mean that the newborn
babe becomes a human being when it takes its first breath.
As an atheist, I'll buy that. (Actually, my view is that the
embryo doesn't become a human being until around
eighteen years of age, and even then, some just become
Republicans.) Certainly, what you do with your womb is no
business of any religious zealots or their political exploiters.

A sane, honest abortion rights opponent would in any
case have to agree that the right's fanatical *cult* of the

1

unborn child—of "life," as they put it in order to define *pro-choice* as *pro-death*—is typically accompanied by much, much less concern about the survival and well-being of the *born* child* (unless it's about protecting the tyke from the influence of the HOMOSEXUAL AGENDA and from the fruit of the tree of knowledge of evolution). Besides favoring capital punishment and opposing gun control, antiabortion protesters don't on the whole feel as stirred to protest their Bushite heroes' needless, criminal sacrifice of lives in Iraq. (Au contraire. For as commentatrix ANN COULTER said—in touch, as always, with her inner terrorist and fearlessly voicing all conservatives' guilty thoughts: "We should invade [Muslims'] countries, kill their leaders and convert them to Christianity." Or at least empower reliably anti-choice, anti-feminist, anti-gay Islamist theocrats in Iraq. . . . Hey—Mission Accomplished!)

For these good folks, it'll be Mission Accomplished back home only when *Roe v. Wade* is overturned and the Constitution has been amended to ban abortion outright. Never mind that year after year, a majority of Americans oppose such a ban. (In an April 2007 NBC/*Wall Street Journal* poll, 55 percent said the choice should be left up to the woman and her doctor.** This figure is roughly the same as it was in 1990, having fluctuated by no more than 5 percent in the

---

*In its first budget proposal (March 2001), the Bush White House sought to cut the Maternal and Child Health block grants and to freeze the Healthy Start program, which had been shown to reduce infant mortality and morbidity. Being "pro-life" means different things to different people.

**Another 30 percent said abortion should be legal in cases in which pregnancy results from rape or incest or when the life of the woman is at risk. Only 13 percent said it should be illegal in all cases. May 2007 Gallup poll: 53 percent said don't overturn *Roe*, 35 percent said do.

intervening years.) By 2006, Bush had given the religious right *minority* the two appointments it needed to attain an anti-choice *majority* on the Supreme Court. (Those poor, persecuted Christians! See **Xmas and Christianity, Democrat-Liberal-Satanist-Secularist War on.**) If *Roe* were overturned, it is estimated that at least twenty-one states and possibly as many as thirty-eight would move quickly to outlaw abortion.

Not, of course, that such action would *end* abortion: Before *Roe*, thousands of American women died every year from botched backdoor abortions—as some eighty thousand women around the world still do. In fact, 43 percent of all abortions worldwide are performed in countries where abortion is illegal. And although the U.S. abortion rate fell about 27 percent during the Clinton years—apparently thanks to improved access to medical care, family planning services, and education—it began to climb again under Bush, as poverty, antiabortion agitation and legislation, and the national stupidity level (NSL) increased.

Gag me. Bush's war on reproductive rights began literally on his first day in the Oval Office, when he reinstated President Reagan's so-called "global gag rule" by cutting off U.S. funding for international organizations that provide abortion counseling. This included groups such as the United Nations Population Fund, which provides family planning services that *prevent* abortions by preventing unwanted pregnancies. These groups also provide AIDS education, sexual violence prevention, maternal care, literacy programs, job training, and emergency disaster relief around the world. UN officials estimated the loss of U.S. funding would result in 800,000 unwanted pregnancies and the deaths of 4,700 women and

77,000 children. The global gag rule led to closed health clinics, dwindling medical supplies, and a *complete* cutoff of United States Agency for International Development (USAID) funds in sixteen countries.[1] "The upshot is that women and babies are dying in Africa" because of Bush's "idealism," wrote the *New York Times*'s Nicholas Kristof.

Next, Bush disbanded the President's Interagency Council on Women, a group appointed by Clinton to implement the 1995 Beijing Declaration on women's rights, which called for governments to close the gender gap in health, education, employment, and political participation and to recognize women's right to "decide freely and responsibly on matters related to their sexuality . . . free of coercion, discrimination and violence." (Obviously, America could have nothing to do with a declaration like *that*.) At a 2005 UN conference, the United States, standing alone, standing tall, opposed by more than one hundred nations, tried to amend this declaration to exclude the right to abortion and "any new international human rights" (God forbid!). And why

Robertson, Relatively Speaking. Who could be more supportive of exporting the American religious right's abortion agenda than tycoon televangelist and Christian Coalition founder PAT ROBERTSON? As it turns out, just about any honest-to-God pro-lifer. Pat, you see, had personal business interests in China, whose government doesn't take criticism so well. Robertson, commenting in 2001 on China's one-child policy—which inevitably results in forced abortion—explained that "China suffers from tremendous unemployment [the official rate was 3.6 percent, vs. 4.8 percent in the United States, but,

were abortion rights to be denied globally? To ensure that U.S. judges could never cite the Beijing document as a basis for protecting abortion rights at home.

The right wouldn't seem to have much to worry about on that score. Out of over 200 judges nominated by Bush in his first term, only two expressed even the slightest respect for the abortion rights protected by the laws they were supposed to uphold.

In other words, Bush broke his promise . . . to appoint *only* 100 percent guaranteed anti-choice judges. In 1999, on the eve of his presidential campaign, Bush addressed a meeting of the COUNCIL FOR NATIONAL POLICY (CNP), an ultra-secretive cabal one might call the Elders of the Religious Right (including Paul Weyrich, Pat Robertson, Jerry Falwell, Tim LaHaye, Phyllis Schlafly, Donald Wildmon, Bob Jones III—plus leading right-wing financiers like Joseph Coors and Nelson Baker Hunt; see AMERICA, HIJACKING OF BY RADICAL CONSERVATIVE WINGNUTS WHOSE POLICY GOALS ARE OPPOSED BY MOST AMERICANS). At this gathering, which was closed to the

whatever] . . . so, I think that right now they are doing what they have to do. . . . I don't agree with forced abortion, but I don't think the United States needs to interfere with what they're doing internally in this regard." (How would a precipitous rise in domestic unemployment affect Pat's views on U.S. abortion policy? one wonders.) Let's review: Depending on . . . various things, it's okay for governments to tell women they *can't* abort or that they *must* abort. Women must never, however, be permitted to decide for themselves. After all, they are the property of men.

press, "Bush reportedly sought to put to rest any notion that he was a moderate," *The Nation* reportedly reported. The rumor was that he'd promised to appoint only antiabortion judges if elected. And the CNP got behind him, and the Lord got behind him, and lo, he was selected president. And the Lord saw that it was bad.

Over the next couple of years, Bush & Co.:

▶ Announced that thenceforth, a fetus would be defined as a "child," for the purpose of entitling poor women to prenatal care under the State Children's Health Insurance Program (SCHIP). So what was not to like? Well, the administration simply could have said pregnant women would be covered under SCHIP—but that wouldn't have helped further define abortion as murder. Which was in fact *all* this move did: SCHIP already had mechanisms to provide prenatal care; what it didn't have was *funding*—and no new funding was provided for this "expansion." In fact, by 2007, Bush budget cuts would result in at least 600,000 children *losing* SCHIP coverage and joining the 8 million American children with no health insurance coverage. Well, *someone* had to pay for Bush's $2-trillion-plus TCFR (Tax Cuts for the Rich) program.

▶ Altered a National Cancer Institute website fact sheet to suggest that abortion could cause breast cancer, a favorite "pro-life" scare tactic. There was no scientific evidence to support this contention. As the fact sheet originally stated.

▶ Signed into law the so-called Abortion Non-Discrimination Act, which allowed Medicare, private insurers, and hospitals to ignore *Roe v. Wade* and to bar doctors from providing abortion referrals or even counseling patients about their options. The act—a mere two sentences slipped into a three-thousand-page appropriations bill by House Republicans in a closed-door session—was "an extraordinary sneak attack on women's rights," said Nancy Pelosi.

▶ Routinely compared the antiabortion movement to the civil rights movement and (as Bush did in a 2004 debate with John Kerry) *Roe v. Wade* to the 1857 *Dred Scott* decision upholding slavery. Just as that court refused to see blacks as human, the same was done to fetuses in *Roe*, claimed rightists. As if the party of STROM THURMOND, JESSE HELMS and TRENT LOTT would have opposed *Dred* in its day.

▶ Repeatedly compared abortion-rights supporters to terrorists. Never mind that it was abortion-rights *opponents* who had bombed clinics and killed doctors. When Bush declared January 22, the anniversary of *Roe v. Wade*, "National Sanctity of Human Life Day," he obscenely twisted and slandered the meanings of *two* important dates: "On September 11," he said, "we saw clearly that evil exists in this world, and that it does not value life. . . . Now we are engaged in a fight against evil and tyranny to preserve and protect life." In response to a huge pro-choice rally in Washington in 2004, Bush adviser KAREN HUGHES said: "The fundamental issue between us and the terror network we fight is that we value every life." (Indeed? See ENVIRONMENT, HEALTH CARE, GUN CONTROL, IRAQ, POVERTY, **VETERANS,** HURRICANE KATRINA.)

▶ Blocked the repeal of a ban on overseas servicewomen or dependents obtaining privately funded abortions at military hospitals. Servicewomen risking their lives in Iraq could now risk their lives at the hands of Baghdad back-alley abortionists. By maintaining the ban, the Bushies only helped the terrorists.

Like walnut shells. In November 2003, Bush signed into law the first-ever federal ban on abortion procedures—a bill banning "partial-birth abortions," an array of abortion methods used in the second or third trimester usually only when there are serious health complications for the mother or fatal abnormalities in a fetus. Although the banned procedures constituted fewer than 0.2 percent of abortions, the bill, commented the *New York Times*, "strikes at the heart of *Roe v. Wade*" by criminalizing many midterm abortions, with no exceptions for pregnancies that endanger the mother's health. The press photos of Bush signing the bill surrounded by an all-male coterie of middle-aged, dark-suited Republicans—looking gleeful as they deprived women of a potentially life-saving medical procedure—spoke volumes. (Thenceforth, the White House would be more careful to include a woman in the picture while amBushing women's rights.)

The bill was not about partial birth abortions, it was about abortion, period: It was the wedge with which *Roe v. Wade* would be split open, its two gutted halves eventually to be discarded like walnut shells. Or any other nut you prefer. "Incrementalism" was the word a delighted "pro-life" activist used to explain the bill's significance. One step at a time. Nothing too radical that will get the public up in arms. Stealth. Subterfuge. Good GOP values.

But people *were* up in arms. Citing a Supreme Court ruling that declared a nearly identical law in Nebraska unconstitutional three years earlier, three federal judges immediately issued restraining orders blocking enforcement of the new law. (Whom did then attorney general **JOHN ASHCROFT** assign to enforce this law, which the courts had deemed a violation of women's civil rights? The Justice Department's civil rights division, of course. See CYNICISM, UNBOUNDED.)

Ritual sacrifice of women. In April 2007, the Supreme Court voted 5–4 to uphold the ban. The (all-male) conservative majority "went so far as to eviscerate the crucial requirement [which dated to *Roe v. Wade*, 1973] that all abortion regulations must have an exception to protect a woman's health," the *New York Times* commented. "As far as we know, Mr. [JUSTICE ANTHONY] KENNEDY [who wrote the majority opinion] and his four colleagues responsible for this atrocious result are not doctors." Maybe they forgot. . . . In any case, they chose to override the mass of medical evidence presented during the preceding trials, instead ratifying "the politically based and dangerously dubious claim that criminalizing [the "partial-birth" method] would never pose a significant health risk." [2]

Actually, it was worse. Contradicting his own written opinion, Justice Kennedy allowed that there was "medical uncertainty" on this question. In other words: When in any doubt about danger to women's health, err on the far-right side and sacrifice the *woman* to the demands of America's antiabortion minority.

Perhaps most amazing of all: Kennedy said if a woman or her doctor felt her health was in jeopardy, she could go to court to challenge the law. Need a medical procedure, fast? Get a lawyer. A first-class constitutional lawyer, preferably. Get a court date. Plead your case. Against a Supreme Court ruling. What's the problem?

Moreover, the *Times* pointed out, Kennedy "actually reasoned that banning the procedure was good for women in that it would protect them from a procedure they might not fully understand in advance and would probably come to regret. This way of thinking, that women are flighty creatures who must be protected by men, reflects notions of a woman's place in the family and under the Constitution that have long been discredited." Dissenting Justice RUTH BADER GINSBURG noted that the new ruling, which "saves not a single fetus from destruction" by banning a single method of abortion, was radically at odds with Court precedent—including an opinion by Reagan-appointed former Justice SANDRA DAY O'CONNOR seven years earlier, when the Nebraska ban was struck down. "The court has handed the Bush administration and other opponents of women's reproductive rights the big political victory they were hoping to get from the conservative judges Mr. Bush has added to the bench," said the *Times*.

There was a wide spectrum of opinion on the ruling among GOP presidential candidates. RUDY GIULIANI: "The Supreme Court reached the correct conclusion." **JOHN MCCAIN**: "A victory for those who cherish the sanctity of life and integrity of the judiciary." **MITT ROMNEY**: "Today, our nation's highest court reaffirmed the value of life in America." SAM BROWNBACK: "This is a great step forward . . . I hope that this decision signals the Court's willingness to revisit and reverse *Roe v. Wade*." Giuliani alone said "it would be okay" if the Supreme Court upheld *Roe v. Wade*. Then again, backpedaled the one candidate with a pro-choice record, "It would be okay to repeal it." The over-turning of "a constitutional decision that secured a fundamental personal liberty to millions of persons would be unprecedented in our two hundred years of constitutional history," wrote former Justice Harry Blackmun. Sam

Brownback: It would be "a glorious day of human liberty and freedom." Only in the strange land called GOPland . . .

And no birth control, neither. Prevent abortions through more effective birth control and sex education? The fact that conservatives oppose this, too, suggests that what they're really against is *sex*, except in marriage and for the purpose of procreation rather than recreation. (H. L. Mencken's famous definition of Puritanism—"The haunting fear that someone, somewhere, may be happy"—applies just as neatly to contemporary Christianism.)

In May 2004, the Bushevist Food and Drug Administration (FDA), caving to pressure from anti-sex conservatives and the White House, refused to permit over-the-counter sales of the "morning-after" birth control pill (brand name: PLAN B)—overruling two FDA scientific panels, which had reviewed forty studies and voted 23–4 that permitting such sales would be safe and effective. In 2000, when it was only available by prescription, Plan B prevented exactly 100,000 pregnancies and 51,000 abortions.[3] Doctors' groups said easier access could reduce the nation's 3 million unwanted pregnancies each year by half. The abstinuts feared that increased access would encourage teenagers to be sexually active. (Like they need encouragement.)

The right's point man on Plan B was DAVID HAGER, an ob-gyn appointed by Bush in 2002 to chair the FDA's Reproductive Health Drugs Advisory Committee, which, in theory, evaluates the safety and effectiveness of drugs used in obstetrics and gynecology. (A *man's* job. Apparently.) Hager was more concerned with drugs' *religious* and *political* safety and effectiveness. Hager is the author of *The Reproduction Revolution: A Christian Appraisal of Sexuality,*

Reproductive Technologies and the Family, which endorsed the medically false claim that oral contraceptives cause early chemical abortion of those pregnancies they fail to prevent. Hager also had spoken out against the use of condoms outside of marriage and recommended reading the Bible and praying as treatment for premenstrual syndrome, postpartum depression, and eating disorders.

The faith healer provided the FDA's pretext for blocking Plan B sales by questioning whether the drug had been adequately tested on adolescents—even though another physician on the FDA panels called Plan B "the safest product that we have seen brought before us," and the FDA did not require age-group-specific testing for other contraceptives or for scores of other drugs. (In 2002, the Bushies *suspended* a Clinton rule that required drug companies to test their products for children!) Oddly enough, nearly a year after the manufacturer proposed making Plan B available only to females over age sixteen, the FDA *still* withheld approval. The Bush administration, having already banned abortion at military hospitals, also overrode Pentagon health officials' approval of stocking Plan B at military medical facilities for America's 350,000 largely postadolescent servicewomen.

In a church sermon, Hager boasted that "[f]or only the second time in five decades, the FDA did not abide by its advisory committee opinion." He had argued "from a scientific perspective," but "[o]nce again, what Satan meant for evil [*science*, presumably] God turned into good." Christians such as himself were at "war" with secular medicine, he added.

"God has called me to stand in the gap . . . regarding ethical and moral issues in our country," Hager declared. His ex-wife saw him rather differently: see SEX PERVERTS.

> ***Abstinut of the Year: Eric Keroack,*** a non-board-certified but totally certifiable ob-gyn who claimed that premarital sex damages women's ability to bond in a successful long-term relationship by altering their brain chemistry. (You look at a lot of conservatives and you have to wonder: Does *lack* of premarital sex cause brain damage?) He was medical director of a Massachusetts-based Christian family planning organization and a leading antiabortion and anti-birth-control advocate. So it was a literal no-brainer for **BUSH**, in 2006, to appoint Keroack to head the Health and Human Services department that oversees federal family planning, teen pregnancy, and abstinence programs. Keroack resigned a few months later after receiving two warnings from the Massachusetts board of medicine ordering him to stop (a) prescribing drugs to people who were not his patients, and (b) providing mental health counseling, an area in which he had no training. At least not as the provider.

Asshole #1; Crime, Corruption, and Cronyism
Case #1:

ABRAMOFF, JACK: The GOP Culture of Corruption, on Steroids

"The Man Who Bought Washington," a *Time* cover labeled Jack Abramoff. (With very few exceptions, he bought *Republican* Washington, thank you.) The former Republican activist/superlobbyist pleaded guilty in January 2006 to felony charges of defrauding American Indian tribes, bribing public officials, and conspiring to commit wire and mail fraud related to the purchase of SunCruz Casinos, the murder of whose owner was allegedly connected with the sale. Abramoff was sentenced to serve 5.8 years in prison and pay $21 million in restitution.

But those charges don't begin to, uh, do justice to this scandal. Bill Moyers gave it a shot: "It's a dizzying scope of perfidy and politics that boggles the imagination. . . . The scale of corruption still coming to light dwarfs anything since WATERGATE." What? That sordid little burglary? *This* is perhaps the biggest political corruption scandal (not counting the Bush administration itself) in U.S. history. Even more than his good friend TOM DELAY, Abramoff was the point where all the vectors of GOP evil and malfeasance intersected. (Note: I can't

---

Assholes. I take the controversial position that not all Republicans are assholes. But scattered throughout this book are thirty-four alphabetically correct little entries about Republicans who are so designated. Why these thirty-four? In the absence of a national political asshole directory, what factors did I consider? What methodology was used?

The asshole candidate must demonstrate competence in at least three of the following areas: arrogance; self-righteousness (faith-based or other); blowhardiness; boorishness; meanness; moral slipperiness or hypocrisy; indifference to suffering; jingoistic nationalism; ethnic, racial, and/or anti-gay bigotry; male-chauvinist pigotry; anti-intellectual, anti-"elitist," faux-populist reverse snobbery. What we want to see is a serious, good-faith effort to emulate BILL "Hot Lips" O'REILLY and RUSH "For the Exits" LIMBAUGH.

begin to cover it all, and so am focusing on the more assholistic and alliterative asspects of the Abramoff affair.)

Abramoff and his coconspirator, former DeLay spokesman MICHAEL SCANLON, double-crossed their Indian tribe clients and bilked them out of at least $80 million for lobbying and PR work, most of which the tribes never received. The demonic duo also directed their clients to donate millions of dollars to GOP politicians, conservative organizations, and a beach house "think tank" run by a lifeguard. Meanwhile, the two exchanged gleeful e-mails mocking tribal leaders as "morons," "troglodytes," and "monkeys." (Abramoff: "I have to meet with the monkeys from the Choctaw tribal council" and "We need to get some money from those monkeys!!" "I want all their MONEY!!!" e-mailed an exuberant Scanlon in the midst of one deal.) Abramoff also had Indian tribe clients donate more than $6 million to the Capital Athletic Foundation, which he founded ostensibly to fund athletic activities for inner city kids, but almost all the money went to an Orthodox Jewish school in Maryland that Abramoff founded and then used as a money-laundering conduit.

In 2002, Abramoff teamed up with Christian Coalition leader/GOP activist **RALPH REED** to charge a Louisiana gaming tribe millions to organize a "Christian" antigambling crusade in Texas in order to shut down a competing casino owned by the Tigua tribe. Abramoff and Reed then turned around and charged the Tigua $4.2 million to lobby lawmakers to reopen it. Payments were laundered through GOP activist/asshole **GROVER NORQUIST**'s outfit Americans for Tax Reform. At Reed's request, his payments were laundered through other organizations to keep his hands Christian-clean.

The three mucketeers. Abramoff, Reed, and Norquist had worked together since college days in the early 1980s, when the "Abramoff-Norquist-Reed triumvirate" took over the College Republican National Committee (CRNC), where they purged "dissidents" and rewrote the CRNC's bylaws to solidify their own control. Little baby Republicans! It was so cute! Like little baby Tyrannosaurus rexes.

In 1983, Abramoff's CRNC passed a resolution condemning "deliberate planted propaganda by the KGB and Soviet proxy forces" against the apartheid government of South Africa. In 1984, Abramoff formed a "nonpartisan," therefore tax-exempt, group to organize campus rallies celebrating Reagan's glorious military victory over Grenada. Abramoff, writing nonpartisanly to campus Republican leaders: "I am confident that an impartial study of the contrasts between the Carter/Mondale failure in Iran and the Reagan victory in Grenada will be most enlightening to voters twelve days before the general election." (Iran: Oil-rich, formidably armed nation of 70 million. Grenada: Impoverished, second-smallest country in the Western Hemisphere; pop. 100,000. National bird: the endangered Grenada dove. Thank you, Wikipedia. Hmm. Maybe they invaded *because* there was a species that needed further endangering. See LITTLE FURRY ANIMALS, HATRED OF.)

Global whoring. The GOP congressional takeover in 1994 and the Bushist putsch in 2000 made Abramoff a player. He was paid $1.2 million to arrange a meeting with Bush for the prime minister of Malaysia, and reportedly asked for $9 million to arrange a Bushez-vous for the president of Gabon, whose government is regularly accused by the United States of human rights abuses. Abramoff offered his services to the government of Sudan, one of five countries on the State Department's State Sponsors of Terrorism list; he sought millions in return for improving the country's image among

American evangelicals who were upset by Sudanese atrocities against Christians in the Darfur region. Abramoff reportedly promised to enlist Ralph Reed in the campaign. Image-buffing PR work for such beacons of democracy as apartheid South Africa, the Nicaraguan contras, and the Afghan Mujahedeen was an Abramoff specialty. "Folks like Norquist and Abramoff," wrote conservative columnist David Brooks, "were talking up the virtues of international sons of liberty like [South African–backed Angolan rebel leader Jonas] Savimbi and Congo's dictator Mobutu Sese Seko—all while receiving compensation from these upstanding gentlemen," notwithstanding "Savimbi's little cannibalism problem . . ."

When proposals were made in Congress to do something about patriotic U.S. companies that were registered abroad simply to evade taxes, the Abster lobbied to help one such corporate piker, Bermuda-incorporated TYCO INTERNATIONAL, keep its tax-exempt status. (He was hired by Tyco executive TIMOTHY FLANIGAN, who had just left his post as Bush White House Deputy Counsel.) Abramoff's assignment was to "Astroturf"—verb: to create a fake "grassroots" campaign opposing the new tax proposals. Without bothering to cultivate *that* green, Abramoff did keep the $1.7 million in fees, allegedly diverting it to "entities controlled by Mr. Abramoff." Somewhat like Tyco CEO DENNIS KOZLOWSKI, who in 2005 was convicted of misappropriation (i.e., keeping and spending*) of company funds and defrauding shareholders of more than $400 million, and sentenced to up to twenty-five years in prison. Of Kozlowski's generous political donations,

---

*On, for example, his $30 million New York City apartment with the $6,000 shower curtain and his wife's famous $1 million "Roman orgy" birthday party in Sardinia, featuring an ice statue of David pissing Stoli.

by the way, 93 percent went to Republicans. So, how many layers of sleaze is that? I count seven.

Abramoff's efforts on behalf of the sweatshop bosses of the Commonwealth of the Northern MARIANA ISLANDS to block any reforms of the abominable labor conditions there cried out in anguish for a separate entry. Worth noting here, however, is that Abramoff got the U.S. territory to award a $1.2 million no-bid contract to his old friend and religious adviser Rabbi DAVID LAPIN for "promoting ethics in government"! Which is akin to talking about government ethics in the antebellum slave states. Besides, if Lapin's ethics are anything like Abramoff's. . . . It *was* Lapin's influence that turned Abramoff into an Orthodox Jew. Supposedly. Abramoff is Jewish like Tom DeLay (to whom Lapin's brother and fellow rabbi, DANIEL LAPIN, reportedly introduced Abramoff) is Christian. God help us. And the Marianas.

"It's the Republicans, stupid." Naturally, once the Abramoff scandal broke open, the White House dropped him

Baseball Bat Republicanism. Like Abramoff, his side-kick Michael Scanlon—who in 2005 pleaded guilty to conspiring to bribe Congress members—was a man of strong beliefs. Scanlon, in an e-mail during the Clinton impeachment trial: "This whole thing about not kicking someone when they are down is BS—not only do you kick him—you kick him until he passes out—then beat him over the head with a baseball bat—then roll him up in an old rug—and throw him off a cliff into the pounding surf below!!!!" (The "pounding surf" is more than a tad clichéd—and *four* excla-

like a soiled diaper. Bush didn't even know him. (He didn't know Enron CEO KEN LAY either.) Naturally, at least five photos of Bush meeting in the Oval Office with Abramoff and/or clients soon surfaced. (The big Bush/GOP contributor who owned the Web site on which some of the photos were discovered immediately removed them.) Abramoff was a member of the Bush 2001 Transition Advisory Team, for God's sake. His own records listed 485 lobbying contacts with White House officials over three years, including ten with Karl Rove Himself. SUSAN RALSTON, a former administrative assistant for both Abramoff and Ralph Reed, had served as special assistant to the president and assistant to Rove since 2001. The first person arrested in the Abramoff scandal, in September 2005, was DAVID SAVAFIAN, then head of procurement policy at the White House Office of Management and Budget. Savafian had helped Abramoff, his old friend and former lobbying colleague, on business deals with the Bush administration while working *in* the Bush administration. (Nothing unusual there.) In March 2006, Abramoff,

mation marks? . . . but all in all, a fine expression of the GOP ethos of our age.)

Signs of such sociopathy often appear in adolescence. In a 2006 radio interview, journalist Jonathan Gold, who attended high school with Abramoff, described him as a school bully— "the sort of person who would walk across the street to be unpleasant to somebody"—and told how Abramoff, a weightlifting jock, once knocked him and his cello down a flight of stairs, then walked away laughing with his friends. You know, that's really rude!

now abandoned by his White House friends, insisted that Bush and other top Republicans knew him very well, and called them liars for denying it.

Of course the Republicans rushed to deny it was a *Republican* scandal. Because "both Democrats and Republicans received money . . . we shouldn't be pointing fingers," Republican National Committee chairman KEN MEHLMAN said in one of his many attempts to de-Republicanize the scandal. Actually, Abramoff gave *no* money directly to Democrats. He did direct Indian tribe clients to give to Democrats—in a 2 to 1 R to D ratio. Oh, yes: Sen. Byron Dorgan (D-N.D.) used Abramoff's skybox. Anyway, it's ridiculous. Abramoff was as Republican as you can be without being Mussolini or LOUIS XIV. All of his close associates, friends, and co-conspirators were GOP zealots like Norquist, Reed, Rove, and GOPs like Senators CONRAD BURNS and RICK SANTORUM and Representatives DeLay, Bob Ney, **JOHN DOOLITTLE**, and DANA ROHRABACHER (who once called Abramoff "a very honest man").

In a January 2006 piece titled "It's the Republicans, Stupid," conservative *National Review* editor Rich Lowry wrote:

The GOP now craves . . . bipartisan cover in the Jack Abramoff scandal. Republicans trumpet every Democratic connection to Abramoff in the hope that something resonates. . . . But this is, in its essence, a Republican scandal, and any attempt to portray it otherwise is a misdirection . . . The GOP members can make a case that the scandal reflects more the way Washington works than the unique perfidy of their party, but even this is self-defeating, since Republicans run Washington.

"Well, it's no surprise Ken Mehlman doesn't want any fingers pointed since one of the big fingers would be pointed at him," blogger Josh Marshall noted. As a favor to his friend Jack Abramoff, Mehlman had blocked a State Department post nominee who had given Abramoff some trouble in keeping the Mariana sweatshops running.

As a fitting sentence for all these shmucks, or whatever rhymes with that, how about twenty-five years of stitching Nike sneakers at the Marianas minimum wage of $3.05 an hour?

Asshole #2:
ALLEN, "MACACA GEORGE"

Former Virginia senator and governor, on his best behavior while running for reelection as governor in 2006: "This fellow here, over here with the yellow shirt, macaca, or whatever his name is. He's with my opponent. He's following us around everywhere. . . . Let's give a welcome to macaca, here. Welcome to America and the real world of Virginia." Allen was (a) assuming that the man, a Virginia native of Indian descent, must be an immigrant, and (b) referring to him by the name of the genus of the macaque monkey. (Allen is evidently a learned man.) The same epithet was used by European colonists for the indigenous population of the former Belgian Congo. The m word cost Allen his reelection, but he can still hold his head high: *Macaca* was named Most Politically Incorrect Word of 2006 from Global Language Monitor, a group that tracks language trends.

Asshole #3:

ASHCROFT, JOHN

Full name John "Police State," Corporate-Gun-for-Hire, How-Much-Would-He-Charge-Not-to-Sing-That-Song, Pass-the-Crisco Ashcroft.* Former Missouri governor and senator and Bush's first-term attorney general. A compassionate evangelical Christian under whose governorship Missouri prison capacity grew by 72 percent. Rather than Hannah Arendt's "*banality* of evil," Ashcroft exemplified the *buffoonery* of evil commonly exhibited by GOP pols (and by dictators from Mussolini to Kim Jong Il). Ashcroft can never be forgotten, no matter how hard one tries—so emblematic was he of the Bush administration in its heyday, and of how low the GOP had sunk. Moreover, he has not gone away: old Republican government officials never die—they become lobbyists. Great Ashcroft moments:

▶ In 1998, praised the pro-Confederate magazine *Southern Partisan* for "defending Southern patriots like [Robert E.] Lee, [Stonewall] Jackson and [Jefferson] Davis."

▶ As a senator, met with Thomas Bugel, president of the Saint Louis chapter of the racist Council of Conservative Citizens (CCC—because KKK was already taken), to discuss the case of Charles Sell, a local dentist and CCC member indicted for plotting to murder an FBI agent and a federal witness. Ashcroft then wrote to the U.S. Justice Department on Sell's behalf. Ashcroft later denied having known about Bugel's connection to the CCC—which was often noted in the media—

*Correction: We learned, too late to change the text, that his real middle name is David.

despite the senator's extensive previous contact with Bugel, which included taking his side when he was vociferously defending segregation as a Saint Louis school board member.

▶ Saw fit to give the commencement speech at Bob Jones University, where interracial dating was officially prohibited until 2000. Orated: "America has been different [from other countries]. We have no king but Jesus." (Some of us, uh, nonmonarchists have a problem with that . . .)

▶ Lost his 2000 senatorial reelection bid* to an opponent who had died two weeks before the election. Despite Ashcroft's campaign cash from corporations such as agribusiness/bioengineering giant Monsanto (which contributed five times more to him than to any other congressional candidate that year), voters preferred the corpse.

▶ Author of several self-laudatory books, including *Lessons from a Father to His Son* (1998), in which he described having *anointed himself with cooking oil* (he was out of holy oil—a common household dilemma) at the start of both of his terms as Missouri governor. (I see he used Christco oil. Sounds close enough.)

As Attorney General:
▶ Oversaw the USA PATRIOT Act and other Bushevist assaults on basic American liberties and rights.

▶ Proposed the creation of OPERATION TIPS, a Soviet-style program in which government and private-sector

---

*Ashcroft had considered running for president in 2000. Can you imagine? A sanctimonious moron, ripe for domination by a crafty, ruthless VP? Could have been a *nightmare*.

employees would inform law enforcement agencies about suspicious behavior they encounter on the job. The U.S. Postal Service refused outright to participate, and the proposal was eventually abandoned. (All the letter carriers would have had to do was peek into windows at each stop! What's the problem?)

▶ Drafted the Domestic Security Enhancement Act of 2003, a plan to curtail or eliminate judicial review of federal law enforcement, so the FBI and CIA could do as they liked, unanswerable to any pain-in-the-butt elected representatives about whatever pains they were inserting in the butts of secretly detained suspects.

▶ Told the *Los Angeles Times* in February 2002 that "Islam is a religion in which God requires you to send your son to die for Him. Christianity is a faith in which God sends His son to die for you." And Ashcroft's was an administration in which the president sends *your* son to die for *him*. But that's neither here nor there!

▶ Waged tireless war on casual soft drug users. In the wake of 9/11, he sent federal agents to the central front of the war on ~~terror~~ drugs—the homes of disease-suffering marijuana users in Oregon, which had legalized medical marijuana. As he had apparently eliminated the threat of terrorism (see fourth bullet point down) and had free time on his hands, he also launched two nationwide investigations, code-named, so help me, OPERATION PIPE DREAMS and OPERATION HEADHUNTER, targeting businesses selling drug paraphernalia, mostly marijuana pipes and bongs. Explained Asscroft: "Quite simply, the illegal drug paraphernalia industry has invaded the homes of

families across the country without their knowledge."
(Take it from me, every thirteen-year-old boy in the
Western world, whether he was ever a Boy Scout or
not, can fashion a rude pipe in minutes, using
everyday household items.)

▶ Spent $8,000 of taxpayer funds on curtains to cover
the partially nude female statue of ~~Janet Jackson~~ the
Spirit of Justice in the Great Hall of the Justice
Department.

▶ Wrote, then repeatedly and publicly sang, a hymn to
America called "Let the Eagle Soar," perhaps just to
show that no display of patriotism, even one whose
unbearable flatulence and sheer ridiculousness would
have embarrassed a 1920s meeting of the Daughters
of the American Revolution, could embarrass *him*.

▶ Issued dramatic warnings of impending al Qaeda
attacks in 2004 to distract from Bush's plummeting
approval ratings in an election year and to remind
voters that they still needed their big strong steadfast
daddy to protect them. As he had protected them in
2001. (See FEAR, POLITICAL SCIENCE AND ENGI-
NEERING OF.)

▶ Only a few months later, wrote in his November 2004
resignation letter that "The objective of securing the
safety of Americans from crime and terror has been
achieved." (Shouldn't there have been some kind of
public celebration or holiday?)

▶ Did as all Republican officials do after leaving
office—cashed in on his government connections by
becoming a corporate lobbyist. His Ashcroft Group
was soon turning down two clients for every one it
accepted. Companies seeking government military

and homeland security contracts were among his leading clients. In May 2006, *The Hill* magazine listed Ashcroft as one of K Street's* top fifty hired guns. Let the eagle soar!

Ass-Holiness: Evil Right-Wing Men of God

When you say "radical right" today, I think of these moneymaking ventures by fellows like Pat Robertson and others who are trying to take the Republican Party and make a religious organization out of it. If that ever happens, kiss politics good-bye.
        —Former Republican senator Barry Goldwater, 1994

These jokers may not be GOP officials, but I don't think any of them vote D; several have the ears of top GOP leaders; and their flocks are, after all, the base of the core of the GOP base. They take credit for putting Bush in office. Let's give it to them.

Philip "Flip" Benham, Methodist minister and national leader of the violent antiabortion group Operation Save America, also known as Operation Rescue, which blockades and sometimes invades clinics and threatens doctors and patients. Recovering saloon owner and alcoholic. (Do "recoverers" *have to*, uh, *flip* to the other extreme?)
► "The problem that America has is they've turned their back on God. Our job is to fall down on the barbed wire, so our kids can run over our backs and storm the gates

*Washington's lobbyist row

of Hell." (See AMERICA-HATERS, CONSERVATIVE. In Palestine, small children being trained for martyrdom are given toy suicide belts. There are lots of good ideas out there that American right-wingers could adopt.)

▶ Front of the group's white-on-black T-shirts: "*INTOLERANT.*" Back: "Homosexuality is a sin. Islam is a lie. Abortion is murder. Some issues are just black and white."

▶ Shouted at Norma McCorvey, the "Jane Roe" in *Roe v. Wade*, upon meeting her at a book-signing: "You are responsible for the deaths of over 33 million children."

Bishop ***Wellington Boone,*** leading African-American evangelical leader, from his book *Breaking Through*:

▶ "I believe that slavery, and the understanding of it when you see it God's way, was redemptive."

▶ "The black community must stop criticizing Uncle Tom. He is a role model, who, when he was stepped on like a worm, at a point of crisis, evidenced the nature of the classic model worm, Jesus."

Bill Donohue, president of the Catholic League for Religious and Civil Rights, which patrols America in search of defamation or discrimination against Catholics. The League has links with Operation Rescue (see **Flip Benham**) and with the Protestant-evangelical right, where defamation of Catholicism as "Satanic" and "a false religion" is commonplace. Clearly a case of my enemy's enemy. To wit, Democrats, liberals, pro-choicers, and *certain* non-Catholics.

▶ "The media elite have an aversion to religion." That must be why Donohue appeared on network and cable news programs at least twenty-three times in 2004 alone.

▶ "Hollywood is controlled by secular Jews who hate Christianity in general and Catholicism in particular. It's not a secret, okay? . . . That's why they hate this movie [The Passion of Mel Gibson]. It's about Jesus Christ, and it's about truth. . . . Hollywood likes anal sex. They like to see the public square without nativity scenes. I like families. I like children. They like abortions." He's merely pointing out that these Jews hate Christianity and children and like anal sex and abortions. The Catholic League fights *defamation*. These are simply *facts*.

▶ "The left won't tell the truth about the gay death style [because] they are censorial at heart." Unlike Bill "Anything Goes" Donohue: This civil rights champion wrote a book attacking the American Civil Liberties Union, which has defended even Nazis' free speech rights. Meanwhile the Catholic League led efforts to ban art works and films dealing frankly with homosexuality, AIDS, and the Catholic Church abuse scandal.

▶ On stem cell research: "[W]e might as well serve [human embryos] as appetizers at a human embryonic cocktail to people" [*sic*, and sick].

Tony Evans, Christian radio broadcaster; pastor; Dallas-based chaplain for the NBA's Dallas Mavericks and formerly for the NFL's Dallas Cowboys:

▶ "It's been too long that three percent of homosexuals control our moral majority." Gimme a break. It's barely been twenty-five years.

▶ Men, arise! Throw off your chains! "Don't you understand, mister, you are royalty and God has chosen you to be priest of your home?"

Rev. **Jerry Falwell,** Moral Majority founder:

▶ "Most of these feminists are radical, frustrated lesbians, many of them, and man-haters, and failures in
their relationships with men, and who have declared
war on the male gender." *Bring it on.*

▶ Muhammad was "a demon possessed-pedophile" and
"a terrorist." (He *was not* demon-possessed!)

▶ On the cause of 9/11: "The pagans, and the abortionists, and the feminists, and the gays and lesbians . . .
the ACLU, People for the American Way—all of them
who have tried to secularize America—I point the
finger in their face and say, 'You helped this happen'
. . . [God allowed] the enemies of America to give us
probably what we deserve."

Rev. **Franklin Graham,** eldest son of Billy Graham;
president and CEO of the Billy Graham Evangelistic Association; friend and confidant of **GEORGE W. BUSH.** Gave the
prayer at Bush's first inaugural.

▶ September 14, 2001: "Let's use the weapons we have,
the weapons of mass destruction if need be and
destroy the enemy." But we have met the enemy and
he is us. It was our *own* fault. Graham, same day: "We
need to confess our sins to God, asking for forgive-
ness as a nation . . ."

▶ Polytheism (and ass-holiness) lives: "The god of Islam
is not the same God of the Christian or the Judeo-
Christian faith. It is a different god, and I believe a
very evil and a very wicked religion. . . . The true God
is the God of the Bible, not the Koran."

▶ During the 1991 Gulf War, when Gen. Norman
Schwarzkopf tried to explain to Graham the problems

he was causing by shipping tens of thousands of Arabic-language New Testaments to the troops in Saudi Arabia to be passed out to the locals, in direct violation of Saudi law and of the U.S. government's promise of no proselytizing: "Sir, I understand that, and I appreciate that, but I'm also under orders, and that's from the King of Kings and Lord of Lords."

▶ On the causes of HURRICANE KATRINA: "[New Orleans] is one wicked city, okay? It's known for Mardi Gras, for Satan worship. It's known for sex perversion. It's known for every type of drugs and alcohol and the orgies and all of these things that go on down there. . . . There's been a black spiritual cloud over New Orleans for years. . . . God is going to use that storm to bring revival."

Pat Robertson needs no introduction, but rather, extradition:

▶ "You say you're supposed to be nice to the Episcopalians and the Presbyterians and the Methodists and this, that, and the other thing. Nonsense. I don't have to be nice to the spirit of the anti-Christ."

▶ After the city of Dover, Pennsylvania, voted out the school board that had instituted the teaching of intelligent design, which led to a federal trial: "I'd like to say to the good citizens of Dover: If there is a disaster in your area, don't turn to God, you just rejected him from your city." (God follows every election closely. His commentaries are featured regularly on Fox News.)

▶ "Just like what Nazi Germany did to the Jews, so liberal America is now doing to the evangelical Christians. It's no different. . . . It is the Democratic Congress, the liberal-based media and the homosexuals who want to destroy the Christians . . . More terrible than anything suffered by any minority in history." African slavery, extermination of native Americans—nothing compares to the way Christians are being forced to occupy the White House, Congress, the courts . . .

Jimmy Swaggart, televangelist, in a church sermon: "If one [gay man] ever looks at me like that [amorously], I'm gonna kill him and tell God he died."

Asshole #4:
BAKER, RICHARD

Ten-term Republican representative from Louisiana. Speaking to lobbyists weeks after HURRICANE KATRINA, September 2005: "We finally cleaned up public housing in New Orleans. We couldn't do it, but God did." (God hates public housing and federal assistance for the poor in general. He is, after all, a Republican.)

Crime, Corruption, and Cronyism Case #2:
BECHTEL: Linking Republican Bigwigs with Big Fat U.S. Government Contracts, Assorted Dictators, and Saudi Oiligarchs for Over Half a Century.

With the possible exception of the CARLYLE GROUP, no company —even HALLIBURTON—better epitomizes CORPORATE-GOP incest and the government-business "REVOLVING DOOR" than Bechtel Corp., the largest U.S. engineering-construction company. "Decades before its comrade in cronyism, the Carlyle Group, made its meteoric, Bush-assisted ascent to global prominence, Bechtel had already perfected the dark art of milking intimate government connections for fat, risk-free contracts."[4]

For decades, Bechtel has built environmentally damaging oil, power, and water projects around the world and screwed up major projects in the United States, including, in the 1940s, Alaska's failed Canol pipeline, which cost taxpayers a fortune (the Truman Committee, citing Bechtel's cost overruns and mismanagement, termed Canol more destructive to the war effort than any act of enemy sabotage); Boston's Big Dig project, whose overruns and accounting irregularities totaled over $1 billion; and trailers for post-HURRICANE KATRINA temporary housing—thousands of which were never used. Thanks to Bechtel's cost-plus contract, the government paid $500 million for the largely empty trailers.[5] Moreover, small local businesses could have used the work, and done it way cheaper. According to a director of the International Forum on Globalization, Bechtel has "proven time and again that it has no concern for the social, environmental or human costs of its operations."[6]

Naturally, Bechtel has been a major political contributor, giving over $1 million between 1999 and 2002, most of it to Republicans. Since the 1940s, Bechtel has also cultivated close ties with the Saudi and Kuwaiti "royals," building pipelines, refineries, factories, and ports in Saudiland and Kuwait, often in partnership with the Saudi Binladin Group.

Top Bechtel Republicans have included:

Riley P. Bechtel, current CEO: net worth, $3.2 billion; 50th richest American; George W. Bush appointee to the Export Council.

George Shultz, former Bechtel director and president (1974–1982): treasury secretary under Nixon; secretary of state under Reagan; member of the Committee for the Liberation of Iraq, a bunch of right-wing bigwigs who lobbied for the overthrow of Saddam Hussein. Mission Accomplished: Bechtel immediately won huge reconstruction contracts in "liberated" Iraq.

Caspar Weinberger, defense secretary under Reagan; previously Bechtel vice president, director, and general counsel.

Nicholas Brady, former chairman of Bechtel-controlled investment bank Dillon, Read; treasury secretary under both Reagan and Bush I; friend and adviser to the latter.

Ross Connelly, former president of Bechtel Energy Resources. Maine campaign director for Bush in 2000. Payoff: appointed to the federal Overseas Private Investment Corporation (OPIC), which provides political insurance to U.S. companies who invest in unstable parts of the world. Companies like Bechtel. (Because why should a big, well-connected corporation have to take *risks* like an ordinary businessperson?) Connelly traveled the world for OPIC, arranging a $130 million loan to a Bechtel joint venture to privatize Lima, Peru's airport and helping Bechtel obtain large highway-building contracts in Serbia. Also see CORPORATE WELFARE.

W. Kenneth Davis, head of nuclear reactor development at the U.S. Atomic Energy Commission under Eisenhower. Joined Bechtel in 1958. A year later Bechtel was selected to build the first U.S. nuclear power plant. Appointed deputy secretary of energy in the Reagan administration.

Jack Sheehan, Bechtel senior vice president; retired
Marine Corps general; served under Rumsfeld and Bush
on the Defense Policy Board, the secretive Pentagon
advisory council that lobbied hard for war in Iraq.

DONALD RUMSFELD, defense secretary under Bush II;
never worked for Bechtel *officially*, but as Reagan's
special envoy to make nice to Saddam Hussein in
1983, tried to sell Saddam on a Bechtel oil pipeline
project for Iraq.

In 1988—just after Saddam gassed thousands of Kurdish
villagers—Bechtel signed contracts with Iraq to build a
chemical plant. After Gulf War I, the Bush I administration
awarded Bechtel contracts to extinguish Kuwait's blazing oil
wells. The company scored even bigger after Gulf War II
(Iraq), winning a secret, closed-bid reconstruction contract
worth more than $700 million for starters, and eventually,
contracts totaling $2.3 billion. Best of times, worst of times,
war and peace, pride and prejudice, friend or foe—these
companies make out big-time either way. Bechtel and Halliburton epitomize what has become known as disaster capitalism. (It could also be called "vulture capitalism": feeding
on the carcasses supplied by U.S. policies.)

Constructus interruptus. Bechtel pulled out of Iraq
abruptly in October 2006, leaving a number of projects unfin-
ished, including construction of a new children's hospital in
Basra. "The hospital, which was trumpeted by Secretary of
State Condoleezza Rice and First Lady Laura Bush, fell a year
behind schedule and overran its original budget by as much
as 150 percent." Bechtel blamed "difficult soil conditions in
the area." [7] (Also see **WAR PRIVATIZATION AND PROFITEERING**.)

Assholes of the Air (and the Press): GOP Loudmouth-Pieces
BECK, GLENN

Conservative radio host whose program is syndicated on more than 160 stations (by the GOP Radio Corporation, a.k.a. Clear Channel Communications): "I'm thinking about killing [liberal filmmaker] MICHAEL MOORE, and I'm wondering if I could kill him myself, or if I would need to hire somebody to do it. No, I think I could. I think he could be looking me in the eye, you know, and I could just be choking the life out—is this wrong?" No-o-o! You're a conservative, man! Previously, Beck accused Moore (*yes*, falsely) of "taking help and money from Hezbollah" and called Michael Berg, who criticized the Bush administration after his son Nick was beheaded in Iraq, "despicable" and "a scumbag." (One should sacrifice one's sons to Bush with a smile and a "thank-you"!)

BENNETT, WILLIAM

Pundit/windbag/hypocrite. Education secretary under Reagan; "drug czar" under Bush I. The fact that he had a long-standing gambling problem—while acting as America's self-appointed morality czar *and* heading an organization opposed to the extension of casino gambling—is probably the *best* thing about him. The worst include:

▶ Acting as America's self-appointed morality czar; authoring books like *The Death of Outrage: Bill Clinton and the Assault on American Ideals* and *The Book of Virtues: A Treasury of Great Moral Stories* and at least four other books with the word "moral" or "virtue" in the title; presuming to know what morals and virtues everyone should embrace—while:

▶ Belonging to the PROJECT FOR A NEW AMERICAN CENTURY (see NEOCONS) and supporting Bush's illegal and immoral invasion of Iraq.

▶ Declaring that beheading drug dealers, as in Saudi Arabia, would be "morally plausible." (I've heard that the Saudis promote puritanical Wahabi Islam globally —I just didn't know how successfully.)

▶ Saying: "It's true that if you wanted to reduce crime . . . if that were your sole purpose, you could abort every black baby in this country, and your crime rate would go down." (If you aborted every Republican baby, the rate of larger-scale CRIME, CORRUPTION, AND CRONYISM would plummet. But those decisions should be left up the woman and her doctor.)

Asshole #5:
BOLTON, JOHN

Former Bush administration undersecretary of state and— as one of the leading UN-haters in a party of UN-haters, known to foreign service officers as the "antidiplomat"— GEORGE W. BUSH's obvious choice for U.S. ambassador to the UN. Following his recess appointment* (Senate confirmation was out of the question), Bolton served from August 2005 to December 2006. (Also see NEOCONS.) Boltonisms:

▶ "There's no such thing as the United Nations."

▶ "The [UN] Secretariat building in New York has 38

*See OVERSIGHT.

stories. If it lost ten stories, it wouldn't make a bit of difference." (Opinions differ as to whether the remark was a signal to terrorist cells.)

▶ Upon arriving in Florida in November 2000: "I'm with the Bush-Cheney team, and I'm here to stop the [vote] count."

Asshole #6:
BUCHANAN, PAT

Commentator, former Nixon adviser and speechwriter, and third-party presidential candidate in 2000, 1996, and 1992 (when he performed the only good service he's ever done for this country—drew votes away from Poppy Bush to the benefit of Bill Clinton). Right-wing "peasant populist," militant Catholic, rabid immigration opponent ("No one American better embodies the link between America's religious right and Europe's fascists than Pat Buchanan," wrote Jason Abaluck in the Harvard *Perspective*), and "anti-Zionist" who frequently rails against the pro-Israel lobby and its supposed control over U.S. foreign policy and once said, "Congress is Israeli-occupied territory." The remark prompted a comradely letter from Russian racist-nationalist-misogynist politician VLADIMIR ZHIRINOVSKY, complaining of the "troublesome tribe" that was causing similar problems in Russia, and endorsing Buchanan's 1996 presidential bid. Manages to dislike Muslims, too. And Mexicans. At least those who come to the United States. Author of the 2006 book *State of Emergency: The Third World Invasion and Conquest of America*. Identifies openly with the isolationist AMERICA FIRST movement (has adopted "America First" as a slogan), whose members opposed U.S. entry into World War II and sometimes expressed sympathy with Nazi Germany (and vice versa).*

As Nixon's adviser, "Buchanan made his specialty 'opposition research,' the backbone of the [1968] Nixon campaign's 'covert ops,'" i.e., dirty tricks against Democrats: staging counterfeit attacks by one Democrat on another; arranging demonstrations and spreading rumors; fouling up scheduled events . . . "Buchanan's strategies were Rove-esque before KARL ROVE had even graduated from high school."[8]

As communications director for the Reagan White House, Buchanan's most memorable act was to press Reagan to stand firm in the face of public criticism and to visit Germany's Bitburg cemetery, where SS and other German troops were buried. From the late 1980s through the '90s, he campaigned against U.S. government actions to deport or prosecute accused Nazi and Nazi-allied war criminals.

Buchanan's 1992 campaign organization evolved into a group called American Cause. Its kickoff event was a conference titled "Winning the Culture War," which Buchanan proclaimed as "the Boston Tea party of the cultural revolution." Speakers included professional homophobe WILL PERKINS of Colorado for Family Values; EZOLA FOSTER of Black Americans for Family Values, who referred to public schools as

---

*The movement's most notable leader, aviator Charles Lindbergh—who asked supporters, "Are we going to let Jews run this country?"—accepted a medal from Hermann Goering in 1938. The movement included prominent industrialists who profited from trade with Germany; German-Americans; and Irish-Catholics such as Buchanan and the far-right, anti-Semitic 1930s-'40s radio demagogue Father Coughlin, who were not particularly eager to rush to the aid of the British *or* the Jews. The Nazi salute was seen at America First rallies.

"socialist training camps"; and home schooling proponent MARY KAY CLARK, who described the National Education Association as "the training camp of the enemy of the family." Buchanan still "works the college circuit, warning of that non-white, non-hetero, non-Christian menace that threatens to corrupt your children and grandchildren."[9]

In 2002 Buchanan, who purports to champion the working class, launched a magazine, *The American Conservative*, in partnership with playboy (small p) columnist TAKI THEODORACOPULOS (or "Taki," as he signs his byline), scion to a Greek shipping fortune—"an unabashed yacht-owning, nightclub-going social snob," wrote Franklin Foer in *The New Republic*. "It is, to say the least, an odd match. . . . While Buchanan rails against the fraying of God-fearing, law-abiding, traditional American culture, Taki was convicted in 1984 for smuggling cocaine. His most penetrating meditation on American cultural decay was a 1982 essay . . . titled, 'Why American Women Are Lousy Lovers.'"

Buchanan's own views on women and other banes:

▶ "Rail as they will about 'discrimination,' women are simply not endowed by nature with the same measures of single-minded ambition and the will to succeed in the fiercely competitive world of Western capitalism."

▶ Multiculturalism is "an across-the-board assault on our Anglo-American heritage . . . Our [American] culture is superior. Our culture is superior because our [American] religion is Christianity and that is the truth that makes men free." (Also see Buchanan on XMAS AND CHRISTIANITY, DEMOCRATIC-LIBERAL-SATANIST-SECULARIST WAR ON.)

▶ "Who are the beneficiaries of the courts' protection?

Members of various minorities including criminals, atheists, homosexuals, flag burners, illegal immigrants (including terrorists), convicts, and pornographers."

▶ "Homosexuality is not a civil right. Its rise almost always is accompanied, as in the Weimar Republic, with a decay of society and a collapse of its basic cinder block, the family." And you know who cleansed Germany of all that . . . decay:

▶ "Hitler was . . . an individual of great courage, a soldier's soldier in the Great War, a political organizer of the first rank, a leader steeped in the history of Europe . . . His genius was an intuitive sense of the mushiness, the character flaws, the weakness masquerading as morality that was in the hearts of the statesmen who stood in his path." Gotta hate that mushiness. But as far as a, um, *solution*, you know what *won't* work? Carbon monoxide. According to Buchanan, the diesel engines used to kill victims at the Treblinka death camp could "not emit enough carbon monoxide to kill anybody." (Some "Holocaust," huh.)

▶ "The War Between the States* was about independence, about self-determination, about the right of a people to break free of a government to which they could no longer give allegiance . . . How long is this endless groveling before every cry of 'racism' going to continue before the whole country collectively throws up?" Some of us are throwing up right now.

*That (versus "Civil War") was the name used by the Confederate government and later formally endorsed by the United Confederate Veterans and the United Daughters of the Confederacy.

Asshole #7:
BUSH, GEORGE H. W.: JESUS *CHRIST*, WHAT A LIAR! (AND IDIOT!)

In comparison with Junior's presidency, Poppy's (1989–1993) has come to look moderate, almost benign. But this is an optical illusion. Don't let President Poppy's goofiness, his addled brain and muddled speech, fool you either. Behind them lurks . . . evil.

As Reagan's vice president, Bush had been the consummate yes-man. He fell straight into line, for example, with Reagan's tax and budget plans, which Bush, while running against Reagan for the presidency, had mocked as "voodoo economics." (When reporters asked the new vice president whether he still believed this, Bush denied ever having said it and defied "anybody to find it." So CBS found and rebroadcast the original footage. This created a widespread belief that he *had* said it and was now lying about it. But that's the liberal media for you.)

"Read my lips—no new taxes," Bush famously pledged during his 1988 campaign. In 1990, he signed into law the single largest tax increase in U.S. history. But his lies about the Reagan administration's secret, illegal proxy war in Nicaragua and the illegal schemes to fund it—i.e., IRAN-CONTRA—were much more serious. As *Online Journal's* Carla Binion wrote: "Reagan and Bush's concessions to terrorists did in fact lead to more terrorism, more kidnapping of hostages, and more killing of innocent civilians in Nicaragua, and they knew it. . . . *Those issues will be the subject of the next article in this series.*" (Italics added.)

Iran-Contra was about secret government, contempt for Congress, total disregard for the laws of the land by its highest officers, and complicity with gangs of murderers in acts of utter savagery designed to overthrow another country's democratically elected government. And Bush, the former CIA director under President Ford, was in all the way on the plot. Even while he headed up Reagan's Presidential Task Force on Terrorism—even as he declared, "Our policy is clear, concise, unequivocal. We will offer no concession to terrorists, because that only leads to more terrorism. States that practice terrorism, or actively support it, will not be allowed to do so without consequence"—Bush was regularly attending White House meetings where he, Reagan, and others in the inner circle plotted to sell weapons to the leading state sponsor of terrorism, Iran. Bush later insisted he was "out of the loop." Minutes of those meetings show clearly that he was in the loop and that the loop all knew that what they were doing was illegal.

Bush also claimed that in the various deals made to fund the Contras, "there was no quid pro quo." There was quid. There was quo. In one instance, Bush delivered the quid personally, traveling to Honduras to offer its government $100 million in weapons and money in return for aid to the Contras. The U.S. government admitted this during Oliver North's trial. Bush continued to deny it. Bush to this day has not admitted he lied about Iran-Contra.

In 1992, in his final weeks as president, Bush bestowed eight presidential pardons. One was to a heroin trafficker, one to oil tycoon Armand Hammer for making illegal contributions to Nixon's 1972 campaign. Six were to Iran-Contra principals for any and all related crimes. Bush also displayed his moral judgment in the equivalence he drew during an interview with CBS's Dan Rather: "It's not fair to judge my whole career by a rehash on Iran. How would you like it if I

judged your career by those seven minutes when you
walked off the set in New York? Would you like that?"

***"Spending caps is good" and other Poppy Bush
pearls***—and remember, we've saved the looniest for
IGNORANCE AND IDIOCY:

Toasting Philippine dictator FERDINAND MARCOS, whose
  regime was renowned for human rights violations,
  massive corruption, nepotism, and the murder of a
  popular, left-leaning political opponent, and who was
  removed from power five years later in a popular
  uprising. "We love your adherence to democratic principles and to the democratic process."

Commenting on the 290 civilian deaths in the 1988
  downing of an Iranian passenger airliner in a commercial air corridor by the U.S. Navy warship *Vin-
  cennes*: "I will never apologize for the United
  States—I don't care what the facts are. . . . I'm not an
  apologize-for-America kind of guy." To the world: On
  behalf of America, I apologize for Mr. Bush.

His inspiring words to the mostly working-class, Latino
  students of an East Los Angeles high school—perhaps
  unaware that 70 percent of its seniors went on to college or that its calculus teacher, Jaime Escalante, was
  the subject of the film *Stand and Deliver*, which at the
  time had been in theaters for two months: "You don't
  have to go to college to be a success. . . . We need the
  people who run the offices, the people who do the hard
  physical work of our society." (Stand and deliver pizza!)

"I don't know that atheists should be considered as citizens, nor should they be considered patriots. This is
  one nation under God."

In front of a live mike, after being booed at an AIDS conference: "Who was that? Some gay group out there?"
During a tour of Auschwitz: "Boy, they were big on cre-
matoriums, weren't they?"
To a reporter who asked what his favorite (and to many,
ominous) new phrase, "New World Order," actually
meant: "Well, I envisage it—one: where the whole—
once we're—let me start over. . . . But I think if we work
cooperatively as our—with our common sights set—
this aggressor [Saddam] will not succeed—it opens up
all kinds of possibilities for a New World Order. We're
already seeing that 'world order' means 'world.'"
Clarifying why he raised taxes after promising not to:
"Total mistake—policy, political, everything else. . . .
But it was—spending caps is good. . . . But . . . I would
say both policy and politically, I think we can all agree
that it's drawn a lot of fire."

It is unkind to mock President Bush for vomiting in the
lap of the Japanese prime minister, then fainting, during a
state function in Tokyo. Worth mentioning, however, is that
in so doing he spawned the Japanese slang verb *bushusuru*—
literally, "Bushing it." (As in, "When I heard the 2000 presidential election results, I bushed.")

Bush's postpresidential career has been further distinguished by the speech he gave to a SUN MYUNG MOON–
sponsored organization and by his peddling of his global
connections as a glorified salesman for the CARLYLE GROUP,
helping the Republican-run defense contractor/investment
bank attract various Middle Eastern despots and bin
Ladens as customers. (See **O.I.L.**) He also helped raise
money to aid Asian tsunami victims, saying: "This is bigger
than politics; this is about saving lives, and I must confess

I'm getting a huge kick out of it." Indeed—fun like that
doesn't come along every day! . . . (Now, which way is the
bushusuru room?)

BUSH, GEORGE W.

Our enemies are innovative and resourceful, and so are
we. They never stop thinking about new ways to harm our
country and our people, and neither do we."
—George W. Bush, August 2004

For its President's Day week issue in February 2007, *U.S.*
News & World Report ran a cover story titled "America's
Worst Presidents." What made them think of *that* topic?

Actually, the article led off:

Is George W. Bush's presidency shaping up to be *one*
of the worst in U.S. history? [Emphasis added.] You
hear the question being asked more and more these
days. And more and more, you hear the same answer.
With Iraq a shambles and trust in the administration
declining . . . it is probably not surprising that 54 percent of respondents in a recent *USA Today*/Gallup
survey said that history would judge Bush a below-
average or poor president, more than twice the
number who gave such a rating to any of the five preceding occupants of the White House, including
Gerald Ford and Jimmy Carter.*

---

*A far better gauge of average Americans' opinion was the February 2007
Nation Magazine online reader's poll on "Worst U.S. President Ever."
Results: Buchanan (D), 5%. Harding (R), 1%. Hoover (R), 2%. Nixon (R), 2%.
George W. Bush (R), 87%.

Don't know how they came up with that 54 percent; Bush's approval ratings at the time were below 30 percent. The article named ten presidents most historians agree were awful, from Pierce and Buchanan to Hoover and Nixon, but of course wimped out by writing: "It's too soon to judge the current one."

Yes, yes, too soon, no doubt. Twenty or thirty years from now, perhaps we'll understand that the Bushies' attacks on environmental protections, on the Constitution and its democratic checks and balances, on civil liberties and privacy, on voting rights, on government accountability, on Social Security, Medicare, and the progressive tax system, on the middle class and poor, on fiscal responsibility, on a country that hadn't attacked and didn't threaten us, on the integrity and honor of the president's office, on truth itself, and, in Bush's particular case, on the English language, was all for the *good*.

So, yes—too soon to judge, to be sure. But let's at least tick off a few of the Bush administration's achievements.

▶ Lost the 2000 election but won the recount (by a 5–4 vote). "Won" the 2004 election thanks to GOP state election officials keeping Democrats from voting and discarding Dems' ballots by the hundreds of thousands.[10]

▶ Used the mandate gained in those landslide victories to drag the country—not kicking and screaming so much as shocked and awed—far to the right. (See AMERICA, HIJACKING OF BY CORPORATE INTERESTS AND RADICAL CONSERVATIVE WINGNUTS WHOSE POLICY GOALS ARE OPPOSED BY MOST AMERICANS.)

▶ Saddled us with a president who majored in IGNORANCE and minored in IDIOCY; who said things like, "Quotas they basically delineate based upon whatever," and "a world that is more interacted"; a man whose chief skill was using family connections first to save his failing business career (see **Bush-Bath** and beyond), then to advance his political career— but who *could* be counted on as a staunch defender of the New Global Corporate Order, Big Oil, and certain oily dictatorships. (See **O.I.L.**)

▶ Gave us GOVERNMENT FOR, BY AND OF BIG BUSINESS and created an epidemic of **Crime, Corruption, and Cronyism.** Systematically filled top administration posts with "former" executives, lawyers, and lobbyists from the industries they were now supposed to oversee in the public interest. It's misleading to say the Bushies betrayed the public trust; they are *in the business of* betraying the public trust.

▶ Set about converting every vital government program and function, from Social Security to homeland security, into a semiprivatized profit generator for GOP-friendly corporations to whom trillions of taxpayer dollars would be diverted and from whom political and financial support (and plummy postpolitical jobs) would flow. (See **GOPonomics** and **War Privatization and Profiteering.**)

▶ Created a mountain of new federal debt, the largest contributors to which were Bush's tax breaks for the rich.

▶ Fed us phony "FAMILY VALUES" talk while creating hardship for tens of millions of American families.

▶ Failed to prevent a preventable terrorist attack, the worst in U.S. history, because they were too busy consolidating their big-business coup d'état, pushing through TAX CUTS FOR THE RICH, and, especially, thinking too much about how fun it would be to invade IRAQ to care much about al Qaeda and multiple terrorism warnings. Then, after 9/11, lionized Bush as the *hero* of the hour.

▶ Shamelessly exploited 9/11, FEAR, and the "war on terror" as a pretext to take the axe to civil liberties; to demand speedier congressional approvals of every bit of Bush's pre-9/11 agenda, from oil drilling in the Alaska National Wildlife Refuge to rubber-stamp confirmation of Bush's far-right judicial nominees; to mythify Bush as a great Leader; and to shroud their policies and actions in secrecy.

▶ *Conspired*, using false and grossly exaggerated intelligence claims, to mislead the public and Congress into a disastrous invasion of IRAQ, for reasons that did *not* include strengthening national security, fighting terrorism, or spreading democracy, but did include winning the 2002 and 2004 elections and establishing a new U.S. military footprint in the world's richest oil region. (See **O.I.L.**) Killed scores of thousands, wasted hundreds of billions of taxpayer dollars, turned most of the world against the United States, destabilized the Middle East, and created a potent terrorist recruiting tool.

▶ Responded to the 2006 Congressional elections, which were largely a vote against the Iraq war, by ordering a troop buildup.

▶ Tirelessly fought every effort by Congress, independent commissions, the press, and citizens groups to obtain information about everything from the administration's pre-9/11 neglect of warnings to Bush's not-so-illustrious military record, from the fabrication of "intelligence" used to justify the Iraq invasion to the firing of U.S. attorneys who just weren't partisan enough.

Against democracy and above the law. Way above. The Bush gang claimed, seized and exercised unprecedented ~~royal~~ presidential powers, using highly original legal reasoning to assault the Constitutional checks and balances that protect against corruption and dictatorship. This epochal project entailed fanatical secrecy; the appointment of proponents of the "UNITARY EXECUTIVE" theory (which invests the president with virtually unlimited power) to key Justice Department posts (MICHAEL CHERTOFF, ALBERTO GONZALES, JOHN YOO) and to the Supreme Court (JOHN ROBERTS, SAMUEL ALITO); ceaseless obstruction of all congressional efforts to investigate administration failures and abuses (see **OVERSIGHT AND ACCOUNTABILITY**); and the ruthless rooting out of nonpartisans, dissenters, and whistle-blowers from federal agencies and their replacement by Bush-loyalist hacks (see **JUSTICE SYSTEM, PARTISAN POLITICAL PERVERSION OF**).

Perhaps Bush's least visible yet most nefarious abuse of power was his habitual use of signing statements. In 2006 the *Boston Globe* reported that Bush had "quietly claimed the authority to disobey more than 750 laws enacted since he took office." What courage! Rather than veto these laws in public view, as Frank Rich noted in the *New York Times*:

> [Bush] signed them, waited until after the press and lawmakers left the White House, and then filed statements in the Federal Register asserting that he would ignore laws he (not the courts) judged unconstitutional. This was the extralegal trick Mr. Bush used to bypass the ban on torture. It allowed him to make a coward's escape from the moral (and legal) responsibility of arguing for so radical a break with American practice.[11]

Asshole #8: George W. Bush

▶ "I trust God speaks through me. Without that, I couldn't do my job."

▶ "And as you know, my position is clear—I'm a commander guy."

▶ "I'm the Decider,* and I Decide what is best," Bush decided in April 2006, adding: "And what's best is for **DON RUMSFELD** to remain as the secretary of defense." Bush would wait until the day after the November 2006 midterm elections to fire Rummy (whom **JOHN MCCAIN** called "one of the worst secretaries of defense in history" and **DICK CHENEY** called the "the best secretary of defense the United States has ever had"), preferring to allow Bumsfelt to continue to screw up and get more U.S. troops killed in Iraq rather than admit to a mistake before an election.

▶ To GOP congressional leaders who warned at a November 2005 Oval Office meeting that his push to renew the more onerous provisions of the USA Patriot Act could alienate conservatives:** "I don't give a goddamn. I'm the president and the commander-in-chief. Do it my way." Reportedly screamed at an aide who, at the same meeting, said, "Mr. President, there is a valid case that the provisions in this law undermine the Constitution": "Stop throwing the Constitution in my face. It's just a goddamned piece of paper!"[12] ***

▶ "You know, when I campaigned here in 2000, I said, I want to

---

*The capital D was distinctly heard by reporters present.
**Prominent conservatives like Phyllis Schlafly and Bob Barr had joined forces with the American Civil Liberties Union and other liberal groups to oppose renewal.
***Attorney General Alberto Gonzales, while still White House counsel:

be a war president. [*A Bushian slip if ever there was one.*] No president wants to be a war president, but I am one." Okay. You're a war president. Now please take your toy soldiers and go home.

▶ "[T]he kind of lessons learned in Iraq . . . we can apply to both Iran and North Korea." Omigod . . . *Why?* Once wasn't enough?

▶ Asked at a 2004 press conference to name his biggest mistake (this would be good on a T-shirt): "I wish you'd have given me this written question ahead of time so I could plan for it . . . I'm sure something will pop into my head here in the midst of this press conference, with all the pressure of trying to come up with answer, but it hadn't yet. . . . I don't want to sound like I have made no mistakes. I'm confident I have. I just haven't—you just put me under the spot here, and maybe I'm not as quick on my feet as I should be in coming up with one." (That bulge in Bush's jacket during a debate with John Kerry *had* to be some kind of radio receiver.)

▶ "Those weapons of mass destruction have got to be somewhere . . . Nope, no weapons over there . . . maybe under here?"—At the 2004 Radio and TV Correspondents' Association dinner, narrating a comic slideshow of himself searching the Oval Office for the WMDs in whose name he had sentenced several thousand American troops and perhaps 100,000 Iraqis to death. . . . Oh, lighten up!

"The Constitution is an outdated document." Bush proposed seven amendments to the Constitution—a record for any modern president—during his first five years of occupation of the Oval Office, including an amendment to define marriage as a "union between a man and woman"—presumably to update the document to the mid-nineteenth century.

▶ Betrayed servicemen and women in Iraq by failing to supply sufficient body armor or even, at times, food and water (thanks to crony supply contractors like HALLIBURTON). Betrayed VETERANS by cutting health benefits and consigning them to the privatized, screwed-up care of Walter Reed Army Medical Center.

▶ Failed utterly in its response to the worst natural disaster in U.S. history, waiting days before taking action while hundreds died and hundreds of thousands remained stranded without food and water. (See HURRICANE KATRINA.)

▶ Worst of all: survived all of the above without getting their collective asses impeached and run out of town.

Coward-in-Chief. In July 2007, pollster Andrew Kohut of the Pew Research Center reported that "when we ask people to summon up one word that comes to mind" to describe George W. Bush, it's "incompetence." A better word, wrote the *New York Times*'s Frank Rich, might be "cowardice." Just a few of Bush's "profiles in cowardice":

▶ Using his family connections to get into the National Guard and avoid serving in Vietnam, despite his avowed support for the war—then failing to complete the National Guard service—then lying about it ever afterward.

▶ His record breaking use of dead-of-night recess appointments to install in office far-right-wingers and unqualified political hacks who would not have won Senate confirmation.

▶ His unwillingness to ask Americans for sacrifice, possibly even to introduce a draft, to supply sufficient troops and resources to actually *win* the Iraq war he should never have dragged us into in the first place.

▶ His refusal to ever admit a significant mistake, whatever the costs to the nation—for example, waiting until after the 2006 election to dump Rumsfeld.

▶ His commuting "**SCOOTER**" **LIBBY**'s sentence rather than granting a full pardon, which would have freed Libby to talk about the White House's pre-Iraq war intelligence shenanigans. To attract as little attention as possible, the White House announced the commutation by press release on the eve of the Fourth of July holiday.

BUSHIT

A popular saying goes: If George W. Bush's lips are moving, he's lying. That, however, is unfair. He could just be reading. "Washington could not tell a lie; Nixon could not tell the truth; Reagan cannot tell the difference," said comedian Mort Sahl. I suspect that Bush, even without Alzheimer's, may also be unable to tell the difference.

▶ Within weeks of seizing office in 2000, Bush broke his campaign pledges to leave the Social Security trust fund "lockbox" untouched* and to regulate carbon monoxide emissions (see **WARMING, GLOBAL**).

▶ A few months after Bush pledged—on Earth Day 2001—to protect wetlands, his administration revoked the tougher rules enacted under Clinton to control

---

*"Finding" the box jimmied open in the Treasury Department building, the Bushies blamed the Clintonites, but classified the police report, including fingerprint results, ostensibly for national security reasons.

wetlands-destroying development. On Earth Day 2002, Bush posed in front of a tree and made a solemn pledge to protect the environment. It must have been an enjoyable break from turning timber companies loose on national forest lands and waging the most ferocious war on environmental protections in U.S. history. (Which is tiring!)

▶ Bush asserted over and over that he had made "HOME-LAND" SECURITY his "highest priority." And over and over, he vetoed or shortchanged critical funding for "homeland" defense—while pressing ever harder for his *other* highest priority—TAX CUTS FOR THE RICH.

Noting this bait-and-switch pattern, CNN *Crossfire* host Paul Begala identified "case by case by case of Bush kissing the program and then killing it. It's the kiss of death. You know," he added, "all across America now, charitable groups are saying to the president, 'please don't come here.'" (Columnist Molly Ivins noted another variation on this theme: "When George W. Bush was governor of Texas, many political observers had a theory that whenever he started holding photo ops with adorable little children, it was time to grab your wallet because it meant some unconscionable giveaway to the corporations was in the wind.")

A pediatric training program to help children with cancer moved Bush to tears during a 2001 visit to Egleston Hospital in Atlanta. After the photo op, he went home and cut funding for it. In February 2003, Bush visited a D.C.-area branch of the Boys and Girls Clubs of America and praised the organization —whose funding his new budget proposal had just cut by $10 million. Bush cut $50 million from the Even Start Family Literacy Project, a program he had previously lauded. In

February 2007, *CongressDaily* reported the announcement of Bush's proposal "to increase the maximum Pell Grant for lower-income undergraduate students was greeted with fanfare." His fiscal 2008 budget, released days later, contained no money to pay for it.

▶ Bush, September 1, 2005: "I don't think anybody anticipated the breach of the [New Orleans] levees." *New York Times*: Hurricane Katrina could bring "a storm surge of 20 feet or higher that would 'most likely topple' the network of levees and canals that normally protect the bowl-shaped city from flooding." And: "The 17th Street levee that gave way and led to the flooding of New Orleans was part of an intricate, aging system . . . that was so chronically underfinanced that senior regional officials of the Army Corps of Engineers complained about it publicly for years." Bush, as quoted by Nancy Pelosi (D-Calif.), after she urged him to fire Michael Brown "because of all that went wrong, of all that didn't go right.": "'What didn't go right?'"

▶ "I will restore honor and integrity to the White House." And: "The administration I'll bring is a group of men and women who are focused on what's best for America, honest men and women, decent men and women . . . who will not stain the house." (See CHENEY, ROVE, RUMSFELD, ABRAMOFF, LIBBY, GATES, GRILES, Stephen Hadley, Douglas Feith, Richard Armitage, Elliott Abrams, Otto von Reich, John Negroponte . . .) And: "No one in my administration was involved in betraying the identity of a CIA agent." And: "Anyone involved in the Plame scandal will be fired." ("Fired," in BushSpeak, apparently means "protected and promoted.")

Iraq. This is where it all began. The cradle of civilization. And the source of a veritable Tigris and Euphrates of Bushit. In fact, IRAQ WAR, CONSPIRACY TO MISLEAD THE COUNTRY INTO is a subject of such Babylonian scale, I'm saying, the hell with it. See my *Bush-Hater's Handbook* and *Bushit!* and/or *The Greatest Story Ever Sold,* by Frank Rich. And see CHENEY, NEOCONS, RICE, and ROVE.

Crime, Corruption, and Cronyism Case #3:
THE BUSH–BATH–BIN LADEN–BCCI–TEXUS NEXUS AND DUMBYA'S RAGS-TO-RICHES BUSINESS CAREER

GEORGE W. BUSH's up-by-the-bootstraps rise from a hard-scrabble youth on the rough-and-tumble docks of Kennebunkport, Maine, and the mean streets of Andover, Massachusetts, with no capital except grit, determination, brains, hard work—

Rewind. "When actually in private business for himself," wrote the *New York Daily News*'s Lars Erik Nelson in 2000,

> Bush was a perennial loser. His profits came chiefly from investors who gave him money because of government tax breaks for the oil industry . . . In these self-proclaimed conservative candidates [Bush and Cheney], we see two of the nation's prime beneficiaries of . . . corporate welfare, or socialism for the rich. Both owe virtually every dime they have earned to the help of government. Bush, who derides Vice President Gore as the candidate of big government, made his own killing from one of government's most

abusive powers, the ability to seize private land from its owners at below market rates.

Dumbya's falls were repeatedly broken by his family's international net of unsavory business associates and political contributors. "The Bushes' shadowy business partners come straight out of the world in which the CIA thrives," wrote Jack Colhoun in *Covert Action Quarterly* in 1992:

—the netherworld of secret wars and covert operators, drug runners, mafiosi and crooked entrepreneurs out to make a fast buck. What Bush family members lack in business acumen, they make up for by cashing in on their blood ties to the former Director of Central Intelligence who became president [GEORGE H. W. BUSH]. In return for throwing business their way, the Bushes give their partners political access, legitimacy, and perhaps protection. The big loser in the deal is the democratic process.

To diagram this chapter's Bushantine complexities, you will need a medium-tipped marker and a 30 by 40-inch, white or pastel-colored poster board.

Bush, Bath, and Beyond. Dumbya's business career reveals much about the Texas ethics he smuggled into Washington, a tiny vial of which could contaminate a hundred-square-mile area.

After his losing run for Congress in 1978, W. started his first failed oil company, Arbusto Energy, with money from his education trust fund, from Bush family friend and reputed CIA operative JAMES BATH, and, it seems likely, from Saudi billionaire Sheikh SALEM BIN LADEN, OSAMA's older half brother and head of the bin Laden business empire, for which Bath was the U.S. business representative. During the Vietnam War, Bath had served (or not served) with Bush in the Texas Air National Guard (both were suspended from flying status for failing to show for their annual medical exams). Bath would come under FBI investigation in 1992, accused of funneling Saudi money through Houston to influence the foreign policies of the Reagan and Bush I administrations.

Bath had been a director of BANK OF CREDIT AND COMMERCE INTERNATIONAL (BCCI) before its 1991 collapse in one of the biggest financial scandals in history, in which depositors took a $10–$20 billion you-know-what. BCCI was founded in Pakistan in 1972 with capital from the emir of Abu Dhabi, Bank of America, and, allegedly, the CIA, which needed a laundry for its funding of the Afghan mujahideen (a U.S.–Pakistani–Saudi–Osama bin Laden coproduction). Then-CIA director George H. W. Bush reportedly recruited Bath into the agency in 1976. BCCI had been "set up deliberately to avoid regulatory review . . . to commit fraud on a massive scale, and to avoid detection," according to a 1992 Senate Foreign Relations Committee report (cowritten by Senator John Kerry). By 1980, BCCI had over 150 branches in forty-six countries and was involved in money laundering, bribery, financing of terrorism, arms trafficking, the sale of nuclear technologies, tax evasion, smuggling, illegal immigration, and illegal bank and real estate deals.

After September 11, 2001, Bush initially denied ever knowing Bath, then backpedaled and said that he did, and knew of Bath's Saudi connections, but denied any ties between Salem bin Laden and Arbusto. You'd think His Sheikship was a pillar of one of the world's most brutal, corrupt, religiously intolerant, and repressive regimes and an

IRAN-CONTRA money-launderer who had helped the Reagan administration secretly funnel $34 million through Saudi Arabia to the Nicaraguan Contras or something!

> *"Doing business with the enemy is nothing new to the Bush family."* So wrote Christian conservative journalist Rick Wiles, apparently alluding to GEORGE H. W. BUSH's involvement in the illegal sale of arms to Iran and Junior's shady Saudi business partners. Going back a generation, much of the Bush family wealth came from supplying raw materials and capital to Nazi Germany. Several companies managed by George W. Bush's grandfather, PRESCOTT BUSH, were seized by the U.S. government during World War II under the Trading with the Enemy Act. Two were charged with being German front organizations.[13]

In 1983, the failing "El Busto," as Arbusto had become known, was bought out by Spectrum 7, a small company owned by Bush billionaire friends and big-time GOP donors WILLIAM DEWITT and MERCER REYNOLDS. Because who doesn't want to own an oil-less, el busto oil company? Do you know *anything at all* about tax dodges? (As president, Dumbya would appoint Reynolds ambassador to Switzerland after he and DeWitt contributed nearly $1 million to the Bush 2000 campaign.) Bush was named CEO and director of Spectrum 7, as befitted his long and successful career in the business.

When Spectrum 7 neared collapse (despite a successful drilling partnership with ENRON Corp., whose CEO, KEN LAY, Bush would later claim he hardly knew), Bush sold it to

Harken Energy, which appointed him a director, gave him $600,000 worth of Harken stock, and hired him as a consultant at an initial $120,000 a year. "His name was George Bush," Harken's founder was quoted as saying. "That was worth the money they paid him."

Beknownst only to insiders, Harken was kept afloat only by Enron-like accounting tricks and infusions of capital from Bush cronies. In 1987, Arkansas investment banker JACKSON STEPHENS, a major Reagan-Bush campaign contributor, arranged for investments in Harken by Union Bank of Switzerland and Saudi tycoon SHEIKH ABDULLAH TAHA BAKHSH. Stephens, UBS, and Bakhsh all had ties to BCCI. Bakhsh's banker in Saudi Arabia was BCCI partner and alleged Osama bin Laden financier KHALID BIN MAHFOUZ, whose sister was one of Osama's wives. In 1991, the *Wall Street Journal* concluded: "The number of BCCI-connected people who had dealings with Harken—all since George W. Bush came on board—raises the question of whether they mask an effort to cozy up to a presidential son."

Help for Harken came from even stranger quarters. Within a month of Bush Jr. joining the firm, Harvard University's $18 billion endowment sank $30 million into the ailing company's stock. The endowment's most influential board member was oil man and Bush contributor Robert Stone. When Harken's creditors began calling in loans, Harvard came to the rescue again. At Bush's suggestion, Harken and Harvard also set up an off-book partnership into which Harken dumped $20 million of its *debts*, which it thereby took off its own books—a move straight out of the Enron book of accounting. "Thanks to Harvard's odd generosity," wrote Matt Bivens in *The Nation*, Harken "had turned itself around on paper.... Investors bid up the stock, and Harken insiders, including Bush, cashed out."

Close brush with a spanking. In June 1990—not long after a Harken committee on which he sat was told that "only drastic action" could save the company—Bush sold two-thirds of his Harken stock for a $318,430 profit. A week later, Harken announced a $23 million loss, which caused its stock to plummet by 60 percent over the next few months.

Then, instead of immediately notifying the Securities and Exchange Commission of the sale, as the SEC requires insiders liquidating large blocks of stock to do, Bush filed eight months late. Now he was in big trouble: The SEC's chairman had been appointed by Bush Sr. and had been his deputy counsel as vice president. What if he told Poppy? A grueling SEC investigation —handled by an SEC lawyer who was previously W.'s personal lawyer, and who neglected to interview any of Harken's directors—concluded there was no evidence of insider selling. Close call! "How does [this story] square with George Bush's expressed sympathy for people who lost their savings to unscrupulous accounting schemes?" Bivens asked. "Does he have any apologies for those who believed Harken was a good company because the president's son worked there—people who invested in Harken and then lost their shirts?"

Buy me some peanuts and Crackerjacks, and a stadium. "Oilman" Bush made his real fortune in base-ball—although "corporate welfare" is a better name for this game. In 1989, he helped assemble a group of investors to pur-chase the Texas Rangers. Bush became part owner. By threat-ening to move the baseball team, Bush & Co. strong-armed the Dallas/Fort Worth suburb of Arlington into building a new $135 million stadium, financed by a sales tax hike. When one family refused to sell the city a thirteen-acre plot at half its appraised value, the city simply condemned the land for the stadium. "Never before had a municipal authority in Texas been given license to seize the property of a private citizen for the benefit of other private citizens."[14]

The stadium—which the team ended up owning for a fraction of its cost—tripled the Rangers' value. When the team was sold in 1998—to Dallas investor THOMAS HICKS, one of Bush's top contributors—then governor Bush's initial $600,000 investment yielded $15 million, "the direct result of government intervention on his behalf"[15] *and* of a bonus 10 percent equity stake the other partners had seen fit to *give* Bush, just for being so . . . *Bush*. He then saved $2.4 million in income tax by declaring his entire proceeds from the sale as capital gains instead of as ordinary income, as per IRS rules.* This was all the less kosher because Bush had signed legislation that reduced the Texas Rangers' property tax, thus increasing his own profit. A former governor of Illinois had been convicted of income tax fraud in 1972 in an almost identical case. But he, I assure you, wasn't a Bush.

Bush's tax legislation also saved $2.5 million for Crescent Real Estate Equities, whose billionaire principal owner, RICHARD RAINWATER, was a top Bush contributor and a Texas Rangers partner. Bush himself held 4,222 shares of Crescent stock. On Bush's watch, the Texas University Public School trust fund invested $20 million in Crescent and the state sold three office blocks to the company in a deal that reportedly *cost* a state pension fund $44 million.

In 1997, Governor Bush backed a bill authorizing Texas cities to impose new taxes to finance sports facilities. Read his lips: *New taxes*. To enrich his friends. A few months later, Dallas voters approved $230 million for a new arena for the

*IRS Revenue Procedure 93-27. Read it and weep.

Stars hockey team and the Mavericks basketball team. The former was owned, the latter part-owned by Tom Hicks. The stadium deal also netted Crescent Real Estate a $10 million bonus. Within six months of Bush's signing the bill, his political fund received $11,000 from Crescent's president and $37,000 from Hicks. Hicks and his brother contributed a total of $146,000 to Bush's gubernatorial campaigns, and Hicks's investment firm was Bush's fifth-largest contributor in 2000.

Right after becoming governor in 1995, Bush signed a bill creating a company to manage the University of Texas's $13 billion endowment, and named Hicks (who had lobbied lavishly for the bill) chairman. Almost a third of the university money secretively invested by Hicks during Bush's first term went to funds run by major GOP donors and Hicks associates. Tens of millions more went to private investment firms tied to Hicks and Bush, including Crescent Equities and the CARLYLE GROUP.[16]

But, hey—this was Texas. And this was a Bush. Comparing Bush's dealings to Bill Clinton's Whitewater affair, *Arkansas Democrat-Gazette* columnist Gene Lyons wrote:

> If Arkansas is "incestuous," it's hard to think what adjective describes Texas, where public and private fortunes are commingled to a degree unknown in other states, and GOP leaders have helped themselves to public-sector capital while lecturing the poor on the virtues of hard work and self-reliance. Under laws enacted at Bush's behest, rich Republicans have used billions in state funds to finance leveraged corporate buyouts and other risky investments to benefit themselves and their friends. If you didn't know better, you'd think [it was a story about] Indonesia or Saudi Arabia.

Oh, but it is! (You thought I'd forgotten?) Bushies and bin Ladens were still in bed as fellow investors in the CAR-LYLE GROUP on September 10, 2001. But at this point, our story spills like a ruptured tanker and spreads like an oil slick over to O.I.L., THE "WAR ON TERROR," THE SAUDI-BUSHI AXIS, AND EXXON-MOBIL-REAGAN-BUSH-NORQUIST FOREIGN POLICY.

Asshole #9:
CHAMBLISS, SAXBY

Senator and former representative (R-Ga.). Never mind the mainstream media's silence on the man's *name*. In November 2001, Chambliss told emergency responders they should "turn the sheriff loose and arrest every Muslim that crosses the state line." In his successful 2002 campaign against incumbent Democrat Max Cleland, a highly deco-rated, triple-amputee Vietnam vet, Chambliss—whose damned *knee* kept *him* out of Vietnam—ran ads saying Cle-land "lacked the courage to lead" and pairing images of him with Saddam Hussein and Osama bin Laden, whom, you see, Cleland had helped by voting "against the president." (How many times must people be told? You're with Bush or you're with the terrorists.) Attacks on Cleland's patriotism, *The New Republic* observed, "formed the subtext of virtually the entire Chambliss campaign" (which was advised by RALPH REED and overseen by BILL FRIST).

Chambliss's rating from NARAL Pro-Choice America (abortion rights): 0 percent. American Civil Liberties Union: 7 percent. League of Conservation Voters (environment): 0 percent. U.S. Chamber of Commerce (business): 91 percent.

Christian Coalition (superstition, self-righteousness, and hypocrisy): 100 percent. National Rifle Association (urban mayhem, sadistic sports): A+.

Asshole #10:
CHAVEZ, LINDA

Conservative commentator and anti-union, anti-minimum-wage, anti-affirmative action, anti-antidiscrimination activist. That's what *made* her George W. Bush's first pick for labor secretary. What killed the nomination was merely the news that she employed an illegal immigrant in her home.

From a 2003 fund-raising letter for her organization Stop Union Political Abuse, which is dedicated to the proposition that unions—whose political donations are one-ninth the amount contributed by corporations—have too much voice and power in politics and the workplace: "The media were calling me 'Big Labor's Worst Nightmare.' . . . AND THEY WERE RIGHT! . . . [AFL-CIO President John Sweeney has] put BILLIONS into pushing the socialist agenda. . . . We can cripple liberal politics in this country by passing the Workers' Freedom of Choice Act [a Republican bill attacking labor's right to contribute to political causes]. . . . *If we stop now, the terrorists win!*" (Remember, children: Unions = Terrorism!)

Chavez on CNN two years earlier, commentating on her failed nomination as labor secretary: "Organized labor, I think quite mistakenly, somehow thought that I was going to be their worst nemesis . . . I think I would have actually been very helpful in trying to bridge a gap . . . between the Republican Party and organized labor. . . . I had a very nice talk with John Sweeney this morning, by the way."

CHENEY, DICK

A tenth circle of hell is under construction especially for
Cheney. (Halliburton has the no-bid contract. See PRIVATIZA-
TION, PERDITION, AND PURGATORY.)

I think the reason that mouth of his is such a cartoonists'
and satirists' delight is that it's understood that an equally
twisted *mind* operates it. As Bill Maher (who does Cheney
really well) said, somewhat wistfully, following the apparent
Taliban assassination attempt on Cheney in Afghanistan in
February 2007: "If Dick Cheney were not in power, people

Asshole #11: Dick "Where the Oil Is" Cheney

▶ Vote for Kerry and we all die! Cheney, 2004: "It's absolutely
essential that eight weeks from today, on November 2, we
make the right choice, because if we make the wrong
choice then the danger is that we'll get hit again and we'll
be hit in a way that will be devastating from the stand-
point of the United States." (We made the wrong choice—
some of us—a minority of us—in November 2000, and we
got hit.)

▶ August 2002: "Simply stated, there is no doubt that Saddam
now has weapons of mass destruction."

▶ Warmonger and former defense secretary Cheney on why he
stayed out of military service and Vietnam with five student
deferments from 1959 to 1966 (at which point he became
exempt because his wife was pregnant). "I had other priorities." (Also see CHICKENHAWKS.)

▶ We used to hold trials to decide things like this: "The important thing here to understand is that the people that are at

would not be dying needlessly tomorrow. . . . More people would live. That's a fact."

Catching on perhaps *a bit* late, *Time* magazine managing editor Michael Duffy wrote in March 2007: "Cheney has become the administration's enemy within, the man whose single-minded pursuit of ideological goals, creaking political instincts and love of secrecy produced an independent operation inside the White House that has done more harm than good." But this "enemy within" more or less *is* the Bush administration. As Duffy acknowledged, in picking Cheney "Bush got exactly the kind of partner he wanted"; indeed, "friends and

Guantánamo are bad people. I mean, these are terrorists for the most part."

▶ Quoting the Bush administration's motto to Sen. Patrick Leahy (D-Vt.), who had had the temerity to raise questions on the Senate floor about Cheney's former company HAL-LIBURTON and its Iraq war contracts (see **WAR PRIVATIZATION AND PROFITEERING**): "Go fuck yourself."

▶ On why Halliburton, while Cheney ran it, did business with Indonesia's Suharto (named "the most corrupt leader in modern history" by Transparency International); Nigeria's rulers and death squads; and—violating U.S. trade sanctions —Saddam Hussein's Iraq and Burma, where Halliburton, complicit with the Burmese military, built a gas pipeline involving forced labor, forced "depopulation" of whole towns, murder, torture and rape[18]—and why all this was cool with the good Lord: "The good Lord didn't see fit to put oil and gas only where there are democratically elected regimes friendly to the United States. . . . we go where the business is."

advisers in the fall of 2002 described Cheney as nothing less than the engine of the Administration. 'There's no way in which he is not driving the train on this,' said one, referring to Cheney's role in pushing Bush and the Administration inexorably toward an invasion of Iraq."[17]

Cheney is "the Democrats' most valuable asset," Duffy added. (Was *that* the "harm" he referred to—rather than, say, the destruction of one country and the imperiling of another's [ours'] democracy through drastically diminished **OVERSIGHT** of White House activities, drastically *increased* government oversight of ordinary citizens' personal affairs, and new presidential powers, undreamt of by the Framers, to arrest and detain anyone secretly, indefinitely, with no right to a hearing or to legal counsel?)

Asshole #12:
CHENOWETH, HELEN

The congresswoman (R-Idaho), during her 1994 campaign: "Don't let anything like trees in the Clearwater National Forest get in the way of providing jobs and fueling the economy, even if that means cutting down every last tree in the state." ("Providing jobs and fueling the economy": GOPspeak for boosting corporate profits.)

Asshole #13:
COBURN, TOM

Senator (R-Okla.). Not one of the brightest bulbs in the . . . GOP chandelier or whatever. A few fries short of a Happy

Meal. An intellect rivaled only by garden tools. Should request a refund from his university. (For more, see "Politically Correct Synonyms for 'Stupid'" at C4vct.com.)

On "the gay agenda": "The gay community has infiltrated the very centers of power in every area across this country, and they wield extreme power . . . That agenda is the greatest threat to our freedom that we face today." (In case you thought it was terrorism or DICK CHENEY.)

On renewed calls for tougher gun control laws following the Columbine High School massacre in 1999: "If I wanted to buy a bazooka . . . to do something, I ought to be able to do that."

The Senate investigation of the Bushies' political firing of eight U.S. attorneys (see JUSTICE SYSTEM, PARTISAN POLITICAL PERVERSION OF) was, according to Coburn, kind of like the (death of) Anna Nicole Smith "story": "If you're sitting out in the middle of this country and this becomes the topic du jour, like Anna Nicole Smith for the last two months, which [is] what the press has run with because it makes for a nice dirty story, what are we doing to our country?" Uh, trying to save it from assholes like Bush, Cheney, and Rove and (speaking of Anna Nicole) *big boobs like you?*

"COMPASSION"

Philosophically, GEORGE W. BUSH's "compassionate conservativism"* could be said to predate even Marie *"laissez-les manger le gâteau"* Antoinette. But let us fast forward past COOLIDGE, Hoover, and the 1930s Republicans who fought tooth and nail against Roosevelt's New Deal and whose cure

---

*Don't complain to me. That's what "Nucular" George Bush calls it.

for Depression was ~~"Let them eat Prozac"~~ to *cut* government spending, when every expert from John Maynard Keynes to John Foster Kane knew the opposite was needed—and jump to the REAGAN depression.

In 1983, two years into Reagan's presidency, the Census Bureau reported that over 35 million Americans, or 15.2 percent of the population, were living in poverty—an eighteen-year high. At a press conference some months later, Reagan declared that "not one single fact or figure" backed up Democratic "demagoguery" that his budget cuts were hurting the poor. The next morning, a congressional study reported that cuts in WELFARE had pushed more than 500,000 people, mostly children, into poverty. But no—you see, that's *good* for them! Tough ~~shit~~ love!

Alternatively: "They *enjoy* being poor!" Reagan again, 1984: "You can't help those who simply will not be helped. One problem that we've had, even in the best of times, is people who are sleeping on the grates, the homeless who are homeless, you might say, by choice." (I don't know—for me, it all depends on the grate.)

The real problem, Reagan complained, wasn't poverty and unemployment but *news coverage of* poverty and unemployment: "Is it news that some fellow out in South Succotash someplace has just been laid off, that he should be interviewed nationwide?" he gipped.

Here is Reagan's attorney general, EDWIN MEESE, responding to criticism of the administration's heartless, Scrooge-like policies toward the poor: "I don't know of any authoritative figures that that there are hungry children [in America]." (Each year from 2001 to 2005, according to Census Bureau figures, nearly one in nine households were considered "food insecure"—they could not always afford sufficient food.

In 2004, four in ten Americans used food stamps.[19]) "I think some people are going to soup kitchens voluntarily," Meese groused. "I know we've had considerable information that people go to soup kitchens because the food is free and that that's easier than paying for it. . . . I think that they have money." (Indeed—why cash in stock options when you can just head down to Skid Row for some nice *consommé au pigeon*?)

Labor Secretary Scrooge? Health and Human Services? Here's Meese again, addressing the National Press Club: "Ebenezer Scrooge suffered from bad press in his time. [*I'm not making this up.*] If you really look at the facts, he didn't exploit Bob Cratchit. Bob Cratchit was paid ten shillings a week [*which had the purchasing power of around $54 today*[20]], which was a very good wage at the time [*which was among the worst of times*]. Bob, in fact, had good cause to be happy with his situation . . . He was able to afford the traditional Christmas dinner of roast goose and plum pudding [*which more than made up for the medical treatment he couldn't afford for the dying Tiny Tim*]. . . . So let's be fair to Scrooge. He had his faults, but he wasn't unfair to anyone." ("Oh! But he was a tight-fisted hand at the grindstone, Scrooge! a squeezing, wrenching, grasping, scraping, clutching, covetous, old sinner!" Bah, that's just the creator's view. What the Dickens did *he* know?)

I'm sorry, this rehabilitation of Ebenezer Scrooge (R-UK) is so deliciously, quintessentially Republican, we must savor it a moment longer. Scrooge, reminded of the plight of the poor, says: "Are there no prisons? Are there no workhouses?" Told that many of the poor would rather die than go to the workhouse: "[Then] they had better do it, and decrease the surplus population." Imagine how irreproachably Republican his views would have been on occupational safety and health regulations, unions, minimum wages, and mandatory paid holidays! (Cratchit needed Scrooge's consent to take Christmas Day off, and was expected to make up the time. And they say *liberals* are waging a war on XMAS ...)

Addressing the slogan gap. "Compassionate conservatism," Bush's 2000 campaign theme, was born out of recognition that the American public had moved to the left (as conservate columnist Fred Barnes put it, "Bush is saying 'I'm not NEWT GINGRICH'") and designed to draw minority voters away from the Democrats. This new Orwellian mask for GOP Scroogery was but an updated version of Bush Sr.'s "thousand points of light" crapola. Same principle: A warm and fuzzy soundbite would suffice to make a cruel, heartless, rapacious, corrupt regime look less so, even as it abandoned the needy, palming them off on private and religious organizations.

But once in office, as Michael Scherer put it in *Salon*, Bush "discarded the slogan like a prom queen's sash."

▶ On Bush's first day in the Oval Office, he cut off U.S. funding for international organizations that provide ABORTION information—groups that also provide AIDS education, maternal care, sexual violence prevention, literacy programs, job training, and emergency disaster relief around the world. UN Population Fund officials estimated their loss of U.S. funding could result in over eighty thousand deaths. Which is equivalent to more than three thousand *American* deaths.

▶ In April 2001, Laura Bush, a former school librarian, visited a neighborhood library in Washington to kick off "The Campaign for America's Libraries." A week later, hubby announced a $39 million cutback in federal spending on libraries. (Maybe when Dumbya said, "Rarely is the question asked: Is our children learning?" he meant, "Is libraries really helping?")*

▶ After pledging in 2000 that "first and foremost" he would "fully fund" the Low Income Home Energy Assistance Program (LIHEAP), Bush slashed its budget by nearly half and repeatedly denied requests for emergency funding for the program during weather extremes—all while fuel costs were skyrocketing. (They actually rub their hands and chortle fiendishly while cutting off poor people's heat. We have video.)

▶ Days before declaring in his January 2002 State of the Union message that his number one economic priority was jobs, Bush visited a youth job-training center in Portland and lauded the program that funded it. A month later, he proposed cutting the program's budget by 80 percent and slashing most other job training as well. (In Bush's first year in office, unemployment had risen by 40 percent.)

▶ In June 2002, Bush held a photo op at an Atlanta housing project built with funding from HUD's Hopes Six program, on which he lavished praise. His next budget proposal eliminated funding for the program.**

---

*That he stressed reading ability is beyond doubt. He even began to learn it himself. *"Reading is the basics for all learning,"* he said. And: *"Reading is the beginnings of the ability to be a good student. And if you can't read . . . it's going to be hard to go to college."* (Unless your name is Bush.) And: *"Teaching children to read . . . will make America what we want it to be— a literate country and a hopefuller country."*

**"Home is important. It's important to have a home."*—Bush, Crawford, Texas, 2001

▶ After 9/11, Bush repeatedly posed with firefighters, praising their heroism and promising first responders funding for equipment and staffing. In August 2002, he effectively vetoed $5.1 billion approved by Congress for homeland security, including $340 million for equipping fire departments.

▶ That same month, Bush met with Pennsylvania coal miners rescued from a flooded mine and applauded their and their rescuers' bravery—even as he was seeking for a second time to cut the budget of the Mine Safety and Health Administration (MSHA).**

▶ In February 2003, the day after Bush exhorted the audience at the National Religious Broadcasters convention in Nashville to "rally the armies of compassion" to ease suffering, his administration announced increased rents for thousands of poor people who were receiving housing aid.

▶ Having doled out some $2.5 trillion in tax cuts that overwhelmingly benefited the richest (see **GOPONOMICS**), Bush couldn't find *one-seventh of one percent* of that amount in his 2003 budget to extend a $400-per-child increase in the child tax credit to 6.5 million minimumwage families, including 260,000 children of active military service personnel. The budget also cut funding for children's health insurance and the School Lunch Program—eliminating up to a million children, or as many as one in five participants.

**To ensure unsafe mine conditions, Bush also appointed a mining exec called Dirk Diggler—correction: Dick Stickler—to head the MSHA. His company had an accident rate three times the national average. Experts said the MSHA's approval of a dangerous mining method caused the Crandall Creek, Utah mine collapse that killed six miners and three rescue workers in August 2007.

▶ While he was at it, Bush announced a plan to dump the Head Start program, which provides medical care and meals for poor preschoolers, in the laps of already financially buried state governments. The plan "would absolutely destroy Head Start," the president of the National Head Start Association said. *Duh.* The Bushies obviously could not leave unmolested a Lyndon Johnson-Great Society program that had been working well for nearly four decades. It just isn't done!

▶ Bush even undermined funding for his own, much-ballyhooed "No Child Left Behind" education program. "As soon as the klieg lights were off and the bunting came down, the Bush administration turned its back on school reform and America's children," said Sen. Ted Kennedy, who had worked closely with Bush on the legislation.

▶ In December 2004, the administration cut U.S. global food aid contributions by $100 million—just as the *New York Times* reported that "the number of hungry in the world is rising for the first time in years and all food programs are being stretched," and as UNICEF estimated that more than 1 billion children were growing up hungry.

"Top-down class warfare in action." That's how the *New York Times*'s Paul Krugman described the 2006 budget plan Bush released in February 2005—a plan that almost literally "takes food from the mouths of babes and gives the proceeds to his millionaire friends."

The plan called for cutting $45–$60 billion over ten years from Medicaid, which provides basic health coverage to the poor; terminating food stamp aid for about 300,000 people; and putting an end once and for all to child care assistance for 300,000 children in low-income working families.

There were substantial cuts to health insurance and emergency medical services for children. The National Youth Sports Program for low-income kids. State education technology grants. Safe and Drug-Free School grants. The Even Start literacy program. Housing assistance for low-income families, people with disabilities, and people with AIDS. The program to prevent lead poisioning in children. Land and Water Conservation grants. The National Science Foundation. The Centers for Disease Control. Food and Drug Administration inspection programs.

The plan included budget cutbacks for 2006–2009 that the White House had kept hidden until after the 2004 election*— cuts in special education funding; Section 8, the nation's principal housing assistance program for the poor, elderly, and disabled; veterans' health services; college grants and Title I education funding for low-income students; Head Start; and the Supplemental Nutrition Program for Women, Infants, and Children. (See "FAMILY" AND "FAMILY VALUES.") Many of these were programs Bush had touted on the 2004 campaign trail.

Though "inspired" by concern about the deficit, all these cuts combined would barely make a dent in it, or pay for Bush's upper-income tax cuts (which accounted for seventeen times as much of the Bush deficits as growth in discretionary spending). A rollback of Bush's cuts to high-income

---

*The Center on Budget and Policy Priorities discovered that the budget tables that would normally show these cuts were "missing from the budget books" issued by the White House in 2004. ("Administration's Budget Would Cut Heavily into Many Areas," CBPP, 3/5/04)

rates, capital gains, and dividend income taxes would have saved nearly twice as much as these spending cuts.[21] Just rolling back the tax cuts above the first $200,000 in income would have saved enough to avoid cuts to veterans' health care, education, and environmental cleanup. Instead, Bush's plan *added* $1.4 trillion in tax cuts, 97 percent of which would go to people with incomes above $200,000, more than half to people with incomes above $1 million.

Talk as empty as the treasury. In Bush's January 2007 State of the Union address, it was the same old game. "The president tosses out 'compassionate'-sounding phrases, from *healthcare for the poor*, to *eliminating poverty*, to *care for the elderly*," wrote Paul Cummins on truthdig.com. "Yet he calls for his usual tax cuts [and says], 'Together we can restrain the spending appetite of the federal government.' Again, let's have it both ways." Bush's speech acknowledged global poverty, but didn't mention the fact that one in six U.S. children lives in poverty. "But of course," Cummins remarked, "when you are trying to correct a deficit you created, to escalate a war and to give tax cuts to the rich, it is rather difficult to have any funds left over for poor children and families."

Indeed, Bush's 2008 budget plan, released just two weeks later, contained so many cutbacks in aid to poor and working class Americans, it prompted Connecticut's Republican governor M. Jodi Rell to say: "These cuts interfere with the fundamental responsibility of government: to safeguard the lives of its citizens." Lowlights:

▶ Medicare and Medicaid cuts totaling $101.5 billion over five years—"far surpass[ing] what [Bush] or any other president has sought," the *New York Times* reported; and higher Medicare premiums—apparently another step in the long-range GOP plan of encouraging wealthier (and usually healthier) people to leave Medicare, leaving behind a poorer pool of less healthy beneficiaries, thus hastening the financial demise of the program. (Bush "contends that he can make the rule changes without any action by Congress," the *Times* noted.)

▶ Another $223 million cut for the federally funded State Children's Health Insurance Program (SCHIP), with additional cuts over the next five years. SCHIP covers children in households that earn too much to qualify for Medicaid but too little to afford private coverage—"exactly the sorts of hardworking citizens welfare reformers claim to love," wrote the *Washington Post*'s E. J. Dionne, who called this the most shameful part of the Bush plan. (When Congress established SCHIP in 1997, Governor Bush opposed its expansion to 220,000 children in Texas. A federal judge had to step in, ruling that Texas failed to provide adequate health care for children. It was, I feel, unfair of the judge to single out that item: Under Bush, Texas ranked near the bottom among states on almost *every* measure of social well-being.)

▶ A less than one percent increase for the National Institutes of Health (NIH) and a $9 million cut for the National Cancer Institute. In a visit to the NIH the previous month, Bush said it was "one of America's greatest assets, and it needs to be nourished," adding, "It makes sense to spend taxpayers' money on cancer research." It was at least the second time he'd praised the NIH, then cut its (inflation-adjusted) funding.

Who's not being asked to sacrifice? In April 2007, Bush warned Democrats not to try to include troop withdrawal deadlines in a spending bill for the war in Iraq (just another $103 billion, to cover the next six months). A fight over timetables, he said, would delay money needed for the troops on the frontlines.* Despite this urgency, Bush threatened to veto the bill if Democrats included an additional $20 billion for such frills as health care for veterans and active-duty military personnel, post-Katrina levee repairs in Louisiana, homeland security, wildfire suppression, avian flu preparedness, health insurance for poor children, and $500 million for LIHEAP.

Let 'em eat faith. You figure, maybe killing all these social programs is okay because they'll be replaced by Bush's "FAITH-BASED INITIATIVES" (FBI)—federal funding of religious groups to provide social services. But because the FBI were (a) a sham, (b) a farce, and (c) a travesty, this assumption would be incorrect. See **"F-ING FAITH-BASED INITIATIVE,"** THE.

Business-Profits-Based Initiatives (BPBI). For corporations, on the other hand, the compassion flowed like milk and honey. Bush:
▶ Signed a bill, lobbied for by the bank and credit card industries, that made it more difficult for poor and moderate-income families to use BANKRUPTCY PROTECTION, while doing nothing about predatory lending practices

---

*Total BS; nor had Bush complained the year before when the Republican-led Congress took two months longer to approve funding for the war.

and while exempting schemes used by wealthy families and corrupt corporations to shelter assets from creditors.

► Opposed an increase in the Scroogelike $5.15 federal MINIMUM WAGE. (See sidebar.)

► Sided with big drug companies to block cheaper generic versions of AIDS drugs.

► Repealed regulations that helped miners dying from BLACK LUNG DISEASE claim benefits from the mining industry.

► Took aim at the FAMILY AND MEDICAL LEAVE ACT. Business said the law hurts profits. Say no more!

Some Bushite compassion had nothing to do with corporate

Minimum wages of sin. When the federal minimum wage was raised to $5.15 in 1997, Governor Bush kept the Texas minimum wage at $3.35. Ten years later, the federal level was still $5.15 and Bush & Co. still opposed any increase.

Due to inflation, the minimum wage would have to be raised to $8.05 just to match the *1968* level in constant-dollar terms. The Republicans—siding with business groups such as the National Federation of Independent Business and the National Restaurant Association—were evidently maintaining the Reagan approach: the chairman of Reagan's Council of Economic Advisers, Murray Weidenbaum, once told the *Wall Street Journal*, "If we would have had our druthers, we would have eliminated" the minimum wage; but, realizing this would have been "a painful political process," his administration decided simply to let inflation erode it away.[22]

profits *or* budgetary window-dressing, but simply flowed from the goodness of the administration's heart, as when it:

▶ Tightened work requirements for WELFARE recipients in the face of the worst job slump in decades—while simultaneously cutting funding for job training.

▶ Exempted "WORKFARE" payments from minimum wage and benefits requirements.

▶ Placed crippling restrictions on STEM-CELL RESEARCH.

▶ Streamlined DEPORTATION procedures, fast-tracking religious and political asylum seekers to torture in their homelands.

▶ Pursued harsh penalties for low-level DRUG CRIMES. This even while Republican state governors were

As always, the right claimed its policy was in workers' best interests: jobs would disappear if the minimum wage made labor too expensive. Business owners perpetually threatened that they'd have to fire millions of workers if the minimum wage went up. In practice, of course, this never happened.

In 2001, 2.2 million U.S. workers, or about 3 percent, were paid at or below minimum wage, while about one-quarter of the workforce (including one-third of women and African Americans and almost half of Hispanics) earned less than the so-called living wage of $8.63—the amount officially deemed necessary to keep a family of four out of poverty.

Polls showed that more than 70 percent of Americans favored a minimum wage increase. It did not go unnoticed that Congress gave itself cost-of-living raises every year.

softening on the use of mandatory minimum sentences for such offenses. As Diana Gordon wrote in *The Nation* about then attorney general JOHN ASHCROFT and Bush's drug ~~potentate emir pasha~~ czar John Walters: "These must be the last two guys in America who don't believe in treatment [for drug users]." (Also see IMPRISONMENT AND PRISON CONSTRUCTION, AMERICA'S GLOBAL LEADERSHIP IN.)

▶ Cracked down on MEDICAL MARIJUANA (which Czar Walters the Terrible likened to "medicinal crack"). In the immediate aftermath of 9/11, an Ashcroft priority was to order Drug Enforcement Agency (DEA) action against doctors in Oregon, after the state had legalized marijuana to ease dying patients' pain. A year later, in September 2002, the DEA, in an early-morning raid, stormed a dangerous medical-marijuana hospice in Santa Cruz, California, that catered to terminally ill patients and was praised by local law enforcement officials for its good works. The agents burst in with guns drawn, cut down the pot garden, and took away ailing patients, including a paraplegic, in handcuffs. (In 2000, Bush—his syntax, as usual, suggesting a little overmedication—had declared: "I believe each state can choose that decision [on medical marijuana] as they so choose.")

Mercy, mercy me. Bush—who signed 152 DEATH PENALTY warrants, more than any governor in U.S. history—also issued fewer pardons than any Texas governor since the 1940s: 16, compared with 70 for his one-term predecessor Ann Richards, 822 for two-term governor Bill Clements, and 1,048 for six-year governor John Connally.

In his first year and a half as (p)resident, Bush denied 508 pardon petitions and 1,346 commutation requests, granting none. Six years into his residency, he had issued 3 commutations and 113 pardons—the fewest of any president since World War II, and all of them to people who had served their entire sentences.[23] (*Or* had served their president and vice president; see LIBBY.) President Clinton issued 456 clemencies in his eight years. Carter: 563 in four years. Truman: 2,031 in eight. Presidents Truman through Ford granted a quarter or more of clemency petitions. The total fell to 12 percent under Reagan, into the mid-single digits under Presidents George H. W. Bush and Clinton, and to less than 2 percent under our compassionate conservative in chief.

"And that's peculiar," a former pardon attorney told the Sentencing Law and Policy blog. "[Bush] has stretched the other powers of the presidency beyond the breaking point. [See PRESIDENTIAL POWER, STRETCHING BEYOND THE BREAKING POINT.] But this one power that really is all his, with no checks . . . he's shown very little interest in it."

CONAN THE REPUBLICAN*

Things have come to a pretty pass when an **Arnold Schwarzenegger** can pass for a moderate, decent, acceptable politician, even to liberals—compared, of course, to just about all other Republican politicians.

Go back to his very first political decision, after arriving in the United States in 1968, hearing a Richard Nixon campaign speech, and being told Nixon was a Republican: "And

*So nicknamed by "Poppy" George Bush.

I said, I am a Republican. . . . Listening to Nixon speak sounded like a breath of fresh air [!!]." (Can the air in Austria have been that bad?) Item 1: Inspired by RICHARD NIXON.

Items 2, 3, and 4: Backed RONALD REAGAN, campaigned for **GEORGE H. W. BUSH** in 1988, and for **BUSH JR.** in 2004—in Ohio, where that election was decided/stolen.

The recall effort that put Arnold in the California governor's mansion was engineered by Republicans and energy industry allies who wanted to stop the lawsuits filed by then governor Gray Davis and Lieutenant Governor Cruz Bustamante, who were seeking to recoup $9 billion in illicit profits generated by ENRON and the other power pirates that engineered the California energy crisis of 2000–2001. That was the purpose of a meeting in May 2001 between Enron CEO Ken Lay, Schwarzenegger, and some of Lay's other political friends. According to Enron e-mails, the agenda was to find a way to end "countless investigations into allegations that suppliers manipulated power prices." Such as, a new, Enron-friendlier governor. As journalist Greg Palast put it, "If Arnold is selected, it's 'hasta la vista' to the $9 billion [threat]."

And so it came to pass. In April 2003, as the prospect of a *Total Recall* election became real, Ahnuld met with . . . hmm, **KARL ROVE** to discuss a possible run. With characteristic dignity, the *Running Man* (1987) announced his candidacy on Jay Leno's *Tonight Show*. "There is a total disconnect," he said, "between the people and the politicians" (as opposed to the close connection "between the people and multi-millionaire Austrian weight-lifters," wrote one blogger).

After running on the *True Lies* promise that he would not "take any money from anybody" because "I have plenty of money myself" and because "the people should make the decisions rather than special interests," Ahnuld proceeded "to collect campaign contributions from private interests at a greater rate than any politician in California history, including Gray Davis, whom he had criticized on that very issue."[24] He amassed some $57 million from real estate, financial, entertainment, technology, and other interests. He proposed further deregulation of energy markets and a "rewrite" of the California law that holds companies (like Enron) liable for illegal profits. Meanwhile, he attacked opponents of his budget measures as "represent[ing] those special interests: the unions, the trial lawyers." *And* he called them "girlie-men."

One of Arnold's chief initiatives as governor was a reform of worker's compensation, whose high costs were in fact hurting small businesses. But you know Republican "reforms": They *always* signal an attack on the nonrich. Although the bill Schwarzenegger signed in 2004 placed strict limits on claims, it didn't require insurance companies to pass their savings on to clients. The insurers stood to save millions, while small business owners saw their premiums go *up* by as much as 50 percent, and permanently disabled employees' benefits were slashed. *Raw Deal* (1986). By the way, apropos of nothing, insurance industry contributions to Schwarzenegger—Mr. Campaign Finance Reform—exceeded $1 million, half of it from workers' compensation insurers.[25]

Yes, he's pro-choice. Supports taxpayer-funded stem cell research. Married JFK's niece. Signed a bill to reduce greenhouse gas emissions. Insisted he was all for gay rights—even as he opposed a move by the mayor of San Francisco in 2004 to allow for same-sex marriages, and vetoed a bill in 2005 that would have legalized such marriages.

But Schwarzenegger swung to the center, sort of, only after his popularity plummeted and voters, in a special election in November 2005, roundly defeated all four of his business-backed ballot initiatives. Among these was his scheme to force the pension plans of nurses, teachers, firefighters, police, and other undeserving state employees to switch to less secure 401k's—a "reform" opposed by the employees' unions but backed by corporate interests, which poured tens of millions of dollars into the campaign. (Schwarzenegger is a *Republican*. Try to remember that!)

Wait. We haven't even mentioned his remark during filming of the 1977 bodybuilding documentary *Pumping Iron*: "I admire [Hitler] for being such a good public speaker and for his way of getting to the people and so on." (In 1991, Schwarzenegger prudently acquired the rights to *Pumping Iron*, including outtakes.) According to a "longtime friend" of Ahnuld quoted by *Spy Magazine*, in the '70s he "enjoyed playing and giving away records of Hitler's speeches." Schwarzenegger supported Kurt Waldheim's campaign for the presidency of Austria in 1986, even after it came to light that Waldheim had lied about his past as a Nazi Party stormtrooper officer. In his speech at the 2004 Republican National Convention, David Kusnet observed in *The New Republic*, Schwarzenegger "condemned communism, terrorism, Austrian social democracy, and the American liberalism of Hubert Humphrey . . . implicitly lumping them all together in a crude ideological analysis [that] recalls Richard Nixon or even Joe McCarthy." But unlike JOHN McCAIN and RUDY GIULIANI the night before, Schwarzenegger "failed to mention Nazism or fascism at all." Kusnet wondered "why Austria's social democrats . . . trouble him more than the likes of Kurt Waldheim." (Both of

Arnold's parents were Nazi Party members, but that's neither here nor there.)

Speaking of the master race, in 2003, two African-American bodybuilders alleged that Schwarzenegger had made remarks such as: "If you gave these blacks a country to run, they would run it down the tubes." The same year, sixteen women came forward with allegations that he was a sexual *Predator* (1987). (See **SEX PERVERTS**.) Arnold's grabbiness—combined with his gabbiness about his ex-fellow Austrian head of state—inspired a new *Doonesbury* character, "Herr Gröpenführer."

Then, just months before the recall election, Ahnuld told *Entertainment Weekly* about his inspiration for a scene during the filming of *Terminator 3*: "I saw this toilet bowl . . . How many times do you get away with this—to take a woman, grab her upside down, and bury her face in a toilet bowl?" That apparently endeared him to the California Republican Women's Caucus, which endorsed him, saying he "supports family." Schwarzenegger, wrote columnist Robert Scheer, "appears [to] delight in the extreme violence he peddles" in his films without making any connection between that and the violence, domestic and other, of our society.

One of Reagan's great contributions to political life was to blaze the trail for candidates for high office whose only qualifications are celebrity, some primitive showbiz skills, a testosterone-based persona, and a populist-conservative, antiestablishment, antigovernment (im)posture. "Arnold" and "Ronald" aren't just anagrams—they're analogs, if not quite *Twins* (1988). Now we have Arnold as a political role model. More clowning; more bluster and bravado; more confusion of politics with showbiz and of celebrity with ability or merit. Another message to the world that in America, muscle beats out brains. Another example for multimillionaires who'd like a governorship, senatorship, or presidency* for Christmas. Just what our political culture needed!

COOLIDGE, CALVIN, MODEL REPUBLICAN

Name two presidents who were heroes to conservatives, who doled out tax cuts mainly to corporations and the rich, put big business in charge of (not) regulating big business, cut secret deals with corporate chiefs in exchange for help at election time, sought to privatize every bit of public property that wasn't bolted down, encouraged stock market speculation, opposed welfare relief for the poor but favored government spending on "character development," denied benefits to veterans, denied public employees the right to strike, refused to fire scandal-ridden cabinet appointees, and did virtually nothing during the worst natural disaster ever to hit the Gulf Coast, while thousands of flooded-out victims, mainly African Americans, were stranded without food and water and tens of thousands of others were left to rot in squalid refugee camps.

Yes, Calvin Coolidge (1923–1929) did all that, too. Or I wouldn't be going to all this trouble. Because it's a really, really nice day out.**

After assuming the presidency upon the death of Warren

Achtung: Already, a leading Republican, (Senator ORRIN HATCH, R-Utah, in 2003) has proposed a constitutional amendment to allow naturalized Austrian Americans to run for president. Okay, it might have applied to other naturalized Americans as well.

**May 7, sunny, around 70°F.

Harding, "although many of Harding's cabinet appointees were scandal-tarred, Coolidge announced that he would not demand any of their resignations."[26] He pushed through tax cuts that overwhelmingly benefited corporations and upper-income earners. "Through his appointees he transformed the Federal Trade Commission from an agency intended to regulate corporations into one dominated by big business."[27] Coolidge "gave aid to private business without accompanying restrictive regulation."[28] His most famous remark: "The chief business of the American people is business."

He vetoed a bill to give World War I vets a bonus. "Whereas Harding had talked of establishing a federal department of welfare, Coolidge called for a department to encourage character development." [29] He favored severe immigration restrictions because, he said, "America must be kept American." (Strictly Sioux, Iroquois, Nez Perce, etc., I suppose.)

Thanks to Coolidge's "unquestioning faith in the conservative business values of laissez faire . . . [h]is reputation underwent a renaissance during the Reagan administration."[30] Hey—what more do you need to know? Well, a couple of things.

"His personal honesty and New England simplicity appealed to the American people." "He restored public confidence in the White House after the scandals of his predecessor's administration." So say *Columbia Electronic Encyclopedia* and Wikipedia, respectively, *and* a bit too respectfully. Coolidge *was* Harding's VP, and was accused by opponents of having had a hand in that admin's biggest scandal, TEAPOT DOME, in which Harding's attorney general, Albert Fall, accepted bribes from two oil tycoons in exchange for leasing rights to government oil reserves in Wyoming and California. (Fall became the first U.S. cabinet member to go to prison for misconduct in office. . . . Some credit, please: Have I punned on his name even once?)

Throughout the 1920s, the auto magnate HENRY FORD wanted to buy and develop the federal land around the Wilson hydroelectric dam at Muscle Shoals, Alabama, which under FDR's New Deal was to become the centerpiece of the Tennessee Valley Authority. According to some historians,[31] President Coolidge promised Ford a deal if Ford would just withdraw from the goddamned 1924 presidential race— which Ford did. After winning reelection, Coolidge, faced with Congressional criticism of the deal as a Bushian (they didn't call it that) giveaway of public resources to big business, reneged. But he did succeed for the rest of his presidency in blocking *government* operation of the site— because, you know: private, good, public, bad. "His attitude toward Muscle Shoals was consistent with his lifelong opposition to the expansion of government functions and the interference of the federal government in private enterprise."[32]

Déjà vu, plus ça change, *and other Cajun* **expressions.** THE GREAT MISSISSIPPI FLOOD of 1927 was the worst natural disaster in U.S. history before HURRICANE KATRINA. State and local officials begged the federal government for help during the flood, which displaced between 700,000 and 950,000 people, 90 percent of them black. As a Republican, Coolidge felt that the government should do as little as possible and leave the cleanup and relief efforts to charities, local authorities, and, especially, business leaders. Business good, government bad. Coolidge refused to convene a special session of Congress to consider a bill to fund disaster relief. (The business community and National

Chamber of Commerce lauded his dismissal of the "all-fathering Federal Government.") He declined even to visit the area, and maintained his steadfast opposition to federal spending on flood control.

Meanwhile, here's how things went: The business leaders who ran the show in New Orleans dynamited an upstream levee, flooding two poor, mainly African-American parishes, to divert the floodwaters from the central business district (which, it turned out, wouldn't have flooded anyway because of other upstream levee breaks. It's been alleged the same was secretly done during Katrina). Over thirteen thousand residents, mainly black, near Greenville, Mississippi, were evacuated to the top of a levee and left stranded for days without food or water while boats arrived to evacuate whites. "White refugees were sheltered in houses and received appropriate aid, whereas blacks were forced to stay in tent camps and engage in slave labor in order to receive rations." [33]

At least 330,000 African Americans were dumped into 154 relief camps, where many still languished years later. Men were segregated from their wives and children. They slept in tents, typically on a piece of canvas on the ground. They were forced at gunpoint by the National Guard to labor on cleanup and levee repairs and even Red Cross work, such as loading supplies; they were beaten or shot if they refused or tried to escape from these *slave camps*, as bolder black leaders called them. "Cleanup was a gigantic task . . . done predominantly by poor people of color . . . loading and cleaning were considered to be 'nigger work' and the police conscripted blacks for work gangs. . . . While white areas of flooded regions were undergoing relatively rapid clean up (done by blacks), the black neighborhoods became the dumping ground for all the trash from the white sections, which rendered these sections as disease breeding and uninhabitable."[34]

One notable "same difference" difference was that in 1927, cheap black labor was still needed in the South—for both postflood cleanup and rebuilding, and general labor; "it was probably because of this . . . that the Red Cross helped flood survivors return and resettle back to their homes once the floodwaters resided." In 2005, under not so different conditions, Latino immigrants performed this work; blacks could be expended and scattered to other regions.

A couple of Coolidge's characteristics were commendable, especially in a GOP president. He spoke as little as possible,* yet spoke well and gave twice-weekly press conferences—the first president to do so. (George W. Bush's are twice-decadely, approximately.) A Vermont farmer's son, Coolidge was as staid as they come—so it might interest you to know that among zoologists, male animals' ability to, uh, perform an almost unlimited number of times *if* it's with different females became known as the COOLIDGE EFFECT. As the story goes, the president and first lady once visited a chicken farm and were given separate tours. Told about the rooster's impressive stamina in performing his roosterly duties, Mrs. Coolidge said, "Tell that to Mr. Coolidge." Told the same thing, the president asked: "Always with the same hen?" No, different ones each time, he was told. "Tell that to Mrs. Coolidge," he replied.**

---

*The possibly apocryphal story goes that the writer-wit Dorothy Parker, seated next to the president at some event, told him she had a bet going that she could get more than two words out of him. His famous answer: "You lose."
**A proposal to rename it the Clinton Effect was rejected at a zoological conference in 1999. Or maybe I just imagined that.

Moral: Don't let an appearance of, uh, Calvinist rectitude fool you. A Republican president will always screw as many Americans as possible.

CORNYN THE (SMOOTH-TALKIN') BARBARIAN

I've hated him since he first arrived on Capitol Hill in January 2003. Hated. Why? What *The New Republic* described as "The Hard Right's Soft New Face" alone would have sufficed. It's the gentle, ever-present smile, the debonair look, the soft, oily voice—combined, of course, with the rotten, barbaric politics behind the gentlemanly facade. Being from Texas didn't help. (Politically, this country needs a de-Tex program urgently.) Nor did the fact that the Dem he defeated for the seat vacated by retiring-none-too-soon Republican **PHIL GRAMM**—the former mayor of Dallas, Ron Kirk—was a contender for whom Dems had high hopes. Anyway, please join me in extending a warm hatred toward Senator **John Cornyn** (R-Tex.).

Seeing **KARL ROVE** behind everything *can* just be paranoia, but not in this case. Rove ran Cornyn's 1996 campaign for the Texas Supreme Court, convinced him to run for state attorney general in 1998, and recruited and reportedly cleared the GOP primary field for him in 2002. Bush Himself raised millions and campaigned repeatedly for him, as did Laura, George Sr. and Barbara, and (ugh) **KAREN HUGHES**. Cornyn's loyalty to Bush was a central theme of his campaign. (We find him guilty already and the trial has barely started.) Cornyn's 2002 campaign, wrote *The New Republic*'s Michael Crowley, was "strikingly reminiscent of the 2000 presidential race, when a deeply conservative Bush used soft rhetoric and easy charm to cast himself as a centrist." But in no time at all,

> [Cornyn] had developed a reputation as the Senate's most ambitious*—and most conservative—new addition.** On issues from gay marriage to judicial nominations to the detainee abuse scandals, he has taken stridently conservative stands that make even other Republicans queasy. . . . The Senate has seen conservative firebrands before. But none as deceptively genial as John Cornyn. . . . If TOM DELAY is the stylistic equivalent of heavy metal, John Cornyn is muzak. For that reason, he could prove a major asset to a party searching for ways to seem more moderate than it is.

While leading the GOP fight for a constitutional ban on gay marriage, Cornyn "did not fulminate over moral depravity or clumsily scorn 'the HOMOSEXUAL AGENDA,'" Crowley noted. "His sunny, calm tone suggested a man of deep benevolence." [35] But religious right leaders like Gary Bauer started getting hot pants for Cornyn when he used his Judiciary subcommittee seat to hold a hearing on the

---

*In 2005, Cornyn's name was floated as possible replacement for O'Connor or Rehnquist on the Supreme Court. In December 2006 his colleagues elected him to the five-person Republican Senate leadership team—the only first-term senator in recent memory to be so honored. Besides the Judiciary Committee and various subcommittees, he sits on the Armed Services Committee, the Budget Committee, and the Select Committee on Ethics (as vice chairman). I'm telling you, this guy will run for president. Sorry, I shouldn't tell you scary stories right before your bedtime.
**In March 2007 *National Journal* ranked Cornyn as the third-most conservative senator.

issue. Followed by one on "Hostility to Religious Expression in the Public Square" (see Xmas and Christianity, Democrat-Liberal-Satanist-Secular War on), starring former Alabama Supreme Court justice Roy Moore, who lost his bench for displaying a Ten Commandments monument in the courthouse. (I believe the Second Commandment says, "Thou shalt not make unto thee any graven image . . . Thou shalt not bow down thyself to them, nor serve them . . ." But that's just me. And God.) What else has Cornyn been calm, poised, benevolent, and sunny about? Let us count the rays:

Torture of detainees at Abu Ghraib. To talk about it is to "help our enemies," said the corn man. When Senate Democrats pushed for a measure that would require the Bush administration to release memos detailing its interrogation policies, only Cornyn dared oppose the move publicly. Even to debate interrogation policies was "just wrong," he declared; it was "a distraction from fighting and winning the war" and was intended only "to score political points." (Also see Democrats, Liberals, and War Critics, Tarring of as Treasonous, America-Hating, Terrorist-Loving, Crypto-French Surrender Monkeys.)

Big Brotherhood. Working the same scam in 2004, during Senate hearings on a possible censure of Bush over his illegal wiretapping program, Cornyn went on the offensive, saying censure would amount to "aiding our enemies during a time of war." (*You dare criticize der Leader? Traitor!*) In September 2005, Cornyn cosponsored a bill that would allow law enforcement to force anyone arrested or detained to provide a DNA sample, which would be recorded in a central database. (Yes, conservative Republicans *are* against big government—but DNA samples and computer data take up *so* little space.)

Judicial nominees. "Nowhere," wrote Crowley, "has Cornyn's smooth style been more useful to the GOP" than in Bush's campaign to fill every federal bench with right-wing judges. Cornyn helped lead the GOP push for the "nuclear option"—rewriting Senate rules to eliminate the filibuster, a two-hundred-year-old check on one-party rule. That drew special praise from Cornyn's old Texas friend, then White House counsel ALBERTO GONZALES.

(Cornyn on the Supreme Court vacancy left by Sandra Day O'Connor's retirement: "I don't know whether [newly confirmed Chief Justice] John Roberts has a twin, perhaps a sister or, uh, someone with a Hispanic last name." "So hilarious, and not racist or sexist or terminally cynical at all," a blogger commented. Not to mention that in Roberts, Bush appointed one of the least capable but most partisan, right-wing chief justices in the court's history.)

Bullying, threatening, and excusing violence against "activist [non-right-wing] judges." In March 2005, in what the *New York Times* called "a moment that was horrifying even by the rock-bottom standards of the campaign that Republican zealots are conducting against the nation's judiciary," Cornyn stood up in the Senate chamber and excused a spate of murderous violence against judges in their courtrooms, saying it might be explained by the frustration that "builds up" about judges who "are making political decisions." Right. That's what motivated a career criminal who killed a judge while trying to shoot his way out of a courtroom, and a deranged man who, furious that a judge had dismissed a lawsuit, executed her mother and husband. Just decent, ordinary Americans driven mad by liberal judges.

The next day, Cornyn stood up again and said, "I regret that my remarks have been taken out of context"*—then *did the same thing*: linked the violence to "activist [i.e., *liberal*] judges." (Activist *conservative* judges—like those, for example, who put George Bush in the White House, and those he has appointed—are great.) Cornyn's obscenities came a few days after TOM DELAY warned the judges who ruled that TERRI SCHIAVO's feeding tube could be removed that "the time will come for the men responsible for this to answer for their behavior." ("Trying to intimidate judges used to be a crime, not a bombastic cudgel for cynical politicians," said the *Times*.)

Attacking the 9/11 Commission to protect the White House. When the GOPies were trying to do just that—undermine the Commission's credibility—*and* shift the blame for 9/11 onto the Democrats, it was a formal request from Cornyn that prompted the Justice Department to release a memo written by Democratic Commission member Jamie Gorelick as deputy attorney general in 1995. The GOPniks falsely claimed the memo proved that the rule preventing information sharing between law enforcement and intelligence agencies had been created on Clinton's watch, when in fact it was on Reagan's.

---

*I'm not for the death penalty, except for these constant, weasely uses of "out of context." By Republicans.

Minimum of principles. In February 2007, Cornyn was among 94 senators to vote for raising the federal minimum wage. One week earlier, he was one of 28 senators who voted to repeal the federal minimum wage.

Environment. Cornyn was rated 0 percent by the League of Conservation Voters, meaning, a maximally antienvironment voting record.

The Abramoff-GOP corruption cesspool. As Texas attorney general, Cornyn led a successful effort to shut down the Texas Tigua Indian tribe's casino— apparently in close cooperation with arch-lobbyist-villains JACK ABRAMOFF, former DeLay spokesman MICHAEL SCANLON, and RALPH REED. Abramoff and Reed then charged the Tigua $4.2 million to lobby lawmakers to reopen their casino. Cornyn denied any contact with the three mucketeers on the issue. Yet e-mails from Reed to Abramoff such as, "I'm scheduled to talk to Cornyn today" and "I think we should budget for *an ataboy for cornyn*" (my italics), strongly suggest *contact* with and some kind of *ataboy* for someone or something called *cornyn*. Not necessarily the professedly antigambling senator *John* Cornyn, although the latter did receive campaign contributions from Abramoff and from Las Vegas casino interests.

Democracy. It's such a nuisance! Cornyn, when asked in 2006 about GOP disunity on immigration in the middle of an election year: "Well, you know, that's the problem in America, we're always having elections." Yeah, when are the Republicans going to do something about that?

CRIME, CORRUPTION, AND CRONYISM, and Assorted 'Gates, Scandals, Flaps, Imbroglios, and Brouhahas

Bush 2004 Campaign Pledges to Restore Honor and Dignity to White House
—*The Onion*, 1/28/04

The Republican Party isn't mired in scandal, it IS the scandal—the system of bribery, kickbacks, and scams that fuel its massive money machine and influence peddling racket.
—Markos Moulitsas Zuniga, DailyKos

It does sometimes seem as though there's just one vast GOP scandal, linking Watergate, Iran-Contragate, Wedtech, BCCI, George Bush, George Bush, Enron, Halliburton, Plamegate, the Gonzales Eight, the 16 Words, the Missing 18 Minutes, the Missing 27 Pages (see **O.I.L.**), the missing WMDs, missing White House e-mail-gate, Abu Ghraib, Walter Reed, Hurricane Katrina, Mark Foley, Jack Abramoff, "Jeff Gannon," the Dulles brothers, Sullivan & Cromwell, Roswell. . . .

It really *isn't* a matter of Thisgate, Thatgate, the Othergate—of isolated scandals that could have erupted in either party. There is a whole here that is not only greater than the sum of the scandals—it is the well-manured soil they spring from. Despite long-gone decades of corrupt Democratic city and state machines *and* the Dems' share of federal scandals, two factors make today's Republicans intrinsically more corruption- and crime-prone: (1) Closer ties to CORPORATE SPECIAL INTERESTS, and (2) The crusader/jihadi zeal that drives the social-religious conservatives, the antitax, antigovernment conservatives, and the NEOCONS alike, and which breeds in all

three factions the attitude that *laws* and ethics rules are tri-
fles next to the urgency and sacredness of the Cause . . . of
electing and protecting Republicans . . . so they can fight for
the Cause. . . . of electing and protecting Republicans . . . and
collecting corporate cash . . . to elect Republicans . . .

So, yeah, Dems do it, too—accept unkosher gifts and
donations, take personal trips on the taxpayer's dime, steer
government contracts to friends and no-show jobs to wives
and sons-in-law, talk dirty to interns, stuff like that—but
Republicans have done so much more of it in recent decades
that one *almost* begins to question one's faith in the honesty
and integrity of Republicans as a whole.

In the early 1980s, *Time* magazine—never a friend of the
Democrats—said of the REAGAN administration that "its
many mistakes form a troubling pattern of insensitivity to
the higher standards of conduct expected in Government
service. Perhaps even more disquieting is the fact that the
amiable President seems oblivious to the problem. Far from
publicly rebuking any wayward officials or nominees, he has
been eager to defend his loyalists."

Citizens for Responsibility and Ethics in Washington
(CREW) documented more than 160 cases of **GEORGE W.
BUSH** administration misconduct from 2001 to 2006. It was
as if word was out that anything went. Censuring conflicts of
interest and other ethics violations in *this* administration
was—to quote *Apocalypse Now* for the second time in this
book—"like handing out speeding tickets at the Indy 500."
(Where it *always* smells like victory, by the way.)

None of the following scandals and scandalettes ranks up
there with Attorneygate (see **JUSTICE SYSTEM, PARTISAN
POLITICAL PERVERSION OF**) or the **ABRAMOFF-DELAY-NORQUIST-
REED**-GOP sale of Congress, never mind IRAQ, CONSPIRACY TO

DECEIVE AMERICA INTO, or ELECTION 2000 AND 2004, THEFTS OF, or CONSTITUTION, ASSAULTS ON; but that's sort of the point—they illustrate that you can turn over just about any GOP rock and find the GOP culture of corruption swarming beneath.

*Crime, Corruption, and Cronyism Case #4:**

Spiro T. Agnew. NIXON's first vice president. Resigned in 1973, charged with tax evasion (Republicans do hate taxes!), money laundering, accepting bribes from the construction industry while governor of Maryland, and continuing to demand payments after becoming VP. In what a former Maryland attorney general called "the greatest deal since the Lord spared Isaac on the mountaintop," Agnew pleaded no contest and was fined $10,000 and put on three years' probation. He was eventually forced to repay the state of Maryland the full $268,482 he was known to have taken in bribes. Agnew "blamed Nixon for releasing the accusations of bribes and tax evasion in order to divert attention from the growing Watergate scandal." [36] (Was KARL ROVE a Nixon adviser, by any chance? Actually, yeah, sort of.[37])

Case #5: Claude Allen. Bush II administration deputy secretary of Health and Human Services (where he advocated for bullshit ABSTINENCE-only AIDS prevention programs), then assistant to Bush for domestic policy, until he resigned in February 2006 shortly before being arrested for stealing merchandise from Target and Hecht's stores. Not by a bit of impulsive, everyday shoplifting, such as you and I do: Allen would buy merchandise, return to the store without it, select the same

*The numbering of these CCC cases is continuous with others scattered throughout this book.

items, bring them to the counter, and use the original receipts to obtain fraudulent refunds, which totaled over $5,000. Sentenced to two years of supervised probation plus forty hours of community service and a $500 fine. Bush's nomination of Allen as a U.S. Court of Appeals judge in 2003 was blocked because of his lack of legal experience. He's gained some since.

Case #6: Rep. Roy Blunt. (R-Mo.), House Minority Whip in the 110th Congress (2007–2008). Protégé of TOM DELAY, from whom Blunt took over leadership of the K STREET PROJECT (see NORQUIST). He and DeLay helped JACK ABRAMOFF, a contributor to Blunt's political action committee (PAC), lobby for gambling laws on behalf of (or was it *against*?) one of his Indian gaming clients. Blunt was among those whom Abramoff took along on an expenses-paid golfing trip to Scotland. In 1999–2000, Blunt's PAC, Rely on Your Beliefs, accepted $3,000 from a MARIANAS garment manufacturer that Abramoff was trying to protect from American labor laws, and at least one $25,000 contribution from ENRON (#11, below).

"Soon after Blunt became DeLay's chief deputy whip," wrote John Judis in *The New Republic*, "DeLay initiated him into the practice of funneling contributions from one PAC to another"— which prevents contributors' knowing where their money is going. In 2000, Blunt's PAC received $150,000 from a fund set up by DeLay's Americans for a Republican Majority PAC (ARMPAC—whose initial funding came from KEN LAY and other Enron execs), while *contributing* around $200,000 to DeLay-connected lobbying and consulting firms, including one set up by former DeLay aide ED BUCKHAM (next scoundrel) that employed DeLay's wife—raising "the question of whether ARMPAC was using Blunt's PAC to recycle contributions to DeLay's family and his political network." [38] Similarly, Rely on Your Beliefs contributed $125,000 to Missouri Republican

Party committees, which in turn contributed more than
$233,000 to Blunt's son Matt's successful campaign for Mis-
souri secretary of state. Federal officials are barred from
using their office to benefit "friends, relatives, or persons with
whom the employee is affiliated in a non-governmental
capacity." But if you *rely on your beliefs*—in yourself, in
cheating, in Jesus Christ—you *can* get away with it.

In the category of general Republican-ness, Blunt attempted
to insert a provision into the legislation creating the Department
of Homeland Security that would have made Internet tobacco
sales more difficult, enabling Big Tobacco to control distribution. At the time, Blunt was dating a Philip Morris lobbyist,
whom he later married. Said in August 2006 he would oppose
any legislative action on global WARMING because "the information is not adequate yet for us to do anything meaningful." Supported a banking industry-backed bankruptcy "reform" law to
better enable lenders to squeeze debtors. (See "COMPASSION.")
Voted to prohibit lawsuits against gun manufacturers and
dealers by victims of crimes involving guns, and to reduce the
waiting period for purchasing a gun from 72 to 24 hours.

Still free at the time of writing. Sharp operator, this Blunt.

Case #7: Ed Buckham. GOP activist, lobbyist, evan-
gelical minister,* former chief of staff and top political

*Buckham formerly served as an elder of the Maranatha Campus Ministries.
MCM, which referred to itself as "God's Green Berets," was a major player
in the Christian right until it folded in 1990 under widespread criticism.
Campus pastors closely supervised the lives of members, who were "led to
believe that disobeying their pastor, or 'shepherd,' was tantamount to disobeying God." [Wikipedia] Members were pressured to tithe, or give 10 percent of their earnings to the "ministry," and were forbidden from dating.
Several universities banned the group, in one instance after a member "sexually maimed himself after reading Jesus' command in Matthew 18:8—'If
your hand or your foot causes you to stumble, cut it off, and cast it from
you.'" One less member for a man, many less members for MCM.

adviser to TOM DELAY. Got his lobbying start in the 1990s
with a huge contract from ENRON secured by DeLay.
Founded, and consulted for, U.S. FAMILY* NETWORK, Inc.
(USFN), a tax-exempt lobbying group that received $1 mil-
lion from JACK ABRAMOFF's Russian clients and $650,000
from MARIANAS tycoon and Abramoff client Willie Tan. Payments to the group "coincided with votes and other actions
taken by Tom DeLay in Congress in favor of the 'donors.'"[39]
Tax-exempt groups are supposed to be nonpartisan. In 1999,
USFN received the largest single donation ever made by the
National Republican Congressional Committee (NRCC),
$500,000, reportedly to turn out conservative Christian
voters on election day. USFN then paid $300,000 for radio
ads accusing Democrats of planning to raid the Social Security fund and use it on other programs—exactly as the Bush
administration would soon do!

A RICO (Racketeer Influenced and Corrupt Organizations) lawsuit brought by the Democratic Congressional
Campaign Committee led to a Federal Election Commission
probe of USFN and its closing in 2001, and to the NRCC
being fined $280,000 for transferring "soft money" donations
to USFN.

Most of USFN's money went to Buckham and his wife;
Buckham's lobbying and political strategy firm, the
Alexander Strategy Group; a Washington, D.C., townhouse;
and a fifteen-year lease on a Washington Redskins skybox
used by Abramoff (who took Buckham and DeLay on free
trips to Russia, Scotland, and Korea). USFN paid Buckham
around $400,000 in 1998 alone for fund-raising work, even

*The Family® label is your guarantee of goodness. (Moral, Christian,
antigay . . .)

though almost all of the "grassroots" group's money came from a few large donors. "Grassroots" work sounds pretty sweet.

Case #8: Laura Callahan. Deputy chief information officer, Department of Homeland Security, with responsibility for national security databases. In 2003, the media revealed that she had obtained her advanced computer science degrees through a diploma mill in a small town in Wyoming. (Cheney country. Heartland. Faith-based computer science. Things that liberal ELITISTS could never understand.)

Case #9: Lester Crawford. Bush could pick 'em. Crawford's appointment in July 2005 as Food and Drug Administration commissioner was delayed in the Senate over an accusation that he'd had an extramarital affair with an FDA employee. Resigned abruptly two months after his confirmation and, in 2006, pleaded guilty to making false statements under oath during his confirmation hearing and to violating conflict of interest laws. Turned out he owned stock in food, beverage, and medical device companies regulated by . . . himself. Sentenced to three years' supervised probation and fined $90,000. Became a lobbyist—a more suitable (if not very different) career. ("Must be comfortable with conflicts of interest.") Named one of the 25 Most Corrupt Members of the Bush Administration by CREW.

Case #10: Randy "Duke" Cunningham. (R-Calif.), former member of the House Appropriations defense subcommittee. Resigned from the House and pleaded guilty in November 2005 to taking more than $1 million in bribes from defense contractor Mitchell Wade; drew an eight-year prison sentence. Indicted in February 2007 for accepting more than $700,000, as well as limousine services and prostitutes, from defense contractor and Wade associate Brent Wilkes, who in return obtained a stream of Pentagon contracts from 1996 to 2004. (Also see KYLE FOGGO, below, and JERRY LEWIS.)

Case #11: Thomas Dorr. Undersecretary of Agriculture, appointed by Bush in August 2002. Some months earlier, federal investigators discovered that Dorr used possibly illegal accounting tricks to get around limits on federal subsidies for his farm operation. Dorr had been known to criticize Democrats for supporting farm subsidies, which he compared (aptly) to corporate welfare. Extra layer of manure: Dorr attributed the economic success of three predominantly white Iowa counties to their being "very nondiverse in their ethnic background and their religious background." The Senate Agriculture Committee rejected Dorr, but Bush went ahead and installed him in a recess appointment.

Case #12: Enron. The energy trading giant's collapse, due to fraudulent financial transactions and accounting, wiped out $60 billion in shareholder investments and thousands of employees' retirement savings. Enron was also implicated in the engineered energy crisis in California in 2000–2001, which cost the state billions in artificially inflated energy costs. Enron's meteoric rise, without which its meteoric fall would scarcely have been possible, was enabled by Republican-sponsored deregulation of the energy industry. (See PHIL GRAMM.) Collectively, Enron executives were GEORGE BUSH's largest campaign contributor; CEO KEN LAY was a leading member of the Bush 2000 transition team and of **DICK CHENEY**'s secret energy task force/conspiracy, and a leading candidate for Treasury secretary. Think. Ken Lay in charge of the United States Treasury.

Case #13: EPAgate. One of the most publicized, and most Bushian, of Reagan administration scandals. It led to the resignation in 1983 of Environmental Protection Agency administrator ANNE GORSUCH BURFORD, along with twenty of her top employees.

The EPA, Congress discovered, was misusing the SUPER-FUND toxic waste cleanup program for political purposes. "If a Republican incumbent was running for reelection, a cleanup might begin with remarkable speed. If a Democrat stood to benefit from the allocation of funds, the process suddenly became arthritic."[40] (Also see ABSOLUTELY EVERY-THING, PERFIDIOUS PARTISAN POLITICIZATION OF.)

More ominous, however, was the White House's refusal, on executive privilege grounds, to release documents requested by the congressional investigators. Congress routinely examined far more sensitive materials; what's more, as Daniel Benjamin reported in *Washington Monthly*, "apparently everyone but Congress had access to the documents, including EPA office help and, strikingly, some companies that were the subjects of [EPA] enforcement proceedings." The administration also claimed release of the documents would jeopardize legal cases it was pressing against polluters, when of course it would have jeopardized the *administration* for being in bed and performing disgusting acts *with* the polluters. Meanwhile, the Justice Department (DOJ) went after the two leading House Democrats requesting the documents by seeking damaging information about their campaign contributions. (None was found.)

A confrontation with Congress was in fact just what the White House was after: A successful executive privilege battle, wrote Benjamin, "would enable the White House to embargo all sorts of materials requested by Congress, thus greatly strengthening its hand in the historic battle between the branches of government." As it happened, the DOJ cabal behind the conspiracy was led by Assistant Attorney General TED OLSON, a leading figure in right-wing, FEDERALIST SOCIETY legal circles who, eighteen years later, successfully argued George W. Bush's case before the U.S. Supreme Court in *Bush v. Gore*, and was rewarded by being appointed solicitor general.

A House Judiciary Committee report later implicated many top Reagan officials in a conspiracy to deceive Congress and obstruct justice. No Republican administration would ever try a stunt like *that* again!

Case #14: White House-manufactured "journalism."

The Bush White House paid columnists ARMSTRONG WILLIAMS, MAGGIE GALLAGHER, MICHAEL MCMANUS, and who knows how many others yet to be uncovered to promote White House policies in their columns, without acknowledgment of their secret sponsor, of course. The Bushist attempt to turn the press—along with Congress, the courts, and the corporate sector—into a political arm of the White House and the GOP is far more portentous and evil than this brief entry suggests.

Case #15: Kyle "Dusty" Foggo.

(Adopted the "Dusty" to distinguish himself from other Kyle Foggos.) CIA procurement officer; promoted to executive director, the agency's third-highest position, in 2004 by Bush-appointed CIA Director PORTER GOSS. Foggo and his buddy BRENT

WILKES, a defense contractor and top GOP fund-raiser, were indicted in February 2007 for fraud and money laundering. The indictment stated that Wilkes paid for meals and lavish vacations for Foggo and his family and promised him a post-CIA job, and that Foggo improperly provided classified information to Wilkes. In 2003, a $2–$3 million contract for the sale of water and supplies to CIA operatives in Iraq and Afghanistan was awarded to a Wilkes-owned company with no known logistics experience. It appears Foggo was behind the fog-shrouded deal—in which the agency allegedly wound up overpaying by 60 percent. Wilkes was in negotiations for a contract worth hundreds of millions to provide covert global air transport for the CIA—despite his having no experience in this field, either. CREW named Foggo—a former CIA ethics official—one of the 25 Most Corrupt Members of the Bush Administration.

Case #16: H. Guy Hunt. Alabama's first GOP governor (1987–1993) since Reconstruction—and straight off, he screws up. Convicted in 1993 for using $200,000 of his inaugural fund to pay personal debts and buy cattle and equipment for his farm. Sentenced to five years' probation and ordered to pay back the stolen money plus a $12,000 fine. Was issued a rare full pardon a few months later by the Alabama Board of Pardon and Parole, two of whose three members were appointed by him. Hunt was an ordained minister of the Primitive (a.k.a. Predestinarian or Old School) Baptist Church, whose members retain original Baptist practices such as a cappella singing, feet washing, and violation of campaign finance laws.

Case #17: Kevin Marlowe. Procurement chief under George W. Bush for the Defense Information Systems Agency (DISA), a Defense Department subagency responsible for communications and computer systems. Over the course of four years, Marlowe steered 31 percent of the agency's contracts to Vector Systems, a small company with no other clients. Marlowe and his family received $500,000 in secret payments and other benefits from Vector, including the use of a company credit card with which he created a secret trust fund for himself and his wife. When his scheme came to light, Marlowe filed a gender discrimination suit alleging that female staff were spreading misleading information about him. In the end, he pleaded guilty to fraud, conflict of interest, and perjury charges and was sentenced in 2006 to twelve years in prison. Another member of the CREW 25.

Also see **Bechtel; Coolidge; Dog Booties; Frist; Gingrich; Griles; Hurricane Michael; Iran-Contra; Oversight; Veterans; War Privatization and Profiteering.**

Death Penalty, Love of

Republicans ♥ the death penalty. ♥ ♥ ♥ it. They are *so* pro-death. Take **George W. Bush**. In the thirteen years from 1982, when Texas resumed executions, until Bush became governor in 1995, Texas carried out 18 executions. In just six years, Governor Bush personally signed death warrants for 152, making him (in just one and a half terms) the killingest governor in U.S. history and making Texas a more prolific executioner by far than any *country* in the Western world outside the United States.

Bush also vetoed legislation to provide funding for legal defense for the poor. (Over 90 percent of defendants charged with capital crimes in the United States cannot afford to hire an experienced criminal defense attorney.*) He called that bill, which had bipartisan support, "a threat to public safety." He opposed legislation instituting life without parole and banning the execution of people with IQs below 65. (He, of all people . . .) Both as governor and as president, he granted far fewer clemency requests than any of his predecessors (see "COMPASSION"), indeed, seemed to enjoy mocking clemency pleas (see *Smirk of Death* sidebar below). And he steadfastly opposed legislation to reform Texas's shocking clemency procedures. (From 1982 through 1999, the state executed 170 people; the Texas Board of Pardons and Paroles recommended commuting the death sentence only once. Of more than 70 clemency petitions, the board didn't consider even one worthy of holding a hearing about.)

"I do not believe we've put a guilty—I mean, innocent—person to death in the state of Texas." So said then governor Bush. Well, from 1976 to 2002, more than 82 people who were sentenced to death in the United States—1 in 7 of those on death row—were released from prison after being fully exonerated. From 1900 to 1992, there were 416 documented cases of innocent persons who were convicted and sentenced to death; 23 of these were executed. There is every reason to believe Texas's record is much worse—and that the former governor has a good deal of innocent blood on his hands. Besides Iraqis', Afghanis', and U.S. soldiers'.

---

*"Number of death sentences upheld by Texas courts since 1990 for men whose lawyers slept during their trials: 3."—*Harper's* Index, 1999.

Under his governorship, Texas ranked first in the nation in executions, but at or near the bottom in virtually every social service area. It had some of the most poorly funded programs to help the mentally ill (who make up a considerable portion of the prison population). Bush's response to these social problems: a demand for a $5 billion tax cut. *Obviously.*

Smirk of Death. In February 1998, Karla Faye Tucker, a Texan convicted of murder and sentenced to death in 1983, was executed. Governor Bush had denied her request for commutation of her sentence to life imprisonment, despite pleas on her behalf from such figures as Pope John Paul II, Newt Gingrich, and Pat Robertson. (Tucker, you see, deserved to live because she had found Jesus.)

From a profile in *Talk* magazine, September 1999, in which conservative pundit and professed Bush admirer Tucker Carlson asked Bush if he had met with any of the protesters who demanded clemency for Tucker:

Bush whips around and stares at me. "No, I didn't meet with any of them," he snaps, as though I've just asked the dumbest, most offensive question ever posed. . . . "I watched [Larry King's] interview with Tucker, though. He asked her real difficult questions like, 'What would you say to Governor Bush?'" "What was her answer?" I wonder. "'Please,'" Bush whimpers, his lips pursed in mock desperation, "'don't kill me.'" I must look shocked—ridiculing the pleas of a condemned prisoner who has since been executed seems odd and cruel—because he immediately stops smirking.

Over his dead bodies. In a speech in Nebraska in March 2001, Bush managed to be simultaneously goofy and blood chilling as he assured the audience that he knew what *really* constituted cruel and unusual punishment: "Those of us who have spent some time in the agricultural sector and in the heartland understand how unfair the death penalty is—uh, the death tax [estate tax] is—and we need to get rid of it. [Pause.] I don't want to get rid of the death penalty. Just the death tax."

Asshole #14; Crime, Corruption, and Cronyism Case #18:
DELAY, TOM

Former Texas congressman (1985–2006) and House majority leader (2003–2005). Living legend. Patron saint of influence-peddling, pay-to-play politics, and CORPORATE-OWNED GOVERNMENT. Nominated *eleven times* for best performance by a corrupt-through-and-through Texas politician in the role of a righteous, God-fearing Christian. Earned four rebukes from the House Ethics Committee over a six-year period during which only five other members of Congress received even one—while telling his evangelical brethren that God was using him to promote "a biblical worldview" in U.S. politics. Godfather of the protection racket known as the K STREET PROJECT (see **NORQUIST**). Serial seller of legislative favors to corporate special interests. Author—with former ENRON CEO KEN LAY—of "the Enron bill," which would have completely deregulated the electricity industry. Implicated up to his porcine eyes, nay, his devilish eyebrows in the **JACK ABRAMOFF** ("One of my closest and dearest friends")

scandal. Resigned the House majority leadership in 2005 and
his House seat in 2006 following his indictment on criminal
charges that he conspired to violate campaign finance laws
to help elect Texas GOP state legislators, who would in turn
redraw Texas congressional districts to favor the election of
more Republicans to Congress. DeLay, said Norm Ornstein
of the conservative American Enterprise Institute, "has
taken every norm the legislature has operated on and
shredded it." ("On a scale of 1 to 10, Democrats abused their
majority status at about a level 5 or 6," Ornstein told *Salon*.
"Republicans today have moved it to about an 11.")

Republicans' admiring nicknames for DeLay: The
Hammer, the Exterminator (his former profession),* the
Meanest Man in Congress, DeLay, Inc., and—for his playboy
ways during the late 1970s-early 1980s, when he reportedly
drank "eight, ten, twelve martinis a night at receptions and
fund-raisers"[41]—Hot Tub Tom.

▶ Avoided Vietnam by use of student deferments (which
he managed to keep even after Baylor University
expelled him for drinking) until 1970, when he
enlisted in the war on cockroaches and termites.
According to the *Houston Press*, DeLay told reporters
at the 1988 Republican convention that *"so many
minority youths had volunteered for the well-paying
military positions to escape poverty and the ghetto
that there was literally no room for patriotic folks*

*DeLay's hatred of government regulation of business reportedly grew out of
an Environmental Protection Agency ban on a pesticide he used in his business. (Pesticide use *can* breed resistant, monster insects, but apparently so
can pesticide *bans*.) His tax-cutting fervor may have originated during the
same period: In the eleven years that DeLay ran the company, the IRS imposed
liens on him three times for nonpayment of payroll and income taxes.

like himself. Satisfied with his pronouncement, which dumbfounded more than a few of his listeners . . . DeLay marched off to the convention." [Italics added.]

▶ Boasting that he'd once again stymied campaign finance reform legislation: "The DeLay strategy worked. Delay, delay, delay." Asked whether he would *ever* require public disclosure of political donors' names—whether he believed "the citizens of this country have the right to know who pays for a campaign ad": "Absolutely not."

▶ The Environmental Protection Agency (1995): "The Gestapo of government." (DeLay's other nickname: The Editor—for his wonderfully concise statements of Republican philosophy.)

▶ On air pollution: "It's never been proven that air toxics [sic] are hazardous to people." (A large body of scientific evidence links air pollution and Republicanism to birth defects, impaired lung development, asthma, pneumonia, bronchitis, emphysema, heart attacks, strokes, lung cancer, and premature death.)

▶ "Nothing is more important in the face of a war than cutting taxes." . . . To help pay for the war, I guess . . . no, wait . . . forget it, **GOP**ONOMICS is beyond me.

▶ DeLay's response to a unanimous rebuke (the second in six days) from the five R's and five D's on the House Ethics Committee: "For years Democrats have hurled relentless personal attacks at me, hoping to tie my hands and smear my name." The two-pronged reprimand was for:

(a) Asking the Federal Aviation Administration to track down a plane carrying Texas Democratic legislators who were leaving the state to avoid voting on DeLay's nakedly political, literally crooked congressional redistricting plan.

(b) Somehow leaving executives of Kansas-based Westar Energy with the impression that the $56,500 they contributed to DeLay's political committees had bought them "a seat at the table" where energy legislation was about to be drafted.

▶ Explaining that the 1999 Columbine High School shooting resulted from the teaching of . . . uh, evolutionization: "Our school systems teach our children that they are nothing but glorified apes who have evolutionized out of some primordial soup of mud, by teaching evolution as fact."

▶ Then House majority leader DeLay to three young HURRICANE KATRINA evacuees from New Orleans at the Astrodome in Houston, September 2005: "Now tell me the truth boys, is this kind of fun?"

DOG BOOTIES

Not *all* Republicans wear them—and neither, it turns out, do the rescue dogs employed by the Department of Homeland Security (DHS). According to a congressional audit released in July 2006, DHS employees purchased more than two thousand sets of dog booties, costing $68,442, which went unused after emergency responders decided they were not suited for canines assisting in post-HURRICANE KATRINA recovery efforts. (Such as they were.)

The purchase was made on a government-issued credit card—as were the following:

$ Three portable shower units for $71,170 from not the fairest or squarest contractor in the land. (Best politically connected?) Similar showers were available, faster, for a third of the price.

$ Flat-bottomed rescue boats at double the retail price.

$ 12 Apple iPod Nanos and 42 iPod Shuffles, $7,000, for Secret Service "training and data storage." "Because the Shuffles cost less than $300 [each], the Secret Service said they were not required to track them to ensure they were used properly."[42]

$ Thirty-seven Helly Hansen designer rain jackets, black, $2,500, for use at a firing range that Customs and Border Protection (part of DHS) later acknowledged shuts down when it's raining. (So? Must *style* shut down, too?)

$ Conference and hotel rooms at a golf and tennis resort at Saint Simons Island, Georgia, for training newly hired attorneys who could have used a nearby federal law enforcement training center.

$ A beer-brewing kit and ingredients, $1,000+, for a Coast Guard official to brew brew while on duty as a social organizer for the U.S. Coast Guard Academy. Coast guard cadets were charged $12 for a six-pack of the suds.

After Hurricane Katrina, at the Bush administration's request, the $2,500 spending limit on government credit cards was raised to $250,000. The hundredfold increase was slipped into a Katrina recovery bill approved in September 2005. The roughly nine thousand DHS employees who carried the cards spent $435 million on "business-related" expenses in the 2005 budget year. Government Accountability Office (GAO) investigators estimated that 45 percent of the purchases were improper, and blamed "poor training, lax oversight and rampant confusion." The audit also cited as missing over one hundred laptop computers that department employees bought following Katrina, as well as twenty-two printers, two GPS units worth $170,000, and twelve of twenty boats bought for $208,000. All together, DHS has been blamed for up to $2 billion of waste and fraud.

It should perhaps be mentioned that DHS's chief financial officer was DAVID NORQUIST, younger brother of antigovernment extremist GROVER NORQUIST. Bush appointed David in January 2006, while Grover's involvement in the JACK ABRAMOFF scandal was coming to light. Those plastic-happy federal employees—you *could* say all they were doing was privatizing bits of their agencies . . . and privatization *is* what Grover Norquist is all about.

But it wasn't just DHS. Since the Bush coup of 2000, GAO audits have found hundreds of thousands of dollars in improper expenditures on government credit cards at the Pentagon and other agencies. Navy personnel used the cards to hire prostitutes—but also to gamble and attend Yankees and Lakers games. "One civil employee ran up nearly $35,000 in personal expenses over two years, including breast enlargement surgery for his girlfriend," AP reported.[43] (Universal coverage of the procedure would stop such abuses. But do Republicans care if American cup sizes lag behind those of other industrialized countries?) Someone even bought a dog. Not a bomb- or drug-sniffer or Abu Ghraib prisoner attacker—just a pet. Well, at least that's one set of dog booties that needn't go to waste.

Will the dog bootie issue hurt the Republicans in November 2008? I think the issue has legs.

Asshole #15; Crime, Corruption, and Cronyism Case #19:
DOOLITTLE, JOHN

Protégé of fellow asshole TOM DELAY. One of JACK ABRAMOFF's closest cronies and the fifth-largest recipient of Abramoff money (as well as free golfing trips, skybox seats at sporting events . . . God knows what else). Named one of "The 20 Most Corrupt Members of Congress" in 2006 by CREW.

Neat, bespectacled, and sporting The HAIRCUT, Rep. Doolittle (R-Calif.) looks like someone you'd trust to administer your estate. (Choose your executor carefully.) Spent two years as a Mormon missionary before attending law school. Began his political career in 1979 as an aide to California state senator H. L. Richardson, founder of Gun Owners of America and the Law and Order Campaign Committee. Began his corruption career no later than 1984, the year an administrative law judge found Doolittle guilty of violating campaign finance laws.

January 2006: "A liberal front is underway to find God and all things pertaining to him unconstitutional." (Also see XMAS AND CHRISTIANITY, DEMOCRAT-LIBERAL-SATANIST-SECULARIST WAR ON.) From Doolittle, we also learn this: "The American public is justifiably outraged to discover that they are financing the erectile dysfunction medication of dangerous sex offenders." Really? Guess I was too busy being outraged by the greatest foreign policy disaster in U.S. history, the White House's assumption of dictatorial powers, and the *wholesale corruption of congressional Republicans* to notice.

D'SOUZA, DINESH

This Indian-born American author-intellectual was formerly a senior policy analyst in RONALD REAGAN's White House and a fellow at one of the most influential conservative think tanks, the AMERICAN ENTERPRISE INSTITUTE, and is currently a fellow at another, the HOOVER INSTITUTION.

In his 1995 book *The End of Racism*, D'Souza presented a novel argument: African Americans are harmed by their own ingrained attitude of defiance, adopted by their slave forebears as a means of preserving some sense of dignity. (In case *you* thought prejudice, lousy schools, and economic inequality were their main social problems.) I just wonder how the civil rights movement would have fared without that very attitude. Perhaps what blacks needed was a little more humility and quiescence in the face of brutal apartheid? But then, D'Souza's term for the civil rights movement *is* "the civil rights industry."

He has denounced feminism for, among other things, devaluing women who work in the home. (Odd—I thought feminists have been insisting for decades that women homemakers are underappreciated.) Articles by D'Souza include "How Ronald Reagan Won the Cold War" (see THE "REAGAN WON THE COLD WAR" MYTH) and "Two Cheers for Colonialism." (Only two? Come on, Dinesh—you're not *trying*.)

But he really *ripened* in 2007 with his McCarthyistically* titled book, *The Enemy at Home: The Cultural Left and Its Responsibility for 9/11*. The "primary cause of the volcano of anger toward America that is erupting from the Islamic world," D'Souza writes, is "the cultural left and its allies in Congress, the media, Hollywood, the non-profit sector and the

*According to D'Souza, Grand Inquisitor McCarthy was "largely right."

universities," along with tolerance of homosexuals and the "left's" "aggressive global campaign to undermine the traditional patriarchal family." There's truth in D'Souza's argument. Islamist fundamentalists (like our own religious right) do hate our liberalism—that is, our individualism, pluralism, tolerance, secularism (or what's left of it), freedom of belief and expression, women's rights . . . (*And* our support for Israel, our army boots on their soil, our hands on their oil spigots and other private parts . . .). But as D'Souza sees it, *they're* not the problem—*we* are. Our liberals, that is. The same dreck has been spewed by other conservatives, including JERRY FALWELL, PAT ROBERTSON, and ANN COULTER, whom D'Souza once dated. (Coulter, not the other two, as far as I know.)

To D'Souza, notes political scientist Alan Wolfe, "Flogging adulterers and that sort of thing simply puts Muslims 'in the Old Testament tradition.'"

Susan Sontag never said we brought Sept. 11 on ourselves. Dinesh D'Souza does say it. . . . America is fighting two wars simultaneously, he argues, a war against terror abroad and a culture war at home. We should be using the former, less important, one to fight the latter, really crucial, one. . . . We should drop our alliance with decadent Europe and "should openly ally" with "governments that reflect Muslim interests, not . . . Israeli interests." And, most important of all, conservative religious believers in America should join forces with conservative religious believers in the Islamic world to combat their common enemy: the cultural left.[44]

Now that you know who was responsible for 9/11, you are ready to accept D'Souza's characterization of OSAMA BIN LADEN as "a quiet, well-mannered, thoughtful, eloquent and deeply religious person" and of A̶YATOLLAH K̶HOMEINI as "highly regarded for his modest demeanor, frugal lifestyle, and soft-spoken manner." D'Souza even expresses admiration for sui-cide bombers. So next time you hear a conservative attack *liberals* as America-Hating terrorist sympathizers . . .

D'Souza may sound radical, but all he has done in *The Enemy at Home*, wrote (ex-?) conservative Andrew Sullivan in *The New Republic*, is "to pursue the logic of Bush-era conservatives all the way to its end"—which is "global theoconservatism," in a "death match" with liberal modernity. "In this sense, it is a mainstream conservative book"; its central arguments are "just as central to the base of the current Republican party."

"E̶LITISM," T̶RADITIONAL B̶ULLSHIT C̶HARGE AGAINST D̶EMOCRATS AND L̶IBERALS W̶HEN R̶EPUBLICANS A̶RE THE R̶EAL E̶LITISTS

Every far-right movement mobilizes popular dislike of cul-tural and intellectual (rather than economic) elites, depicting their members as morally and spiritually corrupt, decadent, unmanly, *foreign* . . . and as always looking contemptuously down their, uh, long noses at us plain, honest, hard-working, patriotic, Christian, *real* Germans/Italians/Americans, as the case may be. (See F̶ASCISM.) It's no longer quite acceptable to openly identify the internal enemy as Jewish (although, see B̶ILL D̶ONOHUE under A̶SS-H̶OLINESS); but "liberal," "Holly-wood," and "French" are all good.

For decades, wrote author Thomas Frank, conservative populists have cast "the average American, humble, long-suffering, working hard, and paying his taxes" against "the liberal elite, the know-it-alls of Manhattan and Malibu, sipping their lattes as they lord it over the peasantry with their fancy college degrees and their friends in the judiciary."

Conservatives "regard class as an unacceptable topic when the subject is economics—trade, deregulation, shifting the tax burden," Frank continued. But from GEORGE WALLACE to GEORGE W. BUSH, "a class-based backlash against the perceived arrogance of liberalism has been one of their most powerful weapons"—a backlash that is "workerist in its rhetoric but royalist in its economic effects," that poses as "an uprising of the little people even when its leaders . . . cut taxes on stock dividends and turn the screws on the bankrupt."[45] (See "COMPASSION" and GOPONOMICS.)

The best-selling 2006 book *100 People Who Are Really Screwing Up America,* by conservative Bernard Goldberg, is heavily populated with rich and famous liberal do-gooders. Liberals "from Beverly Hills to New York's Upper West Side; from Malibu to Martha's Vineyard," writes Goldberg, are

snooty, snobby know-it-alls . . . who think they're not only smarter, but also *better* than everyone else, especially everyone who lives in a "Red State"—a population they see as hopelessly dumb and pathetically religious . . . this elitist condescension—this smug attitude that Middle America is the land of right-wing yahoos who are so damn unenlightened that they probably don't even know where the Hamptons are . . .

One obvious objection to Goldberg's indictment is that "Red State" America *is* the land of hopelessly dumb, pathetically religious, right-wing yahoos. And as blogger Digby Anderson wrote, "Much of what is denounced as snobbery today is simply a thoroughly commendable attachment to elitism, to high standards, and a concomitant rejection or ridicule of low standards." (Also see **IGNORANCE AND IDIOCY**.)

More to the point: Liberals who champion the poor and downtrodden, the environment, and all that liberal crap, are denounced as elitists and sent to the guillotine; Republicans like Bush who give the 226,000 taxpayers earning over $1-million-per-year tax breaks equal to the total received by the bottom *125 million*, who attended Philips Academy and Yale yet pretend to be simple Texas country boys, and whose fathers were president of the United States, yet who pretend to be Washington outsiders, are not. Because *they* drawl, don't know too much, and enjoy working with chain saws. On the poor.

> *Someone needs to stand up and defend the Establishment . . . After all, we conservatives are on the side of the lords and barons.*
> —William Kristol, journalist and former Reagan and Bush I administration aide, 1996

ENERGY POLICY

Discourage alternative energy sources and conservation. Keep us hooked on fossil fuels. Keep the prices, and oil, gas, and coal industry profits, high.* Give those industries billions in tax breaks and subsidies while they're already raking in record profits. Collect their campaign contributions. Get reelected. Help those industries some more. The end.

---

*By, for example, taking oil *off the market* by adding to the Strategic Petroleum Reserve for four straight years while supplies are tight and prices are spiraling; and by taking Iraq offline. See **O.I.L.**

"FAMILY" AND "FAMILY VALUES,"
Hypocritic Oath to Uphold

Families is where our nation finds hope, where wings take dream.

—George W. Bush

Ever since Bush said he knew "how hard it is to put food on your family," I've suspected there is something wrong—and possibly quite kinky—about GOP "family values."

When you're busy (a) wasting your people's lives and treasure on a war for fun and for political and oil industry profit; (b) slashing social spending *and* bankrupting the government to pay for tax breaks for the rich, corporate welfare, and an insane, cold war–style military buildup; (c) reversing a half-century's worth of hard-won environmental protections; (d) awarding no-bid government contracts to your corporate cronies and contributors; (e) ignoring the Constitution, making the president a king, fixing elections—in short, being the GOP leadership—what you really, really need are some "moral values" issues to shroud your wickedness in Godliness, to keep what you're really up to out of sight, out of mind, and *out of the news at all costs.*

Besides, the largest block of GOP voters and activists is religious conservatives, who need constant watering and pandering and real or symbolic government action against the enemy—the liberal, homosexual, abortion-loving, anti-XMAS AND CHRISTIANITY future residents of hell. These good folks are the people officially authorized by God to decide which values *are* "family" and "traditional" values and how everyone in America should live. And their vision, or hallucination, has been enshrined in the official GOP platforms of the past few years:

† "We call for replacing 'family planning' programs for teens with funding for abstinence education." (*Which has just one problem—it doesn't work.*)

† "We encourage states to support projects that strengthen marriage." (*Not for gays, of course. For them, we support projects that strengthen closets.*)

† "Promote committed fatherhood." (Not *better wages, benefits, work conditions, and job security for fathers, so fewer flee their homes in shame and despair. What are you, a commie atheist? If so, are you aware that you are required to register with your local police station, and inform them if you move?*)

Of boobs, Bibles, ballots, and baloney. In widely publicized exit polls on Election Day, 2004, 22 percent of voters cited "moral values" as their main concern. Never mind the 78 percent that didn't: The Republicans jumped all over this stat as proof that America was on their page while the Dems were pages away, hopelessly out of touch. The media quickly bought into this as the story of the 2004 election. Many Dems did, too.

The 2004 "values vote" story began officially on February 1, when a glimpse of Janet Jackson's "bare" breast (the all-important nipple was in fact covered) transformed the annual three-hour orgy of violence and sexual titillation known as the Super Bowl into something unwholesome and un-American. It became the Bushies' pretext for launching an antiobscenity campaign that would please religious and social conservatives while distracting millions of voters from, say, the rising body count in Iraq.

† "Government should work with faith-based groups that provide adoption services." (*Because early indoctrination is the key.*)

† "We call for local efforts to help the children of prisoners." (*Because we want to lock up a lot of people . . . without disrupting the Family.*)

† "We support the traditional definition of 'marriage' as the legal union of one man and one woman." (*So much for Mormon and Muslim tradition—never mind the Masai, the Cheyenne, or the ancient Spartans. Granted, most of us aren't Masai or Cheyenne. Not for lack of trying. Believe me.*)

By that point, Bush's "war president" pose was looking less and less like the best one to strike for his reelection campaign. So, as Arianna Huffington noted: "It appears **KARL ROVE** is planning a small rewrite for his candidate: 'I'm a *culture* war president.'"

Within a month of Breastgate, Bush backed then attorney general **JOHN ASHCROFT**'s efforts to poke around the private medical records of women who've had abortions; doubled spending on anti–sex education programs; pledged $23 million for schools (for badly needed books or repairs? No, to investigate students for drug use); and hinted again that he would support a constitutional ban on gay marriage. "You would think," wrote Huffington, "the Christian right has more pressing matters to worry about. America now has 35 million people living in poverty, many of them working poor. Maybe they should take another look at the Bible." (Also see **"COMPASSION"** and **GOPONOMICS**.)

† "We do not believe sexual preference should be given special legal protection or standing in law." (*So, no special privileges for heterosexuals, such as exclusive rights to marriage and its alleged benefits?*)

† "We stand united with private organizations, such as the Boy Scouts of America." (*That bar gays from membership or employment.*)

† "When government funds privately-operated programs, it must not discriminate against faith-based organizations." (*Only against secular ones: see F-ING FAITH-BASED INITIATIVES.*)

† "We support the exemption [of women] from ground combat units, and call for co-ed basic training to be ended." (*Women could be of more service in kitchen, maintenance, and geisha units.*)

† "We support . . . candid analysis of the consequences of unprecedented social changes in the military." (*Stay in the aforementioned closet.*)

FASCISM, SLIGHT BUT MEASURABLE CREEP TOWARD

George Bush is not Hitler. He would be, if he fucking applied himself.

> —Un-American comedian Margaret Cho, whose suspiciously non-Aryan-sounding name has been duly noted

And conservatism is not fascism (no matter what that guy selling Bush-Hitler T-shirts whom I argued with says). But it's a step in the, uh, right direction.

In a widely e-circulated article in 2003, political scientist

Lawrence Britt examined the fascisms of Hitler, Mussolini, Franco, Indonesia's Suharto, and several Latin American regimes and identified fourteen common characteristics (which I paraphrase rather than parrot verbatim like some fool):

1. Powerful nationalism: ubiquitous, conspicuous displays of patriotic slogans, symbols, flags. (Those fucking flag lapel pins. If you're not wearing one, you're not only less patriotic than me—you probably side with the enemy. And if you put one on, I'll wear two. Cheapest patriotism you can buy!)

2. Disdain for civil liberties: The leaders persuade the people that, with their security in peril, human rights and laws pertaining thereto can and should be ignored. A little secret imprisonment and torture, a few summary executions and assassinations, and the sacrifice of every liberal-democratic principle this country stands for is a small price to pay for our war against . . . whatever is it we're being told we're at war against. (See USA PATRIOT Act, etc.)

3. Use of a perceived common threat or enemy—racial, ethnic, or religious minorities, liberals, communists, socialists, terrorists, Zionists, neoconservatives—as a scapegoat, and eradication thereof as a unifying, patriotic cause. (See LIBERALS, DISSENTERS AND WAR CRITICS, TARRING OF AS TREASONOUS, AMERICA-HATING, TERRORIST-LOVING, BRIE-EATING SURRENDER MONKEYS; **XMAS AND CHRISTIANITY, DEMOCRAT-LIBERAL-SATANIST-SECULARIST WAR ON**; etc.)

4. Glamorization of and heavy investment in the

military, at the expense of domestic, civilian needs. (See **NEOCONS.**)

5. Rampant sexism, homophobia, and patriarchalism; rigidly traditional gender roles (which are really anything but traditional); renewed male domination of the household (witness recent evangelical mass "covenant weddings" in which wives affirm their subservience to their three Lords—their husbands, Jesus, and God). "Divorce, abortion and homosexuality are suppressed and the state is represented as the ultimate guardian of the family institution." (See **ABORTION AND BIRTH CONTROL**; **"FAMILY" AND "FAMILY VALUES"**; HOMOSEXUAL AGENDA, SAVING AMERICA FROM; etc.)

6. Government-controlled mass media, whether through direct government ownership; censorship and intimidation of journalists; or government-aligned media ownership. (See MEDIA-GOP AXIS.)

7. Obsession with national security; fear "as a motivational tool by the government over the masses." (See **FEAR, POLITICAL SCIENCE AND ENGINEERING OF.**)

8. Intertwining of religion and government: Use of religion "as a tool to manipulate public opinion . . . Religious rhetoric and terminology is common from government leaders, even when the major tenets of the religion [*Thou shalt not kill? The meek shall inherit? The rich shall pay tax on what they inherit?*] are diametrically opposed to the government's policies or actions." (See **ASS-HOLINESS** and **"F-ING FAITH-BASED INITIATIVES."**)

9. Corporate power: "The industrial and business aristocracy of a fascist nation often are the ones who put the government leaders into power,

creating a mutually beneficial business/government relationship and power elite." (See Corporate-GOP Merger and Hostile Takeover of America and **GOPonomics**.)

10. Suppression of labor power, "[b]ecause the organizing power of labor is the only real threat to a fascist government . . ." (See **GOPonomics; Linda Chavez**; and Labor, Hitting over the Head with a Two-by-Four, Then Kicking When It's Down.)

11. Disdain for intellectuals and the arts; open hostility to higher education and academia; attacks on, and censorship of free expression in arts and letters. (See **"Elitism"; Ignorance and Idiocy**; and Culture, Reaching for the Revolver upon Hearing the Word.)

12. Obsession with crime and punishment: "The police are given almost limitless power to enforce laws. The people are often willing to overlook police abuses and even forego civil liberties in the name of patriotism." (See **Bush Administration**.)

13. Rampant **corruption and cronyism** (see **Crime**): Groups of friends and associates appoint each other to government positions, appropriate national resources, and protect each other from accountability. (See **Bush Administration**.)

14. Fraudulent elections, including manipulation of political district boundaries, vote suppression, smear campaigns, and "use [of] judiciaries to manipulate or control elections." (See Election Theft 2000, 2004, and 2008; **Justice System, Partisan Political Perversion of; Tom DeLay; Karl Rove**.)

Political figures, even self-professed radicals and revolu-
tionaries such as DELAY, GINGRICH, and NORQUIST, can't be
expected to advertise openly just how far over the right-
wing horizon they dream of leading us. It's better left to
more verbally incontinent media figures to give voice to the
movement's darkest thoughts (while helping their friends in
government look moderate and reasonable by comparison):
SEAN HANNITY, for example, who introduced a weekly
"Enemy of the State Award" on his Fox News talk show.
(Actor SEAN PENN took home the first one for his outspoken
opposition to the Iraq War. It was the first Enemy win for
Penn, who had been nominated twice previously.) Or of
course an ANN COULTER, who speaks of executing liberals
("We need to execute people like ['American Taliban' John
Walker Lindh] in order to physically intimidate liberals, by
making them realize that they can be killed, too") and who
says: "My libertarian friends never appreciate the benefits of
local fascism."

Coulter's remarks can be mapped virtually one-to-one
with Dr. Britt's fourteen-point plan of fascism: "Liberals hate
America" and "There are no good Democrats" (3). "Would
that it were so! . . . That the American military were targeting
journalists," and "My only regret with TIMOTHY MCVEIGH is he
did not go to the *New York Times* building" (6). "Frankly, I'm
not a big fan of the First Amendment [free speech]" (2, 6). "It
would be a much better country if women did not vote" (5).
"We should invade [Muslims'] countries, kill their leaders and
convert them to Christianity" (3, 2, 8). "I have to say I'm all
for public flogging" (2, 12).

Also be sure to visit our Michael Ledeen section at
LEDEEN, MICHAEL dot nothing.

FEAR, POLITICAL SCIENCE AND ENGINEERING OF as Weapon of Mass Distraction and Control

Over the decades, conservatives and Republicans have forged and fueled fears of:

▶ **The Communists,** armed and determined, hiding under your children's beds; posing as their school-teachers; producing the movies and television they see every week.

▶ **The blacks,** coming after your teenage daughters, your wife, your stereo, your tax money, your job, your kids' college admissions, and the music your kids listen to. (See SOUTHERN STRATEGY.)

▶ **The queers,** teaching your kids in school to be queer and taking all those sitcom roles.

▶ **AIDS,** which converted in seconds into a gay-bashing weapon.

▶ **Women,** coming after your job, but also your very manhood—and, at the rate they're going, within a few years' time, impossible to get any sex out of. (Unless *you're* a woman, maybe.)

▶ **Sex, drugs, and rock 'n' roll,** in other words, the complete moral collapse of Western civilization.

▶ **The Mexicans** (plus Guatemalans, Ecuadorians, etc., etc.), in other words, the Hispanization of America, the eventual banning of the English language, and the recapture of everything west of the Mississippi by Mexico. (See PAT BUCHANAN, LOU DOBBS, TOM TANCREDO . . .)

But **terror** (as in "WAR ON TERROR," RELENTLESS POLITICAL EXPLOITATION OF) has been the most versatile of all fear generators in recent years. In its name, wrote Greg Palast, **DICK CHENEY,** "from his bunker . . . has created a government that is little more than a Wal-Mart of Fear: midnight snatchings of citizens for uncharged crimes, wars to hunt for imaginary weapons aimed at Los Angeles, DNA data banks of kids and grandmas, even the Chicken Little sky-is-falling SOCIAL SECURITY spook show."

Consider, and then mock, the much-mocked color-coded alert system the Bush administration introduced in 2002. "Low-threat Orange," wrote Palast, "means that there will be no special inspections of passengers or cargo today. Isn't it nice of Mr. Bush to alert Osama when half our security forces are given the day off?" Palast asked an Israeli security expert why his nation didn't use color codes. "He asked me if, when I woke up, I checked the day's terror color. 'I can't say I ever have [I replied]. I mean, who would?' He smiled. 'The terrorists.'"

What purpose *did* the color-code system serve? Could the following coincidences provide a clue?

▶ The system was introduced just as Democrats were beginning to question aspects of the Bush "war on terror."

▶ A torrent of official warnings followed the revelation, in May 2002, of the August 6, 2001, briefing Bush had received which warned of al Qaeda attacks inside the United States, possibly involving hijacked aircraft and targeting New York City.

▶ In June 2002, Attorney General **JOHN ASHCROFT** announced that an American citizen named Abdullah al-Muhajir, né JOSE PADILLA, was under arrest on suspicion of plotting a terror attack in the United States, possibly using a nuclear "dirty bomb." But Padilla had been arrested more than a month earlier and held secretly. Why the delayed announcement? It "coincided precisely with the moment congressional investigations into the missed warnings before September 11 began to come very close to [Bush] himself," the *American Prospect* noted. (As it turned out, the "plot" consisted of conversations between Padilla and another U.S. prisoner who made threats against the Statue of Liberty and the Brooklyn Bridge that were reportedly based on the movie *Godzilla*.[46])

The 2004 election season brought a fresh series of peculiarly timed terror warnings lacking in detail or guidance on how to respond:

▶ In May, a Gallup poll showed Bush's job-approval rating had fallen to 46 percent. A few days later, information emerged suggesting that responsibility for human rights abuses of Iraqi prisoners went high up in the administration. A few days after that, Ashcroft announced that al Qaeda was "almost ready to attack the United States" and intended "to hit hard." A senior administration official anonymously admitted there was "no real new intelligence . . . no significant change that would require us to change the alert level." Asked to explain his timing, Ashcroft could only say, "We believe the public, like all of us, needs a reminder."

So it continued until election day: Again and again, good news or publicity for Kerry was followed by a vague, unsubstantiated, and/or outdated Homeland Security department terrorism warning. A report by

the Government Accountability Office (GAO) concluded that the lack of specific information and guidance in the warnings undermined their credibility and
hampered authorities' ability to protect the public.
"They didn't say what was new and didn't suggest any
additional measures to be taken other than please be
a little bit more vigilant and please go about your
shopping," a GAO official observed. Not only did
repeatedly raising the warning level induce "terror
fatigue," it also created huge costs for cities and states
(especially "blue" ones like New York, speaking of
color coding)—"for which Washington is not paying
its share," the *New York Times* observed, concluding
that the color-coded threat chart didn't "serve the purpose for which it was invented." Oh, but didn't it?

Slimers, Tricksters, and Backstage Bastards: FINKELSTEIN, ARTHUR

He's been acclaimed as "the architect of JESSE HELMS's polit-
ical rise" and "the guy who slandered the term 'liberal' in
American politics" (see LIBERAL, MAKING A DIRTY WORD OF).
Since working for presidents Nixon and Reagan, he has
helped elect the likes of GEORGE W. BUSH, New York governor
George Pataki and senator Alphonse D'Amato, and Israeli
prime minister Benjamin Netanyahu. He also has advised
Ariel Sharon; helped the Swift Boat Smearers for Bush smear
John Kerry's military reputation; and announced he would be
spearheading the "Get Hillary" campaign in 2006.

"He is the stuff of Hollywood," CNN reported in 1996: "A
man who can topple even the most powerful foes, yet so

secretive that few have ever seen him." CNN captioned its photo, "Only known photo of Arthur Finkelstein." This after twenty years as a leading GOP strategist.

Finkelstein helped direct Republican strategy in thirty-three Senate races in 1996 alone. Typical Finkelstein ad lines: "That's liberal. That's Jack Reed. That's wrong. Call liberal Jack Reed . . ." "That's the Finkelstein formula," Democratic consultant Mark Mellman told CNN: "Just brand somebody a liberal, use the word over and over again . . ." Clients called this "Finkel-think."

A classic Finkel-think tactic was the "independent expenditure" campaign, which, by remaining technically unaffiliated with any candidate, "can avoid spending limits while pummeling Democrats with ads GOP candidates can later disavow," *Time* explained. The beauty of this arrangement, a Fink colleague once explained, is that "a group like ours [Finkelstein's National Conservative Political Action Committee] could lie through its teeth, and the candidate stays clean."[47]

In a 1978 South Carolina congressional race, Finkelstein, who is Jewish, conducted a poll that referred to his Republican client as "a native South Carolinian" and to his Democrat rival, Max Heller, as "a Jewish immigrant." Five days before the election, an independent candidate jumped in—allegedly at the Repugs' behest—and attacked Heller for not "believ[ing] in Jesus Christ." Heller lost by less than six thousand votes.

A Rovian figure . . . but did Karl Rove marry his male partner of forty years—as Finkelstein did, in April 2005, after remaining closeted until 1996, when he was outed by *Boston* magazine? Demonstrating that there's more than one way to betray your own people, Finkelstein had helped elect some of the most outspokenly homophobic members of Congress, including

HELMS, LAUCH FAIRCLOTH (R-N.C.), DON NICKLES (R-Okla.), and BOB SMITH (R-N.H.)—four senators whose opposition helped defeat a bill banning antigay job discrimination. They apparently wanted a version that would only protect gay GOP masterminds. Republicans just don't care about the little gay.

All-Time Worst GOP Senators:
FRIST, BILL: "DR. PERFECT" AND MR. HYDE, THE MEDICAL-INDUSTRIAL COMPLEX, and a Lott of Good Ol' Southern Values

My editors took me down to the basement, tied me to a chair, and demanded to know why I gave this guy so many pages. He isn't even in the Senate anymore. I told them: Beneath his surgeon-turned-senator's halo, and despite some genuinely good deeds, Frist embodies so much of what's repubnant about the Repugs that he serves as the perfect lens through which to view the party as a whole. Moreover: only fifty-four when he retired from the Senate in 2006, he ominously announced he was only taking a "sabbatical." He has, as the *New York Times* said, "a hunger to win and a powerful ambition"—including presidential aspirations. In short, he still must be considered a danger to the republic.

Also, I explained, I don't like him.

As you read the indictment, keep in mind *why* the Republicans elected Frist to succeed the disgraced TRENT LOTT as Senate majority leader in 2002. Frist was not only young-looking, handsome-ish, and rich-issimo to boot. As a former heart and lung transplant surgeon, he had *saved lives*. (His first campaign ads "showed him hard at work in hospital scrubs, with grateful transplant recipients offering emotional tributes to his dedication and compassion."[48]) Dr. Frist lent the Republicans cover on one of their greatest political vulnerabilities—health care. His was "a profession people associate with compassion and intelligence," wrote Jonathan Cohn in *The New Republic*. "He seemed to be Lott's opposite —thoughtful . . . caring . . . smart . . ." "We're going to have to go through a healing process as a result of [the Lott] ordeal," said moderate Republican senator Olympia Snowe of Maine, "and who better to handle it than Bill Frist?" "He's a wonderful face for the Republican Party," gushed former Republican Tennessee governor Lamar Alexander. He was, wrote Maureen Dowd, "Dr. Perfect."

What better healer than Frist—whose voting record ranked among the ten most conservative in the Senate, and whose nomination had garnered widespread support from Republican senators who had considered *Lott* too moderate? Frist, noted National Organization for Women (NOW) president Kim Gandy, "has voted against sex education, international family planning, emergency contraception (the morning-after pill), affirmative action, hate crimes legislation and the Employment Non-Discrimination Act. This is the man who is supposed to save face for the GOP in the Senate?"

Frist was also one of the least experienced senators ever to become majority leader. He had never even voted before he decided to ~~buy~~ run for a Senate seat in 1994 (backed by family wealth and $3.7 million out of his own pocket). But, wrote Joe Conason in the *New York Observer*, he "met the criteria cherished by **KARL ROVE** [who was credited with engineering Lott's exit and Frist's entrance]: He is telegenic, articulate and utterly subservient to the White House." Rove "will be the de facto Senate leader," Kim Gandy remarked.

Pass the disinfectant. This surgeon didn't enter the political theater with very clean hands. The odor of Frist's 1994 campaign ads was rather like the odor Trent Lott left lingering over the GOP in 2002 (for which Frist was like one of those aerosol air fresheners that don't *dispel* the smell so much as *add* a sickeningly sweet one). Frist had won with "a classic anti-Washington campaign with the great Southern code words built in," recalled incumbent Democrat Jim Sasser's campaign manager. (See SOUTHERN STRATEGY.) Frist's ads hammered away at Sasser's sending Tennessee taxpayers' money to Washington, home of Marion S. Barry, and featured "The Ballad of Liberal, Taxing, Two-Faced Jim," which included the lyric "You ran up a tab, sent us a bill/If the taxes don't get us, the criminals will."

Crime family. Frist's wealth (and hence his political career) came from the family business—Tennessee-based Hospital Corporation of America (HCA), the nation's largest for-profit hospital chain, which his father founded and which the Frist family still controlled. Bill's brother Tommy, HCA's CEO and largest shareholder, owned hundreds of millions worth of HCA stock. HCA was a top contributor to Frist's and other Republicans' election campaigns, and spent hundreds of thousands a year lobbying Congress. This background helped Frist to become the party's point man on health-care issues. (In the GOP, if you, your family, and/or your CORPORATE SPECIAL INTERESTS stand to gain from legislation you're pushing, it doesn't *dis*qualify you, it *qualifies* you. We've been over this.) But Frist is "exactly the wrong man to address the nation's health care woes," wrote Jonathan Cohn. "He seems to have inherited from his family ... a tendency to see the market as the solution to most problems, even as the ways the market distorts health care—everything from drug companies pushing unnecessary medications to insurance companies neglecting beneficiaries—are growing ever more evident."[49]

There could be no better example, in fact, than HCA. According to a 1996 *New England Journal of Medicine* article, a typical hospital takeover by Columbia/HCA (its old name) resulted in less charity care, the replacement of senior health professionals with cheaper, less experienced workers, and lower quality service.[50] "How did Columbia/HCA get rich?" asked Nathan Newman, policy director of the Progressive Legislative Action Network: "Raiding nonprofit hospitals, dumping the poor previously served and turning them into profit mills for the family bottom line. . . . Oh yeah, and massive fraud against the Medicare system."

HCA increased its Medicare billings by inflating expenses and billing for services ineligible for reimbursement, such as advertising and marketing costs. Doctors received kickbacks for patient referrals; perks included paid positions as medical directors, "loans" that were never repaid, free office rent and furniture, and free pharmaceuticals. Doctors were even paid for performing unnecessary surgeries.[51] In an ABC News interview, a former Columbia/HCA vice president described "an arrogant corporate culture in which meeting demands for profits became far more important than caring for patients or obeying the law." He himself had "committed felonies every day." In 2000, three years into an investigation by the Clinton Justice Department, the company pleaded guilty to fourteen Medicare fraud–related felonies. The same year, the National Labor Relations Board ruled that HCA had engaged in illegal union-busting against hospital workers.

Would a GOP administration—especially one for which Senator Bill Frist was working overtime—ever have investigated HCA? I can tell you this: In 2002, Republican senator

Charles Grassley felt compelled to warn Bush's Medicare administrator THOMAS SCULLY not to sabotage the still unfolding investigation. Scully, as it didn't just happen, had once served as chairman of the American Federation of Hospitals, a Washington lobbying group whose largest member is HCA.

In December 2002, just as Karl Rove was engineering Frist's elevation to Senate majority leader, the Bush Justice Department abruptly closed the HCA investigation and offered a settlement. HCA would pay $631 million in fines, which, on top of previous fines, brought its total penalties to $1.7 billion, the most ever levied in a health-care fraud case. In short, a sweetheart deal. Why? Because, after years of massively defrauding Medicare *and* Medicaid, which covers the poor *and*—here's a nice patriotic Republican touch—Tricare, which covers the military and their families, not only did HCA executives manage to avoid jail time, the company was permitted to continue doing business with Medicare.

"The Senator from the State of Health-Care Industry." Such were HCA/Frist family values. But were they Bill Frist values? A study by the watchdog group Center for Public Integrity concluded that "Columbia-HCA's staunchest ally in Congress is undoubtedly its CEO's brother." Frist promoted caps on damages awards for victims who sue negligent hospitals. He sided with HCA against a Democratic measure to protect hospital whistle-blowers. He sponsored legislation that would direct billions of Medicare dollars to Columbia/HCA by allowing hospitals and doctors to join together as "provider-sponsored organizations" (PSOs) to compete with HMOs for Medicare patients.

Frist was no foe of the HMO, though. He voted for tax subsidies to HMOs and insurance companies that offer prescription drugs to seniors. He nay'd a Clinton plan to save Medicare $6 billion by reducing payments to PSOs *and* HMOs. He acknowledged that the government was overpaying HMOs for Medicare patients, but actually argued: "That might be a good thing. It will attract more managed-care companies into the market and drive prices down." To drive HMOs' prices *down, overpay* them. See? **GOP**ONOMICS isn't so hard.

A "Patient's Bill of Wrongs." That's what the American Medical Association called the Senate GOP's managed-care bill, which Frist wrote in 1999. He led the successful effort against a rival bill that would have guaranteed patients the right to sue HMOs for failure to provide adequate treatment— a provision backed by the AMA, almost all congressional Democrats, and at least twenty Republicans. That year, Frist was the largest Senate recipient of donations from the "Health Benefits Coalition" (HBC), a group joining managed-care companies with other powerful business associations that spent millions lobbying against patients' bill of rights measures. (More than 80 percent of HBC political contributions went to Republicans. I know, big deal—same with every other industry. See CORPORATE-K STREET-GOP AXIS.) "Frist's opposition has alienated his old medical colleagues," the *Washington Post* reported. "'The people in this room are very concerned that he's forgotten about his patients,'" said a family practitioner at a medical meeting in Memphis.

Patriot-Dr. Frist even managed to insert into the bill creating the Department of Homeland Security a provision barring parents from suing drugmaker Eli Lilly over Thimerosal, a mercury-based vaccine preservative that allegedly causes autism and other neurological disorders. (Because if Lilly can be sued for causing autism, then the terrorists win. I guess.) The pharmaceutical industry was the largest single contributor to the Frist-chaired National Republican Senatorial Committee (NRSC).* Lilly was the industry's single biggest contributor to the GOP, which received 79 percent of Lilly's Largesse.** "Frist isn't the senator from Tennessee," said the executive director of Public Campaign, a campaign finance watchdog group, "he's the senator from the state of Health Care Industry Influence. He's gotten . . . more cash from health-care interests than 98 percent of his colleagues."

To change the subject: A report posted on Democrats.com was titled, "Bill Frist is a Whore for the Medical-Industrial Complex." But that's not quite fair; Frist also took $130,000 from the food-processing industry—"and then helped kill a bill putting teeth into the USDA's [Department of Agriculture] authority to crack down on processing plants that violate federal standards for bacterial and viral infection of meat and poultry."[52]

Smooth operator. In June 2005, Frist sold all his HCA stock (worth tens of millions) as though he was afraid *it* was infected. Two weeks later, HCA issued a disappointing earnings report, whereupon the stock, which was up 40 percent for the year, fell 15 percent. Picked at the peak of perfection. With almost surgical precision. Of course, the stock had been held in a blind trust to avoid a conflict of interest or

---

*In 2002, on Frist's watch, the NRSC oversaw and funded some of the dirtiest Senate campaigns in memory (see **SAXBY CHAMBLISS**). In key races, the GOP systematically used dirty tricks and intimidation to prevent African Americans from voting. The surgin' surgeon-senator was made majority leader partly in recognition of his role in winning the Senate back for the GOP.
**Not, contrary to rumors, the name of a clothing chain catering to tall and "full-figured" women.

appearance thereof. But, although Senate Ethics rules bar communication with trustees of a "blind" trust except to direct them to sell an asset that would create a conflict of interest, Frist's trustees contacted him nearly two dozen times between 2001 and July 2005 regarding his blind trust assets. And apparently Frist was only now realizing that his years spent promoting health care legislation affecting the medical industry might—just might—constitute a conflict of interest. A Securities and Exchange Commission investigation eventually cleared Frist of insider trading charges, but that doesn't mean we have to.

Filibluster. In 2004, when it came to light that GOP staffers had been hacking into Senate Judiciary Committee Democrats' computer system and monitoring their private memos for over a year during the battle over Bush judicial nominees, it was, not too surprisingly, Frist's top aide on judicial nominees, MANUEL MIRANDA, who took the fall. After all, it was the Senate "healer" who led the Republicans in their thuggish threats to deploy the "NUCLEAR OPTION" and do away with the two-hundred-year-old right to filibuster if the Dems didn't bow down before Bush on every one of his far-right wing nominees. The judicial filibuster, which two-thirds of Americans favored keeping, was "nothing less than a formula for tyranny by the minority," said Frist—hoping no one would remember *he* had voted for a filibuster of at least one Clinton nominee. Asked about this apparent self-contradiction on *Face the Nation*, Frist blubbered, "Filibuster, cloture, it gets confusing . . ." *

*Frist's claim that he had voted to filibuster merely for scheduling purposes or to get more information on the nominee (whose nomination had been pending for four years) was a plain lie, documents proved.

In April 2005, Frist addressed the audience at "JUSTICE SUNDAY," a rally organized by the Christianist-right-wing Family Research Council (FRC) to portray Democrats as anti-"people of faith." Dems were said to oppose Bush judicial nominees not because the nominees were, as they say, to the right of ATTILA THE HUN, but because they were (*un*like the Huns) *Christian*. Many of the rally speakers compared the conservative Christians' struggle against oppression to the civil rights movement. Odd, ironic, hypocritical, because the man with whom Frist shared the stage, FRC president TONY PERKINS, had long-standing ties to racist organizations.*

Med evil. Also onstage at "Justice Sunday" was FRC founder JAMES DOBSON, who declared: "The biggest Holocaust in world history came out of the Supreme Court" with *Roe v. Wade.* Frist's voting record on ABORTION, along with his votes against teen pregnancy prevention programs that included contraceptives, earned him a 100 percent score from the National Right to Life Committee and 0 percent from Planned Parenthood and NARAL Pro-Choice America. How much abortion itself earned him is hard to say; HCA hospitals profitably performed abortions while Frist still held his millions in stock—*and* while he voted in favor of (1) a ban on so-called partial-birth abortions, making no exceptions for cases where the woman's health is in danger; (2) maintaining a ban

*In 2001 Perkins addressed a chapter of the Council of Conservative Citizens, America's premier white supremacist organization, the successor to the White Citizens Councils, which battled integration in the South. In 1996 Perkins—then campaign manager for a GOP senatorial candidate in Louisiana—paid former Ku Klux Klan Grand Wizard DAVID DUKE for his mailing list. The Federal Election Commission fined the campaign $3,000 for attempting to hide the purchase.

on abortions on military bases; and (3) applying the same criminal penalties for harm caused to a fetus during the commission of a crime as to a *human being*, even if the perp didn't know the woman was pregnant. *"Human Events*, a rightwing rag, tried to get some clarity on the topic [of Frist's profiting from abortion] from Frist's office, but ran into a wall of obfuscation," Democrats.com reported.

Yeah? Well, try getting some clarity on his position on embryonic STEM-CELL RESEARCH. He actually opposed it (as John Kerry might have put it) before he supported it. Or maybe it was the other way around. Frist also voted to ban human cloning. Except of Republican voters, of course.

Hey: Respect Frist's views on these subjects. He's a man of science. "Creation science." He says creationism ("intelligent design"—same difference) should be taught in public schools alongside evolution because "in a pluralistic society that is the fairest way to go." ("I can only assume," a blogger wrote, "that [Frist] tells patients, 'I recommend heart surgery [but] it's fair that I also tell you about the options of faithhealing, crystals, sacrificing a goat to Odin . . .'"[53])

Still, one can't help feeling that, before he ran off and joined the Republican's TERRI SCHIAVO circus—their disgustingly exploitative, purely political crusade to prevent the removal of the feeding tube from the severely brain-damaged woman, against her husband's and apparently her own wishes—before Dr. Frist saw fit to diagnose Schiavo and to publicly contradict her doctors, who were actually *there* and who, unlike Frist, specialized in neurology—he might at least have actually, like, *examined* the patient?

Perhaps Frist's true views on the sanctity of life were better revealed by his literal stand on GUN CONTROL. In July 2005, he stood up in the Senate chamber and said Congress should quickly pass the NATIONAL RIFLE ASSOCIATION's dream legislation to block lawsuits against reckless gun sellers. Speed was essential, Frist argued, or else the U.S. firearms industry might collapse; the Pentagon, he claimed, "faces the real prospect of having to outsource sidearms for our soldiers to foreign manufacturers." To get the NRA's dream package on the Senate floor, Frist had to push aside less pressing business, including a $491 billion defense spending bill. But without the NRA bill, you see, our troops would be unarmed. Strangely, though, the Defense Department had never mentioned this danger before, nor was there any evidence that any major American gun company was in financial trouble. In fact, U.S. gun manufacturers were reporting record profits; the two publicly traded ones recently had filed statements with the government, contradicting claims that lawsuits posed a financial threat. There was, however, compelling evidence that the NRA gave $1,184,130 to federal candidates in 2005–2006—over 85 percent of it to Republicans.

Sometimes doctors favor gun control because they've seen first-hand what guns do; sometimes they don't. It depends.

Naturally, Frist was 100 percent on board with trigger-happy Bush and Cheney on Iraq—both invasion *and* cover-up. Such as in November 2005, when Minority Leader Harry Reid (D-Nev.) tried to force the Republican-controlled Senate to discuss the status of a promised investigation into the Bush administration's (ahem) use of intelligence prior to the invasion—demanding "on behalf of the American people" that we understand why these investigations aren't being conducted." (Because it *was* the Republican-controlled Senate—that's my theory.) As John Nichols wrote in *The Nation*, Frist "immediately accused Reid of attempting to 'hijack' the Senate by forcing a discussion about accountability in matters of war and peace."

That same month, the healer said he was more concerned about information leaks regarding secret CIA detention centers than about what went on in those prisons. In fact, he categorically told reporters he was "not concerned about what goes on." (A doctor *with* very definite borders.) Frist and House Speaker DENNIS HASTERT (R-Ill.) formally called for a joint congressional investigation into a leak about the prisons to the *Washington Post. They* knew a scandal when *they* saw one.

Frist had been even more pissed about the publicizing of the Bush administration's pre-SEPTEMBER 11 neglect of terrorist threats. When former White House counterterrorism adviser RICHARD CLARKE published his 2004 book *Against All Enemies*, Frist called it "an appalling act of profiteering" and accused Clarke of telling "two entirely different stories under oath" before a joint congressional panel and before the 9/11 Commission. A few hours later, his spokesman admitted Frist had no actual evidence to support his accusations, no idea whether Clarke perjured himself, or whether there were any inconsistencies at all in Clarke's story. (The *Washington Post* reviewed his testimony and found none. Republican Senator Richard Lugar, who served on the joint congressional committee, said he recalled none. But that's the Bushist MO: Do the damage, backpedal if you have to—important thing is, the damage is done.) "Coming from a politician who wrote a quickie book to profit from the anthrax scare," Joe Conason observed, "[Frist's] whine about profiteering is ludicrous. . . . Coming from a millionaire whose family company grew bloated through Medicare fraud, his insinuation of dishonesty is laughable."

I believe I've accused Bill Frist of everything but killing cats. Well, I don't like loose ends. The *Boston Globe* reported in 2002 that, while conducting research, medical student Frist's "dilemma was finding enough animals to kill. Soon, he began lying to obtain more animals. He went to the animal shelters around Boston and promised he would care for the cats as pets. Then he killed them during experiments." See Little Furry Animals, GOP Senate Majority Leaders' Cruelty Toward.

Asshole #16: Senator Bill Frist. To an aide while visiting tsunami-ravaged Sri Lanka and posing for a photo op: "Get some devastation in the back."

"F-ing Faith-Based Initiative," The

George W. Bush's "faith-based initiatives" (FBI) were supposed to be the heart of his "compassionate Conservatism." Under FBI, while the Bush administration cut billions from programs to help the needy, it dropped a few coins, as it were, into the charity boxes of religious groups, supposedly to fill the compassion gap. But not, heaven forfend,* to proselytize, because that would violate the constitutional separation of church and state. Unfortunately, the "initiatives'" actual *purposes* were to (a) violate, indeed destroy forever the constitutional separation of church and state, (b) appease the Christianist right, and (c) make it look as though the

---

*What the *hell* does "forfend" *mean*?

government *wasn't* abandoning the needy but indeed doing even more for them.

After the first head of the newly created White House Office of Faith-Based Initiatives (OFBI), JOHN DIIULIO, quit in disgust in August 2001, he told *Esquire* magazine there was a "virtual absence of any policy accomplishments that might, to a fair-minded nonpartisan, count as flesh on the bones of so-called compassionate conservatism." All there was, he said, was "speechmaking . . . everything, and I mean everything, [is] being run by the political arm. It's the reign of the Mayberry Machiavellis." See KARL ROVE, obviously.

In his 2006 book *Tempting Faith*, former OFBI deputy director DAVID KUO confirmed this view of the Bush compassion racket. He told of meetings with DiIulio's successor, Jim Towey, and White House political affairs director KEN MEHLMAN to plan "nonpartisan" conferences with "faith and community leaders" in 2004 battleground states, to "show minority communities we cared. Evangelicals would be happy, too, because we would emphasize the president's deep personal faith." Mehlman explained how not to "make it look too political." Kuo recalled RALPH REED excitedly phoning Rove from a "faith-based" conference in Atlanta and saying, "Karl . . . you won't believe what we've got here . . . 3,000 people, mostly minorities, applauding a stinkin' video of the president. . . . THIS IS UNBELIEVABLE!!" More than a dozen such conferences were held up to the eve of the 2004 election. "Their political power was incalculable," Kuo wrote.

"Farce." The Bushies had promised religious conservatives a $200-million-per-year Compassion Capital Fund that would award grants to faith-based organizations. After the 2000 election, the amount was cut to $100 million, then $30

million. (It takes a Republican to show that you *can* violate two fundamental principles of American government—no establishment of an official religion and no partisan political use of public funds—*without* costing the taxpayer $200 million.)

Potential grant recipients were scored on a 0–100 scale. The highest scoring organizations "were politically friendly to the administration," wrote Kuo. A newly created group, headed by "one of the most vocal black voices supporting the president during the 2000 election," somehow scored a 98. Another new organization, with a staff of three, "all from the world of Washington politics, and all very Republican," scored 99.67. "It was obvious that the ratings were a farce," wrote Kuo. A former member of the fund's peer-review panel told him, "When I saw one of those non-Christian groups [among the applications], I just stopped looking at them and gave them a zero. . . . a lot of us did." (So? Who *should* get the faith-based pork—Jews and Muslims?)

Rats! Out-Jesused again! The administration also funded "faith-based" groups at the expense of nonsectarian groups that had previously received federal grants, the *American Prospect* reported. "I'm not getting out-Jesused for money ever again," said a veterans' shelter director who was denied a federal grant because he hadn't checked off a box that asked if the shelter was "faith-based." Some groups that got funding, he said, "previously weren't even aware of veterans." After he reregistered as "faith-based," his federal funding nearly tripled.

Kuo described White House staff's privately mocking the religious conservatives they courted—commenting about "how annoying the Christians were or how tiresome . . . or how 'handling' them took so much time," and referring to the faith-based initiative as the "f-ing faith-based initiative." "'The nuts' were politically invaluable, but that was the extent of their usefulness."

White House practice, wrote Kuo, was "to make grand announcements and then do nothing." In May 2001, for instance, Bush announced a new $3 billion drug treatment initiative. By December 2003, "not a dime had been spent. . . . The announcements were smart politics because absolutely no one called them on anything. . . . If the faith-based initiative was teaching me anything, it was about the president's capacity to care about perception more than reality."

And they took the people's money, and they built a fitness center unto the Lord. In its own Constitution-violating initiative (CVI), the GOP-controlled Congress approved more than 450 earmarks (federal grants that bypass normal review and bidding procedures), totaling over $150 million, for religious groups just in the 2003–2004 session, compared to fewer than 60 in 1997–1998. Meanwhile, the *New York Times* reported, the number of religious organizations listed as clients of Washington lobbying firms tripled. Federal money to help these groups feed the hungry and care for the sick? According to the *Times*, many of the earmarks were for such charitable works as construction of new buildings on religious college campuses—including a fitness center at one such college—and expansion of churches' parking space, praise the Lord. Because many of the homeless have no place to park.

Crime, Corruption, and Cronyism Case #20:
GATES, ROBERT

> *It sounds like Donald Rumsfeld. It shows the same kind of*
> *arrogance and hubris that got us into Iraq.*
> —National Security Archive director Thomas Blanton, com-
> menting on a 1984 memo in which then deputy CIA director
> Robert Gates urged a bombing campaign to "bring down"
> the democratically elected government of Nicaragua

The day after the November 2006 midterm election, GEORGE
W. BUSH nominated Gates—a deputy director and director
of Central Intelligence under presidents REAGAN and BUSH
SR. and a longtime Bush crony—to replace defense secretary DONALD RUMSFELD.

The *Washington Post* "touted Gates's extensive government experience, brilliance, bipartisanship, and pragmatic,
consensus-building management style," and included only
one sentence about Gates's role in the IRAN-CONTRA affair,
defense analyst Ivan Eland noted on antiwar.com. Even the
BBC reported that Gates "is widely respected among both
Democrats and Republicans in the Congress, and his appointment is expected to be swiftly ratified by the Senate." It was—
unanimously by the Senate Armed Services Committee, then
by a 95-2 vote in the full Senate. Which only showed how
relieved everyone was to see the backside of Bumsfelt.

Then deputy director Gates and his CIA staff apparently
failed to notice the disintegration of the Soviet Union during
the 1980s; indeed, Gates has been criticized "for concocting
evidence to show that the Soviet Union was stronger than it
actually was, and also for repeatedly skewing intelligence to
promote a particular [hardline] worldview."[54] Gates even

vouched for a BS CIA memo, shown to the Senate and President Reagan, alleging that the Soviet Union played a role in the 1981 shooting of Pope John Paul II—a memo later dismissed as baseless in a CIA internal review.

No shit. Although never indicted for his Iran-Contra role, Gates was at a minimum guilty of, as Eland put it, "looking the other way when unconstitutional acts [were] being committed," acts that amounted to "one of the most dangerous threats to constitutional government in American history."

Come on. How could the number two man at the CIA know about the CIA's role in a high-priority covert operation? So Gates seemed to suggest in sworn testimony before a grand jury and at a confirmation hearing, when he repeatedly, uh, *erred* about when he first heard about proceeds from arms sales to Iran being illegally diverted to the Contras. When Judge Lawrence Walsh, the Republican independent counsel who investigated Iran-Contra, confronted him with a report Gates had received on the illegal operation, Gates claimed to have forgotten about it. (But does a defense secretary really *need* a good memory?) In his final report, Walsh wrote that Gates had participated in briefings in which congressional investigators were misled into believing the CIA was not involved and had been "less than candid" during the investigation.

In fact, in a 1984 memo to CIA director William Casey, Gates had warned that without U.S. funding, the Contras would collapse—but that funding the Contras was not enough. He recommended the United States initiate a bombing campaign against Nicaragua and "do everything in its power short of invasion to put that [democratically-elected] regime out." The Soviet Union, Gates claimed, was arming Nicaragua, threatening the stability of Central

America and, I guess you could say, posing an imminent threat to the United States.

At the time, "most Americans thought we shouldn't be doing anything in Nicaragua," Thomas Blanton told the *Los Angeles Times*, characterizing Gates's ideas as "extreme." At any rate, as the *Times* noted, Gates's predictions didn't pan out. "Nicaragua did not become a communist dictatorship. The Sandinista regime did not lead to the fall of U.S.-backed governments in El Salvador, Honduras, or Guatemala. . . . the Sandinistas were voted out of office in 1990. A year later the Soviet Union ceased to exist."

What will Gates's *next* imminent threat to the United States be? . . . As though we don't know. (Hint: subtract "-Contra.")

GINGRICH, NEWT

Perhaps no one deserves more credit than the former Georgia representative (1979–99) and Speaker of the House (1995–99) for making the GOP the GOP we know and love: a radical, *revolutionary* party characterized by partisanship of almost Bolshevik ferocity, contempt for such scruples as laws and ethics, and an equally Bolshie devotion to the propaganda arts. He infected the body politic with one might call *gingrene*, in effect amputating all decency and honor from the GOP. And, as I write, he's a possible, if unlikely, 2008 presidential candidate.

"Newt," a former college history professor, led the 1994 Republican Revolution which ended forty years of Democratic majorities in the House of Reps, which he turned into a House of ill repute, for which he was elected House Speaker *and* named *Time* magazine's 1995 Man of the Year. With Rep. DICK ARMEY, Gingrich cowrote the Revolution's manifesto, *Contract On America,** a wooden horse of government and welfare "reform" and tougher crime laws (always a popular distraction) in whose hollow interior the GOP smuggled corporate tax breaks and deregulation of corporate polluters through the gates of Troy.

As chair of GOPAC, a powerful, uh, GOP PAC that trains candidates for office (and which he allegedly used as a slush fund), Newton issued a memo titled "Language Matters," in which he described language as "a key mechanism of control used by a majority party. . . . We have heard a plaintive plea: *'I wish I could speak like Newt.'*" There follows a list of "powerful words" that trainees are instructed to "apply to the opponent, their record, proposals and their party." Words such as: *abuse of power* [See BUSH, GEORGE], *anti-* (flag, family, child, jobs), *bureaucracy, cheat, corrupt* (see KETTLE, POT CALLING THE), *criminal rights, cynicism, decay, destroy, devour* (as in what we Dems do to our children, I guess), *endanger, excuses, failure, greed, hypocrisy, ideological, incompetent, intolerant* (why didn't he just tell them, "Whatever *you* are, label your opponent as"? Would have been shorter), *liberal, lie, obsolete, pathetic, permissive, radical, red tape, self-serving, shame, sick, spend(ing), steal, taxes, traitors, unionized, waste,* and *welfare.*

"*Knowledgeable ignorance*" expert. On those two constants in the careers of GOP moralizers and reformers— CORRUPTION and a personal "FAMILY VALUES" deficiency—

*"*With* America"? Whatever.

Newt did not let America down. Democrats filed eighty-two ethics charges against Gingrich just in his first term as Speaker.

The charges that led to his resignation from the House in 1998 and his behavior throughout the controversy said much about the party leader's slippery, cynical, cunning, scheming mind. Gingrich had made his name in the GOP by forcing the 1989 resignation of Democratic Speaker Jim Wright for using a book deal to circumvent campaign-finance laws and House ethics rules. Funny—the Wright business was remarkably like what *Newt* himself would do only a few years later: use contributions to his tax-exempt foundation to finance a "nonpartisan" college course whose purpose, he eventually admitted, was to help elect Republicans to Congress. Throughout a two-year House Ethics Committee investigation, Gingrich denied any wrongdoing, before finally admitting he had given the committee false information. The investigators' final report said Gingrich had flouted House standards of conduct for years, ignoring plain understandings that "you're supposed to keep politics and tax-deductible situations separate." Because GOP committee members declined to accuse him of violating tax laws (which the investigation made clear he had done), Gingrich got off with a reprimand—not the censure that would have required him to step down as Speaker—and a $300,000 fine. But he was the first House Speaker in history to be disciplined in any way.

Was he chastened? Newt at all. Blaming his attorney, Gingrich now claimed he'd been "naive" regarding tax laws—another bald-faced lie: Attorneys had warned him early on not to use tax-exempt financing for partisan activities, and he already was involved with another "nonpartisan" organization the IRS had stripped of its tax exemption. Gingrich practically boasted about his flimflammery, telling a Georgia audience just days after the final Ethics Committee report, "I am an expert in knowledgeable ignorance." Yes, "Language matters."

Having only been reprimanded, Gingrich now went about describing the affair as a *controversy*, which implied nothing had been proven. In a press statement, he said he regretted he had "brought down on the people's House a controversy that could shake the faith people have in their government." Gotta love the guy. Shaking people's faith in government is exactly what Gingrich had devoted his entire political career to: spreading the Reagan message, "Government is not the solution. Government is the problem"—the BS the GOP puts out decade after decade (typically while *expanding* government to benefit corporate friends).

Then, in what *Time* called "a brazen wiggle," Gingrich's office hinted that his fine might be paid from campaign contributions, not out of his pocket, which "would render it all but meaningless—*and* enable his legal-defense fund to become a conduit for influence peddling. As the GOP was at that very moment accusing Bill Clinton of doing.

Alternatively, Gingrich could fall back on the $471,000 in royalties he had earned on his book *To Renew America*. As *The New Republic* pointed out, the book relied heavily on copyrighted material paid for and owned by the same tax-exempt, nonprofit foundation that illegally financed his college course. The commercial use of such material appeared to be yet another violation of tax laws. Paying a fine for ethical misconduct with the profits from other ethical misconduct? Surprised the GOP didn't bestow a medal. (Improper use of book royalties rings a bell . . .

Oh, yeah: Gingrich's charges against Democratic Speaker Jim Wright.)

"When I was praying . . ." The ethics scandal was only part of what brought Gingrich down. After all, he didn't resign for another two years—until after he failed to deliver the smashing thirty-seat GOP gain he had predicted in the 1998 midterm election, when the GOP *lost* five seats. *That's* what Republicans call an ethics lapse.

The failure was attributed to Gingrich's use of the MONICA LEWINSKY scandal as the basis of the party's campaign strategy. Imagine if it had been known then that, even as he led the impeachment charge, even as he devoted several years of the House's life to the most critical issue facing the country—the presidential blow job—he was having an extramarital affair with a House aide twenty-three years his junior. Newtrich admitted to the affair—which led to his 2000 divorce from second wife, Marianne—in a March 2007 radio interview with His **ASS-HOLINESS**, Focus on the Family founder JAMES DOBSON. "There were times when I was praying and when I felt I was doing things that were wrong [and] fall[ing] short of God's standards," family-values guy Newt told Dobson. In other words, this story was really all about Newt's good-Christian-ness. (Could you puke? *I* think you could.)

Gingrich had married Marianne months after his divorce from his first wife, his former high school geometry teacher, Jackie Battley. According to Battley, Gingrich served her with divorce papers and made her discuss settlement terms while she was recuperating in the hospital from cancer surgery, and he refused to pay alimony and child support. She reportedly doesn't plan to vote for him for president.

Gingrich has admitted to sexual indiscretions during that marriage, too. In a September 1995 *Vanity Fair* article by Gail Sheehy, a woman named Anne Manning described an affair she had with Gingrich during that period (when she, too, was married). "We had oral sex," Manning said. "He prefers that modus operandi because then he can say, 'I never slept with her.'" (Or, perhaps, "with that woman, Anne Manning.") "Gingrich pioneered a denial of adultery that some observers would later christen 'the Newt Defense': Oral sex doesn't count," wrote Stephen Talbot in *Salon.com.*

In March 2007, around two months before heading down to hell, JERRY FALWELL wrote, "Mr. Gingrich has dedicated much of his time to calling America back to our Christian heritage. . . . He is becoming one of our great ambassadors for reawakening the spirit of our Founders." I assume the reverend was referring more to the Founding Philanderers and Adulterers—Washington, Jefferson, Franklin—than to the founding Deists, atheists, and anti-Christians—Washington, Jefferson, Franklin . . .

How's this for spirit of our Founders: In a November 2006 speech, Gingrich called for a "serious debate about the First Amendment" right to free speech. "We now should be impaneling people to look seriously at a level of supervision that we would never dream of if it weren't for the scale of the [terrorist] threat," he said. So if you have anything to say about Republicans, better say it before such a "level of supervision" is imposed by Bush or President Giuliani, if not by President Newt himself.

Oh—did I mention Newt dodged the draft during the Vietnam War? (See CHICKEN HAWKS AND CHICKEN NEWTS.)

Asshole #17: Newt Gingrich

► On the election of former Ku Klux Klan leader DAVID DUKE as chairman of the Republican Executive Committee in a Louisiana parish: "We're a party of inclusion."

► "Democrats are the enemy of normal Americans." (Keeping the message simple is one of the secrets of the GOP's electoral success.)

► On billionaire financier/philanthropist GEORGE SOROS,* August 2004: "He wants to spend $75 million defeating George W. Bush because Soros wants to legalize heroin." (Nine years earlier, Soros had suggested establishing "a strictly controlled distribution network" through which drugs would be legally available for registered addicts, at "prices low enough to destroy the drug trade" and discourage crime. "I would use a portion of the income for prevention and treatment [and] foster social opprobrium of drug use." For you Republicans: "opprobrium" means strong disapproval.)

► Gingrich's approach to the drug problem was somewhat different. In 1996, Newt, an admitted former marijuana smoker, proposed "The Drug Importer Death Penalty Act of 1997," with a mandatory *death penalty* for a second offense of smuggling 50 grams (1.76 ounces) of marijuana into the United States, and life in prison without parole for the first offence.[55] I've had some killer weed, but this is ridiculous.

*Also see DENNIS HASTERT.

GOLDWATER, BARRY

Senator (R-Ariz., 1953–1965, 1969–1987); GOP presidential candidate, 1964. Once the symbol of all that was detestable in the GOP; later, a detester of much of what was detestable in the GOP. One thing for sure—unlike almost any other politician, he always said what he really thought. For instance, in 1961: "Sometimes I think this country would be better off if we could just saw off the Eastern Seaboard and let it float out to sea." (Terrible thing to say. It's *Texas* that should be torn off along the perforated line and discarded. Give Arkansas a little seacoast for a change.)

On nuclear weapons: "Let's lob one into the men's room at the Kremlin." (No, he was right! Did you ever use that men's room? It was *disgusting*.)

GOPONOMICS AND CLASS WARFARE 101

As we learned in the first semester, GOP economics is commonly identified with "supply-side economics," "trickle-down economics," "Reaganomics," or, as GEORGE BUSH SR. called it, in his last-ever public moment of candor, while challenging REAGAN for the GOP presidential nomination in 1980, "VOODOO ECONOMICS." Whatever you call it, it means you give tax breaks and whatever other help you can to businesses and the rich (who, conveniently enough, are your most important political contributors *and* often include yourself, family, friends, and business associates) because they will *invest* their tax savings in job-producing enterprises, and the wealth will "trickle down,"* while the nonrich will only *spend* their tax savings on such frivolities as . . . necessities. After all, what good does *buying the goods and services* the economy produces do for the economy?

Actually, most economists agree that, while the rich can just sit on their money, the nonrich are far more likely to spend their tax savings and thus stimulate the economy.[56] And corporations have no reason to hire, and increase production, when there is no increase in demand. (They can, of course, always find other uses for a tax windfall—bigger executive bonuses, for example.)

But GOPonomically speaking, upper-income tax cuts are *always* the answer—or rather, the *question*: How do we justify them *this* time? When Bush first stole the White House and inherited a budget surplus from Clinton, his line was, give it back to the taxpayer; as he said so memorably, "It's your money. You paid for it." (*Bush*onomics is a very . . . *special* branch of GOPonomics. Special as in "special ed.") Within months, Bush had plunged the country into depression (economic and psychological); now we needed economic *stimulus*: Tax cuts. (Economy strong? Tax cuts! Weak? Tax cuts! Bush himself stated it perfectly: "A tax cut is really one of the anecdotes [*sic*] to coming out of an economic illness." As in, "Tell me *another* anecdote.") After September 11, the slogan became "economic security"; the "WAR ON TERROR," too, demanded . . . well, as TOM DELAY put it, "Nothing is more important in the face of a war than cutting taxes"!! Not, as you stupidly may have supposed, *raising*

---

*One appetizing trope for trickle-down economics: You feed the horse, and the little birds peck at what comes out. (Marie Antoinette's response to a report of bread shortages has been misquoted: She did not say "Laissez-les manger le gâteau," but "le caca.")

taxes to *pay* for the war—as in every pre-Bushonomic war in history. (Iraq war? Hasn't cost us a cent. We charged it! Current balance: $396,883,762,378.*)

In 1999, candidate Bush criticized Republicans in Congress for trying to "balance the budget on the backs of the poor." President Bush succeeded in *un*balancing the budget on the backs of the poor, for the benefit of the very, very rich.

No millionaires left behind. Bush claimed repeatedly that most of his tax cuts "went to low- and middle-income Americans," when in actual fact:

▶ In his first, $1.3 trillion tax cut (2001), 38 percent of the benefits went to the richest 1 percent. This group got benefits averaging $100,000 a year, while the bottom half of all households were to get *less than $100*. The bill included a phased repeal of the estate tax, which affected only the richest 2 percent. By one estimate, Bush cabinet members stood to save $5–$19 million apiece from "death tax" repeal. Of course, they'd have to die first, so the plan had *some* merit.

▶ In Bush's Orwellianly titled Job Creation and Worker Assistance Act of 2002, businesses got a depreciation tax cut worth $97 billion—seven times the amount provided for the unemployed, whose numbers were burgeoning.

▶ Bush's January 2003 "stimulus plan," popularly known as the "No Millionaire Left Behind Act," increased the 2001 tax cuts by $727 billion, of which 70 percent would go to the richest 5 percent. The top 226,000 tax filers—

*As of June 12, 2007, 11:13 PM EDT, and rising by around $3,000 per second.

those with incomes over $1 million—would receive as much as the bottom 125 million taxpayers combined.

Bush refused to close tax loopholes for those earning over $200,000 a year "because he acknowledges 'the really rich people figure out how to dodge taxes anyway.'"[57] (Firsthand knowledge?) He had a point: according to IRS data released in 2005, among the top 2 percent of earners, the number who paid *no* federal income tax more than doubled from 2000 to 2002. More than 100,000 in this elite group actually paid less tax per dollar of income than the average taxpayer.

Rewarding the export of U.S. jobs. The Bushite policy was to slash taxes on investment—on stock dividends and capital gains—"even as investment in corporations has less and less to do with creating jobs here at home," the *American Prospect* observed. By 2004, the percentage of federal tax revenue paid *by* corporations neared record lows, partly due to increased "outsourcing" and "offshoring" of business activity and jobs overseas. Around 95 percent of corporations paid less than 5 percent of their income in taxes and more than 60 percent paid no taxes at all—this at a time of rising corporate profits and growing financial strain on the middle class.

No taxes for the rich! That great goal at last seemed in sight. The right was pushing for *zero* tax on dividends, cap-ital gains, and corporate income. That could only mean tax *increases* for the majority—as Bush himself had all but acknowledged when he said his second-term tax changes would be "revenue neutral," i.e., would not reduce total tax revenues. What the wealthy saved, someone else would have to pay. This, the conservative founders of the flat-tax movement had called "an obvious mathematical law."

The administration, wrote John Cassidy in the *New Yorker*, appeared set on undermining the two principles on which the tax system had been based for a century: the tax burden is distributed according to the ability to pay; and capital and labor each carry their fair share. If Bush's economic agenda were fully enacted, corporate profits "wouldn't be taxed at all, and labor would end up shouldering practically the entire burden of financing the federal government." Under such a system, wrote Daniel Altman in his book *Neoconomy*, "The fortunate and growing minority who managed to receive all their income from stocks, bonds and other securities would pay nothing—not a dime—for America's cancer research, its international diplomacy, its military deterrent, the maintenance of the interstate highway system, the space program . . ."

"Screwed as never before." Indeed—in addition to bearing the brunt of Bush's essentially symbolic yet devastating budget cuts to help pay for his GRiFTR (Greedy Rich Folks' Tax Relief) program—middle- and lower-income people were already being targeted for tax increases. Bush's budgets raised fees, such as increased surcharges for veterans' health care, by almost $20 billion. In 2004, the Republicans effectively raised taxes on 4 million low-income families who would see their child tax credit shrink or disappear in 2005. Fixing this inequity would have cost less than 5 percent of Bush's $146 billion 2004 tax bill. The Repugs refused—while adding three times as much in corporate tax breaks.

Millions of middle-class families were getting hit for the

first time by Alternative Minimum Tax. With reduced federal aid, state and local taxes went up. (Local property taxes rose an average of more than 10 percent between 2001 and 2003.) The average family's housing, education, and health-care costs rose by *twice* their tax savings. While Bush was giving a $52,000 tax cut to every millionaire in America and eliminating cleanup taxes on industrial polluters, 1.7 million Americans fell below the poverty line. "Average Americans are being screwed as never before," wrote David Sirota in the *American Prospect.*

While the Repugs zealously protected taxation loopholes used by corporations and the rich, Bush singled out the earned income tax credit, which benefited 4 million working poor, claiming it was plagued with fraud (just another variation on the perennial "the poor have it too good" GOP theme). He asked Congress for $100 million and 650 new IRS employees to examine claims. The IRS subsequently introduced "the most exhaustive proof of eligibility ever demanded of any class of taxpayers," the *New York Times* reported—ensuring that even honest taxpayers who were entitled to the credit would no longer receive it. In Bush's first year, audits of the working poor increased 48.6 percent, and accounted for 55 percent of all audits,[58] whereas, from 2001 to 2004, auditing of corporations and high-income citizens fell to record low levels.[59]

Deficit attention disorder. Thanks to his tax cuts and a 33 percent increase in federal spending (Bush had yet to veto a spending bill, no matter how pork-laden), by 2004 Bush had turned the Clinton budget surplus into the worst deficits in U.S. history, creating debt that could take generations to repay. The national debt, which Bush had promised to "pay down to a historically low level," now stood at an all-time high of over $7 trillion—29 percent higher than in 2001. By 2014, Bush's tax cuts alone would add $5.5 trillion in debt—nearly as much as the U.S. government had accumulated in the two centuries before he stole office. The *New York Times*'s Nicholas Kristof noted that Bush "has excoriated the 'death tax,' as he calls the estate tax. But his profligacy will leave every American child facing a 'birth tax' [share of the debt] of about $150,000." The way the administration "is putting us in hock to China"—the biggest buyer of U.S. debt—is probably a bigger risk to our way of life and our place in the world than al Qaeda or the Iraq war, Kristof added. "If a Democrat had this appalling fiscal record," wrote conservative journalist Andrew Sullivan, "no Republican would defend him."

> *There was a time when Republicans cared about federal spending waste . . . [It was] when a Democrat was President.*—Anonymous blogger
>
> *We've not had one Republican president in 34 years balance the budget. You can't trust right-wing Republicans with your money.*—Howard Dean

In 2004, the International Monetary Fund (IMF), which monitors fiscally irresponsible and debt-ridden governments, warned that U.S. deficits were spiraling out of control, threatening to undermine Social Security and Medicare (funny they should say that! see *"It's the Bathtub, Stupid"* below) and create a global currency crisis. U.S. comptroller general

David Walker said 2004 may have been the most fiscally reckless year in this country's history, and called fiscal irresponsibility "the greatest threat to our future."

Nine cents on the dollar. What about the promised economic stimulus? "The tax cuts are working" was Bush's mantra. According to Mark Zandi, chief economist at Economy.com, for every dollar of tax revenue lost, Bush's tax rate reduction yielded 59 cents of economic stimulus; the dividend and capital gains tax cuts, 9 cents. The tax cuts that went to middle- and lower-income people contributed twice as much to growth as the upper-income and business breaks combined—yet the latter received nearly twice as much of the tax reductions. Most of the economic stimulus came not from tax cuts but from low interest rates—which deficits eventually raise.[60] In any case, Bush ended his first term as the first president since Hoover, in the Great Depression, to preside over a net loss of jobs, which contributed to a record number of Americans—more than 45 million—lacking health insurance.*

Bush's tax cuts would likely *reduce* long-term economic growth, according to government economists. As the Center on Budget and Policy Priorities (CBPP) explained *quite* clearly, in addition to raising interest rates, "Higher deficits reduce national saving and thus result in less domestic investment (and more borrowing from overseas)... Such outcomes lower the nation's future income and standard of living."

It's the bathtub, stupid. But as economist Lawrence Mishel wrote in the *American Prospect*, Bush's policies "were never intended to generate jobs or growth . . . they

---

*Nearly double that number were uninsured at least part of the time.

were always about cutting government revenue and shifting the tax burden away from income from investments (from the few) and onto income from labor (that's most of us)." Why "about cutting revenue"? Well, in GROVER NORQUIST's immortal phrase, "to get the government down to the size where we can drown it in the bathtub." To starve hated social programs of funding; to cripple federal finances to the point where the Republicans could say there's no choice but to scrap or drastically shrink Social Security and Medicare.

Shut his pie hole. There's more to GOPonomics than budget-busting, Robin-Hood-in-reverse tax and budget policies. There's loosening of environmental, health, and safety regulations to benefit business; rampant "privatization," or letting corporations milk every area of government; suppression of organized labor; free trade agreements that encourage the export of industries and jobs to low-wage countries; and importation of abundant cheap labor.

All these policies increase income inequality by putting pressure on wages and by boosting the incomes of those at the top, who own the lion's share of corporate stocks and bonds and therefore reap almost all the gains in corporate profitablity. So when our genius-in-chief says, as he did in a 2000 presidential candidates debate, "We ought to make the pie higher," he leaves out the part about how the pie's entire height increase will be devoured by the already fattest people by far at the table. From 1980, the year Ronald Reagan was first elected, to 2004, the share of U.S. income that went to the top-earning 1 percent went from 8.5 percent to 19 percent; the top 10 percent's share rose from 33 to 44 percent; the bottom 50 percent's share dropped from 17.5 to 13.5 percent.[61]

Thanks to the GOP-engineered upper-income tax cuts, the *after*-tax income figures diverged even more: While the top 20 percent enjoyed a 50 percent increase in real after-tax income and the top 1 percent have seen a *157* percent increase, average income for the bottom 20 percent has stagnated at around $11,000.

Do Republicans really believe that helping those at the top first and foremost is ultimately best for everyone? Most of us are pretty good at believing in whatever best serves our own purposes. And the less we *really* believe, the more forcefully we tend to assert it. GOPonomics has increased economic inequality in America for more than twenty-five years. I don't believe Republicans really believe it will ever have any other result. Instead, they convince themselves that inequality is good. The rich from time immemorial have conveniently believed this, in one form or another: The class structure is simply the natural order of things; it *is*, and is therefore what God intended; the fortunate must (as Puritans believed) be morally deserving; hunger and fear of destitution are the best motivators . . . The big tent of GOPonomics has room for all of these ideas.

"It's your money"? George W. bullshit. This is a favorite self-delusion among conservatives: Your fortunes are of your own making; whatever you have or earn is due to your own abilities and efforts (or at least Dad's or Granddad's: the overwhelming bulk of wealth is inherited). Therefore, the tax you pay is, as Republicans like Bush flatter you, "*your* money"—and your greedy, bloated, inefficient, incompetent government has some nerve taking it from you.

It is *not* your money. You *owe* it for goods and services received: education, legislation, law and order, the roads or rails you ride to work on, defense of the air and sea lanes, maintenance of a stable currency, and much else without which your business and your job could not exist in the first place. In his book *The President of Good and Evil,* philosopher Peter Singer argued that as much as 90 percent of our earnings derive from economic infrastructure provided by government. Ronald Reagan's motto, "Government is not the solution, government is the problem," is *bullshit,* man.

What word best describes the notion that we'd be best off with unrestricted, unregulated capitalism? Answer: *bullshit.* Former *New Republic* editor Larry Beinhart pointed out what you'd think anyone over age five would remember: "Capitalism easily gives way to excesses. It can be manipulated by monopolies and cartels . . . Capitalists can hire armies, police forces, goons and thugs to increase their profits. Fraud and deceit may run wild. Capitalists will sell shoddy, poisonous, destructive and even murderous products." So far, so good, from a GOPonomic point of view. But: Capitalism "goes from booms to busts. And some of those busts . . . can be so severe that they upset the body politic and cause society to run to one of the other isms—communism and fascism mostly." So, "a few relatively bright people came up with the idea of keeping capitalism while trying to get rid of the excesses!" Markets were regulated. Products were inspected. Cartels and price fixing were forbidden. Unemployment insurance, workman's compensation, welfare, social security, and progressive taxation were created. Unions were supported. "All this," notes Beinhart, "was quite successful."[62]

> *Should any political party attempt to abolish Social Security, unemployment insurance, and eliminate labor laws and farm programs, you would not hear of that party again in our political history. There is a tiny splinter group, of course, that believes you can do these things. Among them are . . . a few Texas oil millionaires, and an occasional politician or business man from other areas. Their number is negligible and they are stupid.*—Dwight D. Eisenhower, 1954

"To funnel public wealth to the private sector." But are Repugs really anti-Big Government? Don't say such things! Big government programs are big fat *prizes* to be privatized for the benefit of GOP-friendly industries. As columnist Lars Erik Nelson observed even before the 2000 election: "Bush and Cheney are a new kind of conservative.

Traditional conservatives wanted to reduce, even eliminate, government and cut taxes. These new conservatives want the government to continue to collect taxes—but turn the proceeds over to private industry. Here is the common thread of Bush's major proposals: Government collects Social Security taxes—but gives a chunk of the money to Wall Street. Government collects school taxes—but gives the money out in vouchers that can be used in private schools. Government collects Medicare taxes—but gives the money to private insurers who will provide health coverage.[63]

Using "the government's coercive powers of taxation and legislation to funnel public wealth to the private sector," Nelson added, was "what made Bush and Cheney rich." (See THE

BUSH–BATH–BIN LADEN–BCCI–TEXUS NEXUS AND DUMBYA'S RAGS-TO-RICHES BUSINESS CAREER.) Those powers now would be harnessed to funnel public wealth *through* the private sector and back to the GOP, in the form of contributions from the corporate beneficiaries of GOP privatization schemes. See GROVER NORQUIST AND THE K STREET PROJECT.

If there is a single overriding GOPonomic principle, it's—well, see CORPORATE INTERESTS, SIDING WITH *EVERY* GODDAMN TIME. As *The New Republic* editorialized: "There is a simple way to understand economic policy-making under George W. Bush: Whichever pressure group has the strongest and most direct stake in an issue gets its way. . . . If there's a single prominent case where Bush offended a powerful corporate interest—except to benefit an even more powerful corporate interest—we have not come across it.[64]

Asshole #18:
GRAMM, PHIL,
GOPFather of Antigovernment BS

Former Texas Democratic congressman (1979–1983), then Republican congressman (1983–1985) and senator (1985–2002). A man of principles: small government, balanced budgets—principles to be protected, carefully stored, and never used. A true, anything-to-win Republican in the finest traditions of GEORGE W. BUSH, (who came later, but still) and KARL ROVE, Gramm's strategist in two election campaigns. A "unique mixture of smarts and venom" with "an unparalleled thirst for press . . . a knack for the soundbite and a gift for the partisan snipe," a notorious habit of "stealing credit for bills and ideas he didn't think of" (which became known as "Grammstanding"), "a genius for making himself a player," and "a gift for repackaging pandering as heroism," raved David Segal in *Washington Monthly*. He forgot to mention unparalleled treachery, hypocrisy, and love of the low blow. And that Gramm repeated three grades in school.

How on *earth* could the Democrats have failed for three years to notice that their "colleague" was really a Republican?

They discovered it in 1981 when, after attending House Democrats' budget meetings and promising to vote for the Democrats' budget plan, the DINO (Democrat in Name Only) not only cosponsored REAGAN's feed-the rich, starve-the-poor plan instead but secretly passed the Republicans reports on the Dems' strategy. "In any army," a Democrat leader fumed, "he'd have been shot at sunrise." Unfortunately, the Dems only stripped him of his seat on the budget committee—whereupon Gramm resigned his House seat, forcing a special election, in which he ran and won as a Republican.*

What, after all, could have been more simplistically, idiotically Republican than Gramm's stated political creed, "I believe that government is the problem"? Simple enough for red-state America, or its cattle, to understand. Government not only doesn't but *can't* do anything right; best to just choke off its funds and dismantle as much of it as possible. Anyone's funds in particular? Say, the Pentagon's and its contractors', with their $400 hammers and $600 toilet seats? Gramm's targets apparently lay elsewhere: "We're the only nation in the world where all our poor people are fat," he said in a speech about recipients of federal aid.

---

*He could have just switched parties, but resigning, *Texas Monthly* explained, allowed Gramm "to recast himself as a political martyr who had been driven out of the Democratic party."

Ironic, wrote Segal:

Gramm is a living rebuke to the notion that government is merely in the way. The government helped bring him into this world (he was born in a military hospital), funded his upbringing (his father was an Army master sergeant), paid for him to attend private school and even picked up the tab for graduate school. . . . Gramm got a job at Texas A&M, which is state-run, was elected to the House of Representatives, and then to the Senate. In sum, Phil Gramm joined the government's rolls the first day of his life and has never left.

While posing year after year as Washington's leading balanced budget crusader, the fact was, Gramm was "simply unwilling to pay any political price to achieve it."[65] Rather than attack individual programs and risk losing votes, he proposed across-the-board cuts—which made for good press but would, for example, cut Head Start preschool programs as much as subsidies to sugar growers, and didn't address Social Security and Medicare, by far the largest and fastest growing federal programs. *That* would have taken courage. Gramm's constitutents may have loved his anti-government, anti-spending rhetoric, but don't anyone dare touch *their* "entitlement" benefits.

A National Taxpayers Union survey found that, over the previous two years, Gramm was one of only three members of Congress, and the only Republican, who had failed to sponsor a single bill that cut spending. The bills he did back would have added $8.3 billion to the deficit. (Gramm's staff "summoned the authors of the study up to the Hill for a stern chat and suggested they never publish anything like that again . . ."[66])

Oink! Gramm backed billion-dollar Texas projects such as the Superconducting Supercollider and the Space Station; a plant stress lab at Texas Tech ($100 million a year); a National College of DAs in Houston ($500 million); and the creation of a federal Office of Dietary Supplements. (Can man live on pork alone? We don't know. More research is needed.) Meanwhile, he declined to support a bill to shut down a $34 million a year, 1920s-era program to extract and store helium in case it was needed for

---

Gramm the Campaigner.*** Gramm's style has influenced generations of GOP candidates.

► Favorite sayings: "We're going to keep on building the party until we're hunting Democrats with dogs." A stump speech fixture: "I have more guns than I need, and fewer guns than I want."

► In his first congressional race, in 1976, Gramm—Phil Gramm—charged that his opponent, Senator Lloyd Bentsen, "has no principles," and went around warning that, with Asia already "lost," Italy, France, Spain and Portugal "could fall to the communists at any moment." (Thanks in all likelihood to communist shenanigans, he lost to Bentsen.)

► In 1984 Gramm ran for a vacant Senate seat against Lloyd Doggett, a liberal Democrat whom the gay community supported. Once Gramm learned that Doggett had received a $500 contribution from a gay group that had held a fundraiser featuring a male stripper, that was all he talked about

---

*My own nickname for him, inspired by "Vlad the Impaler," the historical name of Dracula.

blimps. (Insert your own "hot air" or "budget-inflating" joke here.) He fought against bills that would have ended the government's mohair subsidy. ("Itch to spend" joke goes here.) He passed on repealing the Davis-Bacon Act (you don't need my help on that one), which would allow open bidding on federal contracts and save the government billions. And all this was only up to 1993. Gramm himself once admitted, "I'm carrying so much pork, I'm beginning to get trichinosis."

from June to November. His campaign ads turned the stripper into "an all-male strip show" and featured the tag line, "Friends of Phil Gramm paid for this because Phil Gramm supports traditional family values." His TV ads showed the Gramm family on a fishing outing; oddly, however, all you could see of Wendy, Gramm's wife, who is of Korean descent, was the back of her head. (Many GOP voters just aren't ready for interracial marriage, integrated lunch counters, etc.)

▶ When two GOP senators voted in favor of a campaign finance reform bill because they thought there should be *some* limits on the buying of elections, Gramm (who, thanks in good part to Enron, ran for president in 1996 with a bulging war chest) ripped their portraits off the wall of the National Republican Senatorial Committee, telling onlookers, "They're not Republicans anymore." One might almost agree with him.

So—as with George W. Bush—we were somehow to have lower taxes, higher spending, *and* a balanced budget. Read Gramm's lips: No new taxes—literally at all costs. After Reagan's deregulation triggered the SAVINGS AND LOAN collapse of the late 1980s, culminating in a $125 billion federal bailout, "there wasn't a sane person on earth who thought taxpayers were going to dodge this bullet," said Steve Pizzo, author of *Inside Job: The Looting of America's Savings and Loans*. No, but there was Gramm. "And every day the Phil Gramms of Congress denied the size of the problem and refused to close down the thrifts," wrote Pizzo, "we lost millions. At one point, $30 million a day."

Gramm could create a crisis as easily as deny one. In 1993, former Gramm staffers passed the *Dallas Morning News* some internal memos written by Gramm. One said: "We have tried to create a 'BAMC funding scare' while feeling comfortable that BAMC [Brooke Army Medical Center in San Antonio] is safe from the budget knife." "The funding scare was designed to cast Gramm as the knight who rescued BAMC from oblivion," wrote Segal.

Gramm came to the rescue during several other crises of the 1990s and 2000s. In each case, the solution was more of what had helped cause the S&L crisis—or rather, less: less regulation.

Crisis #1: Houston-based energy giant ENRON wanted to make more money. Thanks to deregulation carried out by the senator's wife, WENDY GRAMM—head of the Commodity Futures Trading Commission under President Bush Sr., and a future Enron board member—Enron was able to expand into energy futures and derivatives trading. A bill cosponsored in 2000 by Senator Gramm—

the largest recipient of Enron campaign donations after George W. Bush—removed virtually all remaining regulatory oversight of Enron trading. This freed the company to commandeer a large share of California's energy markets, create (along with other traders) artificial shortages (the CALIFORNIA ENERGY "CRISIS"), drive up prices, and quadruple trading revenues.

Crisis #2: Corporate reform legislation loomed! Corporate America's favorite loophole is to inflate profits by paying employees in stock options, which don't have to be declared as expenses. The resulting "higher profits" in turn make the options a more attractive currency with which to pay salaries and buy up other companies, even as the value of the stock is diluted. This pyramid scheme was at the center of the "dotcom" collapse of 1999–2002. Shareholders of one notorious stock optioneer, Cisco Systems, lost five times as much as Enron's. When Congress hashed out the Sarbanes-Oxley corporate reform act of 2002, Gramm blocked a Democratic measure that merely would have required *study* of the stock options issue.

Crisis #3: A congressional proposal to impose a one-time capital gains levy on rich, patriotic Americans who renounce their U.S. citizenship to avoid paying U.S. taxes. Gramm described the proposal as "right out of Nazi Germany."

Crisis #4: The securities and investment sector—Gramm's largest contributor—*needed to make more money.* Between 1995 and 2000, when he chaired the Senate Banking Committee, Gramm received $1,000,914 from the industry—and obligingly brokered the landmark Gramm-Leach-Bliley Act in 1999, which allowed banks, brokerages, and insurance firms to compete or merge. (Notwithstanding such conflicts of interest as had already led to scandal at Travelers-Smith Barney, whose preexisting merger the act merely blessed.) After leaving the Senate, Gramm himself merged with investment bank UBS Warburg, which hired him as vice chairman. Or was it before leaving the Senate? No, after. I think.

Crime, Corruption, and Cronyism Case #21
GRILES, J. STEVEN

Deputy secretary, Department of the Interior (DOI), 2001–2005. "The poster child of the corporate influence on this [Bush] administration."[67] Formerly one of the coal, oil, and gas industries' most powerful lobbyists. Within weeks of his Senate confirmation, after agreeing "to avoid any actual or apparent conflicts of interest," Griles began a series of at least sixteen meetings with "former" energy industry lobbying clients on regulatory issues affecting them, such as weakening the Clean Air Act to protect operators of coal-fired power plans from government lawsuits. The changes were made in due course. Griles intervened with the Environmental Protection Agency on behalf of "former" clients to, in his own words, "try to expedite drilling" of seventy thousand environmentally damaging coalbed methane natural gas wells in vast, previously off-limits expanses of Wyoming and Montana wilderness. He also helped secure rule changes allowing "former" coal mining clients to destroy wetlands. Griles even continued to receive annual payments of $284,000 from his former lobbying firm throughout his DOI "public service."

Pleaded guilty in March 2007 to lying to the Senate Indian Affairs Committee by denying he had a special relationship with lobbyist **JACK ABRAMOFF**, who obtained help from the DOI's Bureau of Indian Affairs for his Indian gaming clients. At the time, Griles was involved romantically with Abramoff's close associate ITALIA FEDERICI, head of the Council of Republicans for Environmental Advocacy, an industry front ("greenscam") group that received donations from Abramoff and his tribal clients. Federici had introduced Griles to Abramoff and acted as their go-between. DOI's former general counsel testified that he "was alarmed that Mr. Griles all of a sudden had an inexplicable desire" to intervene on issues affecting Abramoff's tribal clients. Griles admitted Abramoff had offered him a postgovernment job at his lobbying firm. A former employee at the firm testified that Abramoff described Griles as "his guy." . . . Named one of the "25 Most Corrupt Members of the Bush Administration" by Citizens for Responsibility and Ethics in Washington (CREW).

HAIR, PERNICIOUS DOUBLE STANDARD REGARDING

As you've no doubt noticed, the MEDIA-GOP AXIS is always making an issue of *Democrats'* hair. Blogging in May 2007 about the biggest political scandal of the election season to date—the shocking revelation that Democratic presidential candidate JOHN EDWARDS had had two $400 haircuts—Eric Boehlert wrote that "the Beltway press corps should consider starting up a new reporting pool [which] would focus exclusively on the grooming habits of leading Democrats. Call it the haircut beat."

In recent years, Boehlert observed, "the press, with the help of mischief-making Republicans, has signed off on the notion that Democratic grooming habits are big news. They *matter*." What's telling is "that the press treats only Democratic haircuts as news."

> Year in and year out, the press uses haircut stories to paint Democrats as vain (read: effeminate) hypocrites . . . hypocrites because Democrats claim they care about working people, but in truth they only care about their appearances. . . . The press *loves* playing Hypocrite Police with Democrats.[68]

In 1993, the Beltway press went bonkers over the fact that President Clinton received a haircut aboard Air Force One from a man known to charge $200 for a trim. The later-debunked report that the haircut had delayed passengers at LAX was referenced by the *Washington Post* as a serious political story fifty-plus times in less than fifty days. At least eight other major U.S. papers, including the *New York Times* and *Los Angeles Times*, played the haircut story on the front page.

Hillary Clinton's coif and salon bills received a lot of media coverage when she was first lady and after she became a senator. In 2000, the press obsessed over candidate Al Gore's wardrobe "in search of clues to his 'character.'" In 2002, GOP dirt-drudger extraordinaire MATT DRUDGE—who doesn't even have the guts to take off his fedora—was fed a Republican National Committee tip that, as Drudge then wrote, "self-described 'Man of The People'" John Kerry "pays $150 to get his hair styled and shampooed, the cost of feeding a family of three for two weeks!!" As Boehlert calculated, that would work out to $1.19—or less than one king-size Snickers bar— per person, per meal. "But no matter, CNN treated the Kerry

haircut story as news," announcing that likely candidate
Kerry "'already is in denial mode.'"

But nothing beat the Edwards buzz. Every major news
outlet in the country picked it up. Faster than you can say
"just a trim," a Google search for "Edwards," "$400" and
"haircut" yielded 187,000 hits. CNN aired more references to
Edwards's haircut than it did to his reaction to the Supreme
Court's decision to uphold the ban on "partial birth" abortions. *Newsweek*, in its Conventional Wisdom Watch, "placed
The Haircut directly behind the Virginia Tech massacre and
Attorney General Alberto Gonzales' Senate testimony as that
week's most important news events," Boehlert noted. On
CBS's *The Late Show with David Letterman*, NBC's Brian
Williams agreed that the story was "silly" and there was "no
reason for us to continue talking about it" (*and* claimed never
to have paid more than $12 for a cut). Two days later, as mod-
erator for a televised Democratic debate, Williams's *second
question* to Edwards was about The Haircut.

Meanwhile: President Bush's $3,000 handmade suits?
LAURA BUSH's $700 haircut from stylist-to-the-stars Sally
Hershberger for the 2005 inauguration? Going back a ways,
Ronald Reagan's pompadour and obvious dye job? Coverage
(no pun intended) ranged from sparser than *my* hair (a *real*
scandal, for which I blame the Republicans) to nonexistent.
Because of liberal media bias, I guess.

What about the whole rogues' gallery of GOP pols who
sport modified JFKs, much like Edwards's, seeking to steal a
bit of Kennedy's everlasting aura of modernity and progressivism? I mean TOM DELAY. RALPH REED. NEWT GINGRICH.
JOHN CORNYN. MITT ROMNEY, totally. JACK KEMP. TRENT fucking
LOTT. Progressive paragons like that. To these men, I say what
1988 Democratic vice-presidential candidate LLOYD BENTSEN

said in a debate with his GOP opponent, **DAN QUAYLE**, who had compared himself to JFK: "Senator, I served with Jack Kennedy. I knew Jack Kennedy. Jack Kennedy was a friend of mine. Senator, you're no Jack Kennedy. And you should really rethink that hair." (He didn't actually say the hair part.)

Our well-coifed Dems don't claim to *be* ordinary working stiffs—only to *stand up* for them. So do Republicans. Which of them really do? Which deserve more to wear a JFK—even a $400 one? Which? *Which?*

Asshole #19:
HARRIS, KATHERINE

Representative (R-Fla.), 2003–2007. In her previous capacity as Florida secretary of state, Harris *tried* to preside fairly and impartially over the November 2000 elections. However, she was coerced by Bush-Cheney Florida campaign cochair KATHERINE HARRIS to, among other mischief, hire a GOP-connected firm to purge the voter rolls of thousands of supposed felons (who by Florida law could not vote). Of these approximately 57,000 "felons," some 97 percent turned out to be guilty only of being African American. One can safely surmise that the vast majority of these votes would have gone to Al Gore—many times more than George W. Bush's official 537-vote margin of victory.

Found by investigators on Harris's state-secretarial computer: "I am a bit biased. I co-chair the campaign effort of George W. Bush. . . . I hope it will be 'W.'" (Well, that would be up to her.) But such moments of Katherinian candor were comparatively few. While campaigning for Bush in

2004, she told an audience about a foiled terrorist plot to blow up the power grid of an Indiana town, which she'd heard about from the mayor. "It was an inspiring story that proved once again that President Bush is Keeping Us Safer," wrote Shelley Lewis in *Naked Republicans*. "Except that she made it up." The mayor told a reporter he'd never met Harris or heard of any such plot.

After defense contractor Mitchell Wade (see **JACK ABRAMOFF** and **JERRY LEWIS**) pleaded guilty to funneling $32,000 to Harris, the congresswoman claimed she didn't know the donation was illegal and that it had nothing to do with her attempt to get a $10 million contract for Wade's company.

Harris didn't care for the constitutional separation of CHURCH AND STATE (which she termed "a lie") any more than for the constitutional separation of Bush campaign and State (which she *made* a lie). Said Harris: "God is the one who chooses our rulers." (Oh, so *He* made her lose those 57,000 votes! And since *He* chose George W. Bush, who are we to hold further elections? President for Life!) And: "If you are not electing Christians, then in essence you are going to legislate sin."

The GOP tried to stop Harris from running for the Senate in 2006. After the Wade bribery revelations, even her campaign manager suggested she drop out. When no one else would give her money, the heiress said she'd spend her own millions (her daddy's, rather). Harris, after virtually her entire campaign staff quit: "We are stronger as a campaign today than we were yesterday."

If you can live with the thought that *this* is the person to whom we owe the George W. Bush presidency, fine. If not, information can be found at assistedsuicide.org.

Asshole #20:
HASTERT, DENNIS

Former House Speaker, R-Ill. (1999–2007).

▶ Implying on *Fox News* in 2004 that pro-Democrat financier GEORGE SOROS is some kind of drug dealer: "I don't know where George Soros gets his money. I don't know where—if it comes overseas or from drug groups or where it comes from. . . . George Soros has been for legalizing drugs in this country." Asked if he meant Soros "may be getting money from the drug cartel": "I'm saying we don't know." And I'm saying we don't know whether Hastert snorts coke three times a day or four. Or whether he molests children. We just don't know.

▶ Hastert in May 2004, after Senator JOHN MCCAIN—a man who spent five years as a POW in Vietnam after being shot down on his twenty-third bombing run (while Hastert managed to avoid military service)—argued against further tax cuts on the grounds that war is a "time of sacrifice": "If you want to see sacrifice, John McCain ought to visit our young men and women at Walter Reed and Bethesda. There's the sacrifice in this country." Let's see—that's insult, hypocrisy, chutzpah, and obfuscation of the issue at hand (tax cuts) all at once. . . . Hastert was always underrated. Only on a bench as deep in talent as the GOP's could a Dennis Hastert molder in the shadows.

▶ On another decorated Vietnam vet, then presidential candidate JOHN KERRY: His response to a terrorist attack would be "to file a lawsuit with the World Court or something, rather than respond with troops."

▶ In September 2005, days after he questioned whether it

would "make sense" for the federal government to spend money rebuilding New Orleans after HURRICANE KATRINA, Hastert, back in his home district, announced that the federal government would provide $1.84 million to build a road extension in the village of Annawan, Illinois. He declared, "Illinois is finally getting their fair share." (One doesn't *like* to call someone an asshole, but you see how it is . . . One's hands are tied.)

Asshole #21:
HELMS, JESSE

Legendary senator, R-CSA (Confederate States of America. North Carolina, actually), ~~1673~~ 1973–2003. Leading figure of the Christian right. Never graduated from college, but holds an honorary doctor of law degree from *Bob Jones University*, so shut up. Career highlights:

► As a strategist for the 1950 Senate campaign of Dixiecrat Willis Smith, Helms helped create an ad that read: "White people, wake up before it is too late. Do you want Negroes working beside you, your wife and your daughters, in your mills and factories? [Opponent] Frank Graham favors mingling of the races." Another ad featured photos doctored by Helms to show Graham's wife dancing with a black man.[69]

► Referred to the University of North Carolina (UNC) as the "University of Negroes and Communists."

► Gave an interview to pro-Confederate *Southern Partisan* magazine, which regularly praised Ku Klux Klan leaders and celebrated the assassination of Abraham Lincoln, and which printed an article saying that "neither 'slavery' nor 'racism' as an institution is a sin" and "there is no indication that slavery is contrary to Christian ethics."[70] *

▶ Sang part of "Dixie" while riding in a Capitol elevator with African-American senator Carol Moseley-Braun (D-Ill.), who opposed Helms's symbolic legislation recognizing the Daughters of the Confederacy.

▶ Had the "humorous habit" of calling all black men "Fred."

▶ Declared: "Democracy used to be a good thing, but now it has gotten into the wrong hands." What could he mean? Corporate special interests? Bigoted religious zealots? Wrong *size* hands? Wrong *color*?

Jobs were getting into the wrong color hands—according to perhaps the most infamous campaign ad in American history, Helms's 1990 "hands" ad targeting his Democrat opponent's support for affirmative action. The spot showed the hands of a white worker crumpling up a job rejection notice, under the message, "They had to give [the job] to a minority because of a racial quota." (Also see SOUTHERN STRATEGY. Helms did hire CLAUDE ALLEN as his press secretary, but it is unclear if this was affirmative action for African Americans or for shoplifters; see CRIME, CORRUPTION, AND CRONYISM.)

Pop quiz: Was Helms consequently (a) driven from the GOP like a leper, or (b) given the chairmanships of the Senate Agriculture and Foreign Relations committees?

In his capacity as agri-chair, Helms did much to benefit his state's tobacco industry, and vice versa. (R. J. Reynolds and

*Granted, Republicans DICK ARMEY, JOHN ASHCROFT, PATRICK BUCHANAN, and TRENT LOTT also deemed it appropriate to lee grant interviews to this magazine.

Philip Morris were among his largest contributors.) As foreign relations chair he blocked U.S. payment of its UN dues, ardently supported Chilean right-wing dictator AUGUSTO PINOCHET, and said of a protest against his own 1986 visit to Mexico: "All Latins are volatile people. Hence, I was not surprised at the volatile reaction." In his capacity as ASSHOLE, he said in a 1994 TV interview, on the anniversary of John F. Kennedy's assassination, that President Clinton had "better not show up around here [Fort Bragg, N.C.] without a bodyguard."

Helms passed few bills of his own, but reportedly delighted in the nickname he earned by obstructing Democrats' bills and appointments: "Senator No." He opposed the Martin Luther King holiday bill and blocked Clinton's appointment of former governor Bill Weld (R-Mass.) as ambassador to Mexico because Weld favored legalizing medical marijuana. Helms also helped defeat a bill banning antigay job discrimination and opposed a bill to pay reparations to Japanese Americans interned during World War II.

Former senator **BARRY GOLDWATER**'s three words about Helms were worth a picture or, at the current exchange rate, a thousand ordinary words: "Off his rocker."

Asshole #22:
HOOVER, HERBERT

President, 1929–1933. On the Great Depression and catastrophic unemployment he helped deepen and prolong: "Many persons left their jobs for the more profitable one of selling apples." In 1932, Hoover campaigned against Roosevelt's New Deal as something that "would destroy the very foundations of our American system." (And so it did . . . by introducing Social Security, unemployment insurance, bank deposit insurance, the Securities and Exchange Commission to help prevent future Wall Street crashes . . .)

I Don't ♥ Huckabee, Mike

Former Arkansas governor (1996–2007); 2008 presidential candidate. Touted right and left—perhaps more left—for his caring, un-Republican record as governor and, as Michael Scherer wrote in *Salon*, his "graceful call for throwing away partisanship," which "wowed" Jon Stewart on *The Daily Show*. Has "the potential to appeal to crossover independent voters" and a "charismatic ability to communicate with the common man . . . just might be able to talk, listen and care his way into the Oval Office."[71] More aptly described by blogger Markos Moulitsas Zuniga (*DailyKos*) as "a scary good politician." Often likened to another former Arkansas governor. Like Clinton, born in Hope, Arkansas. Home of the world's largest watermelon.

When first elected, Huckabee may have been the world's largest governor. After doctors warned him about his obesity, he famously shed 110 pounds. Went from barely able to climb the steps of the Arkansas capitol building in 2003 to running in the 2006 New York City Marathon. Talk about a symbol of Hope for the gravitationally challenged, the horizontally gifted, people of mass . . .

He's a self-styled "COMPASSIONate conservative" (uh-oh). As governor, Huckabee pushed for drug treatment instead of incarceration for nonviolent offenders and was critical of governors who "gladly pull the switch" on DEATH PENALTY cases. (See BUSH, GEORGE W.) On Huckabee's orders, state agencies took exemplary care of the seventy thousand Katrina victims who fled to Arkansas. The Bush administration's response, he said, "made my blood boil." He created a health insurance program for low-income children. He pushed for a plan to dedicate one-eighth of state sales tax revenue to state parks and land preservation, and traveled the length of the Arkansas River by boat to promote the idea. He repeatedly raised taxes—and the ire of conservative organizations like the free-market-worshipping Club for Growth and the libertarian Cato Institute, which graded his spending and tax policy an F in 2006. In 2005, *Time* named Huckabee one of the five best U.S. governors. So what's not to ♥?

Huckabee evidently believes in the power of government to help the poor—except when addressing "Christian" audiences, as follows: "Some people say, 'Are you worried that the government might try to do it,' and yes I am. . . . [Think what] people of faith . . . could do if every believer, instead of sending half of his money to the government in taxes, would give one dime out of every dollar to his church." (See FAITH-BASED TAX EVASION INITIATIVE.) *Which* Huckabee were we to believe? Would his be another MISSIONARY POSITION presidency?

That's what's more to worry about than to ♥. With George W. Bush, a lot of bad shit went down behind the screen of FAITH and God talk, while his corps of political engineers set about demolishing the constitutional levee that keeps the church from flooding the state.

Huckabee's pregubernatorial prep for the presidency: graduated magna cum laude from Ouachita Baptist University; attended Southwestern Baptist Theological Seminary; was a small-town Baptist pastor for twelve years; headed the Arkansas Baptist State Convention; ran a religious TV station. He has "solid-gold Christian-right credentials," wrote Scherer, but "unlike former Sen. RICK SANTORUM or Sen. SAM

BROWNBACK, Huckabee does not spend time pounding the pulpit over baby murder and sodomy." True. He raps on the pulpit gently. As governor, he declared countless statewide "days of prayer" and pushed for "faith-based" prison programs. (Missionaries prefer that the souls they target be unable to escape.) He is of course antiabortion-choice. Oops, sorry: "I don't like it when people say, 'But you're against abortion!'" says the Huckster. "I say, no I'm for life." (See "LIFE," HIJACKING OF.) He's anti-gay marriage—I mean, pro-"FAMILY": "I'm for keeping marriage the only way it's ever been . . . and until Moses brings two stone tablets down from Brokeback Mountain that say we've changed the rules, we're going to keep it that way." (Moses, with his famous lisp, shouldn't talk.) He believes in CREATIONISM and wants it taught in schools. (What about the parts of the Bible that call for stoning blashphemers and adulterers to death? How do these people decide which parts to take seriously?)

He has written several books that explain the importance of God in daily life and the right way to live. *From Hope to Higher Ground: 12 Steps to Restoring America's Greatness* teaches: "Read the Bible more; blogs less"; pay down your debt; avoid pornography; rake your neighbor's yard; buy Girl Scout cookies (I'm serious); report litter (Deuteronomy 2:17?); don't watch TV while eating dinner (would Huckabee destroy the very fabric of American life?), and always say "please."

Huckleberry says he wants the votes of the people "out there in the heartland of America, who shop at Wal-Mart, who go to church, who hunt, who fish, who drive pickup trucks and listen to country music and follow NASCAR"—and then adds, with no apparent sense of irony, "the kind of people who are tired of politicians telling them what they want to hear"!

He supported Bush on Iraq, but tried to blur that fact after launching his presidential campaign. Well, let him deny that he endorsed Bush's TAX CUTS FOR THE RICH. Or that, addressing an industry group, he referred to environmentalists as "wackos" and "fruits and nuts." He has joked that his weight loss resulted from being a hostage in a "concentration camp held by the Democrat Party of Arkansas," then dismissed criticism that he had made light of the Holocaust as laughable. (Note: His saying "Democrat Party" again *will* trigger an automatic "Asshole" designation.)

At a presidential debate, he said "we've had a Congress that's spent money like John Edwards at a beauty shop," keeping the public focused on the **HAIR** issue and painting a potential opponent a bit, you know, pink. Not fuchsia . . . more of a cherry blossom or lavender rose?

Hey—ethics-wise, I'll take Edwards's $400 haircuts anytime over the unreported gifts Huckabee let wealthy benefactors buy him, which led to multiple admonishments from the state Ethics Commission. Or the wedding registries Huckabee and his wife of many years opened at Target and Dillard's so friends could buy them gifts for their new home. Under Arkansas law, wedding gifts are exempt from the $100 cap on gifts to political leaders. "Mike Huckabee has such a sense of entitlement," said the editor of the *Arkansas Times*.

Then there's Wayne DuMond, an Arkansan accused in 1984 of raping a high school student, who happened to be a distant cousin of then governor Bill Clinton. Dumond was sentenced to life in prison without the possibility of parole. But because the victim was related to Clinton, the case quickly became a cause célèbre for right-wing radio hosts and columnists decrying the harsh sentence. Upon becoming governor, Huckabee commuted DuMond's sentence to time served, and he was released. Two years later, DuMond murdered a woman in Missouri. (What use would the Repugs have made of that had the governor in question been a Dem? Hint: Think Willie Horton.) Huckabee tried to shift the blame: "Clinton knew it, [former governor Jim Guy] Tucker did it, and now they try to blame me for it," he complained to Scherer.

Secretary of State Huckabee?It is true that Republican presidents are no longer expected to know anything about distant countries like Canada. They are only expected to threaten, bully, or bomb them. Nevertheless: In a 2001 interview for a Canadian TV special about Americans' knowledge of Canada, comedian Rick Mercer convinced Governor Huckabee that the Canadian Parliament building, or "National Igloo," was made entirely of ice. Huckabee, apparently in full seriousness, said: "Congratulations, Canada, on preserving your National Igloo."[72]

Neither Ouachita Baptist University nor Southwestern Baptist Theological Seminary has ever been really strong in international relations.

Asshole #23:

HUGHES, KAREN, "Mother Hen of Bush's Persona," and Bush Diplomacy, Idiocy of

Former Dallas TV reporter. (Texan: Lose three points.) Longtime GEORGE W. BUSH confidante and flak. Organized the 1994 media campaign that vilified Texas's incumbent Democratic governor Ann Richards as a homo/lesbo-lover and put

Bush in the governor's mansion. As co-leader (with **KARL ROVE**) of the Bush 2000 campaign, Hughes was instrumental in finessing (i.e., lying about) Bush's DUI and National Guard non-service. In 2004—for symmetry—she would help smear **JOHN KERRY**'s distinguished military record. As "counselor to the President"—a position Bush created for her—Hughes "sat in on every meeting, oversaw the offices of press secretary, communications and speechwriting, and had the communications directors of every department reporting directly to her," wrote Laura Flanders in her book *Bush-women*. Described by the *Dallas Morning News* as "the most powerful woman ever to serve in the White House," and by ABC News as Bush's "most essential adviser," Hughes was reportedly the object of Rovian jealousy. Bush, wrote Sidney Blumenthal in the *Guardian*, trusted her "with the tending of his image and words. She was mother hen of his persona."

▶ In response to a 1999 interview by Tucker Carlson describing then governor/presidential candidate Bush "swearing like a truck driver," Hughes claimed she'd never heard Bush use profanity. Carlson, saying he'd *seen* her hear it: "I've been lied to a lot by campaign operatives, but the striking thing about the way she lied was she knew I knew she was lying, and she did it anyway. There is no word in English that captures that. It almost crosses over from bravado into mental illness."[73]

▶ From the jacket of her 2004 autobiography *Ten Minutes from Normal*: "Counselor to the President. Wife and Mother. The woman who left the White House to put family first, and moved back home to Texas." (Then—putting *Bush* first—back to Washington less than a year later.) The book, wrote Tina Brown in the *Washington Post*, "is packed with uplifting boilerplate about a strong, loyal, straight-shooting, decisive boss." A "deeply uninteresting and unrevealing memoir," wrote Blumenthal.

PR Czar Karen the Terrible. Hughes was on the team set up by Rove to plot the deception of the American people into believing Iraq was preparing to attack, or already had attacked, the United States. In 2005 Bush tasked Hughes with buffing America's image abroad and appointed her undersecretary of state for "public diplomacy," or as Shelley Lewis put it, "Ambassador of Why They Hate Us." In effect answering that question, Hughes spoke of creating a "rapid-response unit" and "forward-deploy[ing] regional SWAT teams." One might suppose such militarism was the diplomatic *problem*, not the solution. But so runs the Bushist mind.

Shortly after Hughes took the post, a State Department employee complained that "recently, we've had tremendous amount of difficulty . . . getting clearance for our ambassadors to speak." Commissar Hughes's response was basically that ambassadors are free to talk—as long as they say exactly what she tells them: "If they make statements based on something I sent them, they're not going to be called on the carpet and shot." (She didn't *actually* say "and shot." She just implied it. See Dissenters and Whistle-blowers, Intimidation and Execution of.)

On changing foreigners' "perceptions" of the White House's failure to help Hurricane Katrina victims: "We need to aggressively challenge that idea around the world."

You know, to demonstrate to the world that in America, the government suppresses the truth.*

Upon setting foot in mouth—or rather, the Middle East— for the first time as PR czar (with a coterie of sixteen U.S. reporters in tow to help spread the word back home of the wonderful job she was doing), Hughes teed off an audience of Saudi women, condescendingly comparing them to the "broken wing" of a bird that the United States will help to fly again. America, she added, hoped Saudi women will "spread your wings." (That may not have been wise either. Saudis may not want *anyone* telling their women to spread *anything*.) Perhaps, next time, a different approach to countering other countries' perceptions of U.S. imperiousness—like, maybe, not invading and occupying them?

In Egypt, when a politician asked why Bush mentions God in his speeches, Hughes replied that our Constitution cites "one nation under God." What a wonderful reply. Absolutely incorrect, of course. But Hughes wanted to tell the Muslim world about, in her words, "the important role that faith plays in Americans' lives." In other words, "We're like you." (God forbid!)

"If you set out to help bin Laden, you could not have done it better than Hughes," said Robert Pape, a University of Chicago researcher who studies terrorists' motives. The key conditions that lead to suicide terrorism, he explained, are, first, the presence of foreign combat forces in the terrorists' territory; and second, a religious difference between those

*During a 2005 visit to Indonesia, Hughes claimed Saddam Hussein had gassed "hundreds of thousands of Iraqis." Casualties from the infamous gas attack on Halabja numbered in the thousands. Maybe Hughes was thinking of the number of casualties from the U.S.-led war in Iraq. Or was she just forward-deploying a regional BS team?

combat forces and the local community, which "enables terrorist leaders to paint foreign forces as being driven by religious goals"—a central theme of Osama's speeches. That
argument "is incredibly powerful" to Muslims, and "[e]very-
thing Hughes says makes their case."

And mine: Asshole #23.

HURRICANE MICHAEL (CHERTOFF) WALLOPS WASHINGTON: Federal Emergency Management Crippled; Widespread Looting of Civil Liberties Reported; Justice Submerged Under 15 Feet of Politics

In April 2007, Chertoff, Bush's Homeland Security secretary,
was being touted as a likely replacement for Attorney General ALBERTO GONZALES* in the event Gonzales was scape-
goated for the sins of ROVE, CHENEY, and BUSH**—specifically
the firings of eight U.S. attorneys who just weren't, well,
partisan and political enough. (See JUSTICE SYSTEM, PAR-
TISAN POLITICAL PERVERSION OF.)

The layers of irony here were thicker than the earth's
mostly iron mantle, which overlies a liquid outer core and solid
iron inner core. Chertoff certainly did deserve recognition for
the competence and intelligence he displayed as head of the
federal response to HURRICANE KATRINA (see INCOMPETENCE
AND FAILURE, REWARDING OF) and for his overall success at

---

*Chertoff was described as "as cold blooded as they come," and reportedly
had his eye on the AG post as a step toward an eventual seat on the U.S.
Supreme Court.
**Which finally happened in August 2007, just as this book was going to press.

Homeland Security (DHS). In July 2006, eighteen months after Chertoff took command, the government surveyed employees in all thirty-six federal agencies on leadership and job satisfaction. DHS came in last or nearly last in every category.

But what really made Chertoff attorney general material were his own vital contributions to the JUSTICE SYSTEM, PARTISAN POLITICAL PERVERSION OF—first as a GEORGE BUSH SR.-appointed U.S. attorney in New Jersey in the early 1990s, then, a few years later, as special counsel to the GOP-controlled Senate committee hounding the Clintons over their Whitewater scandalette—and finally, in his extremely *un*-Katrina-like swiftness in breaching the levees of CIVIL LIBERTIES after September 11, 2001, as head of the Justice Department's criminal division. The tons of money he'd raised in 2000 for Bush and other Republicans couldn't have hurt either. Well, it hurt America. Ouch. As for Chertoff's active membership in the FEDERALIST SOCIETY, a vast conspiracy of right-wing lawyers who captured almost every important legal post in the Bush II administration—well, that was more than an asset, it was virtually a prerequisite.

The calm and inertia in the middle of the storm.
In the immediate wake of Katrina, MICHAEL "Heckuvajob" BROWN, Bush's supremely unqualified political appointee in charge of the Federal Emergency Management Agency (FEMA), took most of the media flak and late-night talk-show ridicule for the federal government's outrageous failure to take prompt action. Brown was canned. The Bush administration *always* scapegoats an underling and protects those responsible—in this case, (a) ultimately Cheney and Bush themselves; and of course (b) Chertoff, under whose jurisdiction FEMA lay.

Chertoff waited almost four days after the National Hurricane Center warned that Katrina would strike the Gulf Coast with catastrophic force, and thirty-six hours after it actually struck, before authorizing FEMA to act. All Chertoff had to do was to declare Katrina an "Incident of National Significance," a key designation that triggers swift federal coordination, and to designate Brown as the "principal federal official" in charge of the storm. That's all. A memo from Brown to Chertoff several hours after Katrina made landfall showed that "the FEMA director was waiting for Chertoff's permission to get help from others within the massive department."[74]

But, hey—Chertoff might have been busy. Or, as Knight Ridder speculated, he "may have been confused about his lead role in disaster response and that of his department." A memo Chertoff wrote shortly after receiving Brown's plea for help indicated he was waiting for a meeting with Bush (who also was busy, attending a ceremony marking the sixtieth anniversary of the end of World War II) and expected the White House to take the lead. Chertoff's lead role *was* spelled out in the National Response Plan (NRP)—the government's post-9/11 blueprint for the handling of natural disasters or terrorist incidents—*and* in an order issued by Bush in 2003. But to expect the secretary of Homeland Security to concern himself with such details as his *role* is the height of absurdity. I suppose if he were confused about his "role" following a terrorist attack, the Democrats would make a big deal about that, too. But not *this* Stephen Colbert fan.

White House and DHS officials offered no explanation for Chertoff's failure to act. "Homeland Security has refused repeated requests to provide details. . . . and said it couldn't say specifically when the department requested assistance from the military."[75] What *is* known is that no significant army/National

Guard presence was seen in many affected areas until a full nine days after Louisiana declared a state of emergency.

The buck may eventually stop at the president's desk, but this one was supposed to stop on Chertoff's first and remain there for some time. He could even have had it framed. Instead, he passed it.

As the crisis deepened, Chertoff's grasp of the situation did not. On September 1, he said: "I have not heard a report of thousands of people in the [New Orleans] convention center who don't have food and water," But then, where would a Homeland Security secretary find a *newspaper*? Associated Press, same day:

> Outside the Convention Center, the sidewalks were packed with people without food, water or medical care. . . . Thousands of storm refugees had been assembling outside for days, waiting for buses that did not come. . . . At least seven bodies were scattered outside, and hungry, desperate people who were tired of waiting broke through the steel doors to a food service entrance and began pushing out pallets of water and juice and whatever else they could find.[76]

"Nobody could have predicted . . ." (Or, how the Bushies ignored disaster warnings *again*, then lied about it, *again*.) At a press conference two days later, Chertoff claimed the disaster "exceeded the foresight of the planners, and maybe anybody's foresight. . . . The collapse of a significant portion of the levee leading to the very fast flooding of the city was not envisioned." It was "breathtaking in its surprise."

His *lies* were breathtaking in their flagrancy and fragrancy, and were balder than his head. For years, scientists and "government agencies at all levels, including FEMA itself . . . had identified a disaster such as this as one of the three most likely catastrophes to strike the U.S." [77]

New Orleans's levees were built to withstand only Category 3 hurricanes. Officials had long warned that a Category 4 (like Katrina) could cause the levees to fail. Michael Brown said FEMA had long planned for a Category 5 hitting New Orleans and anticipated the damage Katrina caused. The U.S. Army Corps of Engineers chief confirmed, "We certainly understood the potential impact of a Category 4 or 5 hurricane" on New Orleans. A day before Katrina made landfall, the director of the Louisiana State University Public Health Research Center declared, "This is what we've been saying has been going to happen for years . . . [New Orleans] is definitely going to flood."

Hurricane Katrina and the Seven or Eight Bush-GOP Deadly Sins—Sloth, Callousness, Greed, Cronyism, Envy, Pride, Lust, Incompetence, and Partisan-Extremist Depravity. All of the evils of Republican politics seemed to converge in the Hurricane Katrina disaster:

► Chronic underfunding of domestic needs such as infrastructure maintenance (New Orleans' levees, Minneapolis bridges . . .)

► The diversion of funds desperately needed at home to a desperately *un*needed, illegal, politics- and testosterone-driven military misadventure

► Indifference to the plight of poor and nonwhite Americans

► A bogus philosophy of self-reliance whose insane premise is that the poor are quite able to help themselves (while the Republicans' corporate and billionaire constituents are in constant and urgent need of government relief)

But, CNN noted, "Chertoff seemed unaware of all the warnings."

Chertoff also claimed "it wasn't until comparatively late . . . a day, maybe a day and a half, before landfall—that it became clear that this was going to be a Category 4 or 5 hurricane headed for the New Orleans area." Emergency! Pants on fire! The National Hurricane Center predicted that *three* days before.

The inescapable conclusion: Chertoff was a jerkoff.

Michael Brown "is a convenient fall guy," said a former FEMA deputy chief of staff. "The problem is a system that was marginalized." Translation: The Bush administration under-funded FEMA, appointed morons and partisan hacks to run it, and slashed flood control funding. *All that, however, grew out of the GOP's fundamental political values.* (See sidebar.)

▶ Just as with SEPTEMBER 11, denial, denial, denial and lies, lies, lies: there wasn't adequate warning; "no one could have predicted . . ."

▶ Scapegoating of underlings, refusal to hold accountable those ultimately responsible, and warnings to Democrats not to "play politics" with GOP failures

▶ Exploitation of a disaster for partisan political gain—such as by making permanent the disappearance of the large Democratic voting block that *was* New Orleans, leaving a whiter, more Republican state

▶ Exploitation of a disaster to award fat reconstruction contracts to GOP-friendly and crony-owned companies (like HALLIBURTON in both Iraq and New Orleans)

As a MoveOn official said: *"This is what government looks like when it is in the hands of people who don't believe in government."* (My angry italics.)

Scarier than Ashcroft? Chertoff had zero experience in running anything remotely like DHS, with its 180,000 employees and twenty-two subagencies. Of course, by Chenrovebush criteria, he was the perfect man for the job. It was "as political an appointment as one can imagine," wrote Doug Ireland in *LA Weekly*. It "caused jaws to drop" in New Jersey, where, as a U.S. attorney in the early 1990s, "Chertoff was a political attack dog . . . indicting and convicting a raft of Democratic office-holders . . . a skilled political hitman."[78] (One shouldn't really say "attack dog" *and* "hitman"; a Republican is one or the other.) As head of the DOJ criminal division (2001–2003), Chertoff left no doubt as to his loyalty to Bush and to the Bushist agenda of unlimited, dictatorial expansion of presidential power—to putting and keeping Bush above the law. Chertoff:

▶ Helped weave the legalistic blanket of secrecy with which the administration cloaked its malfeasance. Conservative columnist Robert Novak claimed he heard Chertoff argue that the executive branch *never* need grant Congressional requests for documents. Indeed, Chertoff was often the man who did the rejecting. In 2001, for example, he invoked executive privilege to deny to the House Government Reform Committee materials concerning the FBI's involvement in mob rackets and murder in Boston.

▶ Coauthored Bush's CIVIL LIBERTIES-shredding USA PATRIOT Act of 2001. "He was [then attorney general] JOHN ASHCROFT's honcho in the indiscriminate grilling of over 5,000 Arab-Americans after 9/11."[79]

He cooked up the use of "material witness" warrants to lock up thousands of people of Middle Eastern descent and hold them indefinitely without trial. And he wrote a brief arguing there was no constitutional right to be free of coercive police questioning.

▶ Wrote legislation known as the Feeney Amendment, which barred judges from shortening sentences of convicted criminals and required the names of judges who deviated to be reported to the DOJ—to be, in effect, blacklisted.

▶ Is alleged* to have squelched investigations into Saudi terror financing, money laundering, drug and arms trafficking, and ties to 9/11. Ashcroft put Chertoff in charge of the entire DOJ investigation of 9/11. (Pre-Chertoff) Homeland Security officials accused the FBI and DOJ of sabotaging their "Greenquest" investigations into terrorist financing by not turning over critical information and by covering up the FBI's failure to actively pursue terror finance cases. Putting Chertoff in charge of Homeland Security may have been a fast, effective way to suppress any further whistle-blowing.[80]

▶ Prevented FBI agents from testifying at the 9/11 congressional hearings and kept the infamous twenty-eight missing pages out of the 9/11 congressional report. Know what was in those pages? Most of the stuff about Saudi terror ties and the Bush administration's "failure" to investigate them. Ask then Senate Intelligence Committee ranking Democrat Bob Graham. He saw those pages. *He* knows.

---

*By, among others, former FBI translator SIBEL EDMONDS—whom Ashcroft placed under a gag order—and INDIRA SINGH, former business associate of the Saudi- and terrorist-financed PTECH Corporation.

"[A]s intent on undermining the law and Constitution as Ashcroft" was how law professor Elaine Cassel described Chertoff in 2003, when he was elevated to Court of Appeals judge. "What's so scary about Michael? Well, besides having no judicial experience and being a right-wing radical who does not believe in the Constitution and wants to rewrite federal law and rules of procedure on an ad hoc, case by case basis, as it suits him, nothing I guess."

Leading the government's case against terrorism suspect ZACARIAS MOUSSAOUI in 2003,* Chertoff argued that neither Moussaoui nor his lawyers should be permitted to confront the government's star witnesses. The judge ruled this a blatant violation of the Sixth Amendment right to confront witnesses and said she would not be a party to making exceptions to the Constitution on a case-by-case basis. Chertoff appealed the ruling.

Ashcroft and Chertoff created other innovative legal procedures. Neither Moussaoui nor his attorneys were given access to all documents related to the case. ("National security" interests, naturally.) Witnesses appeared in court behind screens, invisible to the defendant. The appellate court hearing was the first closed one in U.S. history—closed to all but those screened and approved by the feds. The defendant was not allowed to be present. Attorney–client contacts were subject to surveillance. "We have had secret warrants (or no warrants), secret hearings denying bail, secret trials, and now secret appellate court arguments," wrote Cassel. "Next, we can expect the Supreme Court to be closed, can't we?" (Given its present composition, closing it down might not be a bad idea.)

---

*The actual prosecutor, U.S. attorney PAUL MCNULTY, who was later promoted to deputy attorney general, admitted in 2007 to having lied under oath to Congress about the Bushists' political firings of eight U.S. attorneys.

Kafkaesque; Hellerious. Most inspired of all, Chertoff argued that the government could not be ordered to produce its star witness because he was out of the country "at an undisclosed location"—i.e., because he was in the custody of the government! (Franz Kafka and Joseph Heller have been overtaken by reality. Again.) This, Cassel noted, was similar to a recent federal court ruling that Guantánamo prisoners had no access to federal courts to ask that they be charged or released because they were out of the country . . . on a Caribbean holiday . . .

So why didn't the government simply take Moussaoui to Guantánamo and secretly try him there in one of its exciting new military tribunals? Why insist on keeping him in federal court? "The answer," wrote Cassel, "lies in Chertoff." His goal—and Ashcroft's, and Bush's, "is to subject federal trials, as they see fit, to ad hoc exemptions of whatever laws (be they constitutional, criminal code, or rules of procedure) that will suit their purposes. Their grand scheme is to ultimately cripple and dismantle the federal courts as we know them, one brick at a time."[81]

Asshole #24
HYDE, HENRY

Congressman (R-Ill.), 1975–2006. Highlights:
► Sponsored the Hyde Amendment (1976), which cut off funds to pay for abortions for the poor, thus helping to keep them poor
► Was accused of gross negligence in connection with the 1990 collapse of the Clyde Federal Savings Bank, on whose board he served
► Explaining his opposition to embryonic STEM CELL

RESEARCH: "I myself am a 992-month-old embryo."[82] (May he never divide and become twins . . .)

▶ Observed: "There are so many women on the floor of Congress, it looks like a mall."

▶ Led the House impeachment trial of Bill Clinton while hyding his own record of adultery and homewrecking. See **SEX PERVERTS**.

IGNORANCE AND IDIOCY, GOP Pride and Excellence in; America, Chronic Embarrassment of

If a person doesn't have the capacity that we all want that person to have, I suspect hope is in the far distant future, if at all.
—George W. Bush

After years of spectacularly stupid pronouncements from our ignoramus-in-chief, **GEORGE W. BUSH**—statements of "where wings take dream," "putting food on the family," and "is our children learning?" caliber—it is easy to forget that Republicans were voting for morons well before 2000. The great precedent-setter for Bush's preemptive war on coherent thought and speech was of course RONALD REAGAN. As the Repugs saw it, Reagan proved once and for all that not only was any display of intellect an elec-toral liability but, the dumber, more corn-pone, more know-nothing the candidate sounded, the more appealing to the kind of voters the GOP wanted—on the principle that Americans don't like anyone who thinks they're bet-ter'n me, which sets the bar very low indeed. Funny thing about Americans. We seem to have no objections to gross *economic* inequality, but little tolerance for *cultural* inequality—that is, for people who sound, act, and/or *are* brainier, or better educated, than our own dumb-ass-tattooing, NASCAR-watching selves. The notion seems to be that you either speak *well* or you speak *honestly*; fine language—maybe even intelligence itself—is both "ELITIST" and an instrument of deception. (As compared to the instrument of sheer *confusion* that is, say, a George Bush. Any George Bush.)

Tocqueville remarked on this famous American anti-intellectualism way back in 1835. ("One day, perhaps 165 years from now, this country is going to elect a *real* moron as president," he predicted.) In the classic modern work on the subject, *Anti-Intellectualism In American Life* (1963), Richard Hofstadter wrote that "while most of the Founding Fathers were still alive . . . a reputation for intellect [became] a political disadvantage." The democratic spirit was one reason; another was that the founding, patrician elite split into partisan factions, sank into demagoguery, and began "playing politics with little regard for decency or common sense." (Such as by alleging "plots to subvert Christianity," Hofstadter noted. As in XMAS AND CHRISTIANITY, DEMOCRAT-LIBERAL-SATANIST-SECULARIST WAR ON. Faith is perennially and rightly hostile to reason and intellect, its natural enemies.)

The Fatuous Fifties. The GOP has been an enthusiastic exploiter of popular anti-intellectualism since early in the TV Age. Decades before the GOP conquered the South, it dominated the Midwestern agricultural heartland, with its anti-urban biases. The *head*land, the great cultural, intellectual, and media centers of the Northeast and California, offered rich targets for right-wing demagogues like Sen. JOE McCARTHY (R-Wis.). The Democrats' 1952 and 1956 presidential candidate, Adlai Stevenson, suffered a reputation as an intellectual. Eisenhower's running mate RICHARD NIXON labeled Stevenson an "egghead." Stevenson lost both elections by landslides. Because of the "egghead" thing.

Eisenhower himself was renowned for Bushesque remarks like, "Things are more like they are now than they ever were before," and, "This is something, uh, that is the kind of thing that must be gone through with what I believe is best not talked about too much until we know whatever answers there will be." This, historians tell us, was just Ike's wiley way of concealing what he was thinking. Maybe . . . maybe . . . (Eisenhower did, it's true, write of Senate GOP leader William F. Knowland: "In his case, there seems to be no final answer to the question, 'How stupid can you get?'" A half-century later, we are no closer to the answer.)

The Stupid Sixties and Seventies. The 1960 election pitted plain, humble Nixon against wealthy, sophisticated JFK. Throughout the '60s, segregationist Dixiecrat turned third-party presidential candidate George Wallace assailed the "pointy-headed" intellectuals who were running the federal government and regulating the nation to death. Nixon's vice president SPIRO AGNEW—armed with phrases forged by White House speechwriters WILLIAM SAFIRE and PAT BUCHANAN—attacked journalists and Vietnam War opponents as "the liberal intellectuals [with their] masochistic compulsion to destroy their country's strength"; the "nattering nabobs of negativism," "hopeless, hysterical hypochondriacs of history," "effete corps of impudent snobs," and "pusillanimous pussyfoots." Turd-brained, tax-evading twit.

"Facts are stupid things," said the ever factual Ronald Reagan. Reagan's intellectual unfitness for the job was similar to George W. Bush's, and has been similarly glossed by admirers: "He articulated broad, basic themes and left the details to others"—that sort of BULLSHIT. According to pundit David Gergen, who served under presidents Nixon, Ford, Reagan, and Clinton, Reagan delegated too much and "wasn't intellectually curious," but "had a clear sense of what he was trying to accomplish, where he wanted to go and how he might get there." Citing Harvard psychologist Howard Gardner's theory of multiple intelligences, Gergen wrote: "Reagan ranked high in a form of intelligence [Gardner] calls 'interpersonal,' high in 'bodily-kinesthetic intelligence,' high in an aspect of 'language intelligence' and low in the 'logical-mathematical intelligence' at which lawyers and professors usually excel."* Translation: Reagan had a friendly personality; did his thinking with his broad shoulders; read no reports about what was actually going on in his administration, the country, and the world; and, in attempting to respond to questions, stuck to trite formulas and folksy, not necessarily factual anecdotes that illustrated the wisdom and virtue of plain folks like us.

At his first cabinet meeting, Reagan was asked if he intended to issue an expected executive order on cost-cutting (one of his major "themes"). "He shrugs. Then, noticing

---

*"I never knew anything above C's," he bragged in an interview with Barbara Walters.

[White House] Budget Director David Stockman nodding emphatically, he adds, 'I have a smiling fellow at the end of the table who tells me we do.'"[83] Reagan "knows less about the budget than any president in my lifetime," said always-complaining House Speaker Tip O'Neill, then a congressman for thirty years. "He can't even carry on a conversation about the budget. It's an absolute and utter disgrace."

Now hold on! Reagan *was* surrounded by competent cabinet members and advisers. Right? Let's see. Budget Director Stockman: "None of us really understands what's going on with all these numbers." At his hearing to become deputy secretary of state, William Clark could not name the prime ministers of South Africa or Zimbabwe or the European nations that did not want U.S. nuclear missiles on their soil—all of which featured prominently in the U.S. press at the time. Clark was confirmed, *and* promoted by Reagan to National Security Adviser the following year.

Great Communications from the president whom George W. Bush most wanted to emulate and in certain respects surpassed:

▶ "Eighty percent of air pollution comes not from chimneys and auto exhaust pipes, but from plants and trees." So? "So let's not go overboard in setting and enforcing tough emission standards from man-made sources." On conserving forest resources: "A tree is a tree. How many more do you have to look at?"

▶ "I have flown twice over Mount St. Helens. . . . I have a suspicion that that one little mountain has probably released more sulfur dioxide into the atmosphere of the world than has been released in the last ten years of automobile driving or things of that kind that people are so concerned about." At its peak, the volcano belched about 2,000 tons of sulfur dioxide per day, compared with 81,000 tons per day by cars. But facts are *such* stupid things.

▶ "All the waste in a year from a nuclear power plant can be stored under a desk." And I know the perfect one.

▶ "I'm satisfied that we do have a foreign policy." (White House spokesman, when asked whether President Reagan had read the House report on the latest Beirut truck bombing: "I don't think he's read the report in detail. It's five and a half pages, double-spaced.")

▶ To the Lebanese foreign minister during a White House meeting with Arab leaders: "You know, your nose looks just like Danny Thomas's."* "The Arabs exchange nervous glances."[84]

▶ Picked up and broadcast during a microphone test just before a scheduled radio address, at the height of renewed nuclear tensions with the Soviet Union, 1984: "My fellow Americans, I am pleased to tell you I just signed legislation which outlaws Russia forever. The bombing will begin in five minutes." (Never mind the diplomacy—just consider the IQ of the phrase "outlaws Russia.")

▶ "The United States has much to offer the Third World War." True, alas. Reagan repeated this error—or what Freud called a *parapraxis*—nine times in the same speech.

▶ "The Afghan Mujaheddin are the moral equivalent of the Founding Fathers of America." (And *were* the fathers of the Taliban. Did our Founders destroy all

---

*A nasally endowed entertainer of Lebanese background.

vestiges of religions other than their own and decree
that women who exposed their faces publicly were to
be beaten? I forget.)

Gets it from his father. Ever wonder how the Yale-
"educated" son of an elite New England family learned to
talk like such a yahoo? Is it enough to spend part of your
boyhood in Texas? Is it enough just to be an ignoramus?
Maybe it's enough just to have sprung from the loins of
GEORGE H. W. BUSH. Judge for yourself, from *his* family
jewels, I mean, gems and pearls of wisdom:

▶ "I have opinions of my own, strong opinions, but I
don't always agree with them."
▶ "We're enjoying sluggish times, and not enjoying them
very much."
▶ Addressing the American Legion in Louisville, Kentucky, September 7, 1988: "Today, you remember—I
wonder how many Americans remember—today is
Pearl Harbor Day. Forty-seven years ago to this very
day we were hit and hit hard at Pearl Harbor. . . . Did I
say September 7th? Sorry about that. December 7th."
▶ "High tech is potent, precise, and in the end, unbeat-
able. The truth is, it reminds a lot of people the way I
pitch horseshoes. Would you believe some of the
people? Would you believe our dog? Look, I want to
give the high-five symbol to high tech."
▶ "Remember Lincoln, going to his knees in time of trial
and the Civil War and all that stuff. You can't be. So
don't feel sorry for—don't cry for me, Argentina."

No . . . cry for America. For, then we elected the Son. . . .
Wait a minute—no, we didn't. Well, at least Poppy's VP

never became P . . . Dan Quayle was every bit his boss's
equal. But you can only have one little taste—then you
must go QUAYLE-hunting on your own. (Quayle has his
alphabetal uses.)

▶ "The Holocaust was an obscene period in our nation's
history. I mean in this century's history. But we all
lived in this century. I didn't live in this century."

Other GOP geniuses. The Reagan-Bush-Quayle axis of
idiocy dominates, but hardly monopolizes, the Who's Who of
GOP Dodos.

▶ Former House majority leader DICK ARMEY (R-Tex.):
"I've been to Europe once. I don't have to go again."

▶ Rep. BOB DORNAN (R-Calif.): "Men in the pro-choice
movement are either men trapped in women's bodies
. . . or younger guys who are like camp followers
looking for easy sex." (Moron. He left out *older* guys
looking for easy sex.)

▶ Rev. JERRY FALWELL in *Reader's Digest*, 1985: "The
decline in American pride, patriotism, and piety can
be directly attributed to the extensive reading of
so-called 'science fiction' by our young people. This
poisonous rot about creatures not of God's making,
societies of 'aliens' without a good Christian among
them [*Jewish Alpha Centaurians? Who knew?*],
and raw sex between unhuman beings with three
heads and God alone knows what sort of reproductive apparatus keeps our young people from
realizing the true will of God."[85] (Also see ASS-
HOLINESS and FIVE-LEGGED REPUBLICANS FROM
PLUTO.)

▶ Gov. ARNOLD SCHWARZENEGGER (R-Calif.) on the dangers

posed by gay marriage: "All of a sudden, we see riots, we see protests, we see people clashing. The next thing we know, there is injured or there is dead people. We don't want to get to that extent." (Also see CONAN THE REPUBLICAN.)

▶ Pop singer-actress JESSICA SIMPSON may or may not be a politician or government official; but according to her father, "We are huge fans of [President Bush] and of his family, his girls. Jessica loves the heck out of him." And if you look closely, she's really not that great looking. So: Simpson, upon being introduced to Interior secretary Gale Norton while touring the White House: "You've done a nice job decorating the White House."

▶ TED STEVENS (R-Alaska). In government since the *Eisenhower* administration—yet an expert on Internet technology, as he showed during debate on his very own Communications, Consumer's Choice, and Broadband Deployment bill of 2006: "The Internet is not something you just dump something on. It's not a truck. It's a series of tubes. And if you don't understand, those tubes can be filled and if they are filled, when you put your message in, it gets in line and it's going to be delayed by anyone that puts into that tube enormous amounts of material." Now you understand the Internet.*

Stevens on HURRICANE KATRINA: "This is the largest disaster in the history of the United States,

---

*Stevens complained that "an Internet [*sic*] was sent by my staff" but that commercial traffic delayed it by five days. By the way, he sided with the telecom industry in opposing NETWORK NEUTRALITY, the principle that broadband providers should not have the legal power to block others' Web sites, content, and services.

over an area twice the size of Europe. People have to understand this is a big, big problem." (1) Perhaps only one person on earth *didn't* understand that: Ted Stevens, who threatened to resign from the Senate if funds earmarked for his notorious "Bridge to Nowhere" in Alaska (see STEVENS) were used instead for post-Katrina reconstruction. However: (2) An area twice the size of Europe would be more than twice the size of the entire U.S.

KATRINA inspired a veritable Mardi Gras of GOP mindlessness and merriment:

▶ FEMA Director MICHAEL BROWN, in various e-mails to colleagues and friends in the immediate aftermath: "If you'll look at my lovely FEMA attire you'll really vomit. I am a fashion god . . . Do you know of anyone who dog-sits? . . . Can I quit now? Can I come home? . . . I'm trapped now, please rescue me." And: "Considering the dire circumstances that we have in New Orleans, virtually a city that has been destroyed, things are going relatively well."

▶ Former first lady BARBARA BUSH, commenting on the Katrina evacuees at the Astrodome in Houston: "What I'm hearing which is sort of scary is that they all want to stay in Texas. Everybody is so overwhelmed by the hospitality. And so many of the people in the arena here, you know, were underprivileged anyway so this [chuckle]—this is working very well for them." (When Bushies help cause a humanitarian disaster, they know what they're doing!)

▶ Just being *around* Bushes seems to impair mental functioning. First Lady LAURA BUSH, speaking to children and parents in South Haven, Mississippi, September 2005: "I also want to encourage anybody who was affected by Hurricane Corina to make sure their children are in school." (People affected by Corina—as Laura called it twice—might have just lost everything they had, *including* their school and their children.)

▶ GEORGE W. BUSH: "There will be a momentum, momentum will be gathered. Houses will begat jobs, jobs will begat houses." There speaks a Bible reader! ("And Job begat jobs . . . and jobs begat houses . . . And George I begat George II, who was called The Moron, and who reigned for eight years . . .")

OPERATION IRAQI LIBERATION (see **O.I.L.**) proved a real gusher of death and destruction and idiocy (not to mention complete dominance of the BULLSHIT category).

▶ White House press secretary ARI FLEISCHER, July 2003: "I think the burden is on those people who think he [Saddam] didn't have weapons of mass destruction to tell the world where they are." . . . *huh*??

▶ Fox News host SEAN HANNITY, April 2003: "All of these thousands, according to naysayers, of troops are going to die. . . . They've actually made fools of them themselves." November 2005: "We're close to being finished [in Iraq]."

▶ Defense Secretary DONALD RUMSFELD: "Death has a tendency to encourage a depressing view of war." And to obscure all that's wonderful about it!

▶ President Bush, asked in June 2006 if the tide was turning in Iraq: "I think—tide turning—see, as I remember—I was raised in the desert [*thus "George of Arabia"*], but tides kind of—it's easy to see a tide turn—did I say those words?" (He did. And these:

"We're making the right decisions to bring the solution to an end." And these: "The only way we can win is to leave before the job is done.") Much the way *we* can win only if *he* leaves before his term is done.

Is Bush . . . you know . . . dumb? Is anything more irritating than being told by intellectual critics of George W. Bush that his Bushisms don't *really* bespeak a lamebrain? He's a shrewd politician. Amuses and amazes us into a stupor with his stupidity, then cleans us out. Yada yada. We've heard it all. Well, as Freud said, sometimes a stooge is just a stooge. (Oh, *was* it "stogie"?)

Is Bush a shrewd actor and manipulator of popular antielitism, or just a fucking idiot? I believe you can be both. There's no question that Bush's handlers and speechwriters have made a virtue out of a necessity and exploited his synaptic difficulties for ignoramus appeal, in the aforementioned Reagan–Bush Sr. antielitist faux-populist tradition.

Moreover, I suspect Bush's image team fully appreciates, and Bush himself half-consciously does, the irony of his everyman posture, and the *insult* to America. As Robert Parry, author of *Secrecy and Privilege: Rise of the Bush Dynasty from Watergate to Iraq*, writes:

[W]hile Bush may not be the sharpest tool in the shed, it is he who thinks the American people are the real dullards. . . . He also assumes—with some justification—that his listeners don't mind being misled and lied to, as long as he gives them some bromides that make them feel good . . . that the American people are so gullible that they will buy whatever he sells them—as long as he does it with a folksy charm.[86]

Even Bush's commencement address while accepting an honorary degree from Yale, his alma mater, featured, in Swarthmore president Alfred Bloom's words, a "dismaying disparagement of the intellectual enterprise." "And to you C students," Bush sug-jested, "you, too, can be president of the United States." Bush was simultaneously (a) deploying disarming, self-deprecating humor; (b) obscuring *and flaunting* the fact that had he been just any mediocre student, he never would have been at Yale in the first place—implying, as a corollary, that he overcame his limitations by dint of his own hard work rather than his name; (c) saying "nya nya, fuck you" to all those liberals, journalists, and intellectuals who'd made fun of his dumb ass every step of his way to the White House.

But many Bushisms suggest a complete cognitive and emotional disconnect from his own statements, as though they mean as little to him as they do to his audience. To wit(less): "The best way to defeat the totalitarian of hate is with an ideology of hope—an ideology of hate—excuse me—with an ideology of hope." Observing Bush on the campaign trail in 2000, Todd Gittlin wrote:

There was so much ignorance on display . . . Yet none of the easy charges against Bush [*dyslexia; conscious appeal to his audience's anti-intellectualism*] touched upon his more substantial incapacities: his lack of curiosity about the world . . . and the ample evidence that he does not reason. During the debates, he was unresponsive to questions the answers to which he had not memorized. In public appearances . . . the governor lost track of his points, so that items came out nonsensical, as in: "Drug therapies are replacing a lot of medicines as we used to know it."

The 2000 campaign was no fluke. Bush has kept up his batty average season after idiotic season. A few more greatest hits:

▶ "I think it's important for those of us in a position of responsibility to be firm in sharing our experiences, to understand that the babies out of wedlock is a very difficult chore for mom and baby alike. . . . And, you know, hopefully, condoms will work, but it hasn't worked." (There's one time I especially wish it had.)

▶ "This is still a dangerous world. It's a world of madmen and uncertainty and potential mental* losses." (Potential?)

▶ "We must all hear the universal call to like your neighbor just like you like to be liked yourself."

▶ "This is Preservation Month. I appreciate preservation. It's what you do when you run for president. You gotta preserve." (Speaking during "Perseverance Month" at a New Hampshire elementary school.)

▶ "We want our teachers to be trained so they can meet the obligations, their obligations as teachers . . . to know how to teach the science of reading. In order to make sure there's not this kind of federal—federal cufflink." (I saw the Federal Cufflink when I was in Washington. Awesome.)

▶ "I talked to my little brother, Jeb—I haven't told this to many people. But he's the governor of—I shouldn't call him my little brother—my brother, Jeb, the great governor of Texas." Jim Lehrer: "Florida." Bush:

---

*Usually quoted as "mential." I don't know—I wasn't there. Neither, of course, was he, entirely. . . .

"Florida. The state of the Florida." It's as though he's always thinking about himself.

▶ As I was saying: "Actually, I—this may sound a little west Texan to you, but I like it. When I'm talking about—when I'm talking about myself, and when he's talking about myself, all of us are talking about me."

▶ June 2000: "The fundamental question is, will I be a successful president when it comes to foreign policy? I will be, but until I'm the president, it's going to be hard for me to verify that I think I'll be more effective." (With most of the returns in, we are now projecting "ineffective and idiotic" as the winner.)

▶ "[My father asked me] How did you feel when you stood up in front of the people for the State of the Union Address—state of the budget address, whatever you call it."

▶ "I do think we need for a troop to be able to house his family." (And they say he never finished his military service. By the way, Bush *doesn't* think we need to help a troop house his family. See VETERANS, BETRAYAL OF.)

▶ Declining to answer reporters' questions at the Summit of the Americas, Quebec City, April 2001: "Neither in French nor in English nor in Mexican." (Which he doesn't speak as well as people think, by the way. Better than his American, of course.)

▶ Tokyo, February 2002: "For a century and a half now, America and Japan have formed one of the great and enduring alliances of modern times." (We even gave them the atomic bomb!)

▶ "The illiteracy level of our children are appalling."

▶ Asked whether he'd seen *Brokeback Mountain*: "I'll

be glad to talk about ranching, but I haven't seen the movie. I've heard about it. I hope you go—you know—I hope you go back to the ranch and the farm is what I'm about to say." (No. *We* hope *you* go back to the ranch.)

▶ Speaking of *Brokeback*: "I like my buddies from west Texas. I liked them when I was young, I liked them then I was middle-age, I liked them before I was president, and I like them during president, and I like them after president." (I like *after* president best.)

▶ "I believe that a prosperous, democratic Pakistan will be . . . a force for freedom and moderation in the Arab world." (Perhaps—*if* it can be moved *to* the Arab world.)

▶ While showing a German newspaper reporter the Oval Office, May 2006: "That's George Washington, the first president, of course. The interesting thing about him is that I read three—three or four books about him last year. Isn't that interesting?"

▶ Same interview, when asked about his best moment in office: "I would say the best moment of all was when I caught a seven-and-a-half-pound large-mouth bass in my lake." (Coincidence . . . we caught a 175-pound large-mouth ass in the Oval Office.)

▶ At a June 2006 press conference: "Peter. Are you going to ask that question with shades on?" Reporter: "I can take them off." Bush: "I'm interested in the shade look, seriously." Reporter: "All right, I'll keep it, then." Bush: "For the viewers, there's no sun." Reporter: "I guess it depends on your perspective." Bush: "Touché."—Exchange with *Los Angeles Times* correspondent Peter Wallsten, who is legally blind.

▶ "It was not always a given that the United States and America would have a close relationship."

▶ "Make no mistake about it, I understand how tough it is, sir. I talk to families who die."

▶ Addressing a summit on malaria: "Because of your work, children who once wanted to die are now preparing to live."

▶ "I am surprised, frankly, at the amount of distrust that exists in this town [Washington]. And I'm sorry it's the case, and I'll work hard to try to elevate it."

One Bush campaign promise kept.

IRAN-CONTRA: "Far above Watergate"

The contempt for Congress, the defiance of law, the huge mark-ups and profits, the secret bank accounts, the shady characters, the shakedown of foreign governments, the complicity in death and destruction—they did all this in the dark . . . The secret government has no Constitution. The rules it follows are the rules it makes up.
—Bill Moyers, *Frontline*, PBS, 1987

As assaults on our democracy and Constitution go, many historians would concur with University of Utah professor Edwin Firmage in ranking Iran-Contra "far above Watergate":

You have the sale of armaments to terrorists groups, which can only foment more kidnapping and more terror and finance it. You have the doing of this by members of the armed forces, a very scary thing. You have the government . . . doing things that Congress

has forbidden—direct illegality. You have constitutional abuses that are enormous.[87]

For sheer lawlessness and moral corruption, the Reagan
administration rivaled any Third World dictatorship, indeed,
even the **GEORGE W. BUSH** regime. From 1983 to 1986—
despite repeated denials by President Reagan and declara-
tions that he would not negotiate with terrorists—his
administration secretly sold weapons to Iran, sworn enemy
and the leading state sponsor of terrorism, ostensibly to
secure release of Western hostages held by Iranian-backed
Hezbollah in Lebanon. (The operation was a near-total
failure even in that minor regard.) The arms sales violated
the official U.S. embargo on trade with Iran and the government's express policy of not negotiating with terrorists.
Beginning no later than 1985, proceeds from the arms sales
were secretly and illegally diverted to support the
Nicaraguan Contras—barbaric terrorists with no popular
support, formed out of remnants of the former Somoza dictatorship and seeking to overthrow the democratically
elected left-wing Sandinista government—which was
legally recognized by the United States. The Reagan administration had begun funding the Contras in 1981 and continued to support them after this was expressly banned by
Congress in 1983.

Needless to say, Iran-Contra received far less news coverage than Clinton-Lewinsky.

Crack troops. The CIA supplied the Contras with
weapons, training, equipment, intelligence, and specially
built airfields in neighboring Honduras. Assisted by the
State Department and CIA, the Contras also got money

from arms trafficking.* The Reagan administration abetted the sale of crack cocaine on the streets of Los Angeles to fund its own criminal operation.[88]

The plan was for the Contras to capture a border town and set up a provisional government, which the U.S. government would immediately recognize. After their military engagements with Nicaraguan forces failed, the Contras waged economic warfare against farms, coffee plantations, grain storage centers, and road junctions. CIA employees blew up Nicaragua's only oil pipeline, conducted sabotage operations against oil storage facilities, and mined harbors, all in violation of international law and without the knowledge of Congress.

The U.S.-Contra aims were to create food shortages and general hardship and provoke a clamp-down on civil liberties; turn the population against the government; incite Nicaraguan cross-border counterattacks that, as a CIA contract employee testified, would "serve to demonstrate Nicaragua's aggressive nature"; and provoke Nicaraguan reactions against U.S. citizens and diplomatic personnel within the country.

The CIA, as Reagan publicly acknowledged, prepared and distributed to the Contras a manual titled *Psychological Operations in Guerrilla Warfare*, which included instructions in what it termed the "use of implicit and explicit terror" and the "selective use of violence for propaganda effects." Among other terrorist actions, Contras planted bombs in civil

*John Kerry's 1988 Senate Foreign Relations Committee report on Contra drug links concluded that members of the State Department "who provided support for the Contras were involved in drug trafficking . . . and elements of the Contras themselves knowingly received financial and material assistance from drug traffickers."

aircraft and in an airport baggage area. Lawyers who interviewed many Nicaraguan villagers during a fact-finding mission for the International Human Rights Law Group testified that Contras deliberately targeted civilians "who have no connection with the war effort [and] no economic, political or military significance."

Other witnesses attested to scores of indiscriminate acts of violence by the Contras, including murders, rapes, torture, mutilation, and kidnappings of unarmed villagers. The U.S. government never investigated human rights abuses by the Contras because, in the words of a high-ranking State Department official, the government maintained a policy of "intentional ignorance" on the matter; but "it was clear that the level of atrocities was enormous."[89] According to Nicaraguan authorities, Contras killed 3,886 people and wounded 4,731 between 1982 and 1986. Terrorism on a 9/11 scale, underwritten *entirely* by the Reagan administration.

"If such a story gets out . . ." All or most of this was done with the knowledge of Reagan, vice president and former CIA director **GEORGE H. W. BUSH**, and most or all of their national security staff. Bush—who at the time headed the President's Task Force on Terrorism, and perhaps thought its task was to *encourage* terrorism— attended at least five of ten high-level meetings in which top officials discussed the arms shipments to the terrorists. Meanwhile, Bush repeatedly made such public statements as, "Our policy is clear, concise, unequivocal. We will offer no concession to terrorists, because that only leads to more terrorism." To this day, Bush has not publicly admitted he lied.

At a 1984 meeting of the President's National Security Planning Group, the minutes show, Reagan, Bush, National Security Adviser ROBERT MCFARLANE, CIA Director WILLIAM CASEY, UN ambassador JEANNE KIRKPATRICK, and Secretary of State GEORGE SCHULTZ discussed where to find money for the Contras. Schultz told the group that then White House chief of staff JAMES BAKER had warned "that if we go out and try to get the money from third countries, it is an impeachable offense. . . . Baker's argument is that the U. S. government may raise and spend funds only through an appropriation of the Congress." (Uh, that's the *Constitution*'s "argument.") Reagan: "We must obtain the funds to help these freedom fighters." McFarlane: "I certainly hope none of this discussion will be made public in any way." Reagan: "If such a story gets out, we'll all be hanging by our thumbs in front of the White House until we find out who did it."[90] (Reagan must have meant, "until we *decide* who did it, because it sure as hell wasn't *us* who . . . did what we're about to do.")

"We were in business." To run the operation, the White House enlisted a group of in-house operatives who called themselves "the Enterprise." Using a network of arms dealers, fraudulent companies, and secret bank accounts, the Enterprise boldly went where no White House organized crime family had gone before. It made at least $16 million by inflating prices on weapons sales to the Iranians and charging the Contras markups for weapons delivered to them. The profits were kept in a private slush fund. Asked about this during Senate Iran-Contra hearings, Enterprise chief General RICHARD SECORD answered: "We were in business to make a living, Senator."

After the operation came to light, everyone involved, from the president on down, participated in a massive coverup, destroying or withholding evidence and repeatedly lying to the public, Congress, and the independent counsel appointed to investigate the affair, Republican judge Lawrence Walsh.

A White House–ordered "investigation" of . . . the White House was, of course, part of the coverup. (See *The GOP Playbook*, 38–42.) A month before Walsh was appointed in December 2006, Reagan, under growing pressure, set up a Special Review Board chaired by former senator JOHN TOWER (R-Tex.). The Tower Commission was basically a Whitehouse-wash. Bush got off easiest of all. Two years later, President Bush nominated Tower as Defense secretary. (He failed to win Senate confirmation.)

In *his* final report, Walsh wrote that Reagan administration officials "deliberately deceived the Congress and the public about the level and extent of official knowledge of and support for these operations." He concluded that "the policies behind both the Iran and contra operations were fully reviewed and developed at the highest levels." Among those who knew about the Iran operations, Walsh listed Reagan, Bush, Shultz, Casey, Defense Secretary CASPAR WEINBERGER, and national security advisers McFarlane and JOHN POINDEXTER. Reagan, wrote Walsh, "set the stage for the illegal activities of others by encouraging and, in general terms, ordering support of the contras during the period when funds for the contras were cut off [by Congress], and in authorizing the sale of arms to Iran, in contravention of the U.S. embargo on such sales."

Congress's 1988 report on the affair concluded that the administration exhibited "disdain for the law" and that

Reagan bore "ultimate responsibility" for wrongdoing by his aides: "The President did know of the Iran arms sales, and he made a deliberate decision not to notify Congress. . . . and when Congress finally did learn, [it was] from a story published in a Beirut weekly."[91]

Reagan's weaselly, cowardly, BS statement: "A few months ago I told the American people I did not trade arms for hostages. My heart and my best intentions still tell me that is true, but the facts and the evidence tell me it is not." Was he acknowledging it or not? Asshole! Reagan's vaunted, even boasted, style of delegating "details" came in awfully handy at times. (*GOP Playbook*, 46.) Leaving everyone wondering which was worse—his knowing or his not knowing what was going on in his own administration—was still better than, "The bastard! He knew all along!"

In a case brought by Nicaragua, the International Court of Justice found the United States guilty of encouraging terrorism (the only nation ever so adjudged by the court) and of violating international law by supporting rebels against a legitimate government and mining Nicaragua's harbors. Even though the U.S. had signed the treaty accepting the court's decisions as binding, the Reagan administration refused to recognize its jurisdiction, to participate in the proceedings, or to pay court-ordered reparations.

Sentenced to serve in the Bush II administration.
John Pointexter and Lieut. Col. OLIVER NORTH, a National Security Council staffer who ran the Contra supply operation, were indicted on multiple counts of lying to Congress, obstruction of justice, conspiracy, defrauding the

government, and altering and destroying evidence. (His and his secretary Fawn Hall's famous all-night nude shredding party.*) Convicted on several counts, both had their convictions overturned on technicalities. Weinberger was indicted on several felony charges of lying to the independent counsel, but pardoned by President Bush (Sr.), preempting a trial in which Bush was expected to be called as a witness. Bush was the first president ever to grant a pardon on the eve of a trial. He pardoned five others involved in the scandal, including McFarlane and then assistant secretary of state ELLIOTT ABRAMS, who had obtained a $10 million contribution for the Contras from the Sultan of Brunei—money that Oliver North managed to lose . . . Abrams pleaded guilty on two counts of unlawfully withholding information. Ten years later, **GEORGE W. BUSH** would appoint Abrams special assistant to the president and senior director on the National Security Council. Other Iran-Contraveners appointed to the Dumbya administration were Poindexter, **ROBERT GATES**, and CHARLES ALLEN, a CIA official whom CIA director William Webster had formally reprimanded for failing to cooperate in the agency's internal Iran-Contra investigation. Bush (Jr.) appointed Allen chief intelligence officer at the Department of Homeland Security.

As for Reagan and Bush (Sr.) themselves, they "managed to get away with their wrongdoing precisely because they lied, stalled, stonewalled, and participated in a cover-up," wrote Carla Binion in *Online Journal*—"not because they were innocent, as many of their supporters still believe."

---

*"All-night" and "nude" may be inaccurate.

JUSTICE SYSTEM, PARTISAN POLITICAL PERVERSION OF: Alberto Gonzales and Attorneygate

Among all the political hacks and sheer incompetents appointed to the GEORGE W. BUSH administration purely for their eagerness to put their president and party before any and all duties as public servants, ALBERTO GONZALES, although shorter than most, stands a head taller. His partisan loyalty must have been extraordinary indeed to get him appointed, first as White House counsel, then as attorney general, despite his lacking the other vital qualification for a Bush official: Gonzales couldn't lie his way out of a paper bag.*

Only in this administration could the replacement for JOHN ASHCROFT prove even worse: perhaps less of a buffoon (not *much* less), yet a much more devoted agent of the White House-GOP agenda of PRESIDENTIAL POWER, UNLIMITED EXPANSION OF, and ABSOLUTELY EVERYTHING, PARTISAN POLITICIZATION OF.

But make no mistake: Like all other Bush administration CRIME, CORRUPTION, AND CRONYISM, Attorneygate—the

---

*Of his April 2007 Senate testimony on Attorneygate, the *New York Times* said that if Gonzales had gone to the Senate "to convince the world that he ought to be fired, it's hard to imagine how he could have done a better job . . . Mr. Gonzales came across as a dull-witted apparatchik incapable of running one of the most important departments in the executive branch . . . And when it came time to explain his inept decision making to the public, he gave a false account that was instantly and repeatedly contradicted by sworn testimony. . . . At the end of the day, we were left wondering why the nation's chief law-enforcement officer would paint himself as a bumbling fool."

political firing of eight U.S. attorneys in 2006–2007—was anything but an isolated occurrence or the fault of a single lackey. It was just more of the Cheney-Rove-Bush regime at its purest.

It soon became clear that none of the eight were really fired over "performance issues," as the White House claimed (most received positive job evaluations), but rather because they didn't cave to White House pressure—some of it from Bush personally—to pursue bogus "voter fraud" investigations against Democrats, and/or *had* prosecuted corrupt Republicans. (During his Senate testimony on the scandal, the *New York Times* noted, Gonzales demonstrated that "he had no idea whether any of the 93 United States attorneys working for him—let alone the ones he fired—were doing a good job prosecuting real crimes.") There was strong evidence that the purge was directed from within the White House, by KARL ROVE (who else) and then-White House counsel and failed Supreme Court nominee HARRIET MIERS. (One of the fired attorneys was replaced by a former Rove aide.)

U.S. attorneys are supposed to be independent and to guard the judicial system *against* political abuse; they must police the politicians. As Joe Conason wrote in *Salon*, "To ensure that no U.S. attorney could be fired on a whim and replaced with a malleable hack, the relevant statute required that whenever a vacancy occurred in midterm, the replacement would be appointed by federal circuit judges rather than by the president. Getting rid of irksomely honest and nonpartisan prosecutors was difficult if not impossible." That was until December 2005, when, during Senate renewal of the USA PATRIOT Act, at the behest of the Justice Department, an aide* to Sen. ARLEN SPECTER (R-Pa.) slipped in a provision that enabled the White House to fill vacant U.S. attorney positions without Senate confirmation.[92]

Bottom line: the U.S. Justice Department, federal law enforcement headquarters, was to be converted top to bottom into just another arm of the Republican National Committee, another cog in the Republicans' ELECTION RIGGING AND ELECTION THEFT machine. The White House might as well have hung a sign reading "Sold for scrap" on the *Spirit of Justice* statue in the Justice Department lobby. Maybe when Ashcroft spent $8,000 of taxpayer funds on curtains to cover the statue, it wasn't to hide her seminudity from public view so much as to hide his administration from *her* view. This purge was a direct attack on justice itself. Nothing, but nothing—no principles, no standards of decency or integrity, not even the Constitution of the United States—would be allowed to get in the way of the GOP quest for a permanent stranglehold on power.

The rest is details.

Crime, Corruption, and Cronyism Case #22: "KING OF PAYOFFS": JERRY LEWIS

No, not the Telethon Jerry Lewis, the comedian, but Rep. Jerry Lewis (R-Calif.), who never costarred with Robert De Niro and Sandra Bernhard in Martin Scorsese's *King of Comedy*, but has been dubbed (by *Rolling Stone*) the "King of Payoffs" and *is* renowned for raising money for MD—no, not muscular dystrophy, "My (legal) Defense"—and other such noble causes. Though not in ways he'd really want to televise.

*Michael O'Neill, a former clerk for CLARENCE THOMAS.

In his unsuccessful run for the California state senate in 1974, two-thirds of the money Lewis raised came from just 43 donors, 22 of them lobbyists. From that humble beginning would arise one of the great influence peddling careers of our times, stretching over thirty years in the House (and an as yet undetermined stretch in the Big House, maybe) and richly intertwined with a raft of other GOP scandals. More than a great American story, it is a great Republican story.

In 2003, when Lewis headed the Defense Appropriations subcommittee, he and seven congressional colleagues (five Rs and two Ds) flew on official business to Europe, where they were wined and dined by defense contractors and lobbyists in restaurants from Warsaw to Lisbon, the *Wall Street Journal* reported. In addition to violating House rules and possibly federal law, which prohibit members from accepting gifts worth $50 or more (such as a meal at a McDonald's in London), the meals "gave Boeing Co., Lockheed Martin Corp., Northrop Grumman Corp. and others private access to legislators who control billions of dollars in government contracts." It was an "extreme," if far from isolated, example of House members feeding from corporate troughs.

That same year, CERBERUS CAPITAL MANAGEMENT, a New York investment group whose boardroom and executive suites were lousy with former GOP officials, raised $110,000 for Lewis at a fund-raiser. The next day, the House passed a defense spending bill that preserved $160 million for a project critical to Cerberus—a new Navy computer system—despite reports of cost overruns, delays, management foul-ups, and "a pattern of large-scale fraud, security problems, and financial scandals involving GOP lawmakers and lobbyists" in Cerberus-owned companies' defense and intelligence contracts.[93] "The man who protected the Navy

money? Lewis," *USA Today* reported. (See **War Privatization and Profiteering**.)*

Until that fund-raiser, no Cerberus-connected donor had
ever contributed to Lewis or his PAC. In the months that followed, however, Cerberus executives, spouses, etc., forked
over thousands more to his PAC, which in turn helped fund
the 2004 campaigns of sixty-nine Cerberus-friendly GOP
House candidates. (Good thing it's illegal for corporations to
contribute directly to candidates—otherwise corporate
America would exert undue influence on the government.)
In April 2004, Cerberus execs were treated to a speech by
President Bush at a Lewis-chaired fund-raiser for the
National Republican Congressional Committee, which helps
fund House campaigns. Cerberus kicked in $75,000. (For
$150,000, Bush will agree *not* to speak. For $250,000, I hear,
he'll do anything with his mouth that you want.)

And lo, in January 2005, Lewis's GOP colleagues elected
him chairman of the Appropriations Committee itself,
which controls the purse strings to $1 trillion a year in fed-
eral spending. Cerberus's fund-raising efforts "played a very
significant role" in winning the post, Lewis later confessed
under torture.**

In Greek mythology, Cerberus was the three-headed

---

*The contractor on the navy job was Cerberus-co-owned MCI—formerly
known as WorldCom-MCI, before an $11 billion accounting scandal earned
its CEO, Bernie Ebbers, a twenty-five-year prison term. Because of the
scandal, Congress members were pushing to ban MCI from any future federal contracts. Lewis himself had criticized the navy project in 2002; citing
MCI's poor performance, his committee proposed cutting it by $160 million.
And now, here he was, nursing a fully funded version through Congress.
Lesson: A person *can* change—if he really wants to.
**Thanks, ironically, to the Bush White House's sanctioning of aggressive
interrogation techniques.

dog that guarded the entrance to Hades—the place where most of the people described in this book will be reunited, along with their corporate buck-buddies, at a really hot fund-raiser.

By 2006, Lewis was under federal investigation *and* had made the Citizens for Responsibility and Ethics in Washington (CREW)'s elite "20 Most Corrupt Members of Congress" list. In bestowing the honor, CREW cited Lewis's misuse of his committee chairmanships to steer hundreds of millions of dollars in federal projects to the clients of a close friend—lobbyist and former Rep. BILL LOWERY (R-Calif.). Lowery and his firm, Copeland Lowery, earned millions in fees from these clients, mainly defense contractors. In turn, he and they ponied up hundreds of thousands for Lewis's campaign committee and PAC, which Lewis then used to support the Republicans who had helped him become Appropriations chairman in the first place.

Lowery client BRENT WILKES and a second defense contractor, MITCHELL WADE, were named as co-conspirators by former Rep. RANDY "DUKE" CUNNINGHAM (R-Calif.) in connection with the Dukester's 2006 bribery conviction (see "**CRIME, CORRUPTION, AND CRONYISM**). Wilkes and Wade each donated at least $30,000 to Lewis. In February 2007, Wilkes became the third "Bush pioneer," or $100,000-plus fund-raiser, to be indicted. That same month, Cunningham's prosecutor, U.S. attorney CAROL LAM, who had begun to investigate Wade and Wilkes, was abruptly dismissed in the Bush administration's purge of insufficiently partisan U.S. attorneys (see **JUSTICE SYSTEM, POLITICAL PARTISAN PERVERSION OF**). There really is just one big GOP scandal, with no more than two degrees of separation between any two figures, or between any one and Beelzebub.

Investigating Lewis himself was Cunningham's principal

prosecutor, U.S. attorney DEBRA WONG YANG, until *she* resigned in November 2006 and went to work (at a stunning salary) for Gibson, Dunn, the powerhouse L.A. law firm *defending* Lewis. Among the firm's many Bush administration ties: partner TED OLSON, who had successfully argued Bush's case before the U.S. Supreme Court in *Bush v. Gore* and was then appointed solicitor general. Yang in fact became cochair, with Olson, of his firm's "Crisis Management Team. Why would the White House want to buy off Lewis's prosecutor? The Lewis investigation, wrote Laura Rozen in the *American Prospect*, "is of course the big enchilada, the one that would really hurt, and not just Lewis."

In October 2006, Lewis, citing cost, abruptly dismissed 60 of the 72 Appropriation Committee investigators who saved the government billions by rooting out fraud, waste, and abuse. (See **OVERSIGHT**.) Lewis meanwhile employed his wife as chief of staff in his office, at around $120,000 per year. His stepdaughter somehow got in on the action, as well. Perhaps his wife and stepdaughter were not so likely to investigate him.

The American Conservative Union scored Lewis's 2003 voting record 80 out of 100. The liberal Americans for Democratic Action gave him 5. I say he deserves more like 25 to 30.

"Me ne frego"
LEDEEN, MICHAEL

This section not recommended for the nervous or for readers under 14.

Imagine a male, vaguely human ANN COULTER whose views are taken dead seriously, and embraced, by the most powerful

figures in the land. Michael Ledeen, a former REAGAN administration adviser and a scholar at the right-wing AMERICAN
ENTERPRISE INSTITUTE, has been described twice in this book
alone as the driving philosophical force behind the neoconservative movement (vs. only once each for Irving Kristol and
Norman Podhoretz). When the PROJECT FOR A NEW AMERICAN
CENTURY's core ideas (see NEOCONS) were laid out in 1991 in
a planning document drafted by then undersecretary of
defense PAUL WOLFOWITZ, the Bush I administration rejected
them as too radical. A Bush later, Ledeen's even more radical
views infected the White House, transmitted by his admirers
Wolfie, CHENEY, ROVE, and RUMSFELD, who, despite knowing
they were MAL (Michael A. Ledeen)-positive, had unpro-
tected intellectual intercourse with subordinates.*

Like Coulter, only with a bit less craving for attention,
Ledeen says and writes what other Republicans dare not.
Conservative *National Review Online* editor Jonah Goldberg quoted Ledeen as saying: "Every ten years or so, the
United States needs to pick up some small crappy little
country and throw it against the wall, just to show the world
we mean business." Elsewhere, Ledeen wrote: "We can lead
by the force of high moral example . . . [but] fear is much
more reliable, and lasts longer. Once we show that we are
capable of dealing out terrible punishment to our enemies,
our power will be far greater." (You know what's really good
for that? Nuking a city.)

---

*Among the crew that cooked up the "intelligence" to justify invasion of
Iraq, Ledeen was particularly close to Undersecretary of Defense DOUGLAS
FEITH, Cheney chief of staff I. LEWIS "MoPed" LIBBY, and ELLIOTT ABRAMS,
special assistant to Bush and senior director on the National Security
Council. Abrams pleaded guilty in 1991 to unlawfully withholding informa-
tion from Congress in connection with his role in Iran-Contra.

> *Wage a total war . . . and our children will sing great songs about us years from now.*—Michael Ledeen on the eve of the Iraq war

It might be quicker to name the countries Ledeen *doesn't* want to attack than those he does. For Ledeen, war is clearly more than just a necessary evil. In March 2003, he told a forum that "the level of casualties [in Iraq] is secondary" because "we [Americans] are a warlike people . . . we love war." He has made clear that he regrets that the United States won the cold war without a shot being fired. The only way to achieve peace, he has written, "is through total war" (or as Joseph Goebbels called it, *totalen Krieg*). And: "The sparing of civilian lives cannot be the total war's first priority . . . The purpose of total war is to permanently force your will onto another people."

Wikipedia quotes "left-wing" author Jack Huberman, who described Ledeen as "the most influential and unabashed warmonger of our time." But Huberman doesn't know the half of it. "From the other side of politics," says Wiki, John Laughland, writing in *The American Conservative*, "has claimed that Ledeen had strong sympathies for Italian fascism," for which he was "a clear apologist.'" (See **FASCISM, CREEP TOWARD**.)

In 1977, Ledeen penned "an enthusiastic biography" of "the high priest of fascism," the poet-adventurer Gabriele D'Annunzio (*The First Duce*). In his 1972 book *Universal Fascism* (the title refers to the dream of some fascists, extolled by Ledeen, of exporting Italian fascism to the whole world), he wrote that "the old ruling class had to be swept away so that newer, more dynamic elements—capable of effecting fundamental changes—could come to power." (As the author of a 1932 fascist manifesto wrote, the choice was between "old Europe or young Europe"; compare to Ledeen's and Bush's "old Europe–new Europe" nonsense.) Millions of Europeans, wrote Ledeen, supported fascism "not solely because they had been hypnotized by the rhetoric of gifted orators" but because they were "believers in the rightness of the fascist cause." The problem with Mussolini was that "[h]e never had enough confidence in the Italian people to permit them a genuine participation in fascism."

In his 2000 book about another Italian hero of his, *Machi-avelli on Modern Leadership: Why Machiavelli's Iron Rules Are as Timely and Important Today as Five Centuries Ago,* Ledeen wrote that "Change—above all violent change—is the essence of human history." He has characterized America as follows:

> Creative destruction is our middle name, both within our own society and abroad. We tear down the old order every day, from business to science, literature, art, architecture, and cinema to politics and the law. Our enemies have always hated this whirlwind of energy and creativity,* which menaces their traditions (whatever they may be) [*i.e., they're probably worth-less anyway*] and shames them for their inability to keep pace. Seeing America undo traditional societies, they fear us, for they do not wish to be undone. . . . They must attack us in order to survive, *just as we must destroy them to advance our historic mission.* [Italics added.]

*Elsewhere, Ledeen wrote that the Italian fascist movement was "*a gener-ator of energy and creativity.*"

I'm feeling pretty proud of America at this moment. Embarrassed to live on the same *planet* as Michael Ledeen—but proud to be an American.

"The purest ideologues of fascism," Laughland noted, "wanted something very similar to that which Ledeen himself wants now, namely a 'worldwide mass movement' . . . [with the peoples of the world] 'liberated' by American militarism." The right, Ledeen insists, must reclaim its "revolutionary tradition." In his 1996 book *Freedom Betrayed*, he denounced Bill Clinton as a "counter-revolutionary" and wrote, "The people yearn for the real thing—revolution." Well, perhaps soon, if the Republicans stay in power.

From theory to practice. In 1980, Ledeen joined the Reagan administration as an adviser to Secretary of State Alexander Haig, the Pentagon, and the National Security Council. Ledeen, wrote Jim Lobe in *Asia Times Online*, used that position "to boost the notion of a global terrorist conspiracy based in the Kremlin, whose KGB pulled the strings of all of the world's key terrorist groups, especially in the Middle East." Ledeen espoused the theory that it was the KGB that was behind the 1981 attempted assassination by a Turkish right-winger of POPE JOHN PAUL II, "a view he continues to expound today," even though the CIA never bought into the "Bulgarian Connection."[94]

As a consultant to National Security adviser ROBERT MCFARLANE in the mid-1980s, Ledeen used his Israeli intelligence contacts to help broker arms sales to Iran, and vouched for Iranian arms dealer MANUCHER GHORBANIFAR as "one of the most honest, educated, honorable men I have ever known." Ghorbanifar was supposed to act as go-between to obtain the release of U.S. hostages held in Beirut. He failed. He also failed four lie detector tests administered by the CIA, which had long warned that Ghorbanifar "should be regarded as an intelligence fabricator and a nuisance." It was the beginning of the IRAN-CONTRA arms-for-hostages deal. And when it was over, we'd never want another.

In 2002, Ledeen wrote of "the desperately-needed and long overdue war against Saddam Hussein." Asked in an August 2002 interview when we should invade Iraq: "Yesterday." (November 2006: "I opposed the military invasion of Iraq before it took place." As the neocons say: Go figure.) About Brent Scowcroft, the quintessential foreign policy "realist" (see NEOCONS), Ledeen wrote and quoted: "He fears that if we attack Iraq, 'I think we could have an explosion in the Middle East. It could turn the whole region into a cauldron and destroy the War on Terror.' *One can only hope that we turn the region into a cauldron, and faster, please.* If ever there were a region that richly deserved being cauldronized, it is the Middle East today." (Italics added.)

But total warriors don't just sit around *daydreaming* about cauldronizing the Middle East, do they?

The notorious forged documents purporting to prove Saddam Hussein attempted to buy yellowcake uranium in Niger—a claim notoriously repeated by the notorious George W. Bush even after the CIA had rejected it—were widely reported to have come to U.S. intelligence via SISMI, Italian army intelligence.[95] Ledeen worked for SISMI as a "risk assessment" consultant just before joining the Reagan administration in 1981, after spending several years in Rome studying Italian fascism. (Getting a job in your field right

after you graduate is a good idea.) In 1981, SISMI was implicated in an honest-to-goodness vast right-wing conspiracy
centered on a masonic lodge (I kid not) called Propaganda
Due (two), better known as P2, the discovery of which
brought down the Italian government. "Ledeen's right-wing
Italian connections—including alleged ties to [P2]—have
long been a source of speculation and intrigue," Jim Lobe
noted. So have alleged P2-CIA-**GEORGE H.W. BUSH** ties.*

In a 2005 interview, Vincent Cannistraro, former head of
counterterrorism operations at the CIA and intelligence
director at the National Security Council under Reagan, was
asked who forged the Niger yellowcake documents. "If I said
Michael Ledeen?" prompted the interviewer. "You'd be very
close," Cannistraro replied. Former CIA counterterrorism
officer Philip Giraldi, a columnist for *The American Conservative*, more than suggested the forgeries were produced
by "a couple of former CIA officers working with Ledeen."[96]

---

*A 1981 police raid on the Tuscan villa of P2's leader, LICIO GELLI—a one-time
liaison officer between Mussolini and Nazi Germany, and an informant for the
Gestapo—turned up a membership list that included the heads of all three
Italian military intelligence services as well as four cabinet ministers, forty-
four parliamentary deputies, journalists, and industrialists—including media
tycoon and future prime minister SILVIO BERLUSCONI. Police also found a plan
for a coup d'état in the event of a Communist election victory. P2 was allegedly
involved in the 1978 assassination of Italian prime minister Aldo Moro—part
of a plot to carry out terrorist acts and blame them on left-wing groups.
Former CIA agent Richard Brenneke, who was tried and acquitted in 1990 of
lying to a federal grand jury about the 1980 OCTOBER SURPRISE, claimed not
only that P2 was involved in that arms-for-hostages deal with Iran but that P2
was *created by* the CIA to run covert operations in Europe. Brenneke claimed
to have been present at an October 1980 meeting with Licio Gelli, Reagan-
Bush campaign manager and future CIA director WILLIAM CASEY, and CIA operative DONALD GREGG, who was subsequently appointed National Security
adviser to his friend, then vice president GEORGE H. W. BUSH.

"Time to Focus on Iran." Only a month into the Iraq war, Ledeen gave an address by that title, declaring "the time for diplomacy is at an end." Iraq, he said, "is just one battle in a larger war; bringing down the regime in Iran is the central act." According to one observer, Ledeen's attacks on Iran, even when Iran was assisting the United States, "helped keep the Bush administration from seeking any rapprochement with Tehran."[97]

He's also chomping at the bit to do Syria, and, no doubt, countries to be named later. Sooner, rather: In 2003, Ledeen told the BBC that "Iran, Iraq, Syria, and Saudi Arabia are the big four, and then there's Libya."

But there are only so many Middle Eastern countries; what will we do for fun when we run out? Well, in a 2003 column titled "A Theory," Ledeen speculated that France and Germany "struck a deal with radical Islam and with radical Arabs" to use "extremism and terrorism as the weapon of choice" to bring down a potential American Empire. "It sounds fanciful, to be sure," he wrote, "[but] if this is correct, we will have to pursue the war against terror far beyond the boundaries of the Middle East, into the heart of Western Europe." Also see WORLD WAR III, NEOCON YEARNING FOR.

Crime, Corruption, and Cronyism Case #23:
LIBBY, I. LEWIS

Chief of staff to DICK CHENEY and assistant to the vice president for national security affairs, 2001–2005. Leading member of the Project for the New American Century (see NEOCONS) and of the subcabal known as the "VULCANS"

—a group of foreign policy hardliners, including PAUL
WOLFOWITZ, DONALD RUMSFELD, and CONDOLEEZZA RICE,
who formed the core of GEORGE W. BUSH's national security team.

"~~MoPed~~" "Scooter" Libby's "constant presence behind
the scenes" earned him yet another nickname, "Dick
Cheney's Dick Cheney."[98] Unbearable Cheney adviser MARY
MATALIN said Libby "is to the vice president what the vice
president is to the president." So Libby controlled Cheney,
who controlled Bush? Well, well . . . Among other stag-
gering implications, that removes any possible doubt that
Libby was in on every phase of the plot to mislead America
into Iraq.

You could indeed say he'd been in on it for decades.
Libby had worked under Wolfowitz—his former Yale political science professor—in the Reagan administration State
Department and the BUSH SR. Defense Department. In
1992, the two coauthored a secret document that outlined
a radically unilateralist, nay! imperialist, defense policy
whose main elements—permanent, sole superpower status
for the United States; "preemptive" military strikes; some
kind of God-given right to Mideast oil—were later incor-
porated into the so-called BUSH DOCTRINE and saw service
in Iraq from 2003 to 2046, when the last U.S. troops were
withdrawn, the last resident of Baghdad was buried, and
Operation Iraqi Freedom was declared a success by President Bush VI.

In March 2007, Libby was convicted for perjury, obstruction of justice, and making false statements to federal investigators into "Plamegate"—the unauthorized disclosure of
the identity of CIA agent VALERIE PLAME/WILSON by a White
House seeking to cover up its prewar lies about Iraqi

WMDs.* (See **ROVE**. And BUSH-CHENEY-ROVE CRIMES, FALL
GUYS FOR.**) Four months later, Bush bought Libby's silence
by commuting his sentence, sparing "the man who knows
too much about the lies told to sell the war," as the *New
York Times'* Frank Rich put it, from thirty months in federal prison . . . in total contrast with Bush's notoriety for
denying clemency to almost all of the thousands who had
petitioned for it during his presidency and governorship.
(Some of these were murderers. None was complicit in the
wanton waste of *tens of thousands* of lives.)

But why just a commutation, which left Libby's conviction standing—why not a full pardon, as the neocon crowd
wanted? The move, wrote Rich, was "revealing of just how
worried the president is about the beans Mr. Libby could
spill about his and Dick Cheney's use of prewar intelligence." A commutation put up more roadblocks to Valerie
Plame's pending civil suit, and to House Democrats investigating the Bushite uranium hoax that led to the leak
scandal, "by keeping Mr. Libby's appeal of his conviction
alive and his Fifth Amendment rights intact. He can't testify without risking self-incrimination."

Speaking of fabrications and obscentities, Libby was
also a novelist! See **SEX PERVERTS!**

---

*Libby was the highest-ranking White House official convicted in a govern-
ment scandal since John Poindexter in IRAN-CONTRA.
**Libby's attorney alleged that administration officials sought to blame
Libby for the leak to protect Karl Rove, Associated Press stated. After the
trial, one of the jurors, a former *Washington Post* journalist, told the press
the jury believed Libby was guilty as charged but "was the fall guy" and was
"tasked by the vice president to go and talk to reporters."

LITTLE FURRY ANIMALS, and their Environmentalist Friends, and the Environment, HATRED OF

I'm no "four legs good, two legs bad" animal rights extremist; far as I'm concerned, humans have just as much right to live as animals do. In the Republican scheme of things, however, animals in the wild have no rights. They may live, *if* they don't get in the way of logging or oil drilling operations or real estate development or any other industry near and dear to the party's pockets. Otherwise, they have no more rights than a Wal-Mart clerk, Mexican fruit picker, or homosexual. Be they furred, feathered, scaled, shelled, or carapaced, in the face of GOP-abetted predation and oppression, they are all—*we* are all—furry little animals, standing together. *Ich bin ein Eisbär.**

Where did Republicans ever get the idea the earth was put here for us humans? Oh, yeah, I forgot—the Bible. "[A]nd God said unto them, Be fruitful, and multiply, and replenish the earth, and subdue it: and have dominion over the fish of the sea, and over the fowl of the air, and over every living thing that moveth upon the earth." Or as ANN COULTER put it: "God said . . . Go forth, be fruitful, multiply, and rape the planet—it's yours. That's our job: drilling, mining and stripping . . . Big gas-guzzling cars with phones and CD players and wet bars—that's the Biblical view." Well, the Bible's wrong about the dominion over the fish and the wet bars, as about so many things.** We confuse our ability

---

*I am a polar bear.
**Noah and the Ark, manna from heaven, water into wine. . . . According to some scholars, these and many other Bible stories may only be myths.

to destroy animals with the right to. Much like our right to attack other countries. I've coined a phrase for this way of thinking: "Might makes right."

Some 23 percent of all mammal species, 12 percent of the world's birds, and more than one-third of the world's amphibians are threatened with extinction.[99] Yes (God forgive me), the frogs are croaking . . . According to a 1998 survey conducted by the American Museum of Natural History, nearly 70 percent of biologists believe we are in the early stages of a human-caused mass extinction. Biologist E. O. Wilson has estimated that if current rates of human destruction of the biosphere continue, one-half of all species will be extinct within one hundred years. The present rate of species extinctions is estimated to be 100 to 1000 times the average rate throughout the history of the planet and *up to 100 times the rate during prior mass extinctions.* The main causes are believed to be (a) loss of habitat to, well, us (our highways, malls, housing tracts), and (b) Republican nastiness and stupidity.

Seriously—if you were asked to guess which party first sought to block, then to repeal the ENDANGERED SPECIES ACT (ESA), how long would you have to think about it? (I'm assuming you do not suffer from any advanced dementia.)

Goodbye, dwarf wedgemussel. You'd think Repubs would be more concerned about our plant and animal friends. Preservation can mean profits. It can also, secondarily, save human lives. A humble little purple-flowered plant called Heller's blazing star, an endangered species that grows only in northwestern North Carolina, has proved useful in treating cancer. "Species diversity has provided humankind with food, fiber, medicines, clean water, and numerous other services that many of us take for granted," a University of Nevada researcher noted. In fact, if we kill off enough species, *we* may not survive. And that would *really* be bad for business. But other creatures don't deserve to live only because they're useful to us—they just deserve to live.

In the United States, GOP-endangered mammals range from the California bighorn sheep, the jaguar, the cougar, and the wolf to the Gulf Coast beach mouse and the Little Mariana fruit bat. Other vanishing creatures that once roamed the Great Plains in vast herds include the Royal Marstonia snail, the Virginia fringed mountain snail, the dwarf wedgemussel, the turgid blossom pearlymussel, the fat pocketbook clam, the Kentucky cave shrimp (the world's only surviving cave-dwelling shrimp), and Attwater's greater prairie chicken.

The food chain, remember, begins with plants—and endangered plants far outnumber endangered animals. The Zapata bladderpod, Wheeler's peperomia, and the Ventura marsh milk-vetch may soon be but memories. In Hawaii alone, better say aloha (in the good-bye sense) to the olulu, the lo'ulu, the ma'oli'oli, the haha, the honohono, the 'awiki-wiki, and Fosberg's love grass. Try to imagine New England without the Furbish lousewort, Oregon without the Malheur wire-lettuce, or the San Diego area without the button-celery. You can't. No one can. Except Republicans. It's what they dream of.

Let's be honest. When conservationists (*never* to be confused with *conservatives*) seek to protect the snail darter or the spotted owl under the ESA, their main aim is to protect the river, forest, or mountain habitat itself. (Designating "critical habitats" in which commercial activities and development can be regulated is the ESA's chief weapon.) So don't be an asshole like RUSH LIMBAUGH and haha at efforts to protect the honohoho.

And *please* don't be like Rep. RICHARD POMBO (R-Calif.), a rancher who ran for Congress in 1992 expressly to kill or maim the ESA on behalf of agricultural and development interests. Pombo, whose family is one of California's largest real estate developers, became such a leading spokesman for what the *New York Times* called "the extreme property rights movement" that Republican leaders tapped him to head the powerful House Resources Committee.

In 2005, with the ESA up for reauthorization in Congress, the House passed a bill authored by Pombo to (uh-oh—the *other* R-word) "reform" the landmark law. Nearly six thousand scientists opposed to the Pombo bill signed a letter describing the ESA as "the cornerstone of the United States' most basic environmental protections," a "valuable, well-functioning piece of legislation" that "has served our nation well" since its enactment in 1973.

Pombo mumbo jumbo. Pombo argued that the law doesn't work because only a handful of species have ever recovered to the point where they no longer require protection. Conservationists contended that the ESA has in fact done a very good job. It saved our national bird, the bald eagle. (But not, alas, its hair.) "Since it was enacted, less than one percent of species listed under the ESA have gone extinct, while 10 percent of species waiting to be listed have been lost," a University of Washington biologist, Dr. Gordon Orians, told the Environmental News Service (ENS). The ESA's main problem, Orians said, is "that it is seriously underfunded. Species become extinct while waiting for funding."

Rep. Jay Inslee (D-Wash.) agreed: Pombo's bill is "not modernizing the Act, it is euthanizing it . . . putting it down with the guise of kindness." A lawyer for Earthjustice described the Pombo bill as "comprehensive in trying to undo what's been done over the last thirty years." It basically made protection of habitats voluntary (the Republicans' invariable approach to environmental regulations). It eliminated critical habitat protection—a change that Rep. Jim Saxton (R-N.J.) called "a drastic mistake" (and which the Bush administration supported). It limited the types of species and circumstances that qualify for protection, reduced the role of scientists, shortened the deadlines for their reviews, and restricted the methods they can use. Most critical of all, according to the ENS, "it would have set the stage for getting rid of the Endangered Species Act in 2015." The Pombo bill *so* wasn't really intended to protect species more effectively.

"The purpose of this bill," said Pombo, "is to protect my private property owners [so far, so true] and to make them willing participants in protecting species and their habitat." How? By compensating them for lost commercial value—or, putting it another way, paying them to protect endangered species on their land. (*Pay businesses to comply with the law* is another of the GOPies' favorite forms of "regulation." Which I'm all for, provided *I* will be paid to refrain from the murder and mayhem I would otherwise be committing.) According to opponents, the provision would bankrupt the endangered species program by encouraging disingenuous development plans from private property owners in search of financial windfalls. Moreover, Republicans such as former EPA chief Bill Ruckelshaus cited instances when business interests worked with environmentalists to protect a species only because the ESA gun was pointed to their heads, as it were.

Actually, all you really need to know about the Pombo bill is that Senator JAMES "Global Warming is a Hoax" INHOFE (R-Okla.) supported it.

"Appease, abuse, and assault." The Repugs had launched a major attack on the ESA just after taking over leadership of Congress in 1995. That blew up in the party's face; the public strongly supported the law. The **GEORGE W. BUSH** administration, however, gave the ESA a new lease on death. Caving like a Kentucky shrimp to real estate developers, the administration urged federal judges to rescind legal protections for some two dozen endangered species found on millions of acres. Repeat: the administration did not *lose* these cases—they *asked the judges to rule in favor of the developers*. It was part of a pattern in which the Bushies, guardians of the public interest, rushed to surrender to big business in court. (They did the same with CLEAN AIR ACT enforcement actions.) While it was at it, the administration announced it had "little confidence of prevailing" in many other lawsuits brought by developers nationwide. *That* always helps your case. The Fish and Wildlife Service, which administers the ESA, then began inserting a "disclaimer" into critical habitat designations and press releases, saying, "Designation of critical habitat provides little additional protection to species." In 2003, the agency announced it would "temporarily" stop designating critical habitats because it was running out of money. Well, critics noted, the agency hadn't bothered *requesting* additional funding from Congress. "They've engineered a budget crisis," said the director of the Center for Biological Diversity.

Before Bush, the annual rate of completion of endangered

species recovery plans had increased steadily, from the Ford administration (4 per year) through Carter (9), Reagan (30), Bush I (44), and Clinton (72). Under Bush II, that number dropped to 16.*

Said House Democratic leader Nancy Pelosi: "The Bush administration takes the same approach to the Endangered Species Act that it takes to all the other major environmental laws that protect our air, water and lands. Their approach is to appease, abuse, and assault." (Which at least answers the question, is Bush still attending his AAA meetings?)

MARIANA ISLANDS: Unregulated Sweatshops, Sex Slavery, Forced Abortions . . . The Republicans' "Shining Light"

From 1995 until around 2004, GOP activist-superlobbyist-criminal JACK ABRAMOFF and his lobbying firms were paid over $6.7 million to lobby for the Commonwealth of the Northern Mariana Islands (CNMI), a small archipelago north of Guam. Under the terms of its 1975 political union with the United States, CNMI was exempt from U.S. labor, minimum wage, and immigration laws; it could label its products "Made in USA" while banning labor unions and allowing notoriously abusive labor practices in its garment sweatshops and "sex shops."

"Human 'brokers' bring thousands there to work as sex slaves** and in cramped sweatshop garment factories where clothes (complete with 'Made in USA' tag) have been produced for all the major brands [including Ann Taylor, Liz

---

*As of September 2006.

**The CNMI has one of the world's highest female-male ratios—roughly 10:7

Claiborne, The Gap, Ralph Lauren]," the American Progress Action Fund reported. "Workers are paid barely half the U.S. minimum hourly wage . . . forced to live behind barbed wire in squalid shacks minus plumbing [often three women to a bed], work 12 hours a day, often seven days a week, without any of the legal protections U.S. workers are guaranteed . . . Thanks to Jack Abramoff, who lobbied against better worker protections, that's the way conditions stayed."[100]

Abramoff's job: thwart any congressional crackdown on the sweatshops and sex shops. I wonder *which* shops were visited by the GOP House members—including **TOM DELAY** and staffers—whom Abramoff treated to free trips to the islands, along with other gifts, to secure their help on the issue. Rep. **JOHN DOOLITTLE** (R-Calif.), who accepted $14,000 from Abramoff, claimed he saw no evil on his visit. Meanwhile, Abramoff tried to ensure that Congress heard no evil. His lobbying team helped prepare a GOP House member's statements attacking the credibility of an escaped teenage sex worker to discredit her testimony about the islands' sex slave industry.

But a *Ms.* magazine writer saw all the aforementioned evils, and others—including forced abortions—on her visit to the islands in 2006. In a 1998 U.S. Interior Department investigation, "a number of Chinese garment workers reported that if they became pregnant, they were 'forced to return to China to have an abortion or forced to have an illegal abortion' in the Marianas."[101]

Such were the conditions that DeLay and other good "Christian" Republicans—with Abramoff's, uh, encouragements—succeeded in preserving by blocking reform efforts year after year and praising the Marianas as, in DeLay's words, "a petri dish* of capitalism." At a dinner during his 1998 visit, DeLay toasted CNMI's governor thus: "I wanted to see first-hand the free-market success and the progress and reform you have made . . . You are a shining light for what is happening in the Republican Party, and you represent everything that is good about what we're trying to do in America, in leading the world in the free-market system." Scum.

McCain, John

On the Arizona senator's presidential campaign bus in March 2007, a reporter asked him if he supported U.S.-funded distribution of condoms in Africa to fight HIV transmission. What followed, the *New York Times*'s Adam Nagourney reported, was "a long series of awkward pauses, glances up to the ceiling and the image of one of Mr. McCain's aides, standing off to the back, urgently motioning his press secretary to come to Mr. McCain's side." This, mind you, is on the "Straight Talk Express," as McCain called his campaign bus trips. "The upshot was that Mr. McCain said he did not know this subject well, did not know his position on it, and relied on the advice of [Oklahoma] Senator Tom Coburn, a physician and Republican"—and serious, far-right-wing *moron*. McCain's press secretary later reported that the senator had a record of voting against using government money to finance the distribution of condoms.

What kind of moderate, what kind of *mind*, relies on the advice of a Tom Coburn? What kind of *human being* opposes the provision of condoms to save lives—in a region

*A lab dish in which fungus and other GOP scum is cultivated.

where 2 million died of AIDS in 2005 alone, leaving 12 million orphans, and where 25 million are infected with HIV—just to pander to "Christian" wackos who think sex is worse than death?

The exchange continued as follows: "What about grants for sex education in the United States? Should they include instructions about using contraceptives? Or should it be Bush's policy, which is just abstinence?" McCain: (*Long pause*) "Ahhh. I think I support the president's policy." Q: "So no contraception, no counseling on contraception. Just abstinence. Do you think contraceptives help stop the spread of HIV?" McCain: (*Long pause*) "You've stumped me." Q: "I mean, I think you'd probably agree it probably does help stop it?" McCain: "I'm not informed enough on it. Let me find out." Is there a teenager in America who doesn't know that? This is a candidate for *president*. Man, did Reagan, Bush, and Bush lower the standard . . . More "straight talk": "You know, I'm sure I've taken a position on it on the past. I have to find out what my position was. Brian, would you find out what my position is on contraception? I'm sure I'm opposed to government spending on it . . ." The reporter pressed him again on condoms and STD prevention. (*Twelve-second pause*) McCain to aide: "Get me Coburn's thing . . ." This went on for a few more moments, Nagourney reported, "until a reporter from the *Chicago Tribune* broke in and asked Mr. McCain about the weight of a pig that he saw at the Iowa State Fair last year."

Okay—the producers are motioning to me that we have space to mention how McCain . . .

▶ Enthusiastically supported Chenrumbush's illegal and immoral war in Iraq and their twenty-thousand-troop surge in 2007—which, actually, McCain didn't think was big enough. Pour *more* lives down that oilwell.

▶ Termed those who disagreed with his Iraq position "the far left," then, less than a minute later—after being asked if he considered (far-right) Senator SAM BROWN-BACK "the far left"—denied having used those words.

▶ Said in January 2007: "When I voted to support this [Iraq] war, I knew it was probably going to be long and hard and tough." McCain, September 2002: "I believe that the operation will be relatively short . . . I believe that the success will be fairly easy." *

▶ Said he was concerned that a surge in the Iraqi insurgency might "switch American public opinion the way that the Tet Offensive did" during Vietnam. "Note to McCain: more than two-thirds of Americans already oppose the war."[102]

▶ Called on soft money donors to bankroll his expected presidential campaign, despite the fact that he had personally campaigned against the use of soft money, the *Washington Post* noted. McCain called the *Post* article the "worst hit job that has ever been done in my entire political career."

The thought of McCain's famous "short fuse" being connected to America's nuclear arsenal, along with his belief in military solutions. . . . Please, put him on *any* express bus headed away from Washington, D.C.

---

*Straight-talker McCain, wrote Paul Krugman, "appears to share the Bush administration's habit of rewriting history to preserve an appearance of infallibility." Jon Stewart to McCain on Stewart's *Daily Show*: "It appears the Straight Talk Express has taken a detour through Bullshit Town!"

Asshole #25: JOHN MCCAIN, Senator (R-Ariz. 1987–); 2000 and 2008 presidential candidate. On the prospects of the Democrats taking back the Senate in the November 2006 election: "I think I'd just commit suicide." (Just another politician's promise.)

Crime, Corruption, and Cronyism Case #24, and Fourth-Worst U.S. Governor Ever: MECHAM, EVAN

Republican governor of Arizona, 1987–1988. Removed from office following conviction in his impeachment trial for obstruction of justice and misuse of government funds. After just fifteen months as governor, Mecham, a Pontiac dealer, became the first U.S. governor to face removal from office simultaneously through impeachment, a recall election, and a felony indictment. He was charged with failure to report a $350,000 "loan" to his election campaign from a local real estate developer and "loaning" $80,000 in public funds to his auto dealership. A third impeachment charge involved a death threat to a government official made by a Mecham appointee. When Mecham was informed of the threat, he reportedly instructed the state police director not to provide information on the incident to the attorney general.

A devout Mormon who taught Sunday school, the tenacious Mecham ran unsuccessfully for Arizona representative in 1952; U.S. senator in 1962; state Republican party chairman in 1963; and governor of Arizona in 1964, 1974, 1978, and 1982. His platforms called for school prayer, withdrawal from the UN, elimination of income taxes, and an end to federal involvement in education and welfare. In his successful 1986 run for governor (I mean his fifth, not his 1986th), his core support came from fellow Mormons and the ultraconservative John Birch Society. A three-way vote split helped Mecham overcome adverse publicity generated when the Arizona Automobile Dealers Association's ethics committee placed his dealership on probation for failure to respond to customer complaints.

Several days after his inauguration, Mecham fulfilled a campaign promise to cancel a paid Martin Luther King Day holiday for state employees, stating that "King doesn't deserve a holiday" and telling black community leaders, "You folks don't need another holiday. What you folks need are jobs."

Apparently working from a "Groups to Offend" checklist, Governor Mecham:

▶ Defended the use of the word "pickaninny" to describe black children.
▶ Denied he was a racist, saying, "I employ black people. I don't employ them because they are black; I employ them because they are the best people who applied for the cotton-picking job."
▶ Told a Jewish audience America is a Christian nation.
▶ Cited working women as the cause of high divorce rates.
▶ Said a group of visiting Japanese businessmen got "round eyes" after being informed of the number of golf courses in Arizona.
▶ Referred to supporters of a recall election as "a band of homosexuals and dissident Democrats." (The Mecham Recall Committee was headed by Ed Buck, a registered Republican and gay businessman. The committee obtained 388,988 petition signatures, or 45,075 more than the votes Mecham received during his election, and 172,242 more than were needed to force a recall election.)

Don't forget to insult white people. The Martin
Luther King Day cancellation led to a boycott of the state
and the cancellation of forty-five conventions worth over
$25 million to the state. In addition, several corporations
reportedly passed over Arizona as a location for new facilities. But Mecham apparently just couldn't help himself. In
response to the cancellation of the National Basketball
Association convention in Phoenix, he was quoted as saying,
"Well, the NBA I guess they forget how many white people
they get coming to watch them play."

During his fifteen months of fame, Mecham appointed or
nominated:

► A superintendent of the Arizona Department of Liquor
  Licenses and Control who was under investigation for
  murder
► A director of the Department of Revenue whose company was in arrears to the tune of $25,000 on employ-
  ment compensation payments
► A head of prison construction who had served time
  for armed robbery (would he use his inside knowledge of escape methods for good or for evil?)
► A state investigator who, as a Marine, had been court-
  martialled twice
► An education adviser who told a legislative committee, "If a student wants to say the world is flat, the
  teacher doesn't have the right to prove otherwise"
► A special assistant to the governor who was forced to
  take leave after being charged with extortion

God guided his actions, Mecham believed. A staff member
reported "that Mecham believed he had obtained office by
divine right and was thus not overly concerned about the

feelings of others."[103] (The Republicans in a nutshell—if you change "feelings" to "lives" or "well-being.") Another staffer reported hearing a conversation in Mecham's office before entering the room, only to find him alone. (Yet not alone . . .)

Mecham was *sure* his voice was heard from above. On one occasion, a senior staff member broke his leg after falling through a hung ceiling over which he'd been crawling, looking for the eavesdropping devices Mecham believed his enemies had planted. Mecham reportedly said, "Whenever I'm in my house or my office, I always have a radio on. It keeps the lasers out."[104]

After his removal from office, Mecham—the GOP being the GOP—remained active in politics for nearly a decade, serving as a delegate to the Republican National Convention and running again for governor and for the U.S. Senate. In both bids, he was foiled again by the blacks, the queers, the press, the feminists, the Japanese, and the NBA.

NEOCONS, WAR MONGERY, THE PNAC, THE BUSH DOCTRINE, and Some Deep, Dark, Dirty GOP Waters

The reality-based community . . . believe[s] that solutions emerge from your judicious study of discernible reality. That's not the way the world really works anymore. We're an empire now, and when we act, we create our own reality."

—An unnamed GEORGE W. BUSH adviser to reporter Ron Suskind, 2002, making the first known use of the term "reality-based community" (as distinct from the fantasy- and irrationality-based GOP/Bush/neocon community)

We're going to get better over time. The future of war is that these things are going to be much more of a continuum. . . . We'll get better as we do it more often."
—Assistant Secretary of Defense LAWRENCE DI RITA,
July 2003, on the brighter and "more often" tomorrow for
U.S. invasions and occupations[105]

Everyone thinks the "neocons"—neoconservatives—have had Bush foreign policy all to themselves, and therefore deserve all the credit. Not quite. On foreign policy, we continue to have three delicious flavors of Republican to choose from:

1. Old-fashioned, isolationist **"paleocons"** like PATRICK BUCHANAN and journalist ROBERT NOVAK, who tend to oppose U.S. military adventures, particularly Middle Eastern ones, particularly if they are backed by Israel and her supporters (her "amen corner," as Buchanan says). Buchanan vociferously opposed (from the *right*) the Bush-Cheney invasion of Iraq. These folks therefore find themselves at times with strange, left-wing bedfellows, male *and* female. Under the AMERICA FIRST COMMITTEE rubric, the paleocons' Republican forbears fiercely opposed U.S. entry into World War II; some expressed sympathy with Nazi Germany—and vice versa. (See **BUCHANAN**.)*

2. **"Realists,"** who eschew ideology and idealism, such as the neoconservatives' fanatical anticommunism

---

*America Firsters included business tycoons (and their scions, including a young GERALD FORD) but on the very other hand left-liberal intellectuals like Sinclair Lewis and E. E. Cummings. Their motives obviously varied, from profitable trade with Germany (see PRESCOTT BUSH, Dumbya's granddad, in **The BUSH–BATH–BIN LADEN–BCCI–TEXUS NEXUS**) to "We refuse to die in capitalist wars for resources, markets, and bragging rights."

and commitment to spreading what they call democracy (i.e., American-style free market economics) by pretty much any means necessary. Realists say, "Fuck that shit." They'll cut deals with anyone: Soviet and Chinese communists; Iraqi and Saudi dictators . . . in fact, their interests and those of Big Oil are generally in close alignment (see **O.I.L.**); hence, members of the realist establishment that has long dominated the U.S. State Department (as opposed to the Pentagon-based neocons under Bush II and **DONALD RUMSFELD**) are sometimes, with reason, disparaged by neocons as "Arabists." Leading realists types: ZBIGNIEW BRZEZINSKI (I spelled that without having to look it up); **GEORGE H. W. BUSH** (see sidebar) and his foreign policy crew, including JAMES BAKER, BRENT SCOCROFT, and COLIN POWELL; and former CESARE BORGIA adviser NICCOLÒ MACHIAVELLI.

They may advocate more limited goals and accept a balance of power among rival nations, but realists can be plenty interventionist, militaristic, mean and nasty.

Occupying Iraq in 1991 "would have incurred incalculable human and political costs. . . . The coalition would instantly have collapsed, the Arabs deserting it in anger and other allies pulling out as well. . . . [We] would have destroyed the precedent of international response to aggression we hoped to establish . . . [and] the U.S. could conceivably still be an occupying power in a bitterly hostile land."—**GEORGE H. W. BUSH** and BRENT SCOWCROFT, *A World Transformed* (1998)

After all, realism sees politics as nothing but the amoral pursuit of power. America's preeminent *realpolitiker* was Nixon-Ford secretary of state and alleged war criminal HENRY KISSINGER, who okayed or engineered Nixon's overtures to China, Indonesian dictator Suharto's invasion of East Timor, and the Chilean coup that replaced the democratically elected leftist president Salvador Allende with the more capitalist-corporate-friendly murderous dictator Augusto Pinochet. (Also see MURDEROUS DICTATORS, U.S. SUPPORT FOR, and LATIN AMERICA, ENDLESS FUCKING WITH.) Actually, Kissinger's statement that "Victory over the [Iraqi] insurgency is the only meaningful exit strategy" suggests a deficiency in morality *and* realism.

3. The dreaded, hated **neocons**.

What is a neocon? How many chromosomes do neocons have? Can neocons and humans interbreed?

The "neo" refers to the fact that most of the founding 'cons were once liberals, leftists, even Marxists. (There is a

---

"Whose life would be on my hands as the commander-in-chief because I, unilaterally, went beyond the international law . . . and said we're going to show our macho? . . . America in an Arab land—with no allies at our side. It would have been disastrous."—GEORGE H. W. BUSH, statement (obviously written, or it would have been disastrous) to Gulf War veterans, 1999

wormhole through political space that lets you go directly from the far left to the far right without having to cross the middle or exhibit such attributes as moderation, empathy, pragmatism, and common sense.) Although a few made the journey during the 1950s, for most, it was in reaction against 1960s-'70s leftism.* These founders were generally intellectuals, academics, and magazine editors like neocon "godfathers" NORMAN PODHORETZ and IRVING KRISTOL, and "godmothers" MIDGE DECTER, GERTRUDE HIMMELFARB, CHARLES KRAUTHAMMER, and DAVID HORRORWITZ.

A group of neocons is known as a *conspiracy* or, more commonly, by the Hebrew-derived word *cabal*. Neoconservatism is of course part of a much vaster and more ancient conspiracy. If you know what I mean. This is one thing on which the far left and far right can generally agree.

They look much like us, but there, the similarity ends. Neocons, Wikipedia explains, "promote an interventionist foreign policy, including preemptive military action against designated enemy nations"—i.e., any whose leader once forgot to bow before a U.S. official or that wants to control its own oil. Neoconservatives "are willing to act unilaterally when they believe it serves either American interests or a moral position to do so." Or as neocon pundit WILLIAM (ben Irving) KRISTOL said: "American power should be used not just in the defense of American interests but for the promotion of American principles." In other words, to force others to live the way "we" (U.S. right-wingers) think they should

*California governor Ronald Reagan's remark during the Vietnam War— "It's silly talking about how many years we will have to spend in the jungles of Vietnam when we could pave the whole country and put parking stripes on it and still be home by Christmas"—already displayed that neocon je ne sais quoi.

live. (Under free markets unencumbered by health, safety, and environmental rules, labor unions, corporate taxes, democratically elected leaders . . . See **O.I.L.**)

Accordingly, neocons loathe international law (except insofar as it applies to *other* countries, whose violations can be used as pretexts to attack them) and international institutions, particularly the UN. The United States of America, they feel, should not need the permission of countries like Turkmenistan or Bolivia or of any CESM's ("cheese-eating surrender monkeys"—see FRANCE, INCURABLE, OBSESSIONAL HATRED OF) in order to swat a fly like Iraq. Nor should our leaders be liable to prosecution by some fucking Belgians or flying fucking Dutchmen should we happen to be running a secret gulag system and using interrogations methods that might hurt a terrorist's feelings, *boo-hoo.* Or as RICHARD PERLE, a leading neocon Iraq hawk and Bush Pentagon adviser (that's a triple redundancy), said: "We are going to have to take the war against ["the terrorists"] often to other people's territory, and all of the norms of international order make it difficult to do that"; Bush therefore needed to make sure "we" did not "have our hands tied by an antiquated institution." (Much the same way that then White House counsel ALBERTO GONZALES referred to parts of the Geneva Convention against torture as "quaint" and "obsolete.")

Neocon hotbeds include influential right-wing think tanks like the HERITAGE FOUNDATION, the HOOVER INSTITUTION, and especially the AMERICAN ENTERPRISE INSTITUTE (AEI). Bush administration neocons who are AEI alums are simply too numerous to count using any known mathematical system.

Neocon cabalists (and just plain Kabbalists) are found in the editorial offices and boardrooms of leading conservative publications, including Norman Podhoretz's *Commentary* and William Kristol's *Weekly Standard*, and wherever Bush-Cheney-GOP views are passed off as objective, fair and balanced news and opinion. Neocon pundits' and tank-thinkers' frequent guest appearances on news and talk shows have spread the insidious neocon influence far and wide.

'Cons conned their way into the innermost recesses of the Bush White House—among them, NEOCONDOLEEZZA RICE; her protégé and successor as National Security adviser, STEPHEN HADLEY; and former Bush speechwriter/sycophant DAVID FRUM, author of the unforgivably titled book about Bush, *The Right Man*. 'Cons like I. LEWIS **"Mo-ped"** LIBBY (of PLAMEGATE patsyhood) and DAVID WURMSER (an AEI fellow also connected with Plamegate) wurmed their way into DICK CHENEY's office as aides and twisted his formerly noble and liberal mind and mouth. (Actually, quasi-oilman Cheney, already well twisted, plays both sides of the realist-neocon rivalry; see **O.I.L.**)

But the biggest, baddest cabal of the Bush era was the one that invaded and occupied first the Pentagon, then Iraq, transported on the SS *DONALD RUMSFELD*. Its ~~elders~~ members included Deputy Defense Secretary PAUL WOLFOWITZ; Defense Policy Board members RICHARD PERLE (an AEI fellow), ELIOT COHEN, and DEVON CROSS; and undersecretaries of defense DOUGLAS FEITH and DOV ZAKHEIM. They and their minyan—I mean, minions—*they* fomented the Iraq war. Those dumb *sheygetses* Bush and Rumsfeld were just ~~our~~ their puppets. Bush, "on issue after issue, has reflected the thinking of neoconservatives," Perle boasted.

This gang had in fact been pushing for "regime change" in Iraq ever since Gulf War I. (Iraq *had* to be crushed; Saddam was thumbing his nose at us!) In 1996, Perle, Feith, and Wurmser coauthored a notorious paper, for Israel's incoming Likud government, that urged Israel to break off peace initiatives and called for "removing Saddam Hussein from power in Iraq." The "Clean Break" report, as it was known, also recommended "striking Syrian military targets in Lebanon," and possibly "select targets in Syria proper."

Wurmser, as adviser to then undersecretary of state JOHN BOLTON, played a leading role in the creation of Cheney's Pentagon intelligence "boutique,"* which sought to link the Iraqi regime to al Qaeda in the months leading up to the U.S. invasion. Wurmser, who holds dual U.S.-Israeli citizenship, was questioned (along with Wolfowitz and Feith) by the FBI about the passing of classified information to the neocons' Iraqi puppet of choice, AHMAD CHALABI, and/or the America-Israel Political Action Committee (AIPAC).

"What's all this planning and thinking about postwar Iraq?" The role of the American Enterprise Institute and its alums in the Iraq debacle can hardly be overstated. But let's try.

Because it was more wholeheartedly pro-war than the Heritage Foundation, in 2003 then National Security adviser Condoleezza Rice picked AEI over Heritage to be part of a team that was to prepare a plan for postwar Iraq. (Because, said Rice, "We'll be too busy ourselves." Busy with the important part: the *destroying* part and the "Mission Accomplished" BS PR part.) But at the first meeting, AEI president CHRIS DEMUTH immediately interrupted: "Wait a minute. What's all this planning and thinking about postwar Iraq? [*Turning to Rice*:] Does the president know you're doing

---

*Also referred to as Cheney's intelligence *emporium, convenience store,* or *factory outlet.*

this? Does Karl Rove know?" End of project. "Without AEI, Rice couldn't sign on," wrote George Packer in his book *The Assassins' Gate*. "In effect," wrote Gary Kamiya, reviewing Packer's book for Salon.com, "the far-right AEI was running the White House's Iraq policy—and the AEI's war-at-all-costs imperatives drove the Pentagon, too." The neocons over at the Pentagon were "very worried about the realities of the postconflict phase being known" and perhaps slowing the rush to war, a Defense Department official told Packer, "because if you are Feith or you are Wolfowitz, your primary concern is to achieve the war.'"

The Project. The closest thing to a neocon membership card is participation in the PROJECT FOR A NEW AMERICAN CENTURY, a think tank founded in 1997 by a motley crue of desktop warriors, former Reagan and Bush I and future Bush II officials, and other right-wingers whose great fear was that the United States might forfeit its chance at a global empire. Funded by three of the largest U.S. bankrollers of right-wing causes—the Sarah Scaife Foundation, the John M. Olin Foundation, and the Bradley Foundation—the PNAC posse advocated, not to put too fine a point on it, unilateral U.S. military expansion, unchallenged global hegemony—especially in the Middle East—you know, where the oil is—and "preemption" rather than containment of rivals. A Pax Americana; easy on the pax.

Almost to a woman, the architects of the Iraq qatastrophe were PNAC members: Bush, Cheney, Rove, Rumsfeld, Wolfowitz, Zakheim, Bolton, Cambone, Cohen, Cross, Libby, Deputy Secretary of State RICHARD ARMITAGE, and ABRAM SHULSKY, former director of the OFFICE OF SPECIAL PLANS, the Pentagon unit set up by Rumsfeld and Feith to "stovepipe" to Bush Iraq "intelligence" that the CIA *wouldn't* supply.

The PNAC manifesto, a report titled *Rebuilding America's Defenses (RAD)*, issued in September 2000, became the blueprint for the "BUSH DOCTRINE" (which pundit/PNACster CHARLES KRAUTHAMMER termed "a synonym for neoconservative foreign policy"). Invoking "the cause of American political and economic power outside the U.S.," *RAD* called for repudiation of the Anti-Ballistic Missile Treaty (done in 2001) and building of a missile defense system (under way), huge military spending increases (done and done), "preemption" rather than containment of rivals, establishment of a network of "forward operating bases" to increase America's military reach, as well as "a more permanent [U.S.] role in [Persian] Gulf regional security," for which "the unresolved conflict with Iraq *provides the immediate justification*" (emphasis added). As the report made clear, PNAC saw Iraq as merely Act I, with Iran and other unruly nations awaiting *their* turns.

Conspiracy theorists seized on a line in *RAD* as evidence the Bush administration was somehow behind the SEPTEMBER 11 attacks. The "process of transformation" PNAC envisioned "is likely to be a long one, absent some catastrophic and catalyzing event—like a new Pearl Harbor." You *could* almost hear the rueful sigh.

Genotype-cide? There was more substantial conspiracist fodder in *RAD*'s calls for U.S. control of the new "international commons" of cyberspace and outer space, with eventual creation of a new military service—U.S. Space Forces. (Talk about "forward operating bases"!) Because the alternative is Sino-Russo-Franco-Iranian-Mexican control of space, and then, there goes the neighborhood. The report also advocated development of a new generation of small nuclear weapons for actual battlefield use (okayed by Congress in 2002) and stated that *"advanced forms of biological warfare that can target specific genotypes* [races or ethnic groups] may transform biological warfare from the realm of terror to a politically useful tool." (Stunned emphasis added.) That's right, "'race-specific elicitors' produced by the pathogen which are only operational in certain host genotypes"[106] do exist. Hitler sure could have used *that*.

Speaking of the devil: If you like neoconservatism with steel in its spine and a goose in its step, MICHAEL LEDEEN is your man.

NORQUIST, BUSHEVISM, THE K STREET PROJECT, and the Great Groverian Dream of a One-Party State

Conservative commentator TUCKER CARLSON once (admiringly?) described right-wing activist-strategist Grover Norquist as "a mean-spirited, humorless, dishonest little creep . . . an embarrassing anomaly, the leering, drunken uncle everyone else wishes would stay home. Norquist is repulsive, granted."

Granted. Of course. But Norquist is no anomaly. Since the mid-1990s, he has been one of the most powerful and pivotal players in Republican politics. He was House Speaker NEWT GINGRICH's top unofficial adviser, and helped draft Gingrich's CONTRACT ON AMERICA. ("On," "with" . . . whatever.) He said of the newly "elected" GEORGE W. BUSH administration, "We is them, and they is us. When I walk through the White House, I recognize as many people as when I would walk through the HERITAGE FOUNDATION" (a right wing think tank Norquist had long-standing ties to). With his old friends TOM DELAY, KARL ROVE, and JACK ABRAMOFF—who laundered payoffs through his organization—Norquist is the co-architect and co-embodiment of the CORPORATE-K STREET-GOP AXIS of CRIME, CORRUPTION AND CRONYISM (and evil) and the modern GOP's guerrilla/gorilla style of politics.

The *Wall Street Journal* described Norquist as "the V. I. Lenin of the anti-tax movement," in apparent admiration of his Bolshevik zeal, ruthlessness, and strategic wiles. Norquist was in fact said to have a portrait of Lenin prominently displayed in his home, and proudly referred to himself as a "revolutionary." As did his comrades in the mid-1990s Republican Revolution, DeLay, Gingrich, and Rove.

Norquist's base of operations is Americans for Tax Reform (ATR), "a kind of trade union for billionaires," as Greg Palast called it, founded within the Reagan White House, which then tapped Norquist to run it. ATR's chief cause is tax cuts for the superrich. With generous financial backing from right wing foundations, industries such as tobacco, gambling, and alcohol, and companies including Microsoft, Pfizer, and American Express, ATR lobbies for a flat tax rate, whereby the $40,000 per year earner pays the same rate as the $4 million earner (higher, in fact); for "tort reform" (limiting the rights of victims of corporate or medical negligence or malfeasance to sue); and against abortion, gun control, campaign finance reform, and any restrictions on corporations and wealthy individuals sheltering their assets in offshore tax havens such as the Cayman Islands. (Which, with the help of ATR's efforts in promoting skepticism about global WARMING, should soon be under water.)

"Spill their blood!" Norquist's goals are simple enough:
to (a) essentially kill the Democratic Party; and (b) eliminate
three-quarters of the federal government by 2050—from the
Internal Revenue Service (stop cheering, you idiot) to the Food
and Drug Administration. (Test your own medicines, why
don't you. Never heard of trial and error? Shoulder a little
responsibility!) He's not joking. Discussing his state-level
initiatives in 2003, Norquist told the *Denver Post*: "We are
trying to change the tones in the state capitals—and turn
them toward bitter nastiness and partisanship. Bipartisanship is another name for date rape." The "other team" (the
Dems), he added, "isn't stupid, they're evil." His most famous
remark: "My goal is . . . to get [the government] down to the
size where we can drown it in the bathtub." ("Just as soon as
he and Abramoff are done profiting from it," Tim Grieve
griped on *Salon.com*.) It may seem strange that Norquist has
pushed for drastic expansion of military spending—but
without a powerful military, how are we going to impose the
Norquist-GOP agenda on the rest of the world? How?

Norquist says he has grown more radical over the years. He
was apparently more moderate back in the early 1980s, when
he and Jack Abramoff (soon joined by **RALPH REED**) took over
the leadership of the College Republican National Committee
and "instructed organizers to memorize a speech from the
movie *Patton*, [but to] replace references to Nazis with references to Democrats. As in, 'The Democrats are the enemy.
Wade into them! Spill their blood! Shoot them in the belly!'"[107]

In the 1980s and early '90s, Norquist was a registered foreign agent of Angola, promoting U.S. support for, and
serving as an economic adviser to, Angolan rebel leader and
(I don't think I've ever written these words before) known
cannibal Jonas Savimbi, who was backed by the Heritage

Foundation, the Reagan adminstration, and South Africa's apartheid regime.

"The hidden story." From 1992 on, Norquist conducted a weekly "Wednesday Meeting" of his so-called Leave Us Alone Coalition, which included representatives of the Heritage Foundation, the National Rifle Association, the Christian Coalition, the right-wing media, and various corporate lobbies. From 2000 on, Bush and Cheney aides attended every Meeting. That's a lot of evil in one room.

Norquist helped orchestrate the Bush administration's stealth, step-wise elimination of the progressive tax system, beginning with the reduction or elimination of taxes on dividends, capital gains, estates (Norquist has equated the "death tax," which affects only the richest 2 percent of households, with the Holocaust), and all other income that is derived from *wealth* rather than *work*. The shift of the tax burden onto the middle class and working poor would culminate with the replacement of progressive taxation by a flat tax. This, said Stephen Moore of the conservative Club for Growth, is "the hidden story of what is going on under Bush." (See **GOPONOMICS AND CLASS WARFARE**.)

Norquist supported DeLay's infamous Texas congressional redistricting plan, which, although aimed at gaining GOP seats, also created solidly Democratic, largely African-American districts—Democratic ghettos. The strategy was to permanently marginalize the Dems as a minority party in both senses. Norquist, referring to conservative Democratic Rep. Charlie Stenholm, explained: "It is exactly the Stenholms of the world who will disappear . . . the moderate Democrats. They will go so that no Texan need grow up thinking that being a Democrat is acceptable behavior."

Replace "Texan" with "corporate executive or lobbyist" and you have the essence of the K STREET PROJECT, which Norquist and DeLay launched right after the 1994 GOP House takeover. With that victory, wrote conservative columnist David Brooks, they realized "[y]ou could harness the power of K Street [the Washington lobbying community] to promote [conservative] goals . . . And best of all, you could get rich while doing it!"[108]

The Project's twin purposes were:

1. To purge the lobbying community of Democrats. It was made clear that firms could not do business with, contribute to, or employ Dems if they hoped to advance their agendas in the GOP-controlled House. "We will hunt [these liberal groups] down one by one and extinguish their funding sources," Norquist vowed.

2. To put K Street's multitude of trade associations and corporate offices, its armies of lobbyists, lawyers, and public relations experts and hundreds of millions of dollars in political money, at the GOP leaders' disposal, creating one vast influence-peddling machine. Norquist and DeLay effectively converted the lobbyists into aides which they could use to pressure obstinate members of Congress on key votes.

What would the lobbyists and their industries get in return? Why, all the public programs and tax dollars the GOP could pillage and plunder on their behalf. Major programs like MEDICARE, wrote Nicholas Confessore in *Washington Monthly*, were to be turned "into a form of private political spoils." Bush's 2003 Medicare drug bill was a step toward the GOP goal of privatizing Medicare, or turning it into a milch cow for the health insurance industry, which in turn would be "vastly supportive, politically and financially, of the GOP." Similarly, Norquist helped promote Bush's SOCIAL SECURITY privatization scheme, which would divert trillions of dollars in Social Security revenues to the financial services firms that would manage millions of new private retirement accounts. In return the industry would back the Republicans' initiatives and contribute to their campaigns. Think of it as a huge scheme for looting and laundering public funds.

Thus, explained Confessore, the emerging GOP machine "could usher in a new era of one-party government in Washington. As Republicans control more and more K Street jobs, they will reap more and more K Street money, which will help them win larger and larger majorities on the Hill. The larger the Republican majority, the less reason K Street has to hire Democratic lobbyists or contribute to the campaigns of Democratic politicians, slowly starving them of the means by which to challenge GOP rule."[109]

With Abramoff behind bars, his ties to Norquist under federal investigation, and (as I write) the Democrats back in control of Congress, the GOP-K Street machine would appear to be garaged for now. The great worry, of course, is what will become of Norquist's RONALD REAGAN LEGACY PROJECT, which seeks to name "at least one notable public landmark in each state and all 3067 counties after the 40th president," to replace Alexander Hamilton's portrait with Reagan's on the $10 bill, and to add Reagan's head to Mount Rushmore. For, how much longer can the Republic endure a Reaganless Rushmore?

O.I.L. (Operation Iraqi Liberation*), THE "WAR ON TERROR," THE SAUDI-BUSHI AXIS, AND EXXON-MOBIL-REAGAN-BUSH-NORQUIST FOREIGN POLICY

> *[Our people] have been led in Iraq into a trap from which it will be hard to escape with dignity and honor. They have been tricked into it by a steady withholding of information. . . . Things have been far worse than we have been told, our administration more bloody and inefficient than the public knows. . . . We are today not far from a disaster.*
>
> —T. E. Lawrence ("of Arabia"), 1920, on the British occupation and war against insurgents in Mesopotamia (as Lawrence actually called it)
>
> *It'll take time to restore chaos and order . . . but we will."*
>
> —George W. Bush

In his January 2007 State of the Union speech, BUSH said nothing was more important than succeeding in Iraq. He may even have meant it, but, for once, sounded doubtful of success. The following day, on the other hand, CHENEY rejected the idea that there had been any failure in Iraq and claimed "enormous successes." "If [Saddam] were still there today, we'd have a terrible situation," he told CNN's Wolf Blitzer. "But *there is*," said Blitzer. "No," insisted Cheney, "there is not. There is not."

I think he really meant it. So, was Cheney the most out-of-touch person on the planet or in fact one of the most *in* touch and in the loop? Didn't the loop in fact consist of

---

*This was the White House's earlier name for the Iraq invasion, but not even the Bushies were shameless enough to keep it; once someone noticed, "Liberation" was changed to "Freedom."

Cheney's inner circle? If so, what did *he* mean by "success" in Iraq? What do he and I know that you don't?

As I write, it's been four years since Chenrumbush invaded Iraq. Insurgency and civil war grind on. Bombs kill dozens seemingly daily. Hundreds of thousands of civilians have been killed, maimed, sickened, impoverished, made homeless, and/or driven from the country. Death squads are busy. Saddam may be gone, but the torture chambers remain in business. (At least they can't be using much electric shock; Baghdad residents, who before the war received sixteen to twenty-four hours of electricity a day, were down to one or two.) The number of U.S. troops killed rises steadily. In a March 2007 ABC poll, 98 percent of Iraqi Sunnis said the U.S. invasion was wrong; 94 percent said it was okay to attack U.S. troops.

Hundreds of billions of U.S. taxpayer dollars have been wasted—enough to develop alternative energy sources; improve health care, schools, police, and fire departments; and repair crumbling bridges, water and sewer systems across the United States. Billions more will keep flowing down the same drain for years to come.

Incalculable damage has been done to U.S. international relations and to the perception of our military strength, which, after all, is the best use of military strength—the deterrent effect. Instead, by failing to secure and pacify a country the size of California, we've emboldened our enemies by demonstrating the limits of our power—while at the same time draining our military resources.

A powerful Iranian influence and a new "al Qaeda in Iraq" have been established, making Iraq a greater security threat than it was before Chenrumbum set about solving the problems of the ultraflammable Middle East by tossing a bomb into the middle of it. In January 2007—on the same day that the Iranian ambassador to Baghdad told the *New York Times* that Tehran intended to expand its influence in Iraq—the Brookings Institution released a report warning of an all-out Iraqi civil war that would kill hundreds of thousands and could erupt into a regional catastrophe. Such a conflict would disrupt world oil supplies, destabilize Jordan, Saudi Arabia, Syria, Kuwait, and even Iran, and set up a direct confrontation between Washington and Tehran (good news for NEOCONS!), where, since the invasion of Iraq, a fanatically anti-American president has come to power. President Ahmadinejad and his Shiite ally, Hezbollah leader Sayyed Nasrallah, are the two most popular men in the Muslim world. Thousands of Iranian advisers are arming and training Shia militias in Iraq. The United States and the Saudis are funding al Fatah. The Saudis are backing Iraqi Sunnis and insurgents who are fighting the Iraqi Shiites *and* U.S. forces. Meanwhile, bogged down in Iraq, we are losing Afghanistan—remember Afghanistan? Osama bin Laden's neighborhood? And what's the story with *him*—can we *really* not find a six-foot-two Arab with diseased kidneys? Is our good friend Pakistan just looking after him too well?

Well, so are Bush and Cheney: (1) They removed all U.S. military bases from Saudi Arabia—just as Osama had demanded for years. (2) They've helped achieve his other chief goal: higher prices for "Islam's" oil. (3) Pulling out of Iraq, said Cheney, "would simply validate the terrorists' strategy that says the Americans will not stay to complete the task, that we don't have the stomach for the fight." The terrorists' strategy, *Dick*, is to convince the Muslim world that we're after its oil and at war with its religion. Aided by

Bush's blundering reference to the war as a "crusade," his alleged ties to organized religion and organized oil, and his whole administration's MISSIONARY POSITION, the U.S. occupation of Iraq has validated *that* strategy.

If the crazies in Washington who led us to this pass wanted all-out war with half the Muslim world (when what was needed was police and intelligence work to root out a terrorist network), well, then, Bushie, you're doing a heckuva job. But give most of the credit to Cheney and his (former) neocon allies in the Pentagon, who drove the Iraq project from the start. (See **WOLFOWITZ** and **LIBBY**.)

"But Saddam is gone!" How do we know he wouldn't have been deposed by now anyway—without all this frightful cost—by one or another of the willing Iraqi generals with whom one Washington faction wanted to replace Saddam?

But—for a change—our leaders weren't merely after a more pro-U.S. dictator. They were after *democracy*. They told us so—right after their original pretexts (Saddam's WMDs and "symbiotic relationship" with al Qaeda) had been exposed as lies, and before they'd moved on—or back, or whatever—to the "if we don't fight them over there we'll have to fight them over here" line of **BUSHIT**. In fact, Cheney insisted to Blitzer that "there's a democracy established" in Iraq already. I regret to tell the president of vice that a civil-war-torn country ruled, or unruled, by rival militias, a foreign occupation force, assorted kleptocrats, and highly undemocratic laws locked into place by the occupiers' edicts, not by any elected representatives, is *not* a democracy. Not bothering to plan how to keep the postwar peace, despite the obvious likelihood of insurgency and civil war, suggests that (a) the Bushies were extraordinarily self-deluded—blinded by PROJECT FOR A NEW AMERICAN CENTURY

(PNAC) ideology (see **NEOCONS**) and/or their sense of infallibility; or that (b) creating a stable and democratic Iraq wasn't very high on their real list of reasons for going to war. Indeed, as we'll see, democracy was on the Bushite agenda only as a *problem* to be circumvented. (In Iraq. But, yes, at home, too.)

> *You know, one of the hardest parts of my job is to connect Iraq to the war on terror.*—George W. Bush, 2006

So what *is* this whole mess really all about? Are any clues to be found in this section's heading, or in the paintings of Leonardo da Vinci? The *New York Times*'s Bob Herbert summed up the matter thus: "What's driving this is President Bush's Manichaean view of the world and messianic vision of himself, the dangerously grandiose perception of American power held by his saber-rattling advisers, and the irresistible lure of Iraq's enormous oil reserves." Yes. Yes. Sort of.

Is the war really a DEP (disaster of epic proportions)? It depends what the aims were. It depends *for whom*. In the drive to war, a variety of agendas converged in what the *New York Times*'s Maureen Dowd called a "perfect storm of imperial schemes and ideological stratagems."

TOP TEN REASONS CHENEYBUSH INVADED IRAQ. Here at last is the definitive list.
10. *To kill off, once and for all, the "Vietnam syndrome"*—Americans' post-Nam aversion to foreign military adventures—along with all other remnants of hated 1960s–'70s progressivism, pacifism,

and touchy-feeliness. To restore America's virility. Its cojones. America had become too soft. Too flaccid. Militarily/geopolitically speaking.

9¾. *To be bad.* People mistakenly assume baddies don't know right from wrong. Some people *just want to be bad.* Many right-wingers got so sick of liberal goody-goodiness and political correctness that they in fact *got sick* with hatred of all they perceive as weak, soft, and effeminate, including peace, love, and u-understanding. (Granted, to become a Rush Limbaugh, you probably have to be pretty nasty in the first place.)

9½. *For fun.* It was only natural for the draft-evader-in-chief to buy into this macho ethos (see #9¾). Indeed, it was inconceivable that this phony cowboy yahoo president was *not* going to have himself a nice war in which to play hero and strut around carrier decks in flight suits.

9. Not because Iraq *threatened* us but because ***Saddam wasn't showing us enough respect.*** "He thinks he can jerk us around!" For this gangster egotism, a hundred thousand or more had to die.

8¾. *To avenge (and show) Dad.* "After all, this [Saddam] is the guy who tried to kill my dad," said Junior in 2002. At the same time, according to Mickey Herskowitz, ghostwriter for an aborted Bush autobiography, "Bush expressed frustration at a lifetime as an underachiever in the shadow of an accomplished father. In aggressive military action, he saw the opportunity to emerge from his father's shadow."[110] As in the ancient Greek play *George Rex.*

8½. *Closure.* An end to a dozen years of right-wing criticism of Bush *père*, his defense secretary Dick

Cheney, Joint Chiefs of Staff chairman COLIN POWELL, et al. for not driving on to Baghdad and toppling Saddam in 1991.

8. *To make Iraq into a neocon free-market utopia,* with every state-owned asset and industry (especially oil) privatized, no trade barriers, no regulations, no unions, and not too much political or press freedom to muck things up—in short, a model for other nations, especially America, to emulate.

7½.*Contracts for cronies.* So Halliburton and other well-connected companies could get their greedy hands on big, lucrative pieces of the Iraq destruction/reconstruction pie. (See **WAR PRIVATIZATION AND PROFITEERING**.)

7. *A warning to others.* Actually going to war once in a while tells the world's bad guys your threats aren't idle.

6½.*Better than any war games.* There's really no substitute for a real, honest-to-goodness war once in a while for keeping your armed forces in fighting trim, testing new weapons, and showing foreign arms buyers how well they work.

6. *To justify an insane level of military spending.* A war might necessitate big defense budget increases—but it can also work the other way around.

5. *To dominate the news and distract* from the Bushies' plutocratic, business-*über-alles*, help-the-rich/screw-the-rest domestic agenda—their war on workers' rights, women's rights, civil liberties, the environment, science, truth, and a couple of other things.

4¾.*To build Bush up into a "war leader"*—in the public's eyes and his own—with a glorious victory over the inflated bogeyman of Baghdad. To make the

Repugs look like hard-ons in their pursuit of bad guys and the Dems look like . . . well, see DEMOCRATS, PAINTING AS LACY-PANTY-WEARING GIRLY-MEN. Talking to Herskowitz (see #8¾) in 1999, Bush revealingly non-sequitured: "One of the keys to being seen as a great leader is to be seen as a commander in chief. . . . My father had all this political capital built up when he drove the Iraqis out of Kuwait and he wasted it. . . . If I have a chance to invade . . . if I had that much capital, I'm not going to waste it. I'm going to get everything passed that I want to get passed and I'm going to have a successful presidency."

4½. *To win the 2002 and 2004 elections* by means of #4¾ and #5 above.

4. *The FEAR factor:* To prolong indefinitely the so-called war on terror as a pretext for more favors for big business, curtailments of civil liberties, and illegal expansions of presidential power. The Bush team, wrote Maureen Dowd, "thinks the way to galvanize the public is with fear, by coupling Saddam to 9/11 and building him up into a Hitler who could threaten the world." "George Bush and Tony Blair are Al-Qaeda junkies," wrote Greg Palast. "They've sold us on everything from fingerprinting five-year-olds to invading Baghdad to tolerating plummeting paychecks in the USA all on the slick line that we are under attack."

3. *An alternate base for U.S. oil-regional military forces,* allowing their withdrawal from Saudi Arabia, where their presence inspired Muslim fury. This, said then deputy Defense secretary PAUL WOLFOWITZ, was an "almost unnoticed, but huge" reason for war. Interesting assumptions: the presence of U.S. forces

in Iraq (a) would *not* infuriate Muslims, and (b) was to be more or less permanent. Well, satisfying one of Osama's chief demands—getting the United States out of Saudi Arabia—*would* help keep the Islamist–al Qaeda wolves from our allies', the Saudi dictators', door.

We're down to the final two reasons and we haven't used the O word yet.* Conquest of Iraq *would* mean U.S. control of the world's second largest oil reserves. And, as author Thom Hartmann pointed out, "Transferring the money from Iraq's oil to large corporations that heavily support Republican candidates has obvious benefits to those currently in control of the White House, Senate, House, and Supreme Court."[111]

But first I have 20 questions—starting with this stupid one:

(1) Control of Iraq's reserves *for what*?

(2) If this was "blood for oil," why couldn't we just keep doing business with Saddam as we'd always been happy to do with him and other blood-soaked tyrants? Simply lifting the sanctions on Iraq would have doubled its oil exports to the United States.

(3) If the war was about filling our SUVs at good old-fashioned American prices, not these fancy European-style prices we have now, why did the price of oil more than double over the four years following the invasion?

---

*I forgot one: "To protect Israel"! Which the war in Iraq has accomplished by installing Iranian-backed Islamists within Scud range of Tel Aviv and giving Muslims a whole new reason to believe in a Zionist-U.S. plan to take over the entire Middle East.

(4) If the Bush administration wanted lower oil prices, why, instead of *releasing* oil from the Strategic Petroleum Reserve, did Bush keep adding to it right through to April 2006, a policy that added $10 a barrel to the price in 2002 alone, according to the conservative Cato Institute?

(5) Why, in April 2004, when Saudi Arabia forced OPEC to cut production to keep the price soaring, did Bush "refuse to lean on the oil cartel"[112]—despite having declared during his 2000 campaign, "The president of the United States must jawbone OPEC members to lower the price," and promising that as president he would "convince them to open up the spigot"? What happened to the spigot?

(6) Why would we *expect* Bush and Cheney to want lower oil prices? When have oilmen ever wanted lower prices?

(7) Why, despite (a) friendly Saudi aid to the U.S. economy in the form of higher oil prices, (b) those fifteen Saudi 9/11 hijackers, (c) the Saudis' refusal to turn over information about Saudi links to terrorism, (d) their support for the Taliban and (e) refusal to let U.S. planes targeting the Taliban take off from Saudi soil, (f) their spreading of an extreme form of Islam and (g) "funneling hundreds of millions of dollars to jihad groups and al Qaeda cells around the world,"[113] (h) their torpedoing of U.S. plans for an Israeli-Palestinian peace summit in February 2007, (i) their repression of Saudi women, (j) their predilection for beheading people (more than one hundred a year), and (k) their permitting no religious expression but Islam and no independent newspapers or political parties—despite all this, why were we looking at those photos of Bush and Saudi crown prince Abdullah holding hands as they strolled around the Crawford ranch in

April 2005? Just how close *were* the two men—at least one of whom wears a sort of dress? Why did the White House continue "to treat the spoiled princes of the House of Saud as bosom brothers" (Arianna Huffington) and "to fawn on this disgusting dynasty" (Christopher Hitchens)? Did Bush feel some special affinity for hereditary dynasties?

(8) Why—despite the bin Laden-connected bombing of the World Trade Center in 1993, destruction of American troop barracks in Saudi Arabia in 1996, bombing of U.S. embassies in Africa in 1998, and attack on the USS *Cole* in 2000—did the incoming Bush administration direct the CIA and Defense Intelligence Agency to "back off [on investigating] the Saudis"—including the investigation, begun by Clinton, of Pakistan's Saudi-funded atomic bomb program*—and not rescind that order until *months* after 9/11?

(9) Why did the Bushies try to halt Clinton administration efforts to tighten lax international banking laws that enabled terrorist money-laundering schemes?[114]

(10) Why, in the first days after 9/11, while other U.S. flights remained grounded, did the White House help 160 Saudis—including bin Laden family members—fly home to Saudi Arabia without first interviewing many of them, "leaving open the possibility," the *New York Times* reported, "that some departing Saudis had information relevant to the Sept. 11 investigation?" This while other Arabs around the

---

*Soon after, program director Dr. A. Q. Khan sold the blueprints and materials to Libya and North Korea. After 9/11, Bush posed arm-in-arm with Khan's personal patron and our good ally, Pakistani president Pervez Musharraf. The Saudis had funded an "Islamic bomb" program in Iraq until Saddam invaded Kuwait.

country were being rounded up and interrogated almost indiscriminately? "How could officials bypass such an elemental and routine part of an investigation during an unprecedented national-security catastrophe?"[115]

(11) Why did the White House edit out of an Osama videotape released in December 2001 footage showing a Saudi visitor assuring bin Laden of continued support by clerics on the Saudi government payroll?[116]

(12) Why did the FBI wait until May 2004 to raid the Virginia offices of World Assembly of Muslim Youth (WAMY), which distributed literature encouraging suicide attacks on Jews and Americans and praising that "compassionate young man, Osama bin Laden"—and which was founded by a nephew of Osama, funded by the Saudi royals, and in the business of recruiting jihadis?

(13) Why, in 2003, did the White House insist on editing out of the congressional report on 9/11 the 27 pages that dealt with the Saudis' role—pages that officials who'd read them said showed "that not only Saudi entities or nationals are implicated in 9/11, but the [Saudi] government, [which] not only provided significant money and aid to the suicide hijackers but also allowed potentially hundreds of millions of dollars to flow to Al Qaeda and other terrorist groups"?[117]

(14) Why did the Bush Justice Department refuse to declassify evidence concerning Washington, D.C.–based Riggs Bank, which federal regulators eventually fined $25 million for "willful, systemic" violation of anti-money-laundering laws, citing the bank's failure to monitor withdrawals of tens of millions of dollars by the Saudi embassy and large

monthly payments from the account of Saudi ambassador Prince Bandar's wife, which ended up in the accounts of two of the 9/11 hijackers? Was it only because Riggs's president, Joe Allbritton, was a longtime Bush family friend and contributor and Bush's uncle, Jonathan Bush, was CEO of the bank's investment arm?

(15) Why did the Bush administration assign twenty-one full-time treasury agents to investigate Cuban embargo violations and just four to track Osama bin Laden's money?[118]

(16) Why did the administration fight tooth and nail against an independent 9/11 commission?

(17) When Bush said, "I'd like to speak to the Iraqi people" on national television at the start of the Iraq invasion, why was his urgent message *not* "join with us," or "please don't shoot at our troops," or "I'm sorry I'm going to have to kill so many of you, but that's life," but rather, "Listen carefully to this warning. . . . *Do not destroy oil wells*"?

(18) Why did the Saudis act to lower the price of oil only twice in the past decade: once, briefly, in the months before the U.S. invasion of Iraq—their promised contribution to the war effort—and then again in the final months before the 2004 U.S. presidential election—as they'd promised the White House, according to Bob Woodward?

(19) Finally (almost), can all these questions be answered by one vast conspiracy theory which, as a bonus, yields something that eluded Einstein—a unified field theory of gravity and electromagentism? Yes, in fact! (Except for the unified field theory.)

The coziness with the Saudis is the easy part. In a sense, everyone on earth is a subject of King Abdullah, because Saudi Arabia controls OPEC (it *is* OPEC, people of oil often say) and thus the price of oil. But in the United States— home to three of the Big Five international oil companies— the oil industry has gained control of a major political party *and* occupies the White House. The last three or four Republican administrations have been lousy with oil persons and others with business connections to feudal Gulf regimes, especially the Saudis'.

And no U.S. royal family has been closer to the Saudi royals than the House of Bush. In his book *House of Bush, House of Saud*, Craig Unger traced millions "in investments and contracts that went from the Saudis over the past 20 years to companies in which the Bushes and their allies have had prominent positions—HARKEN ENERGY, HALLIBURTON, and the CARLYLE GROUP among them." (See **The BUSH–BATH–BIN LADEN–BCCI–TEXUS NEXUS**.)

"We made money and we made it fast." As every Michael Moore fan knows, on the morning of 9/11, 2001 (it was actually 9/10, but what's one day compared to a good story?), top Carlyle executives, including **GEORGE BUSH SR.**, met in Washington, D.C., with Carlyle investors, including the Saudi Binladin Group's SHAFIQ BIN LADEN, Osama's half-brother. The Carlyle Group is a $12 billion investment firm with major stakes in U.S. defense firms that equipped and trained the Saudi military. As a Carlyle senior adviser from 1998 to 2003, Bush Sr. specialized in attracting Saudi investors. "The idea of the President's father, an ex-president himself, doing business with a company [Saudi Binladin Group] under investigation by

the FBI [in connection with 9/11] is horrible," hissed Larry Klayman of Judicial Watch.

Carlyle chairman FRANK CARLUCCI had been defense secretary under Reagan and college roommate under former defense secretary DONALD RUMSFELD. Board member RICHARD DARMAN was a Reagan aide and Bush I's budget director. Carlyle board member, senior counsel, and $180 million equity owner JAMES BAKER was—despite not being Sicilian—the Bush family consiglieri; he served as Bush I's secretary of state and 1988 campaign manager, and counsel/ass-saver to the Bush 2000 campaign. In the years since 9/11, Baker has been busy defending Saudi Arabia and the Saudi defense minister against a lawsuit brought by the families of 9/11 victims over Saudi financing of al Qaeda and other terrorist groups. In 2004 a Carlyle-led consortium used Baker's name eleven times in a proposal to the government of Kuwait to collect billions owed Kuwait by Iraq (which also owed billions to the Saudis)—this while Baker served as Bush's special envoy to obtain debt *relief* for Iraq, the most debt-laden country in the world.

Carlyle-owned arms manufacturer United Defense "is making a gold-plated mint off the war in Iraq," TruthOut.org reported. "It's the best 18 months we ever had," a Carlyle exec told the *Financial Times* in November 2004. "We made money and we made it fast."

As for Dick Cheney, while he was CEO of Halliburton in the 1990s, the company partnered with the Saudi Binladin Group in a pipeline construction joint venture. As Cheney once said, "You've got to go where the oil is": Bush-Cheney foreign policy in a nutshell. (See CHENEY for other rotten regimes he did business with. Also see BECHTEL.)

Rome vs. the Persian Empire. Some things don't change. In the 1980s, wrote conspiracy theorist Greg Palast in his book *Armed Madhouse*, "America's policy was bent to this purpose: stopping the Iranians from supplanting the Saudi's control over OPEC." Here's what another conspiracy theorist said in February 2007 about Gulf War II (2003–2073): *"American forces are in Iraq to prevent the Iranian[s] from dominating the energy supplies of the industrial democracies."* That was actually conspira*tor* HENRY KISSINGER—a strong supporter of Junior's war.

When Islamist revolutionary Iran attacked Iraq in September 1980, its Shia-crats dreamed of joining Iraq (and its Islamic oil) with Iran and seizing control of OPEC. The Reagan White House decided to back Iraq when Iran appeared poised to win, threatening the whole Gulf region. In 1982, the United States removed Iraq from its list of state sponsors of terrorism, even though, according to then assistant secretary of defense Noel Koch, "No one had any doubts about [the Iraqis'] continued involvement in terrorism." The message of friendship that Donald Rumsfeld, as Reagan's special envoy, brought Saddam in 1983 was followed by military aid, including satellite maps to help Iraq target Iranians for poison gas attacks in 1988.

Saddam remained, to borrow Lyndon Johnson's phrase, *"our* bastard" until 1990, when he met with U.S. ambassador April Glaspie and asked politely whether the United States would have any objection to his "defend[ing] our claims on" Kuwait. Glaspie: "We have no opinion on your Arab-Arab conflicts . . . Secretary Baker has directed me to emphasize . . . that the Kuwait issue is not associated with America." Thinking he knows green from red, Saddam overruns Kuwait. Color blindness? Misunderstanding? Misunderestimation of

President Poppy Bush because he seemed like such a *wa gha 'bi* (moron) and *dajaaj* (wuss)? Some Machiavellian U.S. machination? At any rate, Bush sends in the troops— among other reasons, out of fear that Saddam might push on to the Saudi oil fields. The purpose of Gulf War I, said Bush I, was "to maintain our [gas-guzzling] way of life."

Another U.S. protégé during the Reagan and Bush I years was Osama bin Laden, whose largely Saudi mujahideen the CIA helped arm and train to fight the Soviets in Afghanistan, where the Russkies had seized a planned oil pipeline route. But the Russians weren't the only worry. After failing to conquer Iraq, Iran turned its attention to Afghanistan, with its Shia minority. Control of the Afghan corridor to the oil-rich Caspian basin would have made Iran the "swing" producer* and effective controller of OPEC. The United States, the Saudis, and bin Laden "could not let that happen," wrote Palast. "Here was something [they] could all agree on: No 'Shia dogs' (the Iranians, in al Qaeda terminology) were going to control a new oil caliphate from Kazakhstan to the Tigris."

So, beginning in 1993 (the year of the al-Qaeda-funded World Trade Center bombing), Pakistan, Saudi intelligence, and Osama bin Laden—with U.S. consent and/or aid— financed, armed, and trained the puritanical Sunni Taliban.** In 1996, U.S.-based Unocal sought a deal with the Taliban to

---

*Even modest changes in output by a single unruly OPEC member can effect large changes in the world's oil prices.
**The CIA's top oil expert, Robert Ebel, wrote in 2000: "[The Taliban] are part of the post-1992 U.S. strategy to maintain a high level of influence in the energy belt from the Caspian Sea to the Persian Gulf. . . . The question whether the United States actively supported the Taliban or, as one U.S. ex-official put it, merely 'winked' as Pakistan and Saudi Arabia did the actual work, is controversial and difficult to resolve."

run a pipeline through Afghanistan—a project in which Halliburton and Enron also had major interests. The pipeline project is allegedly the reason why, shortly after taking office, the Bushies slowed down FBI investigations of al Qaeda activities in Afghanistan. Indeed, the Taliban was receiving financial aid from the Bush administration up until 9/11. The Taliban's terrorism, opium production, and massive human rights violations, a Republican member of Congress observed at the time, were the sort of things international oil companies and U.S. governments learned long ago to overlook. The 2001 U.S. invasion of Afghanistan may have been aimed both at clearing out al Qaeda and securing access to the Caspian oil reserves.

Former FBI deputy director John O'Neill, the bureau's chief bin Laden hunter, explained in the summer of 2001 that the main obstacles to investigating Islamic terrorism "were U.S. oil corporate interests, and the role played by Saudi Arabia in it . . . All the answers, everything needed to dismantle Osama bin Laden's organization, can be found in Saudi Arabia."[119] In a tragic irony, O'Neill, disgusted by the Bush administration's refusal to investigate Saudi ties to al Qaeda, quit the FBI two weeks before 9/11 and became director of security at the World Trade Center, where he was killed in the attack.

But we didn't invade Saudi Arabia after 9/11—we invaded Iraq. Why?

THE TOP TWO TOP TEN REASONS:

2. *To seize Iraq's oil industry, privatize it, ramp up production, and flood the world market*, driving the price down, the Saudis to their knees, and OPEC out of business.

1. *To get control of Iraq's oil and keep it in the*

ground at all costs, to keep the price *up* and *protect* OPEC and the Saudis' control of OPEC—and, by extension, Sheik George ibn Bush's virtual seat on OPEC.

According to Palast, Bush did not have a plan to control Iraq's oil—he had two plans. Actual documents. They were based, respectively, on objectives #2 and #1 above. But #1 is, well, #1: "The war is about the oil, for certain—not to get it for our SUVs, but to prevent us from getting it."

The real Iraq war is "between two political armies arrayed across opposite banks of the Potomac":

A. The State Department-Big Oil establishment, traditionally dominated by "Arabists" and "realists": good friends with the Saudis, willing to deal with any regime, favoring stability and the status quo, and represented by such figures as George Bush Sr., his national security adviser, BRENT SCOWCROFT, James Baker, and former secretary of state COLIN POWELL (a regular tennis buddy of Saudi ambassador PRINCE BANDAR); versus:

B. The applecart- and oil-barrel-upsetting neocons, based in (but now largely ousted from) the Pentagon and in various think tanks and journals; supportive of Israel, hostile to the Saudis, and intent on changing the map, politics, and economics of the Middle East and the world; represented by **PAUL WOLFOWITZ**, RICHARD PERLE, DOUGLAS FEITH, ELLIOT ABRAMS, **"SCOOTER" LIBBY**, as well as figures who have *never* been indicted, convicted, circumcised, or investigated for conflicts of interest . . . basically, the whole PNAC crowd. (See **NEOCONS**.)

Dick Cheney, a PNAC member, ran with the Pentagon neocons, but played both sides. Junior did what Cheney and Rove told him.

When the Saudis raise the price of crude, profit-sharing agreements give the major oil companies a slice of the higher price. Naturally, the Saudis want higher prices—just not *so* high as to encourge energy conservation and alternative sources. The Saudis' vast oil and cash reserves allow them to set and enforce production quotas for every OPEC member: Any member overproduces and the Saudis open The Spigot, driving the price so low, they bankrupt the disobedient government while their own cash reserves let them ride out the slump. They've done it before—to Venezuela and the Soviet Union.

In 1927, the oil bigs jointly bought Iraq's drilling concession to seal it up and keep it off the market. An international industry policy of suppressing Iraqi oil production has been in place ever since. Since OPEC's birth in 1960, the Saudis had assigned Iraq "a humiliatingly small quota" exactly equal to that of the despised Shia of Iran, whose reserves were only half as large as Iraq's.

Plan A—the Big Oil plan for ousting Saddam—would have maintained this fine tradition. It was outlined at a confidential gathering in February 2001—seven months before 9/11—at the California home of oil industry intelligence consultant FALAH ALJIBURI, formerly Reagan's and Bush Sr.'s back-channel to Saddam. Attendees included the father of Plan A, Secretary of State COLIN POWELL (who, despite his later claims to the contrary, did not oppose the *invasion* of Iraq—only the occupation), and PAM QUANRUD of the National Security Council.

Plan A was basically a coup that would replace Saddam with a new Baathist strongman—it didn't much matter who.

"Bring him in right away," said Aljiburi, "and say that Iraq is being liberated—and everybody [else] stay in office . . . everything as is"—including the oil ministry and state oil company. The whole thing was supposed to take two or three days. Aljibury, wrote Palast, "wanted us to know that the oilmen's plan would not have left us with what we have today: a tribal, shattered, blown to hell Iraq."

As **Plan B**—the Pentagon-neocon plan—has done. It was all in a 101-page document drafted within the Pentagon in November 2001. But the plan's core idea dated back to the 1990s and was the brainchild of ARI COHEN of the Heritage Foundation.

Its real target was not Saddam but the Saudis. We would essentially do unto them as they had done in the past unto OPEC members who exceeded their quotas: We'd ramp up Iraqi oil production, flood the market, and drive down the price, leading to rampant cheating by OPEC members, which would overproduce, drive the price down further, and dissolve any semblance of OPEC order. End of Saudi control, end of Saudi wealth, end of Saudi regime. The key to the whole plan was to end the Iraqi state oil monopoly and sell off all oil assets: competing, private producers, not governable by OPEC, would maximize production.

A regime change "that 99 percent of the people of Iraq wouldn't vote for." The so-called "Economy Plan" (Plan B) outlined a complete rewrite of Iraq's laws and regulations to create a U.S. right-wingers' economic utopia: A big income tax cut for Iraq's wealthiest; elimination of taxes on business revenues and of tariff barriers to imports; the sale of Iraq's infrastructure to foreign operators; the sell-off ("privatization") of *all* state-owned companies—i.e., just about the entire Iraqi economy—but *"especially,"* the plan stressed, *"assets, concessions, leases [etc.] in the oil and supporting industries."* [Italics added.]

As Palast observed, "it was more like a corporate takeover than an invasion plan." It contained little about how to deal with insurgents and private militias, "and not a thing about elections or 'democracy.'" Instead, "there was much about securing a 'market-friendly regulatory environment.'" There were even new copyright laws protecting foreign (i.e., American) software, music, and drug companies. "This was undoubtedly history's first military assault plan appended to a program for toughening the nation's copyright laws."

This economic conquest—sorry, "liberation"—obviously could not be achieved in three days. The plan would require U.S. forces to remain in Iraq and in control for nine months to a year. (A year. . . . would the American people stand for that?)

Of course, until all the new laws were locked in and the assets looted, elections were out of the question. "They have Wolfowitz coming out saying it's going to be a democratic country," an insider reportedly said, "but we're going to do something that 99 percent of the people of Iraq wouldn't vote for." In other words, the will of the Iraqi people mattered every bit as much as that of the American people.

Why, then, *shouldn't* GROVER NORQUIST be the man to plan Iraq's economy?

"Asset sales first." Yes, who should claim credit for the Economy Plan but Norquist, "the rottweiler of the radical right"! His model, Norquist said, was Chile under AUGUSTO PINOCHET, the right-wing dictator who came to power in 1973 by murdering Chile's elected president, Salvador Allende,

and executing three thousand dissidents. "The right to trade, property rights, these are not to be determined by some democratic election," said Norquist. "Asset sales and free markets must come first." *Über alles*, baby!

The first U.S. occupation chief, General JAY GARNER, didn't agree. "It's their country . . . their oil," he said. Two weeks after taking command and promising Iraq free and fair elections within ninety days, he was canned.

Plan B was in effect, in effect, for thirteen months under Garner's successor, Viceroy PAUL BREMER III, who "had no experience on the ground in Iraq, no training to fight a guerilla insurgency, and no background in nation-building." But Bremer *had* served as managing director of Kissinger and Associates. It was, incidentally, Herr Kissinger who greenlighted the Allende assassination, saying, "These issues are too important to be left to the voters."

Bremer appointed the entire Iraqi government himself. National elections would have to wait until 2005. "U.S. forces imprisoned all those we [Iraqis] named as political leaders," Aljiburi grieved. The entire board of the Iraqi Workers Federation of Trade Unions was arrested. Bremer imposed a flat tax on corporate and individual income capped at 15 percent (a Norquistian scheme Congress had rejected for the United States; at least it didn't go completely to waste). He sold off Iraqi banks to hand-picked foreign financiers, eliminated the Islam-based prohibition on charging high interest rates, and made Iraq the world's first large economy with no tariff protection. Iraqi industry was immediately crushed under an avalanche of cheap Chinese goods. A year after liberation, Iraqi unemployment was at 60 percent.

But Bremer never privatized the oil industry. The mere rumor that he would prompted the wholesale bombing of oil facilities and pipelines by insurgents, who gained popular support. Houston, we have a problem. Houston (i.e., Big Oil) dispatched Philip Carroll, former CEO of Shell Oil USA and of Fluor Corp.—the biggest contractor in Iraq after Bechtel and Halliburton—to quietly take charge of the Iraqi oil ministry and lay down the law to Bremer, to whom he made "very clear that there was to be no privatization of Iraqi oil resources or facilities while I was involved. End of statement."[120]

I owe you a twentieth question, don't I? It's this: If Big Oil wanted Iraq's oil industry to remain unchanged—right down to its Baathist oil ministry officials and technical experts—*why did Saddam have to go*? Because he was almost literally yanking OPEC's chain. That was basically the conclusion of the Joint Task Force on Petroleum of the James A. Baker III Institute and the Council on Foreign Relations, which was set up as soon as the 2000 election was fixed (by James Baker) and the Bushies were able to hand control of the planet over to the oil industry. Saddam was jerking the oil market up and down, according to whim and political circumstance. He was off the reservation, a "destabilizing influence . . . to the flow of international markets from the Middle East," concluded the Joint Task Force report.

Big Oil wanted him gone, the neocons wanted him gone—just for different reasons. Americans got the worst of both worlds: the neocons' long war and Big Oil's high prices.

After September 11, it was often said that to fight terrorism, the West needed to wean itself from oil, to stop enriching exporters of oil and radical Islam—meaning, principally, the Saudis. Here's what Bush's war in Iraq accomplished for his people: with Iraq's pipelines in flames, the price of oil rose. The Saudis then withheld more than a billion barrels a day from the market, driving the price even

304 Oversight and Accountability, Murder of

higher. In 2004 alone, the Saudis reaped an estimated $120 billion windfall, tripling its oil revenues. The rise in prices over the first three years of the war cost Americans $305 billion and 1 million jobs. But the Big Five oil companies' profits soared from $34 billion in 2002 to $113 billion in 2005, while the value of their reserves rose by $2.3 trillion.[121] That's what Bush accomplished for his people.

Keeping Congress and the Public Out of the Government's Goddamn Business:
OVERSIGHT AND ACCOUNTABILITY, MURDER OF, and the Bush-Cheney coverup industry

> But the true threats to stability and peace are these nations that are not very transparent, that hide behind the—that don't let people in to take a look and see what they're up to. They're very kind of authoritarian regimes."
> —George W. Bush, 2001
> There is a problem with the government knowing too much about you, but the real problem is that you don't know enough about the government.
> —Rush Limbaugh

(When we're agreeing with Rush on something, you know things aren't good.) You know how eager Republicans always are to protect their industry friends from government regulation (typically by putting them in charge of overseeing themselves; see HENHOUSES, FOXES GUARDING THE). So why would GOP officials be any less eager to conceal their own dirty dealings—those thoughtful little things they and their corporate pals do for each other, sometimes just to say, "I love you"?

If you're the Bush administration, for example, *you're* not letting any congressional riffraff, Democrat or Republican, poke their noses into *your* affairs. Let them get their own country to play with. This one's yours. Not that Republican lawmakers have shown much interest in doing their constitutional duty and checking up from time to time on what their sovereign liege, King George, and his ministers are up to. (See ROYAL, I MEAN, PRESIDENTIAL, POWER, RELENTLESS, ILLEGAL EXPANSION OF.)

Is the administration, perchance, trading arms to embargoed Middle Eastern countries in return for help in winning a U.S. election? Fomenting an unnecessary war and fabricating evidence to justify it? Blocking investigations of terrorist-connnected persons, companies, and governments because they're, say, Bush-connected? Doctoring scientific reports to benefit corporate friends and contributors? These are obviously far-fetched scenarios, but without a properly functioning system of oversight, they could become less far-fetched in a hurry.

IGnorance (of corruption and waste) is bliss.
Irritatingly enough (for Bushies and GOPies), each federal agency has within it an inspector general (IG) who is charged with investigating waste, fraud, and abuse. Congress requires that presidents appoint these IGs "without regard to political affiliation" and "solely on the basis of integrity and demonstrated ability." Bush's rule was *nearly* identical: His went, "without regard to integrity and demonstrated ability, and solely on the basis of political affiliation."

In 2004, the then-GOP-controlled House Committee on Oversight and Government Reform, at the request of Democratic member (and later chairman) Henry Waxman, reviewed the forty-three IGs appointed by Presidents Bush and Clinton over the preceding twelve years. Whereas Clinton "typically appointed nonpartisan career public servants as IGs," Waxman found that Bush "has repeatedly chosen individuals with Republican political backgrounds." Although 64 percent of the IGs appointed by Bush had prior *political* experience, such as service in a Republican White House or on a Republican congressional staff, just 18 percent had prior audit experience. In contrast, 66 percent of Clinton-appointed IGs had prior audit experience, whereas 22 percent had prior political experience. Over a third of the IGs appointed by Bush previously worked in Republican White Houses. Clinton appointed *no* IGs who had worked in a Democratic White House.[122]

Waxman noted several "high-profile instances of questionable actions" by Bush administration inspectors general:

▶ The former IG of the Department of Health and Human Services (HHS), JANET REHNQUIST (daughter of former Supreme Court Chief Justice WILLIAM REHNQUIST), delayed the release of an audit critical of Florida's pension system until after the reelection of Governor JEB BUSH.

▶ Rehnquist's successor, DARA CORRIGAN, refused to investigate whether HHS Secretary **TOMMY THOMPSON** or White House officials participated in the decision to hide the true cost of Bush's Medicare drug plan from Congress until after the bill was approved.

▶ The U.S. Army IG, Lt. Gen. PAUL MIKOLASHEK, reported that the abuses at ABU GHRAIB were the result of "unauthorized actions taken by a few individuals," not the fault of senior military officials or Defense Secretary **DONALD RUMSFELD**, as *so* proved to be the case . . .

"These actions," wrote Waxman, "may be a symptom of the increasing politicization of IGs under President Bush." You think? (See ABSOLUTELY EVERYTHING, PARTISAN POLITICIZATION OF.)

Doan ask, Doan tell. Within months of taking over in 2006 as head of the General Services Administration (GSA), which procures the office space, equipment, supplies, and services used by the federal government, LURITA DOAN proposed cutting $5 million from the budget of GSA's Office of the Inspector General (OIG), whose staff investigates fraud and waste in the $56 billion per year worth of contracts awarded by the agency. IG audits had enabled GSA to recover billions from naughty* contractors. But Doan wanted to outsource some of this work to private auditors. (Who, one wonders, would audit the contracts with these auditors? *Quis custodiet ipsos custodes?* Answer me that.) Why? The IGs, Doan explained, were *terrorists.* They were "intimidating to the GSA workforce." There are, she said, "two kinds of terrorism in the U.S.: the external kind; and internally, the IGs have terrorized the Regional [GSA] Administrators." The IGs are backed by Iran, or so I understand.

Coincidentally, Doan proposed the budget cut shortly after the OIG opened an investigation into *her* attempt to sidestep federal laws and award a no-bid contract to a PR firm founded and operated by a friend.

Doan could not, however, cut the budget of the House Committee on Oversight and Government Reform** when,

---

*From *naught*, meaning *zero*; ergo, contractors who add zeros to the left of the decimal point.
**She could, I suppose, have seen to it that their paper clip shipments got lost, or something like that.

in January 2007, the committee (under new, 'Crat management) opened its own investigation into what Doan done done, including intervention on behalf of five major contractors—accounting giants KPMG, ERNST AND YOUNG, PRICEWATERHOUSECOOPERS, and BOOZ ALLEN HAMILTON, and consulting firm BEARINGPOINT INC. (see **WAR PRIVATIZATION AND PROFITEERING**)—that had allegedly ripped off GSA. The agency's debarment office was considering blacklisting these companies when Doan asked that that process be halted.

Who's ever heard of Pentagon waste? Writing in the *American Prospect* back in 2001–2002, Jason Vest called it "curious" that George Bush professed outrage at the ENRON/ARTHUR ANDERSEN scandal while shoveling unquestioned billions into the Pentagon, whose accounting practices "make Enron and Andersen look like sticklers for detail." Trillions of dollars were unaccounted for because the Pentagon's books were "in such disarray that the Defense Department can't even be effectively audited."[123]

But the Bushies wanted even *less* oversight of the Pentagon. In 2003, a bill that would have been better named the Colossal Pentagon Waste Protection Act, but was for some reason called the "Defense Transformation for the 21st Century Act," was proposed by defense secretary **DONALD RUMSFELD** and introduced in the Senate by then Armed Services Committee chairman JOHN WARNER (R-Va.). This . . . this *act* would have exempted the Department of Defense (DOD) from:

▶ Congressional review of major contracts
▶ Notification to Congress of significant cost increases in weapons programs
▶ Rules giving DOD employees union rights, annual pay

raises, whistle-blower protections, and the right to appeal disciplinary actions

▶ Environmental protection of 23 million acres of public land controlled by the Pentagon

▶ Congressional oversight of the MISSILE DEFENSE PROGRAM—thus granting the DOD's Missile Defense Agency spending authority "reaching far beyond that of any other federal agency."[124] Exempting this program from oversight was important because the damn missile-interceptor missiles didn't even work, and never would—in other words, a *hell* of a lot more money was going to have to be poured into the program. Which happened to be Rumsfeld's pet project.

Spend more now—get hired later. At the time, the Pentagon was arranging a sweetheart deal with BOEING whereby the Air Force would lease one hundred converted Boeing 767s for use as fuel-tanker aircraft for $23 billion—billions more than it would have cost to buy the planes outright. While negotiating the deal in 2002, the Air Force's number two acquisition executive, DARLEEN DRUYUN, was also negotiating jobs with Boeing for herself, her daughter, her son-in-law, and her dog-walker. (Well, all except the last.) In 2004, Druyun pleaded guilty to criminal fraud and conflict of interest charges related to the deal and to three other contracts she had given Boeing. She was sentenced to nine months in prison, fined $5,000, and ordered to perform 150 hours of community service. (Tutoring aspiring young Republican officials?) A subsequent Pentagon investigation found that at least four other contracts Druyun oversaw deviated from proper procedure "because Druyun was allowed to amass significant authority with little oversight."[125]

Yet Rumself wanted *less*. This *act* of his—this great big FY to Congress and taxpayers—died somewhere in Congress. Still. It goes to show.

Anyway, some of what Rumsfeld wanted was later accomplished at the funding end: In October 2006, Rep. JERRY LEWIS (R-Calif.), then chairman of the powerful House Appropriations committee—the valve through which all discretionary federal spending, including defense spending, passes—abruptly dismissed sixty of the committee's seventy-two investigators responsible for rooting out fraud, waste, and abuse. The sixty were contract workers "brought on to handle the extraordinary level of fraud investigations facing the panel."[126] (This *was* after all the Bush era.) "This eviscerates the investigatory function," one of the dismissees, a former FBI agent, told *Congressional Quarterly*. "There is little if any ability to do any oversight now. . . . This staff has saved billions and billions of dollars, we've turned up malfeasance and misfeasance. . . . I have no idea why the chairman would do this." (Uh, see immediately preceding sentence?)

Habeas corpse of civil liberties and rule of law. That same month, on October 17, Bush signed into law two bills further expanding his increasingly dictatorial powers, weakening oversight, and attacking Americans' constitutional liberties. The notorious MILITARY COMMISSIONS ACT OF 2006 (MCA) established procedures for secret military tribunals to try alleged "unlawful enemy combatants," and suspended the most fundamental civil liberty of all, habeas corpus—the right to challenge one's detention in court, the right not to simply be locked up indefinitely—for anyone so labeled by the Executive Branch. It could be applied to U.S. citizens as well as noncitizens. According to congressional critics and legal scholars, the MCA violated the constitutional prohibition of ex post facto laws by allowing conviction of defendants for actions that were not illegal when they were taken. And—thanks to a "compromise" negotiated by John Warner*—it gave a nine-year retroactive immunity to U.S. officials who authorized or committed acts of torture and abuse; permitted the use of statements obtained through torture in military tribunals; and authorized the president to "interpret the meaning and application" of the Geneva Convention—that is, to decide what is torture and what isn't; in other words, we accept international law when we accept it and we don't when we don't. (Why can't all statutes end with the words, "But it's up to you"?)

The other bill Bush signed that day went far less noticed. THE JOHN WARNER DEFENSE AUTHORIZATION ACT OF 2007,** named for its chief promoter, expanded the president's power to declare martial law and take charge of National Guard troops without state governor authorization, and eliminated the position of the Special Inspector General for Iraq Reconstruction. (The last thing the Bushies needed was effective monitoring of its out-of-control, corruption-ridden WAR PRIVATIZATION AND PROFITEERING.) In the usual Bushite fashion, these provisions were embedded in a $500 billion defense spending bill to make them less conspicuous *and* harder to vote against.

---

*Warner has been vilified for years by the conservative "wing" of the GOP for his "moderate" social views.
**It was to take effect in 2007.

Bush's favorite period: Recess. The Bush administration vastly increased the use of regulatory action, exempt from congressional oversight, instead of legislation, to implement far-reaching policy changes in everything from environmental, health, and safety regulations to public funding of religious groups. Repeatedly—a record-breaking 167 times in his first six years in office, twenty times in one week in August 2004 alone—Bush ignored the Senate's advise-and-consent role and used RECESS APPOINTMENTS to install, in the dark of night, as it were (and as it often *was*), officials who were too ideologically extreme or conflict-of-interest-laden to win Senate approval.

Live free or Diebold. As if having to work with Congress wasn't bad enough for the Bushies, we still had these damn *election* things every other year. Ah—but there are elections and there are "elections." Republicans are not helpless before the will of the people, you know. They *don't* just have to sit there and take it. When we try to vote them out.

The Repugs, of course would have preferred to leave election supervision in the hands of reliable Republican state officials like **KATHERINE HARRIS** and her 2004 counterpart, Ohio secretary of state KENNETH BLACKWELL. Unfortunately, the 2000 election fiasco had drawn attention to many of their favorite ELECTION THEFT techniques. The HELP AMERICA VOTE ACT (HAVA) of 2002 was supposed to fix the problems revealed in November 2000—or rather, make it appear something was being done. Under HAVA, a new Election Assistance Commission (EAC) was charged with setting standards and scrutinizing the security of voting technology. But Bush delayed appointing a commissioner for nearly a year. And with just seven full-time staffers, EAC was too underfunded to test new electronic voting computerized machines. What was advertised as "federal testing" was actually secretively conducted by three private companies paid by the (GOP-supporting) manufacturers themselves. Bottom line: Oversight of these systems remained "illusory," the California Voter Foundation said. GOP motto: If it's broke, don't fix it. And so, by November 2004 (and November 2006, and . . .), it was still broke. Or should we say, "fixed"?

Stonewall isn't just the name of a famous riot in New York City. None of this should come as a surprise to anyone old enough to remember the Bushies' largely successful effort to prevent any investigation of the pre-9/11 "intelligence failures" (i.e., the Bushies' downgrading of counterterrorism work upon taking office, the halt they put to investigations of Saudi radicals and terror financiers, and their inattention to the almost ridiculous *abundance* of intelligence warnings they received nonetheless). But those of you under age seven may not remember.

First, the White House delayed a joint investigation by the House and Senate intelligence committees. Then **DICK CHENEY** twice pressured then Senate majority leader Tom Daschle to shut it down, or at least "assure me you won't do anything." The Justice Department and CIA didn't quite cooperate. The administration opposed bipartisan congressional demands for an independent investigation.

The Bushies didn't oppose *all* oversight: When the media reported that the National Security Agency had intercepted two warnings on September 10 that something big was about to happen, the White House ordered the FBI to investigate—not the intelligence lapse, but rather, which members of Congress had leaked this information to the press.

When the White House could no longer stave off formation of a bipartisan 9/11 commission—and had failed to install as commission chairman HENRY KISSINGER, a man with no business being at the investigat*ing* end of *any* investigation—the Bushies got busy stonewalling it. They refused to release documents or to let White House officials testify, and imposed strict conditions (e.g., no written transcript) on their appearances. When those efforts began to fail, the administration launched a campaign to discredit the commissioners and witnesses. Never mind that the commission was chaired by Republican former governor Thomas Kean of New Jersey or that its R and D members were requesting the same documents and voicing more or less the same frustrations; the White House's congressional allies accused the Democrat members of slander, describing them as, in the words of Sen. MITCH MCCONNELL (R-Ky.), "the partisan gallery of liberal special interests seeking to bring down the president" and charging, like **TOM DELAY**, that the investigation "undermines the war effort [in Iraq] and endangers our troops." Yes, the commission's real purpose was to (1) embarrass Republicans and (2) endanger our troops. (And *you* thought it was to embarrass Republicans *and prevent another 9/11*.)

"Don't dare question." If the 9/11 cover-up was the father of all Bushite cover-ups, the mother was the cover-up of the administration's pre-Iraq war "intelligence failures" (see IRAQ WAR, CONSPIRACY TO MISLEAD THE COUNTRY INTO). Cheney's attempt in October 2003 to shut down the Senate Select Committee on Intelligence inquiry into prewar intelligence on Iraq enraged even some Republicans, such as committee member Chuck Hagel of Nebraska. When asked about Rumsfeld's warning that criticism of U.S. policy in Iraq might embolden terrorists (see DEMOCRATS, LIBERALS, DISSENTERS AND WAR CRITICS, TARRING OF AS TREASONOUS, AMERICA HATING, TERRORIST-LOVING, CRYPTO-FRENCH SURRENDER MONKEYS), Hagel, a Vietnam veteran, said: "I heard that same argument in Vietnam for eleven years: 'Don't dare question. Don't dare probe.'" Congress, he added, "is the only thing that stands in the way between essentially a modern-day democratic dictatorship and a president who is accountable to the people."

In November 2005, when Senate minority leader Harry Reid (D-Nev.) took to the Senate floor, demanded "on behalf of the American people that we understand why these investigations aren't being conducted," and tried to force a discussion of the question, then majority leader BILL FRIST (R-Tenn.) immediately characterized the demand for *accountability* about mere matters of war and peace as an attempt to "hijack" the Senate.

The Bush administration even managed to export its oversight practices—i.e., its culture of secrecy, evasion, subterfuge, and deceit—*to* Iraq. In the first year of occupation, instead of spending $18.4 billion appropriated by Congress, the Coalition Provisional Authority (CPA) doled out nearly all of the $20 billion in the Development Fund for Iraq—Iraqi oil money, intended to help Iraqis rebuild their own economy—to American contractors like Halliburton. (See WAR PRIVATIZATION AND PROFITEERING.) The use of Iraqi money allowed the CPA "to bypass U.S. contracting rules on competition, oversight and monitoring for controversial projects," the *Washington Post* noted. Iraq became the Bushies' laboratory for the kind of unregulated "free market" corporate welfare state they want to impose at home and throughout the world. (See **O.I.L.**)

Asshole #26:
PACKWOOD, BOB

U.S. Senator (R-Ore., 1969–1995). Accusations by at least twenty-nine women of sexual assault, harrassment, and abuse going back many years began to surface in 1992. Packwood's exquisitely assholistic "apologies": "I'm apologizing for the conduct that it was alleged that I did." And: "Am I sorry? Of course. If I did the things that they said I did." When the Senate Ethics Committee subpoenaed a daily diary Peckerwood had kept for more than twenty years, reportedly detailing his relations with almost one hundred women, Packwood made it known that the diary also described the sextracurricular activities of at least two other legislators. To make his point perfectly clear, he assured the Senate: "I have no intention of ever using it for blackmail, graymail or anything else." Portions of the diary turned over to the committee also indicated some illicit *non*sexual intercourse with lobbyists whom Packwood allegedly encouraged to offer him "financial assistance"—lobbyists with interests in legislation he could influence. Resigned in 1995 and, surprise! became a lobbyist! Senator BOB DOLE's PAC donated $10,000 to Packwood's defense.

From his infamous diary: "God, was she a good [bridge] player. I was so fascinated in watching her bid and play that I could hardly concentrate on her breasts." (Idiot. *Every* breast-watching manual warns against playing bridge at the same time. . . . Also see **SEX PERVERTS**.)

The Quintessentially Quotable
QUAYLE, DAN

Why? Because long before "I suspect hope is in the far distant future, if at all" (GEORGE W. BUSH), there was, "The question is: Are we going to go forward to tomorrow, or past to the back?"

Because as addled as GEORGE H. W. BUSH was (see IGNORANCE AND IDIOCY), and despite his sad attempts at a folksy drawl, the GOP yahoo base saw him as too Northeastern and patrician; they didn't trust him to be conservative enough; they didn't believe he had the real, rock-ribbed, heartland, bag-o'-hammers dumbness to be one of them. It was after all Reagan's act that Bush had to follow. The year was 1988, and George Bush needed Dan Quayle on his ticket.

Because a *potato* could spell *potatoes* better than the young Indiana senator.

Moreover, a Vice President Quayle made Bush impeachment-proof—a vital consideration for *any* President Bush. (See CHENEY.) As a 1988 Democratic campaign ad said, "Quayle: just a heartbeat away."

▶ Vice President Quayle, first chairman of the National Space Council, on sending humans to Mars: "Mars is essentially in the same orbit [as Earth]. . . . Mars is somewhat the same distance from the Sun,* which is very important. We have seen pictures where there are canals, we believe, and water.** If there is water, that means there is oxygen. If oxygen, that means we can breathe." (And if no oxygen, brain damage follows swiftly.)

---

*For Republican readers: Mars is around 62 million miles or 66 percent farther.
**Uh, no canals.

▶ "Welcome to President Bush, Mrs. Bush, and my fellow astronauts." And space cadets.

▶ "For NASA, space is still a high priority."

▶ "[It's] time for the human race to enter the solar system."

▶ He's stronger on terrestrial geography. In Hawaii in 1989: "Hawaii has always been a very pivotal role in the Pacific. It is in the Pacific. It is a part of the United States that is an island that is right here."

▶ Commenting on September 11, 2001: "There were no Palestinians riding on planes on September 9th."

▶ Speaking to the United Negro College Fund: "What a waste it is to lose one's mind. Or not to have a mind is being very wasteful. How true that is."

▶ Asked during the 1988 campaign about his use of his wealthy family's connections to get into the National Guard in 1969 and avoid service in Vietnam: "I do—I do—I do—I do—what any normal person would do at that age. You call home. You call home to Mother and Father and say, 'I'd like to get into the National Guard.'" (A week later: "I did not know in 1969 that I would be in this room today, I'll confess.")

▶ "We are on an irreversible trend towards more freedom and democracy—but that could change."

▶ "I have made good judgments in the past. I have made good judgments in the future."

▶ The Quayles' 1989 Christmas card: "May our nation continue to be the beakon of hope to the world."

Learn more about Quayle at the The Dan Quayle Center and Museum in Huntington, Indiana.

Dan Quayle. Because "the future *will* be better tomorrow."

Asshole #27:
REED, RALPH

GOP-Christian-right activist/lobbyist/self-described "guer-rilla fighter"; former executive director of PAT ROBERTSON's Christian Coalition; campaign adviser for segregationist Senator JESSE HELMS and for GEORGE W. BUSH; ABRAMOFF crime family member; Boy Scouts of America regional board member; and former aspiring president of the United States.

On this, and this alone, we can agree with Reed's fellow Georgian, Steve Scoggins of the far-right Georgia Heritage Council: "There was always something just a little phoney about him. Was it his sissie GQ baby-face? Or maybe the oiliness of his diction? To me he just came across as a carica-ture, too much of the exaggerated Boy Scout with a phoney 'aw-shucks' that alternated with righteous confidence." Said the Religious Freedom Coalition, which in 1998 awarded Reed its Lifetime Achievement Award for Bigotry and Villainy: "Reed, who has the aura of a choirboy who slips behind the rectory to strangle cats, is one of the most sinister figures ever to gain power on the Christian Right." Jack Abramoff—*Jack Abramoff*—told his accomplice Michael Scanlon that Reed "is a bad version of us!"

***Gandhi-basher, body-bagger* . . .** In the early 1980s, when the "Reed-Abramoff-NORQUIST triumvirate" took control of the College Republican National Committee (CRNC) and purged it of "dissidents," Reed was known as the hatchet man. Soon after, he himself was axed from the University of Georgia student newspaper for writing a column (titled "Gandhi: Ninny of the 20th Century") that allegedly plagiarized another article. Later the CRNC determined that

Reed had rigged the election of an ally to succeed him as president of the local chapter.

Reed was clearly destined for great things in the conservative movement. But first, he clearly needed help. *Spiritual* help. And behold, just a few months later, "the Holy Spirit simply demanded me to come to Jesus." The epiphany occurred in a Capitol Hill pub aptly called Bullfeathers. It is not known *how much* spirit filled Reed that night; but the next morning he went to an evangelical church and enrolled as a born-again Christian.

After that, his moral decline accelerated. As executive director of PAT ROBERTSON's Christian Coalition (CC), Reed repeatedly made comments like: "The most important strategy for evangelicals is secrecy . . . I want to be invisible. I do guerrilla warfare. I paint my face and travel at night. You don't know it's over until you're in a body bag." (Very much as Jesus would have put it.) He was widely credited with helping the GOP win control of the House in 1994. However, in 1996, the Federal Election Commission alleged that on Reed's watch, CC violated federal campaign finance laws in 1990, 1992, and 1994. The Internal Revenue Service then revoked CC's tax-exempt status (which it had enjoyed by virtue of being, you know, nonpartisan and nonpolitical). Reed, too, came under investigation for financial mischief involving CC payments to a close friend.

He resigned in 1997 and set up shop as a political consultant and lobbyist. Reed was responsible for some of 1998's most vicious and racist campaigns, such as that of the wonderfully named MITCH SKANDALAKIS for lieutenant governor of Georgia, who charged his primary opponent with desecrating Indian graves and ran ads in the general election calling the black mayor of Atlanta a "buffoon," promising to "kick Atlanta's ass," and accusing the Democratic candidate of drug abuse.*

Humping. With Abramoff's help ("Hey," Reed e-mailed him, "now that I'm done with the electoral politics, I need to start humping in corporate accounts! I'm counting on you to help me with some contacts"[127]), Reed went on to lobby for such distinguished clients as ENRON; the cable TV industry, which hired the Christian activist to fight *against* proposed federal decency standards; Chris Whittle's "educational" Channel One News, which even a conservative group complained pumps classrooms full of "commercials for junk food and sleazy movies"; the Internet gambling firm eLottery ("come on, Jesus, snake eyes!"); at least two Indian gaming tribes introduced to Reed by Abramoff; and Microsoft, which was being prosecuted for antitrust violations. Well, as Reed reminded Enron in an October 2000 memo soliciting more business, "It matters less who has the best arguments and more who gets heard—and by whom."

As a consultant to the 2000 Bush-Cheney campaign, Reed was credited with orchestrating the successful attacks on Senator **JOHN MCCAIN** in the crucial South Carolina primary, included allegations that McCain begat an illegitimate black child.

In 2001, Reed was elected state chairman of the Georgia Republican Party with the help of secret financing from the Choctaws, an Indian gaming tribe represented by Abramoff, and a large block of pro-Confederate "heritage activists," to

*Skandalakis was promptly sued for libel on the latter charge and paid $50,000 in damages. He subsequently pleaded guilty to lying to federal investigators in a public corruption investigation and was sentenced to a six-month prison term.

whom Reed promised to restore the Confederate battle emblem to the state flag. They later said he double-crossed them on the issue. (Does double-crossing scum make you more scummy or less?)

In 2002, Reed helped Republican asshole SAXBY CHAMBLISS unseat Georgia's Democratic senator Max Cleland. Chambliss, who never served in the military, ran ads that questioned the patriotism of Cleland—a decorated, triple-amputee Vietnam veteran—and juxtaposed images of him and Osama bin Laden. And in *that* year's Ralph Reed financial scandal, he was accused by Republicans of diverting state party funds to his own firm.

Too extreme and corrupt for the GOP!!! Leading Republicans opposed Reed's run for lieutenant governor of Georgia in 2006, fearing he would hurt the GOP ticket. Former Georgia House Republican leader Bob Irvin described Reed as "someone who is available for hire to influence political outcomes . . . [whose] M.O. is to tell evangelical Christians that his cause of the moment, for which he has been hired, is their religious duty . . . I resent Christianity being used simply to help Reed's business."[128] During an appearance in Georgia, Bush "pointedly ignored Reed, who attempted to get his attention by jumping up and down and waving, during his speech."[129] Endorsements from ZELL MILLER and RUDY GIULIANI, who traveled to Georgia to campaign for Reed, failed to save him from defeat in the primary, after which he indicated he would not seek elected office again. However, until he signs a sworn statement to that effect, no citizen can truly feel safe.

Marcy Reed, Ralph's mother: "I used to tell people he was going to be either president of the United States or Al Capone." He was smart to get such an early start on plan B.

RICE, CONDOLEEZZA

Upon Rice's promotion to secretary of state in November 2004, the *Washington Post* commented that "many experts consider her one of the weakest National Security Advisers in recent history." Right . . . So what was their point? Rice earned the government's highest foreign policy post (after vice president and White House deputy chief of staff [next entry]) the way all Bush-Cheney officials earned their positions: through incompetence combined with absolute loyalty to Bush and party.

Rice has been there for Bush every step of the way. She refused for as long as possible to testify before the 9/11 Commission, then served the commissioners at least fifteen serious lies[130]—indeed, almost nothing *but* lies, distortions, evasions, and selective amneezzia. To come clean would have meant confessing that Bush and Cheney and especially the National Security adviser (i.e., *she*) downplayed terrorism from their first days in office and ignored warning after increasingly urgent warning during the summer of 2001.

Rice told a large share of the lies with which the administration misled Congress and America into the black hole of Iraq (the "mushroom cloud"; the uranium story she "didn't know" was bogus; the aluminum tubes that "are only really suited for nuclear weapons programs," something she knew the government's experts had denied). Almost as many lies as she previously told about how no one could have predicted 9/11—and which she has peddled ever since to cover her beloved boss's and her own culpability.

In April 2007 (just before the fourth anniversary of "Mission Accomplished" in Iraq), Rice was making the Sunday morning talk show rounds to preempt former CIA director

324 Rice, Condoleezza

GEORGE TENET's appearance that night on *60 Minutes* to discuss his new book absolving himself while blaming Rice, Cheney, and Bush for the 9/11 and Iraq intelligence failures. On ABC, Rice claimed that back in 2002–2003—when she was evoking her image of the cloud that would mushroom if we didn't invade Iraq immediately—she never meant to imply that Saddam was an imminent threat. On CBS's *Face the Nation*, she claimed the Iraq intelligence errors were "worldwide," even though, as Frank Rich noted, "the International Atomic Energy Agency's Mohamed ElBaradei publicly stated there was 'no evidence' of an Iraqi nuclear program and even though Germany's intelligence service sent strenuous prewar warnings that the CIA's principal informant on Saddam's supposed biological weapons was a fraud."

On CNN, Rice told Wolf Blitzer she would have more to say on these issues "when I have a chance to write *my* book." Ha-ha-ha, thank you for being with us. At the time, Rice—invoking separation of powers and executive privilege Bushit (see PRESIDENTIAL POWER, ILLEGAL AND DICTATORIAL EXPANSIONS OF)—risked being held in contempt of Congress for stonewalling an investigation by House Oversight Committee chairman Henry Waxman, who had been trying to get answers from her about the uranium hoax since 2003. Thanks to Rice and her crew, Americans were dying daily in Iraq, yet she still wouldn't explain to Congress why they were really over there—which might have some bearing on whether they should stay and keep getting killed; but apparently she would be happy to tell all once she was out of office and could cash in.

When pressed by reporters in 2006 about the administration's Middle East failures, Rice got up on her doctorate and condescended, "I'm a student of history, so perhaps I have a little more patience with enormous change in the international system." According to former Rice speechwriter Adam Garfinkle, editor of the foreign-policy journal *The American Interest*, "No one in a senior position in this administration seems to have even the vaguest notion of modern Middle Eastern history." Garfinkle was referring to Rice's and Bush's favorite analogy for their project in the Middle East: post–World War II Europe. "Critics dismiss Ms. Rice's references to the Cold War as both convenient and a sign of her limited frame of reference," the *Wall Street Journal* reported in January 2007. "The challenges facing Europe in 1946, they say, bear little similarity to those of the Middle East in the 21st century." Aaron Miller, a public policy scholar at the Woodrow Wilson Center and former adviser to two Republican Secretaries of State, George Schulz and Colin Powell, said Rice's comments on the subject were so misguided, he "nearly fell off [his] chair" when he read them. Actually, "off their rocker" is a very common reaction to Bush policy.

Serious worry #1:
ROMNEY, MITT

You know, he almost escaped inclusion in this book? It was a last-minute thing. But all the while, the specter haunting Europe (and me) was a Romney presidential nomination. Because the Repugs would nominate him as the best, most "presidential"-*looking* of their lot, recognizing, of course, that in this country, looks can trump almost all other qualities. Besides looking like a president out of central casting, the former Massachusetts governor could also, on occasion, speak well, *and* had introduced a form of universal health-care coverage in his state; it might be tough for presidential candidate Romney's Democrat opponent to make health care her main campaign issue.

So here's what she *should* remind voters of: In his presidential campaign, Romney ran to the right of everyone but Sam Brownback, completely disowning his moderate-Republican record, if not his home state. He did everything he could to de-Massify his image, comparing being a conservative Republican in Massachusetts to being "a cattle rancher [ooh, how Bushy!] at a vegetarian convention"; portraying himself as the right's champion against "the Kennedy-apologist, knee-jerk Clinton supporters"; coming out, as it were, as a vehement opponent of same-sex marriage and gay adoption; and evolving miraculously into an abortion and stem-cell-research *opponent* (praise the Lord!).

All these positions were at odds with his record as governor. "In any flip-flop contest," wrote Ellen Goodman on TruthDig.com, "Romney makes [John] Kerry look like he wears Timberlands. . . . Did he lie to us then or is he lying to you now?" As a former venture capitalist, she noted, Romney was adept at "doing and saying whatever it takes." (Remember those last three words.)

Steve Crosby, dean of the McCormack Graduate School at the University of Massachusetts and an aide to two previous Republican governors, described Romney's governorship as being like "a corporate takeover. . . . He took over the asset, stripped it of what it was worth to leverage him into another asset, the presidency. There's no way to think he has any core beliefs other than leveraging to the next acquisition."[131]

By the way, Romney, curiously, chose to announce his candidacy at the Henry Ford Museum in Dearborn,

Michigan, a place the National Jewish Democratic Council (NJDC) immediately decried as a "testament to the life of . . . a notorious anti-Semite and xenophobe." Some observers, wrote Rick Perlstein in *The New Republic*, "wondered if perhaps this wasn't intentional: If you want to prove to conservatives you're no liberal, what better way than to announce on the former estate of a man who, as the NJDC also pointed out, was 'bestowed with the Grand Service Cross of the Supreme Order of the German Eagle by Adolf Hitler'?"

Perlstein's take was that, while Romney was certainly not reaching out to anti-Semites, his campaign had calculated—correctly, it turned out—that mainstream media criticism of his provocative choice of venue would win him right-wingers' knee-jerk support by demonstrating that he had "the tribal stuff right, the us-versus-them stuff." Moreover, "an alert and ambitious Republican pol like Romney" must have been aware that, fueled by anti-immigration sentiment (a button Romney pushed in his announcement speech), "*that* Ford—the xenophobe—has been making a comeback in Republican circles." In his 2006 book titled—hmm—*Whatever It Takes*, former congressman and honorable-mention asshole J. D. HAYWORTH (R-Ariz.) quoted *that* Ford as a hero. Romney, wrote Perlstein, will "prove he's part of the conservative tribe—whatever it takes."

Was Romney swinging right just to win the primaries? Probably. But: A scion of an important GOP political family (his father was Michigan governor George Romney)—a former "moderate" governor with no core beliefs who, with his eyes on the prize, swings far to the right? Been there, done that, barely survived that . . .

ROVE, KARL, and the Art of Dirty, Filthy, Anything-To-Win, Take-No-Prisoners Political Warfare

A long, wormlike thread of lawlessness, lies, corruption, and partisan fanaticism runs through four GOP administrations, connecting GOP scandals from ancient Watergate to Plamegate, Attorneygate, and the slime attacks on JOHN MCCAIN in 2000 and on John Kerry in 2004. What thread? What worm? As political analyst and recovering Republican Marshall Wittmann said: "In Bush World, all low roads lead to Rove."

Master of Machiavellian machinations. Doctor of dirty tricks. Sultan of smears. King of character assassination. Devout evangelical Christian. Actually, he talked the talk—to every right-wing Christian group in America, before every election—but, according to Christopher Hitchens, it was an open secret that Rove was not a believer. His middle name, however, is Christian; he was born on December 25; and he came to save Republican sinners from electoral defeat. He taught them to turn the other ass cheek and be *complete* asses, and to really do it unto others.

Campaign adviser to NIXON, REAGAN, PHIL GRAMM, JOHN ASHCROFT, JOHN CORNYN, and BUSHES *père et fils*. Chief political adviser to George W. Bush and, in Dumbya's words, "the architect" of his election victories; "the boy genius"; "turd blossom" (Texas-speak for a flower that grows from cow shit). Or as James Moore wrote in *Bush's Brain*, "The most powerful political consultant in American history . . . in essence, a co-president."

The "Mayberry Machiavelli," as a former Bush official called Rove, was said to reread his Machiavelli "the way the devout study their Bibles."[132] Also a fan of right-wing guru David Horowitz's book *The Art of Political War*, Rove said politics *is* "a gigantic war." What he meant is clear: war first and foremost against the Democratic Party; against liberalism in all forms; and against all remnants of moderation and bipartisanship. Under his direction, the administration's highest purpose was not to serve the country but to achieve permanent Republican rule. He was indeed not just the brain but the heart and soul of the Bush administration, which, following a long illness, died the day Rove announced his resignation in August 2007.

"Somehow, when Rove's candidate needs a boost, an opponent is attacked with a whisper campaign; rumors and innuendos emerge that have nothing to do with the issues . . . yet have a strong, visceral influence on voters," wrote one blogger.[133] Rove, wrote the *New York Times*'s Paul Krugman, "understood, long before the rest of us that . . . there are few, if any, limits to what conservative politicians can get away with [and that] attacks don't have to be true, or even plausible," to get results. They just have to get a lot of media play.

"All politicians operate within an Orwellian nimbus where words don't mean what they normally mean," wrote Neal Gabler in the *Los Angeles Times*, "but Rovism posits that there is no objective, verifiable reality at all. Reality is what you say it is."

As far as we know, Rove's dirty tricks career began in 1970, when he used a false identity to gain entry to Illinois Democrat Alan Dixon's campaign offices, stole some letterhead stationery, and sent out one thousand fake rally fliers promising "free beer, free food, girls and a good time for nothing." Eight months later, he was hired as executive director of the College Republican National Committee.

Speaking of breaking into Democrats' offices, in 1973, the *Washington Post* reported that Rove, a protégé of Watergate conspirator Donald Segretti, toured the country during the 1972 presidential campaign, training young Republicans in "dirty tricks" while boasting about the Dixon caper.

While working on the 1980 vice-presidential campaign of George Bush Sr., Rove introduced the candidate to Rove's mentor LEE ATWATER—"the Darth Vader of the Republican party"; "the very definition of smashmouth politics, in which every effort is made to destroy the reputations, careers and lives of political opponents"; "the guy who went negative for the sheer joy of it," in the words of admirers. In 1988, Atwater would put Poppy Bush in the White House in one of the dirtiest campaigns in U.S. history.

While running the 1986 Texas gubernatorial campaign of Republican Bill Clements, Rove claimed his office had been bugged by the Democrats. Police and FBI investigators suspected Rove of planting the bug himself. In 1992, Rove was fired from Poppy Bush's presidential campaign after he leaked a story to right-wing columnist ROBERT NOVAK about Bush's dissatisfaction with his chief fundraiser (who, Novak wrote, had "shoved [Rove] aside"). In 2003, Rove would reveal to Novak the identity of CIA operative VALERIE PLAME, in retaliation against her husband, former ambassador JOSEPH WILSON, for contradicting Bushite claims that Saddam Hussein tried to purchase nuclear weapons fuel in Niger. Rove then told MSNBC's Chris Matthews that Wilson's wife was "fair game." In 1994, a campaign Rove ran for a Republican candidate for the Alabama state supreme court featured charges of financial improprieties against the Democratic incumbent and a whisper campaign that he was a pedophile. No wonder

Nixon White House counsel John Dean said that Rove makes Nixon aide Charles Colson—who once said he would run over his grandmother to get Nixon reelected— "look like a novice."

1994 was also the year Rove directed George W. Bush's first Texas gubernatorial campaign. Rove made "tort reform"—i.e., making it harder for victims to sue corporations like, say, Rove's lobbying client PHILIP MORRIS—the campaign's centerpiece. As Rove boasted, "business groups flocked to us." Next a rumor began that incumbent Democratic governor Ann Richards might be a lesbian. A Bush campaign "push poll" asked voters whether they would be "more or less likely to vote for Governor Richards if [they] knew her staff is dominated by lesbians." A regional Bush campaign chairman criticized Richards for "appointing avowed homosexual activists" to state jobs.

Six years later, during Bush's crucial South Carolina primary campaign against John McCain for the 2000 Republican presidential nomination, Rove was allegedly behind another push poll that asked potential voters, "Would you be more likely or less likely to vote for John McCain for president if you knew he had fathered an illegitimate black child?" The mother, it was rumored, was a prostitute. Actually, McCain had adopted his dark-skinned Bangladeshi daughter from Mother Teresa. Not a prostitute in any real sense. The Bush campaign also attacked McCain's military service and questioned his mental stability. (The crackpot calling the kettle cracked. Or something.) In December 2000, Rove masterminded the emergency airlift of Republican politicians, supporters, and thugs to Florida to assist the Bush campaign by intimidating local election officials during the recount fight.

In January 2002, Bush promised he had "no ambition what-
soever to use the war [on terrorism] as a political issue." It
was about to become his *only* issue. That month, Rove
advised GOP operatives to tell the American people they
could "trust the Republican Party to do a better job of . . .
protecting America." In a talk on White House strategy for the
2002 midterm elections, Rove said the focus on Iraq was key
to maintaining "a positive issue environment." Rove chaired
meetings of the secretive White House Iraq Group, whose purpose was to devise ways of deceiving the country about the
alleged threat from Iraq and need for war.

In June 2005, Senator Richard Durbin (D-Ill.) read on the
Senate floor from a report about torture at Guantánamo, and
said, "If I read this to you and did not tell you that it was an
FBI agent describing what Americans had done to prisoners
in their control, you would most certainly believe this must
have been done by Nazis, Soviets in their gulags, or some mad
regime—Pol Pot or others—that had no concern for human
beings." Rove responded*: "Al Jazeera now broadcasts the
words of Senator Durbin to the Mideast, certainly putting our
troops in greater danger. No more needs to be said about the
motives of liberals." Got that? The motives of liberals are *to*

---

*Fellow asshole **NEWT GINGRICH** piled on: What Durbin did was "to
endanger young Americans and defame America." For the other ninety-
nine senators not to denounce him—excuse me, "to defend America and
to defend the reputation of our young men and women in uniform"—
would be "the shame of the Senate." Actually, as is quite well known, the
shame of the Senate is its failure to impeach Bush and Cheney.) Fox News
host CHRIS WALLACE said the abuses described by the FBI agent "would
be considered a day at the beach in the Soviet gulag . . . I think they
would have been very happy to be allowed to defecate on themselves."
(That indeed is freedom. In America, our Republican leaders insist on
doing it for us.)

put our troops in danger. The strategy of conservatives is to denounce those who denounce those who, on false pretenses, *sent* our troops to die in an unnecessary and illegal war *and* okayed the kind of barbarism Durbin described. (*Damn*—why do Repugs always have the simpler message?)

Asshole #28, Karl C. Rove, In His Own Inspiring Words

▶ George W. Bush is "one of the most intellectually gifted presidents we've had."

▶ On Bush's call for a constitutional amendment banning gay marriage: "We should not carve out special privileges for people on the basis of sexual orientation." In GOPspeak, *equal* treatment becomes "special privileges."

▶ "Conservatives saw the savagery of 9/11 and prepared for war; liberals . . . wanted to prepare indictments and offer therapy and understanding for our attackers." What Rove and his crew *actually* saw in 9/11 was a domestic political opportunity; and what every Democratic senator voted for was military force against al Qaeda. (The White House called Rove's comments "very accurate" and said the calls for an apology were "somewhat puzzling.")

▶ At the March 2007 Radio and Television Correspondents' Association dinner, Rove performed a mock hip-hop song-and-dance routine in which he rapped: "Listen up suckas, don't get the jitters, but MC Rove tears the heads off of critters." When asked if he has any hobbies, Rove, demonstrating the motion with his hands, said he enjoys "ripping the tops off of animals." Another reported hobby is hunting doves. Symbols of peace.

Asshole #29:
RUMSFELD, DONALD

Former Bush defense secretary (2001–2006). Got so excited on September 11, 2001, he was ready to attack Iraq that afternoon. Why Iraq, which had nothing to do with the attacks? Why not Afghanistan, where al Qaeda's training camps were? Because, said Donald Duck–Reality Rumsfeld, "there are no good targets in Afghanistan."

What a Kant: "We know there are known knowns: there are things we know we know. We also know there are known unknowns: that is to say we know there are things we know we don't know. But there are also unknown unknowns—the ones we don't know we don't know." *I* know that I know that I know he's an asshole.

SEX PERVERTS: Hypocritical, Bible-Thumping, Gay-Bashing, Purity and Family-Values Preaching, Philandering, Child-Molesting Republican Whores

"Porn star Mary Carey, meanwhile, was eager for her chance for a one-on-one with [President George W.] Bush this week. For the second year in a row, the former California [GOP] gubernatorial candidate accepted an invitation to press the flesh with GOP bigwigs at a NRCC [National Republican Congressional Committee] fundraiser hosted by Bush. 'I actually get hit on more in Washington D.C. by Republicans that are drunk than I do by porno fans in Vegas,' said Carey, whose film credits

include such productions as Dual Airbags* *and* Some Like
'Em Big."[134]

Why most Republican politicians are sex perverts remains a
mystery, but it seems to have something to do with the
prevalence of fundamentalist religion and moral sanctimony
amongst them. One unconsciously rebels against one's own
moral and religious strictures, or breaks under the strain of
having to be so, uh, upright. Or the pious *pose* is just that—
and what kind of morals can you expect to find behind
phony piety? In addition, most Republican politicians are
already whores—for business special interests—so, like,
WTF . . . go the whole nine yards toward eternal damnation.

Yes, the Democrats have their perverts too. But *this*
many? I don't think so. Besides, theirs are just practicing
what, as any Republican will tell you, Dems believe in and
preach: promiscuity, adultery, homosexuality, bestiality,
environmental protection, economic fairness . . . *Their*
affairs therefore lack that special ingredient, hypocrisy,
which raises a mere peccadillo to a true scandal.

Think it only started with Larry Craig or Mark Foley?
Uh-uh.

▶ Rep. **Robert Bauman** (R-Md., 1973–1981). Devout
Catholic; founding member of several conservative
activist groups; publicly denounced homosexuality;
received a perfect 100 on the Christian Voice Morality
Rating. Voted out of office a month after his arrest for
"oral sodomy" and attempting to solicit sex from a
sixteen-year-old male prostitute. Renominated by the

*More hypocrisy. The introduction of mandatory airbags in the 1980s was
opposed by the Reagan administration and most Republicans, who naturally sided with the auto industry.

ever-forgiving (of Republicans) GOP in 1982, but withdrew from the race. Later came out as gay. Became legal counsel for the Sovereign Society, a group dedicated to the avoidance of taxes through offshore accounts. A man's gotta have a vice!

▶ Sen. **Larry Craig** (R-Idaho, 1991–2007). Among the most rabid Bill Clinton hounders during the Lewinsky imbroglio. Called Clinton "a bad boy, a naughty boy . . . a nasty, bad, naughty boy." (An attack from which Clinton may *never* recover.) Supported a constitutional amendment banning same-sex marriage. Opposed extending the federal definition of hate crimes to cover sexual orientation. Arrested in June 2007 for "lewd conduct" in a Minneapolis airport men's room for allegedly making advances to a (male) undercover officer. Pleaded guilty in August to disorderly conduct and resigned from the Senate.

▶ Rep. **Dan "Slamming Dan" Crane** (R-Ill., 1979–1985). Accused in 1983 of having a consensual sexual relationship with a seventeen-year-old female congressional page; censured by the House. A dentist before and after his political career. No drilling, filling, or cavity jokes, *please*. Origin of his nickname: Probably best left to the imagination.

▶ **Brian Doyle**, deputy press secretary, Department of Homeland Security, until arrested in April 2006 and charged with seven counts of using a computer to seduce a child and sixteen counts of transmitting harmful materials to a minor. He had initiated a sexually explicit online conversation with a Polk County, Florida, detective who was posing as a fourteen-year-old girl. Doyle sent her hard-core porn films, asked for naked pictures of her, and offered to send naked pictures of himself. Sentenced to five years ~~of masturbation~~ in prison and ten years of probation, and required to register as a sex offender.

▶ **Frank Figueroa**, head of the Tampa, Florida, office of U.S. Immigration and Customs Enforcement until 2005. Previously led Operation Predator, a federal program that deports foreigners convicted of sex crimes. Arrested for exposing himself and masturbating in front of a sixteen-year-old girl at a mall. Pleaded no contest in ~~food~~ court.

▶ Rep. **Mark Foley** (R-Fla., 1995–2006; R-closet, ca. 1969–2006). One of the House's leading fighters against child pornography. Served as chairman of the House Caucus on Missing and Exploited Children. Introduced a 2002 bill to outlaw Web sites featuring sexually suggestive images of preteens. Got a tougher federal sex offender law passed. Was the GOP front-runner for a vacant Florida Senate seat in 2004 until rumors surfaced that he was gay or bisexual. The unmarried Foley called the questions about his sexuality "revolting and unforgivable."

Resigned in September 2006 and came under FBI investigation for allegedly sending sexually explicit e-mails and, worse, instant messages, to young men who had formerly served as congressional pages, two of whom said they had had sex with him. Others alleged inappropriate conduct by Foley dating back at least ten years. Authorities said Foley might be prosecuted for the pornograms under some of the laws he helped enact. (Should have kept his petard in his pants.) His attorney told reporters Foley was gay, had an alcohol problem, had written the e-mails while drunk (the modern devil-made-me-do-it defense), and as a teen had been sexually abused by a clergyman. A Florida newspaper reported that a Catholic priest had confessed to an intimate two-year relationship with altar boy Foley. A *Catholic priest* . . . can you believe it?

More important for our GOP-trashing purposes, House Speaker **DENNIS HASTERT'S** three top aides appear to have known of Foley's hanky-panky for years and just stood around in a circle jerk, so to speak, watching while he continued to prey on boys. Hastert was, after all, only the most senior Republican in Congress, so *he* couldn't possibly have known about Foley.*

▶ **James Guckert/"Jeff Gannon."** For nearly two years, until February 2005, Jeff Gannon was "Washington Bureau Chief" for the right-wing Web site *Talon News* and a fully credentialed White House correspondent whom Bush called on for questions with a regularity the *Washington Post* or *New York Times* might envy. (Not too surprising: they were questions like, "How are you [Bush] going to work with people [Senate Democrats] who seem to have divorced themselves from reality?") Only, Gannon turns out not to be Gannon but Guckert, working under an alias for a fake news organization. Guckert had "an apparently promising career as an X-rated $200-per-hour [gay] 'escort'" which he advertised by posing nude on his Web sites, such as Hotmilitarystud.com, where he described

---

*Speaking of immorality: One of those three Hastert aides—his counsel and top aide on ethics matters—had previously helped engineer the effort to save House Majority Leader TOM DELAY by changing GOP ethics rules to allow an indicted lawmaker to remain in the leadership.

himself as "military, muscular, masculine and discrete [*sic*] . . . Position: Top."[135] *Talon* and GOPUSA, another site that used Gannon's stuff, were owned by BOBBY EBERLE, a wealthy Texas GOP donor, delegate to the 2000 Republican National Convention, and member of Texas Christian Coalition and Texas Right to Life.

"Gannon" was real enough for RUSH LIMBAUGH and SEAN HANNITY to cite repeatedly as a source. Fox News's Hannity described Gannon as "a terrific Washington bureau chief and White House correspondent" and invited him onto his show. The *New York Times*'s Maureen Dowd, who was denied a White House pass after Bush took over, was mystified by how "someone with an alias, a tax evasion problem and [nude] Internet pictures . . . is credentialed to cover a White House that won a second term by mining homophobia and preaching family values." How did Guckert/Gannon get through the normally months-long Secret Service background check and retain his pass for two years? "If Gannon was using an alias," wrote former Reagan and Bush I official Bruce Bartlett, "the White House staff had to be involved in maintaining his cover."[136] (In return for which of his various services?)

► Rep. **NEWT GINGRICH** (R-Ga.). House Speaker, 1995–1999. Extramarital affair with a congressional staffer twenty-three years his junior from 1993 to 1999, during which time he led the Republican jihad for the impeachment of Bill Clinton over the Lewinsky peckerdillo.

► **David Hager**, Bush-appointed chair of the Food and Drug Administration's Reproductive Health Drugs Advisory Committee; born-again Christian; fanatical

ABORTION AND BIRTH-CONTROL opponent. An ob/gyn
who prescribed prayer as the cure for many female
health problems and authored *As Jesus Cared for
Women*. His ex-wife of thirty-two years, Linda Davis,
claimed he repeatedly sodomized her between 1995
and their divorce in 2002. It was "painful, invasive,
totally nonconsensual," she told *The Nation* in 2005.
(Hager—an ob/gyn—claimed the *rear* entry was *acci-
dental*!) She alleged that he pressured her to let him
videotape and photograph them having sex, and said
she let him pay her for oral and anal sex because he
kept such a tight grip on the family purse strings.[137]

▶ Rev. **Ted Haggard**, founder and former pastor of Colorado Springs–based New Life Church; president of
the National Association of Evangelicals, 2003–2006.
Advised George W. Bush on the "Christian" agenda; frequently visited, and teleconferenced weekly with, the
White House. Removed from his positions in
November 2006 when a former male prostitute, Mike
Jones, accused him of drug abuse and of having sex
with him on a monthly, pay-as-you-go basis over the
previous three years. Insisting "I'm faithful to my wife,"
Haggard initially denied knowing Jones or ever having
had a gay relationship,* but later admitted to having
bought methamphetamine from him and, eventually,
copped to "sexual immorality": "There is a part of my
life that is so repulsive and dark that I've been warring

---

*JAMES DOBSON, head of Focus on the Family: "It is unconscionable that the
legitimate news media would report a rumor like this based on nothing but
one man's accusation. Ted Haggard is a friend of mine and it appears
someone is trying to damage his reputation as a way of influencing the out-
come of Tuesday's midterm election."

against it all of my adult life," he said—talking about his Republicanism instead of addressing the issue at hand. Was declared "completely heterosexual" after three weeks of religious counseling. So, the rest of you queers: No more of that "just the way I am" shit.

▶ President **Warren Harding** (1921–1923). At least two extramarital affairs. One, with Carrie Fulton Phillips, his friend's wife, lasted fifteen years. The Republican National Committee sent Phillips and her daughter off to Japan for the duration of the 1920 election season, gave her $50,000, and made monthly payments thereafter. Harding's affair with a friend's daughter, Nan Britton, produced a daughter—conceived, according to Britton, in his Senate office in 1919. The affair reportedly continued while he was president, using a closet adjacent to the Oval Office. ("Closeted" apparently applies to both wings of the GOP—gay and straight.)

▶ Rep. **Jon Hinson** (R-Miss., 1979–1981). Conservative. Admitted during his 1980 reelection campaign that he had been arrested for exposing himself to an undercover policeman at the Iwo Jima Memorial in Washington. (Must have gotten carried away, swelling with pride at the sight of those big, strong marines raising their great big flag pole.) Hinson denied being gay; blamed his behavior on—class?—alcoholism; won reelection. Arrested again a month into his second term, charged with performing oral sex on a male Library of Congress employee in the House restroom (where a sign clearly reads, "No Oral Sex"). Resigned; acknowledged he was gay; said he was "into heavy denial" when first elected. (That's right: at the time, he still believed in deregulation, privatization, upper-income tax cuts, etc.)

▶ **LEWIS "SCOOTER" LIBBY.** Chief of staff to Dick Cheney and adviser to George Bush, 2001–2005. While coauthoring the future Bush foreign policy with his mentor, **PAUL WOLFOWITZ**, Libby also found time to write a novel, *The Apprentice*, published in 1996 and described in the *Guardian* (UK) as "an everyday tale of bestiality and paedophilia in 1903 Japan . . . packed with sexual perversion, dwelling on prepubescent girls and their training as prostitutes."[138] One passage describes a girl being thrown into a cage "with a bear trained to couple with young girls. . . . Groups of men paid to watch." Reprinted after Libby's PLAMEGATE-related indictment generated renewed interest. Speaking of cages, in 2007, Libby was sentenced to thirty months of undisturbed writing time. Bush commuted the sentence because his already weakened presidency might not have survived another Libby novel.

▶ Rep(robate) **Donald "Buz" Lukens** (R-Ohio, 1967–1971, 1987–1990). Convicted in 1989 of contributing to the delinquency of a minor—a sixteen-year-old girl to whom Lukens, then age fifty-eight, gave $40 and gifts in exchange for sex. The relationship allegedly began when she was thirteen. Lukens's defense: the girl was already a delinquent! Refused to resign his House seat until the following year, when a Capitol elevator operator accused him of fondling her. Sentenced to thirty days in jail and ordered to see a psychologist. Convicted in 1996 on five counts of bribery and conspiracy for his part in the House banking scandal.

▶ Rep. **HENRY HYDE** (R-Ill., 1975–2006). Chairman of the House Judiciary Committee, 1995–2001. Lead House manager for the Clinton impeachment trial, 1998–1999.

Adulterer, 1965–1969. In 1998, while Hyde was playing Great White Clinton-Hunter, the liberals over at Internet magazine *Salon.com* decided to smear him by publishing a story titled "This Hypocrite Broke Up My Family." From 1965 to 1969, Hyde conducted an extramarital affair with Cherie Snodgrass, a married mother of three. When the story came out, Hyde, who was forty-one and married when the affair began, dismissed it as one of his "youthful indiscretions."

▶ Rep. **Steven LaTourette** (R-Ohio, 1995–). Voted to impeach Clinton. Lost his place on the House Ethics Committee—and his wife—after he was outed in 2003 for an affair with his former chief of staff, Jennifer Laptook, who by then was a lobbyist with business before a subcommittee chaired by LaTourette. (Don't even *think* of saying "in bed with special interests.") He's a twofer—sex scandal and financial scandal: LaTourette lobbied to promote a regulation change that would help JACK ABRAMOFF's tribal clients.

▶ Rep. **Bob Livingston** (R-La., 1977–1998). Conservative. Very. Succeeded GINGRICH as House Speaker in 1998, only to be sunk within weeks by his own scandal even as he was howling for Clinton's impeachment for occupying the White House while being a Democrat. Livingston knew he was among the GOP politicians whose sexual indiscretions were about to be detailed in *Hustler* magazine. He was resigning, he said, as an example to Clinton. (Hypocrite! Calling himself a Republican yet practicing what he preached!) Became a lobbyist, obviously.

▶ Sen. **BOB PACKWOOD** (R-Ore., 1969–1995). Accused by

at least twenty-nine women of sexual assault, harrassment, and abuse.

▶ Rep. **Ed Schrock** (R-Va., 2001–2005). Opposed various gay rights causes, including same-sex marriage and gays in the military. In 2004, blogACTIVE.com posted links to audio recordings of what the site said was Schrock soliciting male prostitutes on a gay phone-sex chatline. Schrock announced that he would abort his 2004 reelection campaign amid ugly, ugly rumors of *homosexuality*.

▶ Gov. **Arnold Schwarzenegger** (R-Calif., 2003–). His gropes gave our language the term Gropegate. (California produces more gropes than any other state. They are the basis of the whine industry.) During his 2003 campaign, sixteen women came forward with allegations about Ahnuld's handiwork, ranging from breast-grabbing to spanking to wild orgies. In 2005, the *Washington Post* reported that the publisher of two bodybuilding magazines for which Schwarzenegger was executive editor had paid a former TV actress $20,000 to keep silent about a seven-year extramarital affair they began when she was sixteen years old. As the age of consent in California is eighteen, Ahnuld may have committed statutory rape.[139] (See CONAN THE REPUBLICAN.)

▶ Rep. **Don Sherwood** (R-Pa., 1999–2007). One of the worst things that can happen to an election campaign is for a woman who is not the candidate's wife to lock herself in his apartment bathroom, dial 911, and report that he just assaulted her. This happened to Sherwood's campaign in September 2004. When police arrived, Cynthia Ore said he had choked her. He said it was only a backrub. The two were irreconcilably far apart on the issue. No charges were filed. When the incident was publicized, Sherwood initially claimed Ore was just a "casual acquaintance." This turned out to mean a five-year extramarital affair. Ore filed a $5.5 million lawsuit against Sherwood, accusing him of repeatedly assaulting her. Under the terms of a settlement, the Associated Press reported, Sherwood agreed to pay Ore $500,000, of which she would receive the second half *after* the November 2006 election. Peculiar arrangement . . . Anyway: Sherwood received strong support from Republican leaders, including GEORGE BUSH, and campaign contributions from several other House members' PACs.

▶ Supreme Court Justice **Clarence Thomas**: See **THOMAS**. See Thomas lie.

Asshole #30:
Shays, Christopher

Congressman (R-Conn., 1987–). Moderate Republican but self-described "stalwart supporter" of the Bush-Cheney war in Iraq. April 2003: "The war plan has been nearly flawless." August 2004: "We're on the right track now." June 2005: "We've seen amazing progress." Early August 2006: "To have a timetable [for withdrawal of U.S. troops] is absolutely foolish." Late August 2006, upon returning from a trip to Iraq (and with a tough reelection fight drawing near, in a heavily antiwar district): Said his views had changed; now called for a timetable for withdrawal; but "I am not distancing myself from the President. . . . I totally support the war." Have it both ways. I mean, your way.

▶ October 2006: "Abu Ghraib was not torture." It was "a sex ring." Off-the-cuff, unthinking remark? Apparently not. . . . Next day: "I saw probably 600 pictures of really gross, perverted stuff. [*A good hundred more than most people would want to see.*] The bottom line was it was sex. It wasn't primarily about torture."

Forced masturbation. Simulated fellatio. Smearing feces on prisoners. Forcing them to wear women's underwear while chained in stress positions. Pouring cold water and phosphoric liquid on naked prisoners. Threatening them with dogs, with loaded pistols, with rape. Beating them with broom handles and chairs. Sodomizing a prisoner with a broomstick. . . . Is that Shays's idea of sex? We liberals try to keep a broad mind about sexual preference, but these Republicans go too far.

▶ Not *all* cruelty is excusable: "I am committed to animal welfare because I believe humankind has an obligation to all animals."

▶ Most damning of all: "**NEWT GINGRICH** is my hero."

SOUTHERN STRATEGY, THE

Republicans would be shortsighted if they weakened enforcement of the Voting Rights Act. The more Negroes who register as Democrats in the South, the sooner the Negrophobe whites will quit the Democrats and become Republicans. That's where the votes are."

—NIXON strategist KEVIN PHILLIPS (who popularized the phrase "Southern Strategy"), 1970

You start out in 1954 by saying, "Nigger, nigger, nigger." By 1968 you can't say "nigger"—that hurts you. Backfires. So you say stuff like forced busing, states' rights and all that stuff. . . . you're talking about cutting taxes . . . a byproduct [of which is that] blacks get hurt worse than whites.

—LEE ATWATER, campaign manager to **GEORGE H. W. BUSH**, mentor and friend to **KARL ROVE**, in a 1981 interview[140]

How to win control of Washington: Beginning in the 1960s, simply determine that you, as a GOP election strategist, will concentrate on Southern whites, appealing to their:

▶ Resentment of the growing legal equality and social status of blacks, which offends the crackers' sense of the proper social order and threatens a vital pillar of their self-esteem—their imagined racial superiority—as well as, they believe, their jobs

▶ **FEAR** of violent revenge at the hands of emboldened and embittered blacks

▶ Belief that a substantial portion of their tax dollars go to undeserving (i.e., black) **WELFARE** recipients

▶ Dismay at the decline of religion, growing sexual permissiveness, and crumbling racial barriers—which all add up to only one thing: your daughter in bed with a black man

▶ Rage at the northern and Hollywood and northern Hollywood white liberal Jewish intellectual commies who are responsible for all of the above because they want to *destroy white Christian America* (see **XMAS AND CHRISTIANITY, DEMOCRAT-LIBERAL-SECULARIST SATANIST WAR ON**)

The white South was solidly Democratic from the Civil War

until after World War II. The Civil Rights Act (CRA) of 1964, like all previous civil rights legislation, had more support among Republicans than among Democrats.[141] But President Lyndon Johnson supported it; and in 1964, his Republican opponent, **BARRY GOLDWATER**, who opposed the CRA and championed "states' rights" (code for "no forced federal desegregation")— and whose all-white primary delegation was filled with segregationists—became the first Republican since Reconstruction to carry the Deep South states (Louisiana, Georgia, Alabama, Mississippi, and South Carolina). That same year, archsegregationist Senator **STROM THURMOND** (D/R-SC) switched to the GOP—one of the first conservative Dixiecrats to do so.

In 1968, Nixon, by exploiting the widening cracks in the Solid South and pressing all the right white buttons—"states' rights," "law and order," "busing"—picked up Virginia, Tennessee, North Carolina, South Carolina, and Florida, and won, despite the independent candidacy of the rabidly anti–civil rights former Alabama governor GEORGE WALLACE. In 1972, Nixon swept the South, winning over 70 percent of the popular vote in the Deep South states and Florida and over 60 percent in all the other states of the former Confederacy.[142]

In 1980, RONALD REAGAN kicked off his successful presidential campaign by declaring support for "states' rights" in a speech near Philadelphia, Mississippi, the site of the notorious murder of three civil rights workers in 1964.

GEORGE H. W. BUSH Southern-Strategized his way to victory in 1988. "By the time this election is over," Bush campaign manager LEE ATWATER promised, "WILLIE HORTON will be a household name." Horton was a convicted murderer who had committed rape and armed robbery after his release under a Massachusetts weekend furlough program. Bush's Democratic opponent, Michael Dukakis, who was governor at the time, had supported the program—which a Republican predecessor had signed into law. No matter: Horton became the recurring theme of the Bush campaign. Bush's media consultant ROGER AILES—later head of Fox News—reportedly remarked, "The only question is whether we depict Willie Horton with a knife in his hand or without it."

The Strategy reared its Southern head again in 2000, when the GEORGE W. BUSH campaign—managed by Atwater disciple KARL ROVE—conducted a "push poll" that asked voters how they would feel if told that JOHN MCCAIN (Bush's front-running opponent in the crucial South Carolina primary) had fathered an "illegitimate black child."

How do *you* feel knowing that the Southern Strategy fathered an illegitimate presidency?

Crime, Corruption, and Cronyism Case #25:
STEVENS, TED

463-term U.S. senator (R-Alaska). Citizens Against Government Waste (CAGW) has ranked Alaska #1 in federal "pork per capita" every year since it began ranking porkosity in 2000, and has honored Stevens with the OINKER AWARD each year since 1998, crediting him with roughly half a billion dollars in pork each year. (How did Stevens thank the group? By calling it "a bunch of psychopaths.")

Stevens is perhaps best known for threatening in 2005 to resign from the Senate if the federal money earmarked for two Alaskan bridges—the Gravina Island "BRIDGE TO NOWHERE," as critics labeled it, and the Knik Arm Bridge— was rerouted to repair HURRICANE KATRINA damage. The proposed Gravina Bridge connecting Ketchikan (pop. 8,000) to nowhere, a.k.a. Gravina Island, would be nearly as long as the Golden Gate Bridge and higher than the Brooklyn Bridge and cost $315 million, or $4.5 million for each of the island's fifty residents. (Existing ferry service, which runs at least every half-hour, takes between three and seven minutes.) The Knik Arm Bridge would connect Stevens's arm and hand to campaign contributions from Alaskan real estate and construction interests. Anyway, Alaska got the money. (Also see FISCAL RESPONSIBILITY, THE PARTY OF.)

Some of Stevens's other notable achievements in the categories of federally funded bacon, ham, spare ribs, pork chops, and lard: $500,000 for Alaska Airlines to paint a giant king salmon on one of its jets and to distribute fishing industry-themed bookmarks to passengers; hundreds of thousands for the Reindeer Herders Association; $1,480,000 for berry research; over $1 million for the Wasilla (pop. 7,700) Police Department for technology upgrades (Baltimore, Maryland, received a $100,000 earmark for the same purpose); $1,000,000 for Emmonak (pop. 767) street lighting; and $100 million for a project to harness the aurora borealis to heat up the ionosphere and improve military communications, which a University of Alaska Geophysical Institute professor stated would require that they "flatten the entire state of Alaska and put up millions of antennas, and even then, I am not sure it would work." But if that's what it takes, Stevens *will* secure the federal funding for it.

In other mischief, Stevens:

▶ Secretly placed a hold on a bill to increase accountablity in federal funding. (I wonder why.)

▶ Pushed tirelessly to open the Alaska National Wildlife Refuge to oil and gas drilling.

▶ Became a millionaire "thanks to investments with businessmen who received government contracts or other benefits with his help," according to a 2003 *Los Angeles Times* exposé.[143] In one example, Stevens preserved a Defense Department contract for an Alaskan developer who in turn cut Stevens in on an office building deal that earned him a $700,000 profit on a $50,000 investment.

▶ Set up a *charity*, if you please, called the Ted Stevens Foundation. It is "nonpartisan and nonpolitical" (making donations to it tax-deductible), said its chairman—a lobbyist who was treasurer of Stevens's 2004 reelection campaign. The charity's stated purpose is to "assist in educating and informing the public about Senator Ted Stevens." I gave at the office.

THOMAS, CLARENCE, AND THE GOP SLEAZE MACHINE v. Hill, Decency, Truth, Honor, et al.

During the Senate confirmation hearings of George the First's Supreme Court nominee Clarence Thomas in 1991, Anita Hill, a member of the University of Oklahoma law school faculty, testified that Thomas had sexually harrassed her when she worked for him at the Education Department and the Equal Opportunity Commission (EEOC) in the 1980s. Hill alleged that after repeatedly asking her out and being rebuffed, Thomas began to make crude sexual comments "about my anatomy . . . about women's anatomy quite often," about pornographic films and "his own sexual prowess"—and continued despite Hill's protestations. She claimed he hit on other women in the office and that one night he came by her apartment unannounced and uninvited. Her most famous recollection to the Senate panel:

"[Thomas] got up . . . went over to his desk to get the Coke [he was drinking], looked at the can and and asked, 'Who has put pubic hair on my Coke?'"

Reason to believe Thomas's denial of Hill's story: As a member of the Vast Right-Wing Conspiracy, Thomas would not have needed to ask who planted the pube; he would certainly have known about the GOP plot to put pubic hair on every can of Coke in America because Coca-Cola Inc. continued to donate to Democrats (see K STREET PROJECT, PUBIC HAIR PLOT, and **KARL ROVE**).

Reasons to believe Hill: Who could or would make up an incident like that when, if the purpose was to sabotage the guy, a standard grope tale would have sufficed? Moreover, Hill "was drawn *reluctantly* into the national limelight when she was *subpoenaed* regarding her accusations."[144] [Italics added.]

In any case, Thomas's GOP supporters smeared Hill as a fruitcake, nutcake—every kind of pastry and tart imaginable— and hinted that she was your typical, angry, vengeful, "woman scorned" feminist bitch who must have been sweet on Thomas and been rejected. Or in the phrase coined by then conservative journalist DAVID BROCK, author of *The Real Anita Hill* (1993): "a little bit nutty and a little bit slutty."

At the time, Brock was the star reporter for *The American Spectator*, a magazine financed by right-wing billionaire RICHARD MELLON SCAIFE. In Brock's later book *Blinded by the Right*, the recovering right-winger described *The Real Anita Hill* as a "character assassination"—a hit he was *commissioned* to carry out and had written as "a witting cog in the Republican sleaze machine."

Brock has claimed he helped Thomas threaten another witness into backing down and that the White House helped him smear still another witness to Thomas's conduct: Angela

Wright, a former EEOC PR director who told the Judiciary Committee that Thomas fired her after years of hitting on her and making inappropriate comments. According to Brock, the White House sent him to the Judiciary Committee's chief Republican counsel, TERRY WOOTEN, who supplied him with confidential FBI files containing derogatory remarks about Wright by former employers and co-workers. In *The Real Anita Hill*, Brock quoted from an FBI file that referred to Wright as "vengeful, angry and immature."

Brock told about Wooten's help in a sworn statement in 2001, after GEORGE W. BUSH nominated Wooten as a U.S. district judge. Another fine Bush nominee. Wooten, who denied giving Brock any files, was an aide and protégé of Sen. STROM THURMOND. When, in 1991, Anita Hill sent the Judiciary Committee a statement accusing Thomas of harassment, Wooten, in what he later described as "an effort to control the damage," withheld the information even from the Republican committee members (who were furious when it was leaked on the eve of the Senate vote for Thomas) and from Thurmond.[145]

A second witness against Thomas, Wooten well knew, would have spelled d-o-o-m for his confirmation. In deposing Angela Wright, Wooten referred to her six times as having "come forward," as if politically motivated, when in fact, as she pointed out, she had been subpoenaed.* Wooten then asked Wright, a registered Republican, "who you voted for in '80, '84 and '88." In the end, Wright was never called to testify before the Senate; when Thomas was confirmed, most of the Senate and even some Judiciary Committee members remained unaware that Wright even existed. Wooten has said he did his part to keep her story under wraps.[146]

---

*That's a damn hard word to spell.

But for sleaze, nothing in the Thomas-Hill affair could top Thomas's own denunciation of the Judiciary Committee for its *presumption* in inquiring into a Supreme Court nominee's qualifications and character. The statement epitomized what has become a classic GOP strategy in judicial confirmation fights: to claim that the Dems oppose minority and women nominees that are not Democrats. Or oppose them just because they *are* minorities or women. Said Thomas:

As far as I'm concerned, it [the investigation of Hill's claims] is a high-tech lynching for uppity blacks who in any way deign to think for themselves, to do for themselves, to have different ideas, and it is a message that unless you kowtow to an old order, this is what will happen to you. You will be lynched, destroyed. . . .

To belabor the obvious: a *disgusting* insult to the memories of lynching victims such as could come only come from a sick, sick man. And a sick, sick party. (Also see PERSONAL DESTRUCTION, POLITICS OF.)

Crime, Corruption, and Cronyism Case #26:
THOMPSON, TOMMY*

GEORGE W. BUSH's first-term secretary of Health and Human Services (HHS); previously governor of Wisconsin; above all, exemplary Republican. I believe a man who would run for president with a record like his is a man with the courage to stand up to America's enemies at home (Democrats) and abroad (the French).

*Written before Thompson's August 2007 withdrawal from the 2008 presidential race.

For a sense of the man's mental powers and judgment, here's what Thompson told the audience at a Reform Judaism convention in April 2007, just after announcing his candidacy for president in 2008: "I'm in the private sector, and for the first time in my life I'm earning money.* You know that's sort of part of the Jewish tradition . . ." The audience was aghast. "It's a very sinister, dangerous compliment, because it builds on a stereotype that has been very costly to the Jewish people," said Anti-Defamation League (ADL) national director Abraham Foxman. In the same address, Thompson mistakenly referred to the ADL as the Jewish Defense League, a notorious militant group; to Israeli bonds as Jewish bonds, and (??!) to WINSTON CHURCHILL as the first leader of Israel. (Another Bush! A shoo-in for president! See IGNORANCE AND IDIOCY.)

Whatever he was smoking that night, the nation's former top health official had an especially warm and long-standing relationship with tobacco giant PHILIP MORRIS—a major contributor to his gubernatorial campaigns and to the costs of overseas trips Governor Thompson took in connection with Wisconsin foreign policy. A Philip Morris vice president was among his office's thirty most frequently called individuals and organizations.

But the governor's lines of communication were wide open to lots of business folks. In an eight-month investigation in 1997, the *Milwaukee Journal Sentinel* found "an administration marked by the strong appearance of favoritism . . .

A close-knit group of lobbyists, corporate executives and friends . . . pull the strings of government, with many

---

*Thanks in good part to his very close relations *with* the private sector while he was in the *public* sector, as we shall see!

moving in and out of state jobs ... trading on their access to the governor and blurring the line between government and private interests. ... Becoming a "friend," in the code of Thompson insiders, requires loyalty, deference and never publicly criticizing the governor ... Those who are seeking government assistance are expected to "help," which means making a donation. ... [C]ampaign donations often correlate with success in winning state contracts, direct aid and other favorable treatment.[147]

Another Bush! Examples:

$ The day after Green Bay-area entrepreneur Ron Van Den Heuvel donated $10,000 to Thompson's campaign fund in 1996, he was awarded $9 million in tax-free state bond financing—and eventually another $15 million, saving him a total of $2 million on financing costs—to help him open a factory. It was among the largest such approvals ever made by the state.

$ Executives of four road-building companies that won $218 million in state contracts donated at least $119,000 to Thompson.

$ Thompson and his aides "pressed state utility regulators on issues worth millions to large utilities, including Ameritech and Wisconsin Energy Corp., both major donors to the governor."

Aides and advisers *offered* access to Thompson to firms seeking contracts, favorable regulatory decisions, and other state aid, the *Journal Sentinel* reported. When Thompson allowed the governor's mansion to be used for a charity event, his paid fund-raiser called executives of large Wisconsin firms and offered a one-on-one with the governor for a $5,000 donation to the "charity" (the fund-raiser's mother's lumber museum). "The fund-raising events are sold as prime opportunities to bend the governor's ear on state issues— often worth millions to major players in issues ranging from utility regulation to Indian gaming."

"It's wonderful, the access that's provided," one lobbyist told the paper. Another anonymously said Thompson's fund-raising machine "systematically and methodically" milked firms with state business for donations.

Thompson's other chief accomplishments as governor were WELFARE "reform" (kicking more of the poor into the street) and a nice-sounding "school choice" program that paid for children from low-income families to attend private school. Perennial conservative goal: Make public schools appear increasingly unsalvagable and superfluous by siphoning off their funding to private schools. (Thompson made voucher systems, charter schools, and other forms of school choice a centerpiece of his presidential platform. His thoughtful answer to critics who say Bush's No Child Left Behind law stifles creativity and promotes rote learning: "If they're learning, what's wrong with that?") Thompson, said the *Journal Sentinel*, "has cut taxes and welfare, relentlessly boosted business, tamed the state bureaucracy and whipped the Legislature into submission." Another Bush!

Another Bush. When Thompson announced in December 2004 that he was resigning as HHS secretary "to get into the private sector"* of the health-care industry ("formally," he should have added), the *Progress Report* observed that he "has spent

---

*In an effort to elude federal rules that bar top officials from actively seeking jobs while they are in office, Associated Press reported, Thompson hired two attorneys to "sift through job offers."

the last four years delivering favors to insurance, pharmaceutical and other health care corporations"—such as shepherding Bush's Medicare bill into law; preventing importation of cheaper medicines; and presiding over a Food and Drug Administration that allowed dangerous drugs to stay on the market for years after studies revealed serious problems.

As HHS secretary, Thompson:

▶ Announced in 2002 that, thenceforth, a fetus would be defined as a "child" for the purpose of entitling poor women to prenatal care under the State Children's Health Insurance Program (SCHIP)—thus defining abortion as murder—without providing any additional *funding* for prenatal care; in fact, Bush's budgets repeatedly cut SCHIP funding.

▶ Designed Bush's pro-death restrictions on STEM CELL RESEARCH and his MEDICARE DRUG BENEFIT plan, which should have been advertised as a drug *company* benefit: It barred the government from using Medicare's huge size to negotiate lower prices, as private insurance companies do. The pharmaceutical industry lobbied heavily for the bill and—this being the Age of Bush—got what it wanted. In a legendary (but factual) instance of Bushite deception, before Congress voted on the bill, Thompson's Medicare administrator, THOMAS SCULLY, threatened to fire Medicare's chief actuary if he revealed the bill's true cost, which was $150 billion or nearly 50 percent more than Congress had been told.

▶ Urged the junk food lobby to wage war on critics who blamed the food industry for obesity. Speaking in 2002 to the Grocery Manufacturers Association (GMA), whose members include such companies as the Coca-Cola Company, Mars, Inc., PepsiCo, Inc., and Philip Morris (which owned Kraft Foods, Oscar Mayer, Nabisco, etc.), Thompson urged these manufacturers to "go on the offensive."

This was the country's top *health* official siding with pushers of sugar, fat, and empty calories in the midst of a national obesity epidemic—telling them the problem was their *critics* instead of asking them why they barrage kids with advertising for the garbage they manufacture. Noting the size of the soft money contributions that GMA members had made to the GOP, the director of the consumer group Commercial Alert wrote to Thompson that perhaps "it is time for you to clean out your desk and join the corporate lobbyists on K Street." Which he essentially did.

▶ Oversaw FDA approval of human implants of the VeriChip, a microchip that stores medical and other data. A series of studies dating to the mid-1990s found that chip implants had induced malignant tumors in lab animals—something neither the FDA nor VeriChip Corp. mentioned. Two weeks after the approval, in January 2005, Thompson left the agency, and within a few months was a VeriChip part-owner and board member. While publicly declaring the device "important and secure," Thompson declined to have a VeriChip implanted in himself because of, according to critics, "private concerns he had about the safety of the device."[148] *

After leaving office, Thompson promoted a number of eyebrow-raising changes to Medicaid:

*Why can't VeriChip invent a tiny electronic lie detector that could be implanted in every GOP politician?

▶ More electronic medical record-keeping. (See VeriChip, above.)

▶ Moving more Medicaid patients and the uninsured into commercial health insurance plans—the kind operated by Saint Louis–based Centene Corp., on whose board Thompson sits.

▶ Moving Medicaid beneficiaries under sixty-five from federal to (financially strapped) state care. Well, help in improving states' Medicaid programs *is* available from consulting firms like Deloitte & Touche and its Center for Health Solutions, whose chairman is a man with extensive experience on Medicaid issues— Tommy Thompson.

Let Thompson make all the money he wants in the private sector—so long as he leaves "the Jewish tradition" out of it, thank you. His practices aren't kosher.

Asshole #31:
THURMOND, STROM

South Carolina senator and strombosis in the body politic from 1954 until his death, in 2003, at age 100. Like virtually all Southern whites, a Democrat until 1964, when Southerners like him began to realize they belonged in the GOP.

Ran for president in 1948 as the candidate of his own, newly formed States Rights Democratic Party, whose aim was to preserve segregation. "I wanna tell you, ladies and gentlemen, that there's not enough troops in the army to force the Southern people to break down segregation and admit the nigra race into our theaters, into our swimming pools, into our homes, and into our churches."—Thurmond, 1948. And as former Senate majority leader TRENT LOTT (R-Miss.) declared in 2002, "When Strom Thurmond ran for president, we voted for him. We're proud of it. And if the rest of the country had followed our lead, we wouldn't have had all these problems over the years, either."

Conducted the longest filibuster ever by a U.S. senator in opposition to the Civil Rights Act of 1957. Voted against the Civil Rights Act of 1964 and the Voting Rights Act of 1965.

Fathered an out-of-wedlock child by his family's sixteen-year-old African-American maid when he was twenty-two, when "miscegenation" was illegal under South Carolina law. The daughter, Essie Mae Washington-Williams, gave Thurmond the highly undeserved courtesy of going public with the story (which Thurmond's family confirmed) only after his death. Thurmond's family once owned an ancestor of AL SHARPTON. Ahh, those were the days!

UNCOOL, UNLOVED, AND UNLAID: ROGUE NATIONHOOD and its Discontents

The day after September 11, 2001, was September 12, 2001, and that day's headline in Paris's *Le Monde* proclaimed: "*Nous sommes tous Americains.*" "We are all Americans." That was in *France, putain.* For an all-too-brief moment, America's allies, and even some of her not-so-allies, were actually on America's side.

Well, *that* wouldn't do. Republicans (especially NEOCONS) *don't like* U.S. international popularity any more than they like international laws, treaties, and courts. If Europe, in particular, likes us, we must be doing something wrong.

Cheney, Bush, & Company to the rescue! Thanks to America's rogue nationhood under the Bushies—with their Bushit invasion of Iraq; their rejections of international organizations* and of international treaties on global WARMING, treatment of war prisoners, and arms control; their mindless, chest-beating, flag-waving, lapel-pin-wearing, ally-insulting, God-is-on-our-side, narcissistic, solipsistic, jingoistic "patriotism"; their aid-the-rich, fuck-the-poor, big-business-*über-alles* GOPONOMICS; their all-around mendacity and vileness; and above all, their Idiot-and-Liar-in-Chief—America's international prestige and popularity suffered, you could even say *plummeted to unprecedented depths.*

According to a 2004 poll,[149] a majority of people in Australia, Britain, Canada, France, Japan, Spain, and South Korea shared "a rejection of the Iraq invasion, contempt for the Bush administration [and], a growing hostility to the U.S." In a Canadian poll, nearly eight out of ten said Bush runs "a rogue nation," and most adults under thirty-five believed America had become "a force for evil in the world"[150] and must never again possess the Stanley Cup. Naturally, it was even worse in Muslim countries. In Saudi Arabia and Egypt, two key U.S. allies, a Zogby poll found 94 and 98 percent, respectively, holding an "unfavorable" view of the United States. In Jordan, Pakistan, and Morocco, "a clear majority" said suicide bombings against Americans in Iraq were justified.

The U.S. public seemed to get it: as early as August 2004—just a year and a half into the Debaq**—a Pew Center poll found that 67 percent said the United States was "less

*In 2004, the Texas Republican Party platform called for the United States to leave the UN. And I called for Texas to leave the United States. Also see JOHN BOLTON.
** "The greatest foreign policy disaster in American history."—Everyone

respected" in the world than ten years earlier. And we were literally less loved, according to the *Onion*, which reported the direst diplomatic impact of all: "REPORT: U.S. FOREIGN POLICY HURTING AMERICAN STUDENTS' CHANCES OF GETTING LAID ABROAD." But, for $25—for real—American travelers could simply order the "Going Canadian" kit, including maple-leaf-emblazoned T-shirt and luggage patch and *How to Speak Canadian, Eh?* guidebook.

Bush foreign policy exacted an economic price as well as a, um, social one. *The New Republic*'s Clay Risen reported how, in overseas marketing, U.S. corporations began to conceal their products' American-ness, which had become a liability. An October 2004 poll by market-research firm Global Market Insite (GMI) found "a consistent direct correlation between how closely international consumers associate companies with the U.S. and the likelihood they'll avoid purchasing their brands in the near future." Such sentiment "gained new energy" after the November 2004 election. "American multinational companies will need to mount a valiant effort to distance themselves from the image of the U.S. federal government and its unpopular foreign policies or risk continued brand erosion and ongoing boycotting," GMI declared.

Our pariahhood, pleasing as it may be to Republicans, has more serious diplomatic and national security costs, however. Foreign governments became less eager to go home with us *or* cooperate with us in eradicating terrorist groups. Terrorists no doubt have been gratified and emboldened by our isolation; they may believe *they* brought it about, that their strategy is working. And terrorism *isn't* something we can hide from behind a red maple leaf, eh?

VETERANS AND SOLDIERS, BETRAYAL OF by Their Leaders After They've Risked Life and Limb "For Their Country" (Or at least for Exxon, Chevron, Shell . . .)

The Republican Party, the Republican-dominated Congress, has absolutely been the worst thing that happened to the United States military.

—Ret. Gen. Paul Eaton on HBO's
Real Time with Bill Maher, 3/9/07

Despite all the Bush administration scandals that preceded it, despite all the prior evidence of Bushite indifference to the well-being of ordinary Americans (see "COMPASSION" and GOPONOMICS and HURRICANE KATRINA for some of it), the February 2007 revelation of the conditions under which injured Iraq veterans were "cared for" at WALTER REED ARMY MEDICAL CENTER (WRAMC) induced particular shock and revulsion. Cheney and Bush—those great friends of the serviceman and woman (in photo ops)—had put these soldiers in harm's way for the sake of oil industry profits, neocon fantasies, Bush's vanity, and Rove's election strategies —then discarded them like trash.

At WRAMC, *Washington Post* reporters found rodent and cockroach infestation, stained carpets, cheap mattresses, and black mold, among other signs of neglect. Soldiers reported no heat or water. "Disengaged clerks, unqualified platoon sergeants and overworked managers" made navigating the complicated bureaucracy to obtain medical care even more daunting. Drug dealers worked the corner right outside the unmonitored entry. "Struggling, injured soldiers, most suffering from paranoid delusional disorder and traumatic brain injury, are forced to 'pull guard duty' to obtain a level of security."[151]

Shocking, yet not surprising. As in all Bush scandals, this one wasn't the result of error or oversight but of deliberate policy: in this case, the Bushies' fanatical push to privatize virtually every area of government and, in the process, award lucrative contracts to GOP cronies. Which is why Bush's appointment of a commission *and* an interagency task force of seven Cabinet secretaries to "find out what went wrong" was the usual Bushite postscandal farce.

What "went wrong" was this: In 2004, Bush called for half of the Defense Department's 452,000 civilian positions to be privatized. As a result, in January 2006, the Army awarded a five-year, $120 million contract to run WRAMC to IAP Worldwide Services, Inc., which is majority-owned by screw-up-ridden CERBERUS CAPITAL MANAGEMENT (see **WAR PRIVATIZATION AND PROFITEERING**) and run by AL NEFFGEN, a former senior official at HALLIBURTON, **DICK CHENEY**'s firm. Neffgen had testified before the House Oversight Committee in defense of Halliburton's exorbitant charges for fuel delivery and troop support in Iraq. IAP had itself botched the job of delivering ice as part of Katrina relief operations. (To qualify for a Bush administration contract, a company must have at least one recent significant failure to its credit.)

An army memo "describes how the Army's decision to privatize support services at [WRAMC] was causing an exodus of 'highly skilled and experienced personnel,'" wrote Oversight Committee chair Henry Waxman (D-Calif.). The day before IAP took over, WRAMC's staff dropped from over 300 to less than 60. "Yet instead of hiring additional personnel, IAP apparently replaced the remaining 60 federal employees with only 50 IAP personnel."152

Bush, during a photo op at WRAMC, July 2007: The scandal was just "some bureaucratic red-tape issues."

The WRAMC story was of a piece with the chronic shortages of body armor, vehicle armor, and even drinking water for U.S. troops in Iraq. It was of a piece with Bush budget cuts, year after year, to a broad range of programs intended to protect or improve the lives of veterans and active-duty soldiers. And with Bush-GOP COMPASSION for the little guy in general.

In Year One of the Iraq war, 2003, the White House pushed to cut $75 a month in soldiers' "imminent danger pay" and a $150 family separation allowance, deeming these "wasteful and unnecessary." Democrats fought to block these cuts. After a $3 billion Bush budget cut to Veterans Administration hospitals, VA spending averaged $2,800 less per patient in 2005 than nine years earlier. Bush's 2008 budget shortchanged vets' health care needs by more than $100 million, according to Sen. Charles Schumer (D-N.Y.).153

Perhaps the most sickening part of the scandal was the way Republicans tried to twist it into a lesson about the evils of "big government" and "socialized medicine" and the need for *more* privatization. How? By encouraging the widespread misconception that WRAMC is part of the Veterans Administration—whose hospitals, among the country's best, are not privatized—when in fact it is run by the army. This is why Bush announced an investigation into both military medical care *and* VA medical care. Cunning. Repubnant, but cunning.

WAR (and Peace) PRIVATIZATION AND PROFITEERING

I'm getting a *little* tired of repeating this. Republicans today don't want smaller government—they just want to *shift the benefits* of government to their elite supporters: big business and the wealthy. Privatization of government assets and functions has been a vital part of the GOP-corporate money-power machine. Under GOP rule, companies that contribute to Republicans (and have cushy post-government jobs waiting for them) get government contracts. (Under an administration run by industry executives, lawyers, and lobbyists, this is guaranteed.) The more of the public sphere the Republicans privatize, the more favors and patronage they have to dispense. Paradoxically, by "shrinking" government, Republicans become more powerful. (See **GOPONOMICS**; **DELAY**; **NORQUIST**; **CRIME, CORRUPTION, AND CRONYISM**.)

Nowhere has the cronyism been more flagrant than in the war business. "Companies awarded $8 billion in contracts to rebuild Iraq and Afghanistan have been major campaign donors to President Bush, and their executives have had important political and military connections," according to a 2003 study by the Center for Public Integrity (CPI). The more than seventy contractors studied gave more to the Bush-Cheney 2000 campaign than they did collectively to any other politician over the previous dozen years.[154]

As has been proven time and again—particularly in Iraq—under a regime so joined at the hip to business and so **OVERSIGHT AND ACCOUNTABILITY**-resistant, private contractors need not actually *perform well* to win government business. The GOP's biggest and closest corporate friends—the Halliburtons, **BECHTELS** and ChoicePoints—usually don't even have to compete for contracts, which are generally written to guarantee enormous profits no matter how badly they screw up. Under Bush, half the Pentagon's roughly $400 billion budget went to private contracts, of which only 40 percent were conducted under "full and open competition," the CPI found.

Corruption and cronyism is bad enough in civilian programs. When it endangers the lives of servicemen and women and the success of military operations, it begins to look like carelessness. Examples:

▶ DONALD "BOYSIE" BOLLINGER, a longtime friend of GEORGE W. BUSH, owns Bollinger Shipyards, which is responsible for some of the worst problems plaguing the Coast Guard's fleet-replacement program, DEEP-WATER. "Even as contractors built patrol boats with buckling hulls and a large new cutter with structural flaws," the *Washington Post* reported in February 2007, the Coast Guard extended their deal for nearly four years and paid them a multimillion-dollar bonus.

▶ From 2002 to 2005, BOEING and Integrated Coast Guard Systems (ICGS) paid more than $250 million to settle charges of defrauding the Pentagon—and received nearly $700 million in Department of Homeland Security (DHS) contracts, making them the two largest DHS contractors. In late 2004 DHS's inspector general reported that Boeing overcharged the department $49 million on a contract to install and maintain bomb detection and other screening equipment at U.S. airports, and that an ICGS deal to install new engines in Coast Guard helicopters would take longer and cost more than if the Coast Guard did the work itself.[155]

▶ By 2004, HALLIBURTON, formerly headed by DICK

CHENEY, was squeezing around *$1 billion a month* from Iraq contracts—more than one-fifth of the money the United States was spending in Iraq. Under an open-ended, "cost-plus" contract, Halliburton's KBR subsidiary was billing the army $6 billion a year for services such as food, laundry, and trash collection—services that the army initially estimated at $3.6 billion. Congressional and military reviews found the army being billed $100 per fifteen-pound load of wash, generating $1 million a month in overcharges, as well as vast quantities of lint. Halliburton charged the army for meals it never served to troops. It fell behind in delivering drinking water. It overcharged the army by $61 million for gasoline, a Pentagon review concluded. A third or more of the government property Halliburton was paid to manage for the Coalition Provisional Authority (CPA)—including over $18 million worth of vehicles, generators, and computers—was missing, the CPA inspector general reported in November 2004. A Government Accountability Office (GAO) report in July 2004 said Halliburton overcharged the government by more than $165 million. (And the war was still young.)

The same month, Senate Republicans voted down stiffer penalties on contractors who overbill. In February 2005, the army, ignoring its auditors' counsel, decided not to withhold payments to Halliburton while these issues were pending. In fact, that month the administration budgeted an additional $1.5 billion for Halliburton services and awarded the firm $9.4 million in bonus payments. The Army Corps of Engineers' chief of contracting alleged that officials tried to fire her after she raised questions about Halliburton contracts. (Cheney: "Halliburton gets unfairly maligned.")

▶ In 2004, the U.S.-led occupation authorities in Iraq—using Iraqi oil money taken from the Development Fund for Iraq, which was intended to help rebuild the country—awarded a no-bid contract to CUSTER BATTLES LLC to provide security for the main U.S. military base in Baghdad. That October, two Custer Battles managers accused the company of defrauding the U.S. government out of millions by inflating prices or billing for nonexistent services. The Justice Department declined to prosecute. Custer Battles partner MICHAEL BATTLES "is very active in the Republican Party and speaks to individuals he knows at the White House almost daily," said a Pentagon report cited by the *Washington Post.*

▶ The stock price of ENGINEERED SUPPORT SYSTEMS, INC. (on NASDAQ, EASI, as in "money") more than doubled in the first six months of the war thanks to contracts to refit military vehicles and build $19 million worth of protective shelters against Saddam's dreaded chemical and biological weapons. . . . In January 2005, WILLIAM H. T. BUSH—or "Uncle Bucky," to W.—who sat on EASI's board, cashed out a half-million stock options for a $450,000 profit.[156] Lucky timing, maybe; some of EASI's sole-source contracts were under investigation by the Pentagon.

▶ In **LEWIS, JERRY**, you read how CERBERUS CAPITAL MANAGEMENT won a crucial navy contract a day after hosting a fund-raiser for the California Republican, who chaired the House Defense Appropriations

Subcommittee. In 2005, Cerberus was the subject of a Business Week article titled "What's Bigger Than Cisco, Coke, Or McDonald's?" That's right—$30 billion in sales, more employees than ExxonMobil, and *you* never heard of it. While sucking up Defense Department contracts for projects such as setting up military-base camps in IRAQ and "managing" WALTER REED ARMY MEDICAL CENTER (ring a bell? Well, you can ring the bell all you want—no nurse or doctor will come; see VETERANS AND TROOPS, BETRAYAL OF), Cerberus-owned companies have been found "to have a common pattern of large-scale fraud, security problems, and financial scandals involving GOP lawmakers and lobbyists," Mark Levey reported on DailyKos. But Cerberus was also found to have then Defense secretary DONALD RUMSFELD among its investors and former VP DAN QUAYLE as its chairman of global investments. In October 2006, the firm named former Bush treasury secretary JOHN SNOW as its new chairman. Cerberus lobbyists included former senator JAKE GARN (R-Utah) and a former aide to two members of the House Armed Services Committee. Of course, Cerberus has been a generous contributor to GOP campaign committees. (That's how the pay-to-play GOP system *works*, dummy.) Cerberus execs earn up to $40 million a year. (Maybe Dan Quayle isn't so dumb after all.) That means plenty of leftover grocery money for GOP contributions.

▶ After ten years and $1.7 billion, the Marine Corps got a new amphibious vehicle "that breaks down about an average of once every 4½ hours, leaks and sometimes veers off course," the *Post* revealed. "And for that, the contractor, GENERAL DYNAMICS, received $80 million in bonuses."

Coincidence. . . . GOP ethics also break down about once every 4½ hours, and *always* veer off course.

WARMING, GLOBAL

[Global warming is] the second-largest hoax ever played on the American people, after the separation of church and state.

—Senator James Inhofe (R-Okla.)

In February 2007, the Intergovernmental Panel on Climate Change (IPCC) released a report that was hailed as "history's most definitive statement of scientific consensus on climate change."[157] Its conclusions: global warming is "unequivocal," human activity is the main driver, and if left unchecked, it will destroy our habitat.

The 1,600-page report was authored by 150 scientists, with another 400 as contributing authors. A team of some 600 reviewers conducted two rounds of reviews. A supercomputer ran models for the report continuously for a year. "The really chilling thing is that it is the work of several thousand climate experts who have widely differing views [on the subject]," said "a senior UK climate expert." "Only points that were considered indisputable survived this process. This is a very conservative document—that's what makes it so scary."[158]

Sen. JAMES INHOFE: The report is "a political document, not a scientific report."

Talk about high standards. Or mental retardation.

Insane as Inhofe (as usual) sounded, his reaction was no crazier than the Bush administration's was to every previous IPCC report. All along, Bush maintained it was unclear whether human activity caused global warming, if he acknowledged it was occurring at all. (Save the planet, or protect fossil fuel industry profits? *Fuck* the planet! We hate the *word* "planet"!)

With the 2007 report, however, Bush admitted his past errors. . . . *Not!* The new Bushit line was that, as the White House complained, the media "perpetuated inaccuracies that the President's concern about climate change is new" when actually, Bush "has consistently acknowledged climate change is occurring and humans are contributing to the problem," and "climate change has been a top priority since the President's first year in office."

George W. Bush, June 26, 2006: "[There is] a debate over whether [global warming] is man-made or naturally caused."

Meanwhile, Bush had cut NASA's earth science budget by 30 percent; yanked the Yanks from the 160-nation Kyoto Protocol on reducing greenhouse emissions; and consistently rejected any other serious measures to combat "climate change"—including, in 2007, the creation of a new global body aimed at cooling the warming. Even in his famous February 2007 State of the Union "turnaround" on the issue, Bush never once pronounced the magic words, *global warming*, but stuck to the deliberately vague "climate change."

Energy Secretary SAMUEL BODMAN that same month: "We [the United States] are a small contributor to the overall [problem]." Actually, the U.S., with 5 percent of the world's population, emits one-quarter of global greenhouse gases. And more than half of *that* is emitted by the Bush White House.

Asshole #32:
WATT, JAMES

Reagan's legendary first Interior secretary (1981–1983), a post that gave him authority over the nearly one-third of the United States' territory that is federally owned, and all its vast water, forest, and wildlife resources. Appointed for his solid record of radical anti-environmentalism and support for unregulated commercial exploitation of privately *and* publicly owned land. Previously founded the MOUNTAIN STATES LEGAL FOUNDATION, which represents the oil, gas, mining, ranching, and logging industries in cases against the government. The foundation became a training ground for such future Bush administration pro-industry, antienvironmentalist zealots as Interior Secretary GALE NORTON and Agriculture Secretary ANN VENEMAN.

Congress's chief environmental adviser during the Reagan administration, Greg Wetstone, called Watt and Environmental Protection Agency administrator ANNE GORSUCH BURFORD (see **EPAgate** under **CRIME, CORRUPTION, AND CRONYISM**) the two "most blatantly anti-environmental political appointees" in U.S. history. They personified Ronald "Trees Cause Pollution" Reagan's environmental IGNORANCE, wrote *Grist*'s Amanda Griscom.[159]

At his Senate confirmation hearings, Watt, a born-again Christian, was asked whether he believed that natural resources should be preserved for future generations. He repled: "*I do not know how many future generations we can count on before the Lord returns.*" [Italics added.] After his appointment, he stated his mission: "We will mine more, drill more, cut more timber." True to his faith and his word, Watt:

▶ Cut funding for environmental programs; opened vast

wilderness areas and shorelands for oil and gas drilling; quintupled the amount of federal land leased to coal companies for strip mining; tried to eliminate the Land and Water Conservation Fund, which supports National Wildlife Refuges; even refused donations of *private* land to be used for conservation purposes; and recommended that all 80 million acres of undeveloped U.S. land be opened for drilling and mining by the year 2000.

► Ordered the buffalo on the Interior Department seal turned to face right instead of left. Yes, ass-backwards in *every* way.

► Explained that he wasn't such a bad guy; on his staff, "I have a black, a woman, two Jews and a cripple." (Asshole. Show us at least *two* blacks and *two* cripples—then we can talk.)

That remark led to Watt's resignation in 1983. Naturally, he became an industry lobbyist. In 1995, he was indicted on twenty-four felony counts of perjury and obstruction of justice in connection with his role in the HUD SCANDAL, in which Reagan administration officials steered federal subsidies intended for low-income housing to GOP contributors. Sentenced to five years probation and a $5,000 fine.

In 1991, Watt told an audience of cattlemen: "If the troubles from environmentalists cannot be solved in the jury box or at the ballot box, perhaps the cartridge box should be used." Turned out he did *not* mean ink cartridges—which are deadly enough when fired at high velocity—but rifle cartridges.

Applauding the **GEORGE W. BUSH** administration's energy and environmental policies: "Everything Cheney's saying, everything the president's saying—they're saying exactly what we were saying 20 years ago . . . It sounds like they've just dusted off the old work." (Also see Environment, Rape, Pillage, and Plunder of.)

Welfare Bugaboo, The

Perhaps more than any other issue, welfare is what *built* this party we're trashing here today. From the 1960s into the 1990s, the belief that a large class of mainly black people who were too lazy to work were living off *my earnings, my tax dollars, stolen* from me by liberal Democrats to maintain, you know, *them* in the nonworking style to which they'd grown accustomed—probably drove more Democratic voters into the ~~arms~~ jaws of the GOP than any other issue.

But perceptions are interesting things, compared to boring old facts. In a major 1995 survey, Americans were asked which they thought were the two largest areas of federal spending: 41 percent named foreign aid* (which was actually around 0.2 percent of our GDP); 40 percent named welfare. (The actual largest, defense, came in fourth on the survey.)[160] In fact, federal welfare spending had peaked two years earlier—when the main welfare program, Aid to Families with Dependent Children (AFDC), and food stamp assistance together accounted for less than 3 percent of federal spending. Even if you add in Medicaid, public housing assistance, and child nutrition

---

*In foreign aid as a percentage of GDP, the United States has long been *the* least generous of the industrialized nations. The United States rose to second-to-last place in 2004, but Iraq accounted for most of the rise and might in fact have reduced our aid to other countries.

programs, federal assistance to the poor totaled 10 percent of federal spending, or less than half of the defense budget (pre-Bush-Cheney buildup). But, priorities *are* priorities. And WAR PRIVATIZATION AND PROFITEERING is what Republicans call a *priority*. (Judging by federal dollars spent, the United States considers invading Iraq to get those damned, elusive WMDs ten times as important as feeding the poor.)

The number of welfare* recipients in America has fallen by around 60 percent since its 1994 peak, from approximately 14 million per month to 5.6 million, in some measure because of the welfare reform bill signed by Clinton in 1996, which forced many recipients off the rolls. (Actually, the booming Clinton economy had a lot to do with it; some critics said the prosperity accounted for the *entire* drop in food stamp assistance.) For reasons far too complicated to explain, the new law also resulted in many welfare recipients' being denied Medicaid and food stamp assistance; eliminated guaranteed child care; and required at least 50 percent of all families on welfare and 90 percent of two-parent families to be working. By 2004, only 30 percent of U.S. welfare recipients were working. In Texas, Maryland, and Massachussetts, fewer than 8 percent were employed.

With the law set to expire in 2002, there arose a new debate on welfare—and new GOP demands for getting tougher on the poor, in case the Bush recession wasn't already accomplishing that. With unemployment way up, the National Governors Association urged that work requirements for welfare recipients be relaxed, saying they

*AFDC and its successor, Temporary Assistance to Needy Families (TANF).

were unrealistic and that welfare recipients needed more
education and training to secure jobs. (The governors also
opposed a Bush proposal to take $300 million out of welfare
funds and spend it on programs aimed at "encouraging
healthy, stable marriages"; see **"FAMILY" AND "FAMILY
VALUES."**) Two days later, Bush proposed *increasing* the
work requirements, from 50 percent of recipients to 70 percent and from 30 to 40 hours per week. He also called for
closing loopholes in the work requirements, lest any of
those lazy bums escape the dragnet. The director of the
National Campaign for Jobs and Income Support called the
Bush proposals "welfare reform in Wonderland. . . . We're in
the middle of a recession. Now is a strange time to be
arguing we ought to toughen work requirements on poor
families."

By the way, the majority of mothers on welfare are not
black and never have been black in their lives.

WHITMAN, CHRISTINE TODD

Her book *It's My Party Too: The Battle for the Heart of
the GOP and the Future of America,* published in 2005,
two years after she resigned as **GEORGE W. BUSH**'s Environmental Protection Agency (EPA) administrator, was
hailed as a declaration of independence from the party's
dominant right wing. "The Republican Party at the national
level is allowing itself to be dictated to by a coalition of
ideological extremists," she wrote, "groups that have
claimed the mantle of conservatism and show no inclina-
tion to seek bipartisan consensus on anything."

Indeed. Why, then, was the former New Jersey governor

willing to serve in, and lend a veneer of moderation to, the administration that *heads* that coalition of extremists—*the* most partisan, political, *anti*consensus administration in U.S. history *and* the most *antienvironmental* administration in our history? Why didn't she quit and speak out, once she discovered she was just "moderate" window dressing, helpless to stop the administration from demolishing decades worth of hard-won environmental gains and from denying global WARMING?

Actually, she did speak out on that last issue. *She helped do the denying* by challenging the validity of a government-commissioned report that said human activities have contributed to global warming.

Her denial skills were in demand again during the week following September 11, 2001, when Whitman assured New Yorkers three times that the toxins released by the attacks posed no threat to their health. In a report two years later, the EPA's inspector general determined that the agency had not had "sufficient data and analyses" to justify such assurances —and that the White House had "convinced EPA to add reassuring statements and delete cautionary ones." *That* would have been a pretty good moment to blow the whistle on the motherfuckers. Instead, Whitman did the Bushies' bidding and knowingly told their lies.

Whitman worked under DONALD RUMSFELD during the NIXON administration, and she's related by marriage to the Bush family. So if her record seems at odds with her words, perhaps it's not so surprising; she's been breathing toxic political air for a long time. On the other hand, as governor, Whitman's removal of excise taxes on professional wrestling led the World Wrestling Federation to once again hold events in New Jersey.

Midnight rider. If you were a state governor, how would *you* encourage local police to practice RACIAL PROFILING? In 1996, Governor Whitman was riding along in a patrol car in Camden, New Jersey, as a PR stunt, when the officers stopped a black sixteen-year-old for "suspicious activity" and frisked him. After they found nothing, one of the officers photographed a smiling, frisky Christie as *she* frisked the suspect. The picture was published in newspapers statewide, no doubt boosting her standing with many white voters. (In her book, Whitman criticizes the Bushies' electoral strategy as "divisive.")

WOLFOWITZ, PAUL

Deputy secretary of defense under DICK CHENEY and BUSH I (1989–1993) and under DONALD RUMSFELD and BUSH II (2001–2005); "architect of the Iraq war," a title he seems to share with DICK CHENEY and nine or ten other Bushies. President of the World Bank (2005–2007). But never mind about his being bounced from that position following the disclosure that he helped obtain a promotion and pay raise for his girlfriend, who was World Bank Senior Communications Officer for the Middle East. Let's talk instead about his "architectural" background.

In 1992, in the waning days of the first of a seemingly endless series of Bush presidencies, then-deputy defense secretary Wolfowitz and deputy undersecretary of defense I. LEWIS LIBBY coauthored the innocuously titled "Defense Planning Guidance for the 1994–99 fiscal years" for then

Defense secretary Cheney. This radically noninnocuous document was too radical for public release; when leaked to the press, it caused such an outcry that it was hastily rewritten. But it was simply eight years ahead of (or one hundred years behind) its time; the "WOLFOWITZ DOCTRINE" was the germ, or bacillus, of the "BUSH DOCTRINE," the Cheney-Bush foreign policy madness that propelled America into Mess-o-potamia.

Most popular features: unilateralism (we do whatever the fuck we want and pay no mind to other countries) and "preemptive" military action against potential threats (we *attack* whomever we want). A U.S.-run "new order" would "deter potential competitors from even aspiring to a larger regional or global role" unless they wanted their ass kicked but good. In the Middle East, "our overall objective is to . . . preserve U.S. and Western access to the region's oil." Not much beating around the bush *there*.

Other items on Wolfie's resume: decades of support for "the strong and remarkable leadership" of Indonesian dictator Suharto, who was accused of genocide and named "most corrupt leader in modern history" by Transparency International; pressuring U.S. intelligence agencies to produce false links between Saddam Hussein and 9/11; minimizing the number of troops that would be needed in Iraq (Wolfowitz attacked Gen. Eric Shinseki's much higher and, in turned out, much more accurate estimate as "wildly off the mark"), resulting in severe shortages of troops and equipment, and excess casualties; attempting to impose radical free-market economics on Iraq (see **O.I.L.**); and reportedly approving the harsh interrogation methods that led to abuse and torture in U.S. prisons. "Wolfie's biggest qualification to run the World Bank? His prediction that Iraqi reconstruction would pay for itself with Iraqi oil revenues," wrote Maureen Dowd. "A man of good experiences," said President Bush, who picked the Wolfman for the job.

Apart from girlfriend troubles—and who doesn't have those—Wolfowitz alienated World Bank staff and board members by, among other things, imposing Bush administration policies to eliminate family planning from World Bank programs, and appointing a managing director who opposed serious action on global WARMING. Well, things were soon to get a little too warm for Wolfowitz. No, not in the afterlife— that would be *much* too warm; rather, at the Bank.

XMAS AND CHRISTIANITY, DEMOCRAT-LIBERAL-SATANIST-SECULARIST WAR ON

Democrats and Liberals must be in league with the Jews, the Muslims, Satan, or all three (mainly the Jews, though). In any case, they—I mean, we—are out to destroy Christianity. That's right: 77 percent of Americans are professed Christians; all other religions combined make up just 3 percent (while 14 percent claim no religion); you can hardly get elected dog catcher without first proclaiming Jesus Christ as your personal savior—yet we few, we happy, secular few, we band of non-Christians, are plotting to destroy Christianity and to install statues of Marx, Allah, Darwin (good idea, that one), Madalyn Murray O'Hair, and Satan in the U.S. Supreme Court lobby. This shouldn't come as news—the right has been warning you about it for years.

We began, stealthily, with a War on Christmas. Meaning, the preference for "Happy Holidays" over "Merry Christmas" by satanic chain stores like Wal-Mart. Whether they simply wanted to include, or not *ex*clude, Jews and Muslims from their holiday season well-wishing, or we secularist communist Jewish Christmas-haters were holding their children hostage, I am not at liberty to say.

The phrase and the fantasy "war against Christmas" reportedly originated in 1999 with conservative journalist Peter Brimelow, who, likening the imaginary anti-Christmas forces to Nazis, wrote of "the ongoing Kulturkampf against Christmas," and referred to other December holidays (Hanukkah, Ramadan, Kwanzaa, and the Native American celebration of the winter solstice) as "holidays," in quotes. Brimelow's Web site VDare.com hosts an annual "War Against Christmas Competition" for the best "anti-Christmas" incident report. (First prize is thirty silver pieces and a Service to God and Fatherland Medal.)

Our kampf, and Pat's. In 2001, right-wing commentator PATRICK BUCHANAN wrote of an event you may not have heard about—"the abolition of Christmas." (Sorry now, aren't you, that you wasted all that money on gifts?) What sparked Buchanan's rage? Seek and ye shall find: Amid a nationwide ocean of public Christmas decorations, Christianist jihadis had found the village of Kensington, Maryland, whose council (or as Buchanan labeled it in fine Orwellian fashion, "the Kensington Taliban") had just voted "to purge Santa from its 30-year-old tradition of lighting a pine tree in front of town hall." Note to the ACLU: The village of Kensington, Maryland, continues to allow sectarian religious displays—to wit, one Christmas tree—on public property. Note to Buchanan: In the 1960s, Gerald L. K. Smith, a Disciples of Christ minister and founder of the America First Party (which you so admire), "argued that the Jews introduced

Santa Claus to suppress the New Testament accounts of Jesus."[161] (I *told* them . . . simply rearranging the letters of "Satan" was too obvious!)

Buchanan, who evidently believes in imaginary figures other than Santa, fingers the culprits: the "multicultural-ists." "Their agenda is to purge from public life the Christian faith that gave birth to Western civilization. For they believe Western civilization was a blight upon mankind." (Buchanan identifies only one "they" by name: Jesse Jackson. Yes, the *Reverend* Jesse Jackson.) It *might*, by the way, be argued that ancient Greece and Rome gave birth to Western civ, 500 or so years B.C., and that for the *past* five hundred years (think rise of science), Western civ has been progressively freeing itself of the *Middle Eastern* religions of Judaism and Christianity. Who's for Western civ? We secularists! We patriots of the Enlightenment! *We're* for Western civ! (MEL GIBSON and his fellow religious conservatives, on the other hand, want us to center our civ on images of a guy having his flesh torn off his body and nails driven through him.)

According to Buchanan, Americans "are not free" to celebrate publicly "the birth of our Savior, the day God became man." (Have the churches been shut down? Are those millions of lights festooning my local main street and my neighbors' houses every December actually Hanukkah lights?) Why? "Because our Constitution has been hijacked by bigots in black robes, who perverted it to de-Christianize America." I knew it! Those must be the same people who erased all mention of God or Christianity from every copy of the Constitution *and* revised all the history and civics books accordingly. The bastards!!!

Crazy like Fox. Buchanan's battle cry was picked up, amplified, and made into an "issue" by the great right-wing media echo-chamber, in particular Fox News hosts BILL O'REILLY, SEAN HANNITY, and JOHN GIBSON, author of *The War on Christmas: How the Liberal Plot to Ban the Sacred Christian Holiday is Worse Than You Thought.* O'Reilly: "I am not going to let oppressive, totalitarian, anti-Christian forces in this country diminish and denigrate the holiday and the celebration. I am not going to let it happen. I'm gonna . . . bring horror into the world of people who are trying to do that." (He'd merely have to show up.) In one five-day period in 2005, Fox, a.k.a. the GOP Channel, aired fifty-eight different reports, interviews, and debates about the War on Christmas[162]—this while dozens were dying each day in another, somewhat more real and bloody war. (Correction— not *while*, but *because*: A weapon of mass distraction was urgently needed from *that* war and other GOP-made calamities.) Among several "War on Christmas" incidents O'Reilly reported that were denied by those involved was Saginaw, Michigan's vehement opposition to "red and green clothing on anyone." That *should* be a fashion crime, but the story was "flat-out not true," the town supervisor responded, adding that town hall was adorned by red and green Christmas lights.[163]

No matter—by late November 2005, a Fox News/Opinion Dynamics poll found that *42 percent believed "there is a War on Christmas in the U.S. today."*

Every company in America, O'Reilly argued, should be "screaming 'Merry Christmas'" and "be on their knees thanking Jesus for being born. Without Christmas, most American businesses would be far less profitable." And that is, after all, what Jesus came to Earth for. But if he hadn't, I wonder: Might merchants have invented some other mass-shopping-binge holiday, as they invented Mother's and Father's Days? Indeed, might a holiday *not* based on a Savior who taught disregard for worldly possessions have made better commercial sense?

The Bible (Wikipedia) tells us that, before the Victorian era, Christmas in the United States "was often considered secondary to Epiphany and Easter.... [T]he current state of observance of Christmas is largely the result of a mid-Victorian revival of the holiday inspired by Charles Dickens' novel *A Christmas Carol.*" "Seasons Greetings" has been in wide use since that period, however, and even appeared on White House, uh, holiday cards as far back as COOLIDGE.

But Christmas was only the wedge in our wider war. In March 2006, the *Washington Post* reported that "the 'War on Christmas' has morphed into a 'War on Christians.'" The story described a two-day conference in Washington, D.C., on "The War on Christians and the Values Voters in 2006." Speakers included former House majority leader TOM DELAY (R-Tex.), Senators JOHN CORNYN (R-Tex.) and SAM BROWNBACK (R-Kans.), and Christian Right leaders such as PHYLLIS SCHLAFLY and GARY BAUER.

The opening session was devoted to "reports from the frontlines" on the persecution of North American Christians. Cited examples included the reported barring of religious themed paintings from a municipal art show in Deltona, Florida, and a U.S. Navy chaplain who said he was punished by a commander for offering Christian prayer services. The chap showed a photo of himself next to one of an Afghan Christian who faced possible *execution* for converting from Islam. Two martyrs.

These people complain more than did the Christians who

were fed to the lions and then burned alive in ancient Rome. "To claim that these examples amount to religious persecution disrespects the experiences of people who have been jailed and died because of their faith," the general counsel of the Baptist Joint Committee for Religious Liberty told the *Post*.

To me, the insult is even more intolerable when it comes from a Jew. Michael Horowitz, a senior fellow at the conservative Hudson Institute, told the conference audience of four hundred: "You guys have become the Jews of the twenty-first century." Apparently the Jews of the twentieth century *governed* Germany from 1933 to 1945.

To see "a skirmish over religious pluralism . . . as a war against Christianity strikes me as a spoiled-brat response by Christians who have always enjoyed the privileges of a majority position," said a Church of God in Christ minister and social ethics professor who spoke anonymously for fear of reprisals by Christianist extremists. (Just kidding. He gave his name. Very, very big mistake.)

Victimhood is the best offence. The "war on Christianity" game has obvious political aims. Consider the explanation offered by Bill Donohue, president of the Catholic League for Religious and Civil Rights (see **Ass-HOLINESS**), for some (far too few) Democrats' opposition to Bush Supreme Court nominee JOHN ROBERTS. Never mind that many other Catholic judges had been confirmed: It was "Catholic baiting," insisted Donohue. "Roberts is Catholic. There is no other plausible reason." (Uh, how about *he wouldn't tell the Senate anything about his legal opinions?* Or maybe it was his *positions* on abortion, school prayer, the environment, voting rights, and presidential powers, all of which placed him far to the right of the public at a time when the Court was already skewed to the right?) The Catholic conservative group Fidelis warned Senate Democratic leaders to "keep religion out of future Supreme Court confirmation hearings." Of course, it was precisely Roberts's religious views that sold him to Christian conservatives in the first place. (Would the religious right still demand that religion be ignored if an enlightened president were to nominate an avowed atheist?)

At the height of the judicial nominee battles, in April 2005, the Christianist right-wing Family Research Council (FRC) organized "Justice Sunday," a rally portraying Democrats as "against people of faith." Speaker after speaker (including **BILL FRIST**) compared the plight of conservative Christians to the civil rights movement. Granted, discrimination was being practiced on a massive scale in the government itself—with conservative Christians forced to occupy all the offices of power in Washington while Democrats, liberals, centrists, and secularists remained outside in the fresh air, at their leisure. . . . Still, there was irony here, because FRC president **Tony Perkins** had long-standing ties to organizations such as the Council of Conservative Citizens, America's premier white supremacist organization.

The right used similar tactics to combat objections to other Bush far-right judicial nominations, regardless of religion, race, color, or creed. (Isn't "creed" the same as "religion" and "race" much the same as "color"? Well, never mind.) When Democrats opposed the confirmation of Miguel Estrada, the right accused them of being "anti-Hispanic." With other nominees, it was because Democrats were either anti-African American, anti-Arab, and/or antiwoman. The *Democrats.*

But the "anti-Christian" canard has a special place in the right's bag of tricks. It is part of a larger strategy in which conservatives, after decades of political dominance, pretend to be a beleaguered minority and demand "equal" rights in order to achieve *exclusive* rights and complete political, social, and cultural hegemony. The right has adopted the very strategy of victimhood that it has long accused various minority groups of fraudulently exploiting.

No doubt many truly believe in a "war on Christianity." I'm reminded at times of a charming anecdote told by the Argentine-Jewish crusading liberal newspaper editor Jacobo Timerman about his imprisonment and torture at the hands of Argentina's military junta in the 1970s. His torturer told him Karl Marx destroyed the Christian idea of society, Sigmund Freud destroyed the Christian view of the family, and Albert Einstein destroyed the Christian understanding of space and time. (Argentina seems to have employed a decidedly more intellectual caliber of torturer than we do. Lynndie England hardly ever discussed Freud and Einstein with the naked Abu Ghraib prisoners on her leash.)

By the way, *you* may be a Christophobe (the Christianists' word) without realizing it. Ask yourself these questions: Do you have even one Christian friend? Have you ever *hired* a Christian? Do you think the Christian lobby has too much influence in Washington? Do you believe Christians' consistently lower IQ scores are due in part to genetic factors? Have you ever said, "Nero also did some *good* things . . . He built the Appian Way . . ."?

Oh: Happy Holidays!

Asshole #33; Crime, Corruption, and Cronyism Case #27:
YOUNG, DON

Sole congressman from Alaska since 1973. "[W]ell-known for his sharp elbows and generous appetite for legislative pork," according to *The New Republic*. "His reputation for steering federal dollars to Alaska is almost as legendary as that of [Alaska senator TED] STEVENS."[164] In the 2005 Highway Bill, Young—who then chaired the House Transportation Committee—secured $941 million for 119 special projects, including a $231 million bridge in Anchorage which a rider in the bill required be named for him.[165] Porkmeister Bridge. Young's role in earmarking federal funds for the fabulous "Bridge to Nowhere" in Ketchikan, Alaska (see STEVENS) earned him a spot on *Rolling Stone*'s Ten Worst Congressmen list, and its 2006 "Mr. Pork" title.

Days after Florida real estate developer Daniel Aronoff held a fund-raiser for him in 2006, Young added to a transportation bill $10 million earmarked for construction of a Florida interstate interchange for a short stretch of road along which Aronoff owned 4,000 acres, as well as $81 million for expansion of the interstate. (Young's spokeswoman initially insisted that local Republican congressman Connie Mack had requested the funding; in fact Mack and other local Republicans opposed it.)[166]

In February 2007, Young said: "Congressmen who willfully take action during wartime that damage [sic] morale and undermine the military [such as criticizing the Iraq war] are saboteurs, and should be arrested, exiled or hanged," and misattributed the quote to Abraham Lincoln. When the "mistake" was pointed out, Young's spokeswoman—splitting an infinitive with typical Republican callousness—said, "He continues to totally agree with the message of the statement." Yes: GOP members of Congress want to make like Nazis and *hang* war critics.

A tireless proponent of despoiling the Arctic National Wildlife Refuge with oil drilling, Young has said: "Environmentalists are a self-centered bunch of waffle-stomping, Harvard-graduating, intellectual idiots [who] are not Americans, never have been Americans, never will be Americans." (They are, with few exceptions, Nepalese. Proven fact.)

And: "If you can't eat it, can't sleep under it, can't wear it or make something from it, it's not worth anything." As far as his beliefs and values go, I agree . . . but can he eat, sleep under, wear, or make something from his parents or children? You know, I bet he could . . .

Asshole #34:
Zell

Zell Miller ("D"-Ga.), DINO (Democrat in Name Only) U.S. senator, 2000–2005; governor, 1991–1999. From his opposition-to-Bush-is-treason keynote speech at the 2004 *Republican* National Convention: "Now, at the same time young Americans are dying in the sands of Iraq and the mountains of Afghanistan, our nation is being torn apart and made weaker because of the Democrats' manic obsession to bring down our commander in chief." Guilty as charged.

ACKNOWLEDGMENTS

Thanks to Shelley Hopkins, Carl Bromley, Ruth Baldwin, Iris Bass, and Meredith Smith for their editorial guidance; Evangeline Sicalides for keeping me smiling and relatively sane; and George W. Bush, Dick Cheney, and crew for giving me a reason to get out of bed and, after seeing the headlines and remembering who's in charge, to immediately go back to bed. (Or hit the bottle.) Never slept so much, or so badly, as during the last seven years. WMWIO (wake me when it's over)!

NOTES

1. "Report: Global Gag Rule Spurring Deaths, Disease," Women's eNews, 9/25/03.
2. "Denying the Right to Choose," *New York Times*, 4/19/07
3. "Christian Science?" *Mother Jones*, September/October 2004.
4. "Group Therapy: Bush, Bin Laden, Bechtel and Baghdad," *Counter-Punch* 5/12/03.
5. "Controversy Continues over Post-Katrina Spending on Trailers," PBS *NewsHour* transcript, 4/9/07.
6. "Bechtel to Get Richer in Post-War Iraq," *San Jose Mercury News*, 3/25/03.
7. "The List: Private Profits in Iraq" *ForeignPolicy.com*. November 2006.
8. CampusProgress.org, 10/16/06.
9. Ibid.
10. Greg Palast, *Armed Madhouse*, 2006, provides an excellent account of the election thefts.
11. "Profiles in Cowardice," *New York Times*, 7/8/07.
12. Doug Thompson, "Bush on the Constitution: 'Just a Goddamn Piece of Paper,' CapitalHillBlue.com, 12/9/05. Thompson said he heard it "from two White House sources who claim they heard [it] from others present in the meeting."
13. "Bush Family's Dirty Little Secret," *American Freedom News*, September 2001.
14. Joe Conason, *Harper's*.
15. "Bush and Cheney Self-Made Men? They've Got to Be Kidding," *New York Daily News*, 10/11/00.
16. "New Facts About Bush's 'Whitewater,'" Bushwatch.com, 1/12/00.
17. "Cheney's Fall from Grace," *Time*, 3/8/07.
18. EarthRights International.
19. "Hunger in America," CommonDreams.org, 12/10/04.
20. MeasuringWorth.com.
21. "Bush's Class-War Budget," *New York Times*, 2/11/05.

22. *Wall Street Journal*, 07/19/01, quoted in "Bush Placing Roadblocks in Front of Minimum Wage Hike," Labor Research Association Online, 7/30/01.

23. Wikipedia.

24. Ibid.

25. "Party Is Over on Workers' Comp," ArnoldWatch.org, 12/3/04.

26. Wikipedia.

27. *Columbia Electronic Encyclopedia*, 2007.

28. en.citizendium.org/wiki.

29. presidentprofiles.com.

30. Wikipedia.

31. Some historians.

32. Encarta.

33. Prita Lal, "The Great Flood of 1927 through a Post-Katrina Lens," leftturn.org, 12/31/2005.

34. Ibid.

35. "Lone Star: The Hard Right's Soft New Face," *The New Republic*, 8/16/04.

36. Wikipedia.

37. Rove Strategy Paper Found in Nixon Archive," *New York Times*, 7/14/07

38. "PAC Man," *The New Republic Online*, 10/8/05

39. Wikipedia

40. Daniel Benjamin, "Mutually Assured Corruption: The Justice Department and Anne Burford's EPA," *Washington Monthly*, January 1986.

41. "Absolute Truth," *Washington Post*, 5/13/01.

42. "Credit Card Fraud at DHS," AP, 7/19/06.

43. "Government's Katrina Credit Cards Criticized," AP, 9/15/05.

44. "None (But Me) Dare Call It Treason," *New York Times*, 1/21/07.

45. "What's the Matter with Liberals?" *New York Review of Books*, 5/12/05.

46. "DEFCON Artists," *American Prospect* online, 6/12/02.

47. "The Mystery Man Who Inspired Dole's Latest Strategy," *Time*, 10/7/96.

48. "Senator Is Challenged on His Medical Opinions," *Washington Post*, 10/5/99.

49. "Dr. Feelgood: Bill Frist, Heal Thyself," *The New Republic*, 1/27/03.
50. "Frist Aid," *Mother Jones*, 5/1/98.
51. *Issues Berkeley Medical Journal*, Spring 1998.
52. "The Bad Doctor: Bill Frist's Long Record of Corporate Vices," *LA Weekly*, 1/9/03.
53. whateveritisimagainstit.blogspot.com, 8/20/05.
54. Wikipedia.
55. "Gingrich Urges Death Penalty for Illegal Drug Smugglers," *Washington Post*, 8/27/95.
56. "The Heavy Long-Term Toll of the Bush Tax Cuts," *Business Week*, 6/9/03.
57. "It's a Pattern," AmericanProgress.org, 9/20/04.
58. "I.R.S. Audits of Working Poor Increase," *New York Times*, 3/1/02.
59. "Corporate Risk of a Tax Audit Is Still Shrinking, I.R.S. Data Show," *New York Times*, 4/12/04.
60. "Assessing President Bush's Fiscal Policies," Economy.com, August 2004.
61. "Summary of Latest Federal Individual Income Tax Data," Tax Foundation, 9/25/06.
62. "Capitalism 104," Huffington Post, 2/13/07.
63. "Bush and Cheney Self-Made Men? They've Got to Be Kidding," *New York Daily News*, 10/11/00.
64. "Priceless," *The New Republic*, 11/8/04.
65. "The Real Leader of the Opposition: Republican Party Leader Phil Gramm," *Washington Monthly*, March 1994.
66. Ibid.
67. Kristen Sykes of Friends of the Earth, on Bill Moyers's PBS show *Now*, 5/30/03.
68. "What Haircut Stories Tell Us about the Press," Eric Boehlert's Blog, 5/2/07.
69. FAIR, 9/1/01; Raleigh *News and Observer* 8/26/01.
70. Quoted in "Ashcroft Whistles Dixie," *Salon*, 1/3/01, among other places.
71. "Can Mike Huckabee Out-charm the GOP Big Three?" *Salon*, 3/5/07.
72. http://video.canadiancontent.net/16321139-talking-to-americans-capitol-building-is-an-igloo.html.
73. SourceWatch.org.

74. "Chertoff Delayed Federal Response, Memo Shows," Knight Ridder, 9/14/05.

75. Ibid.

76. "Anger and Unrest Mount in Desperate New Orleans," AP, 9/1/05.

77. "Hurricane Katrina," Wikipedia.

78. "Mike Chertoff's Dirty Little Secrets: Bush's New Homeland Security Czar," Direland/LA Weekly, 1/12/05.

79. Ibid.

80. Patrick Briley, Newswithviews.Com, 2/21/05.

81. "Michael Chertoff: Ashcroft's Top Gremlin," *CounterPunch*, 6/11/03.

82. "Think Again: Has the Media Learned a Lesson?" AmericanProgress.org, 6/2/05.

83. Michael Crane, *The Political Junkie Handbook*, New York: Specialist Press International, 2004, 250.

84. Ibid.

85. "Can Our Young People Find God in the Pages of Trashy Magazines? No, Of Course Not!" *Reader's Digest*, August 1985.

86. "Is Bush Stupid, or Is America?" ConsortiumNews.com, 1/18/06.

87. "George H. W. Bush's Many Lies," *Online Journal*, 1/18/00.

88. "Cocaine Pipeline Financed Rebels," *San Jose Mercury News*, 8/22/96.

89. Terry Gill, *Litigation Strategy at the International Court: A Case Study of the Nicaragua v. United States Dispute.* Dordrecht (1989), 187–91; cited by Wikipedia.

90. "George H. W. Bush's Many Lies," *Online Journal*, 1/14/00.

91. *Report of the Congressional Committees Investigating the Iran-Contra Affair*, New York: New York Times Books, 1988.

92. "Alberto Gonzalez's Coup d'État," *Salon*, 2/9/07.

93. "Larger CIA and DoD Privatization Scandal Emerging from Walter Reed Story, US Attorneys Firing," Daily Kos.com, 3/10/07.

94. "Veteran Neo-Con Advisor Moves on Iran," *Asia Times Online*, 6/26/03.

95. "Intel Probe: The Yellowcake Mystery," *Newsweek*, 11/14/05.

96. http://weekendinterviewshow.com/audio/giraldi_ledeen_clip.mp3.

97. "The Unknown Hawk," Pacific News Service, 5/8/03.

98. "Lewis 'Scooter' Libby, a Quiet Force," MSNBC, 10/28/05.

99. Environmental News Service, 9/23/05.

100. "Rep. Doolittle: A Devoted Friend of Sex Slavery," ThinkProgress.org, 8/7/06.

101. Rebecca Clarren, "Paradise Lost: Greed, Sex Slavery, Forced Abortions and Right-Wing Moralists," *Ms.*, Spring 2006.

102. AmericanProgress.org, 2/13/07.

103. Ronald Watkins, *High Crimes and Misdemeanors: The Term and Trials of Former Governor Evan Mecham*, New York: William Morrow & Co, 1990, 27–28; cited by Wikipedia.

104. "Inside the Wacky World of Evan Mecham," *U.S. News & World Report*, 2/22/88.

105. "Pentagon Prepares for Endless War," *Los Angeles Times*, 7/18/03.

106. Wikipedia.

107. "Writers' Bloc: Abramoff's Shadow Lobby," *The New Republic*, 5/16/05.

108. "Masters of Sleaze," *New York Times*, 3/22/05.

109. "Welcome to the Machine: How the GOP Disciplined K Street and Made Bush Supreme," *Washington Monthly*, July/August 2003.

110. "Bush Wanted to Invade Iraq If Elected in 2000," Guerrilla News Network, 10/27/04.

111. "Blood, Oil, and Tears—and the 2004 Bush Campaign Strategy," CommonDreams.org, 9/4/03.

112. "Bush Refuses to Lean on Oil Cartel," *Miami Herald*, 4/01/04.

113. 1998 National Security Council report quoted in "9/11: The Saudi Connection," Center for American Progress, 3/11/04.

114. "The Complete Saudi Primer," AmericanProgress.org, 6/24/04.

115. Unnamed law enforcement officers quoted in "The Complete Saudi Primer," AmericanProgress.org, 6/24/04.

116. "Tape Missing Subtleties: Bin Laden Translation Omitted Sections," ABCNews.com, 12/21/01.

117. "Saudi Government Provided Aid to 9/11 Hijackers, Sources Say," *Los Angeles Times*, 8/2/03.

118. "More Agents Track Castro Than Bin Laden," AP, 4/29/04.

119. Jean-Charles Brisard and Guillaume Dasquie, *Forbidden Truth: U.S.-Taliban Secret Oil Diplomacy and the Failed Hunt for Bin Laden*, Thunder's Mouth Press/Nation Books, July 2002.

120. Greg Palast, *Armed Madhouse*, 2006.

121. Ibid., 87–89, 102.

122. "Politicization of Inspectors General," oversight.house.gov, 10/22/04.

123. "Costs a Bundle and Can't Fly," the *American Prospect*, 3/11/02.

124. "Concern over Rumsfeld Transformation Grows," Project on Government Oversight, 5/13/03.

125. "Pentagon Probe Flags 8 Deals," *Los Angeles Times*, 2/15/05.

126. tpmmuckraker.com, 10/19/06.

127. "Panel Says Abramoff Laundered Tribal Funds," *Washington Post*, 6/23/05.

128. "Reed an Albatross for GOP," *Atlanta Journal-Constitution*, 6/15/05.

129. Wikipedia.

130. "Claim vs. Fact: Rice's Q&A Testimony before the 9/11 Commission," AmericanProgress.org, 4/8/04.

131. "Mitt Romney's Hypocritical Turnarounds," truthdig.com, 1/31/07

132. "Clarke's Public Service," *Minneapolis Star Tribune*, 3/28/04.

133. "Bush's Brain," blogcritics.org, 9/4/04.

134. Daniel Kurtzman, About.com, 3/16/06.

135. "The White House Stages Its 'Daily Show,'" *New York Times*, 2/20/05.

136. MediaMatters.org, 2/10/05.

137. "Dr. Hager's Family Values," *Nation*, 5/30/05.

138. "Indicted Libby's Publishers Plan 25,000 Reprint of 'Steamy' Novel," *Guardian* 11/11/05.

139. Wikipedia.

140. Published in Alexander Lamis, *Southern Politics in the 1990s*.

141. Wikipedia.

142. Wikipedia.

143. "Senator's Way to Wealth Was Paved with Favors," *Los Angeles Times*, 12/17/03.

144. Wikipedia.

145. "Anita Hill Writer Says Judge Leaked FBI Files," *Los Angeles Times*, 8/25/01.

146. "Judging Terry," *Salon*, 9/1/01.

147. "It Pays to Know Wisconsin Gov. Tommy Thompson," *Milwaukee Journal Sentinel*, 11/2/97.

148. Wikipedia.

149. "Kerry Leads Overseas," *Salon*, 10/15/04.
150. "Welcome to Canada!" *Salon*, 11/15/04.
151. "Walter Reed Army Medical Center Scandal," sourcewatch.org.
152. "Bush Administration Push for Privatization May Have Helped Create Walter Reed 'Disaster,'" rawstory.com, 3/3/07.
153. "Walter Reed Army Medical Center Scandal," sourcewatch.org.
154. "Report Links Iraq Deals to Bush Donations," AP, 10/30/03.
155. "Homeland Security Business Faulted," AP, 1/3/05.
156. "If You Can't Find Something Nice to Say," AmericanProgress.org, 2/23/05.
157. "IPCC Report Fails to Capture Media or Public Agenda," *Framing Science*, 2/5/07
158. "Global Warming: The Final Verdict," *Guardian*, 1/21/07.
159. "How Green Was the Gipper?" *Grist*, 6/10/04.
160. Kaiser/Harvard Program on the Public and Health/Social Policy Survey, January 1995.
161. Wikipedia.
162. "Battlefront Fox: Cable Network Aggressively Promoted Idea of Christmas 'War'," *Media Matters*, 12/7/05,
163. "O'Reilly's Claim About Michigan Town's Opposition to Christmas Colors Is 'Flat-out Not True,'" MediaMatters.org, 12/13/05.
164. Wikipedia.
165. "After 2-Year Wait, Passage Comes Easily," *Washington Post*, 7/30/05.
166. "Alaskan Gets Campaign Cash; Florida Road Gets U.S. Funds," *New York Times*, 6/7/06.

INDEX

Davis, W. Kenneth, 33
Davis-Bacon Act, 179
DEA. *See* Drug Enforcement
Agency
*The Death of Outrage: Bill
Clinton and the Assault on
American Ideals* (Bennett), 35
Death penalty
for abortion, 1
Bush, G. W. on, 82, 110–113
Huckabee on, 192
Defense Information Systems
Agency (DISA), 110
Defense Policy Board, 34
Defense Transformation for the
21st Century Act, 308
DeLay, Tom, 14, 20, 93, 102,
113–116, 119
Buckham and, 104
Christians and, 386
on cutting taxes, 164
in Mariana Islands, 257
Norquist, G., and, 275
Democracy, 98, 266
in Iraq, 283
DeMuth, Chris, 271
Department of Agriculture
(USDA), 144
Department of Homeland Security (DHS), 54
Chertoff and, 201–207
color-code system of, 134–136
contracts from, 368
Department of Justice (DOJ),
107–108. *See also* Gonzales,
Alberto
Department of the Interior
(DOI), 182–183
Development Fund for Iraq, 370

DeWitt, William, 59
DHS. *See* Department of Homeland Security
Di Rita, Lawrence, 265
DISA. *See* Defense Information
Systems Agency
DNA database, 95–96, 134
Doan, Lurita, 307–308
Dobson, James, 146, 160
DOI. *See* Department of the
Interior
DOJ. *See* Department of
Justice
Domestic Security Enhancement Act, 24
Donohue, Bill, 27–28, 387
Doolittle, John, 20, 119, 257
Dorgan, Byron, 20
Dornan, Bob, 217
Dorr, Thomas, 106
Doyle, Brian, 336–337
Drudge, Matt, 184
Drug Enforcement Agency
(DEA), 82
Drugs. *See also* Medical
marijuana
Ashcroft on, 24–25
Gingrich and, 162
Iran-Contra and, 228
penalties for, 81–82
Druyun, Darleen, 309
D'Souza, Dinesh, 120–122
Duke, David, 146, 162

EAC. *See* Election Assistance
Commission
Earned income tax credit
(EITC), 168
Earth day, 53–54
Economy Plan, 300–301

nuclear weapons and, 330
OPEC and, 303
overthrow of, 33
Hyde Amendment, 209
Hyde, Henry, 209–210, 342–343

IAP Worldwide Services, Inc.,
365
ICGS. *See* Integrated Coast
Guard Systems
IG. *See* Inspector general
IMF. *See* International Mone-
tary Fund
Immigration, 89
Inhofe, James, 255
on global warming, 372–373
Inspector general (IG),
305–306
Integrated Coast Guard Sys-
tems (ICGS), 368
Intellectuals, 131, 212, 222, 265,
268
Intelligent design, 30, 147
Intergovernmental Panel on
Climate Change (IPCC), 372
International Forum on Global-
ization, 32
International Monetary Fund
(IMF), 169
Investigations, 313–314
IPCC. *See* Intergovernmental
Panel on Climate Change
Iran, 43, 281–282
Bush, G. W. on, 50
Ledeen on, 247
OPEC and, 295
Iran-Contra, 41–42, 226–233
drugs and, 228
Gates and, 154–156
terrorism and, 229

Iraq, 270–271. *See also* Hussein,
Saddam; Operation Iraqi
Liberation
AEI and, 271–272
Bechtel Corp. in, 33, 34
Bush, G. H. W. on, 266
Bush, G. W. and, 48, 56
cover-up of, 314–316
democracy in, 283
Economy Plan for, 300–301
invasion of, 284–292
Ledeen on, 245
McCain and, 259–260
Norquist, G. and, 301–302
oil and, 288–293, 297–300
Operation Iraqi Liberation,
280–304
al Qaeda and, 271, 281
terrorism and, 284
*It's My Party Too: The Battle
for the Heart of the GOP
and the Future of America*
(Whitman), 378

Jews, 28
Buchanan on, 37
faith-based initiatives and,
151
Thompson and, 355
Xmas and, 383–384
Job Creation and Worker Assis-
tance Act, 165
John Birch Society, 262
John Warner Defense Autho-
rization Act, 311
Jones, Bob III, 5
Journalism, 108
Justice system, 234–236. *See
also* Courts; Department of
Justice (DOJ)